Atlantic France

Cruising Ouessant to the Spanish Border

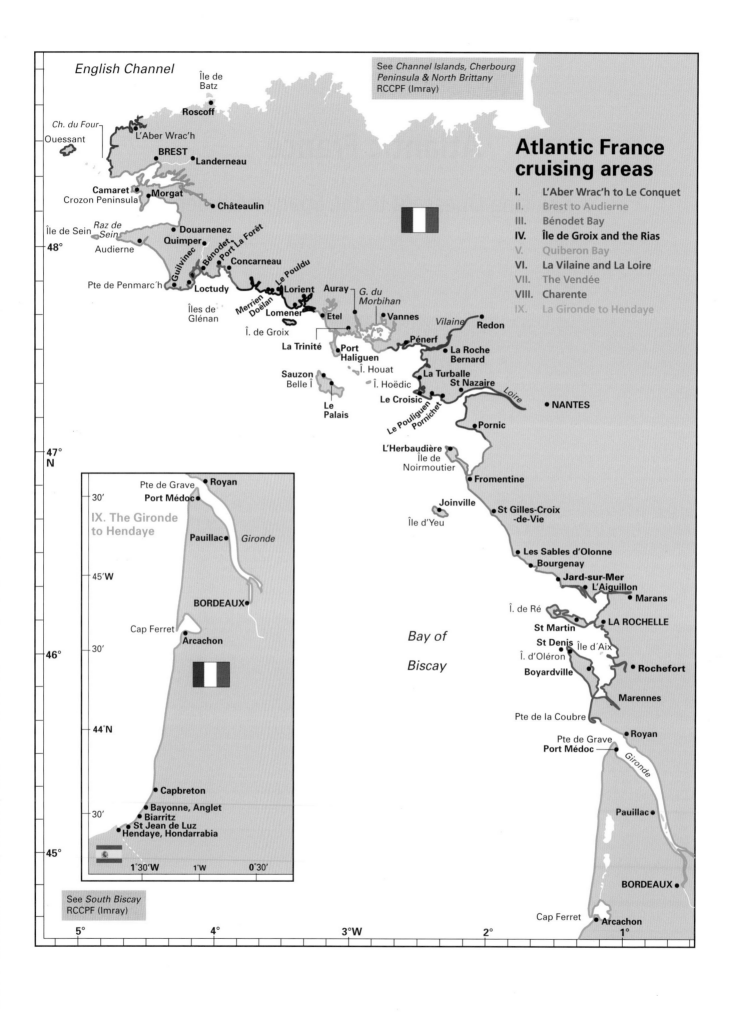

English Channel

Île de Batz

Roscoff

Ch. du Four
Ouessant

L'Aber Wrac'h

BREST
Landerneau

Camaret
Crozon Peninsula
Morgat
Châteaulin

Île de Sein
Raz de Sein
Audierne

Douarnenez
Quimper
Guilvinec
Bénodet
Port La Forêt
Concarneau

Pte de Penmarc'h
Loctudy
Le Pouldu

Îles de Glénan
Merrien
Doëlan
Lomener
Lorient

Î. de Groix

La Trinité
Port Haliguen

Sauzon
Belle Î

Le Palais

Auray
G. du Morbihan
Etel
Vannes

Î. Houat
Î. Hoëdic

Vilaine
Redon

Pénerf
La Roche Bernard

La Turballe
St Nazaire
Le Croisic
Le Pouliguen
Pornichet

Loire
NANTES

Pornic

L'Herbaudière
Île de Noirmoutier
Fromentine

Joinville
Île d'Yeu

St Gilles-Croix-de-Vie

Les Sables d'Olonne
Bourgenay
Jard-sur-Mer
L'Aiguillon
Marans

Î. de Ré
LA ROCHELLE
St Martin
St Denis
Î. d'Aix
Î. d'Oléron
Rochefort
Boyardville
Marennes
Pte de la Coubre

Bay of
Biscay

Pte de Grave
Royan
Port Médoc
Gironde

Pauillac

BORDEAUX

Cap Ferret
Arcachon

See Channel Islands, Cherbourg Peninsula & North Brittany RCCPF (Imray)

Atlantic France cruising areas

I.	L'Aber Wrac'h to Le Conquet
II.	Brest to Audierne
III.	Bénodet Bay
IV.	Île de Groix and the Rias
V.	Quiberon Bay
VI.	La Vilaine and La Loire
VII.	The Vendée
VIII.	Charente
IX.	La Gironde to Hendaye

48°

47°N

46°

45°

IX. The Gironde to Hendaye

30'
Pte de Grave
Royan
Port Médoc

Pauillac
Gironde

45'W

BORDEAUX

Cap Ferret
30'
Arcachon

46°

44°N

30'
Capbreton
Bayonne, Anglet
Biarritz
St Jean de Luz
Hendaye, Hondarrabia

45°

1°30'W   1'W   0°30'

See South Biscay RCCPF (Imray)

5°   4°   3°W   2°   1°

Atlantic France

Cruising Ouessant to the Spanish Border

ROYAL CRUISING CLUB
PILOTAGE FOUNDATION

Nick Chavasse

Imray Laurie Norie & Wilson Ltd

Published by
Imray Laurie Norie & Wilson Ltd
Wych House The Broadway St Ives Cambridgeshire
PE27 5BT England
☎ +44 (0)1480 462114
ilnw@imray.com
www.imray.com
2023

Partly based on *Harbours and Anchorages of North
Biscay Vols I* and *II* by K Adlard Coles, first published in
1959 and 1960 as *North Biscay Pilot* published by Adlard
Coles Ltd. Revised by Professor A N Black
Second edition 1977
Reprinted with amendments 1978
Third edition 1982
Revised by the RCC Pilotage Foundation
Reprinted with amendments 1985
Reprinted with amendments 1987
Fourth edition 1990
Sixth edition 2000
Seventh edition 2005

As *Atlantic France*
First edition 2010
Second edition 2018
Third edition 2023

ISBN 978 178679 374 4

British Library Cataloguing in Publication Data.
A catalogue record for this title is available from the
British Library.

Printed in Malta by Gutenberg Press Ltd.

Front cover photo
The author's yacht, *Wild Bird* entering Les Sables d'Olonne
Julian Lyne-Pirkis

CAUTION

Positions and Waypoints
All positions and waypoints are to datum WGS 84. They
are included to help in locating places, features and
transits. Do not rely on them alone for safe navigation.

Bearings and Lights
Any bearings are given as °T and from seaward. The
characteristics of lights may be changed during the
lifetime of this book. They should be checked against the
latest edition of the UK Admiralty *List of Lights*.

TRINITY HOUSE

The Royal Cruising Club Pilotage
Foundation is privileged to have Trinity
House as its Patron. The ongoing safety of
navigation and education of mariners are
common goals of both organisations.
www.trinityhouse.co.uk

Contents

BOOK SUPPLEMENTS WITH UPDATES AND CORRECTIONS

The quality of Imray and Royal Cruising Club Pilotage Foundation publications is enhanced by contributions from sailors visiting the area. We welcome all feedback for updates and new editions. If you notice any updates, errors or omissions, please let us know via info@rccpf.org.uk or www.rccpf.org.uk/Provide-Feedback

Reports are posted on the Cruising Notes page of the Pilotage Foundation website and incorporated into an annual supplement available free of charge from **www.imray.com** or **www.rccpf.org.uk**.

Printed copies are available on request from Imray.

ROYAL CRUISING CLUB PILOTAGE FOUNDATION

The Royal Cruising Club Pilotage Foundation was established in 1976 and is a registered charity with the charitable objective 'to advance the education of the public in the science and practice of navigation'.

The Foundation's principal activity is to collate and publish pilotage information for the benefit of cruising sailors worldwide. A team of dedicated authors and editors, all of whom are experienced sailors, work with the Foundation's publishers to update and develop its portfolio of pilot books and cruising guides.

In line with its charitable status, any surplus generated finances new publications and subsidises those publications that cover the more remote areas where commercial publication is not viable.

The Foundation's website gives full details of its activities and provides a portal for the sale or download of its books and passage planning guides, as well as Cruising Notes comprising up to date navigational and other reports.

www.rccpf.org.uk

Imray is the leading publisher of nautical information for leisure sailors. Combining the latest official hydrographic data with verified first-hand research, Imray charts, books and digital products present quality information to the highest standard.

Imray was formed in 1904 when three nautical publishing firms, each with a history from the mid 18th century, joined. Today, it works with well-known authors and organisations, covering popular sailing areas worldwide. It has been publishing Royal Cruising Club Pilotage Foundation books since the 1970s.

www.imray.com

THE AUTHOR

Nick Chavasse was cast off in a clinker-built dinghy on the Norfolk Broads aged 6 years. He learned to sail dinghies on the Helford River in a series of Wayfarers, an Enterprise and a sporty Fireball.

He was introduced to offshore sailing whilst in the Army. His first yacht was a Westerley Centaur. He later started an affair with France in his Dufour Classic 38 and more recently in *Wild Bird*, a Bowman 40. He is a Yachtmaster and Cruising Instructor.

The attraction of the cruising area Atlantic France drew Nick in, being within easy reach of England's south coast. Beautiful islands with sandy beaches combined with French cuisine and delicious wines had him hooked.

Nick has sailed the French Atlantic coast many times and explored all the islands and rivers as well as the 106 ports covered in this book. The Morbihan inland sea with about 40 islands and fast-moving currents provides world class pleasure for him and his family. He has always found that the challenges of the tidal range, limited air draught for some bridges and the Gois Causeway all contribute to his love of this area and its fun cruising, often blessed with a fresh breeze and beautiful sunshine.

Nick is the current Commodore of the Royal Cruising Club.

The Pilotage Foundation remains profoundly grateful to Nick for his upbeat and thorough approach to the authorship of Atlantic France. Huge thanks also to Nick's wife, Margie, who has shared much of the exploration and supported in a multitude of ways over several years.

Nick at the helm on *Wild Bird* *Julian Lyne-Pirkis*

Wild Bird in Les Sables d'Olonne *Julian Lyne-Pirkis*

PREFACE

Welcome to the third edition of *Atlantic France*. It is five years since the last edition was published and there are many more changes than I had envisaged, including 260 new photographs. Some changes are minor but others very important such as the complete removal of a sand bank from the approach to Loctudy Marina!

The cruising ground runs from L'Aber Wrac'h in the north, including Ouessant, all the way down the coast as far as Hendaye on the Spanish border. Research for this edition entailed sailing our Bowman 40, *Wild Bird* down the coast as far as Rochefort. The remaining ports going south were visited by car.

The Atlantic coast of France offers so much variety, with 12 islands off the coast and many more if you include all the islands in the Îles de Glénan and the Morbihan. Furthermore, there are at least 20 rivers which are navigable depending upon the boat's draught and air draught. If you like a challenge, then crossing the Gois causeway east of Île de Noirmoutier and taking the short cut east of Île d'Oléron through the Pertuis Maumusson, when heading to Bordeaux or further south, should be included in your passage plan.

This cruising ground, particularly the northern part, is very much in reach of the south coast of England and superb for cutting one's teeth before expanding horizons with ocean sailing: Islands with magical beaches and rivers with idyllic villages. It is well within reach for a two-week holiday.

The purpose of a pilot book changes as technology develops. Most yachts now have at least one chart-plotter on board, and many have one on the binnacle and another one at the chart table, as well as a tablet and phone. However, in my view a chart-plotter should complement and not replace a paper chart. They should also be used in conjunction with an almanac and a pilot book. In this edition, waypoints have only been used if thought to be helpful, for example as a start point when about to follow some pilotage instructions.

This pilot book has been written with the whole crew in mind. It gives pilotage information including the description of a transit, which has the effect of encouraging visual observation, guidance on entering ports and suggestions as to where one might find a berth or anchorage. In addition, there are plans and photographs to help with familiarity, as well as some information on what you might find ashore.

I take pride in the fact that I have visited every port in this book and the vast majority by boat. It has been very reassuring that the book is used by yacht sailors and motor boaters too. I know that to be true having met during our recent research French, German, Belgian and Dutch crews, many of whom recognised our boat, *Wild Bird,* and enquired if I was the author.

It is my hope that the book should be left open at the appropriate page, on the chart or saloon table, for all the crew to dip into as desired. The very nature of a book such as this means it will not be perfect and feedback is welcome. There is a cumulative update document in the form of a Supplement which may be downloaded for free at www.imray.com, so that you can be made aware of any changes as they occur.

In trying to encourage you to visit the ports and harbours, I have included some personal stories, in the side panel, which vary from navigational to geographical and historical interest, and even some notes on wildlife. I hope that these will add depth to the book and inspire you to explore a wonderful cruising ground.

Acknowledgements

A pilot book such as this is the culmination of effort by several successive authors over many years. It was in the 1960s that the pilot book for this area evolved, under the title *North Biscay*. After seven editions, many of them by Adlard Coles, Jeremy Parkinson combined North and South Biscay to produce the first edition of *Atlantic France* in 2010. I remain indebted to all my predecessors for the foundations on which this cruising guide continues to grow.

Managing a 40' yacht on one's own when dodging in and out of harbours and under low bridges is a special challenge, and I was therefore very grateful to receive help from family and friends. A big thank you to my wife Margie who came with me for most of the time. Many thanks also to our friends who came out to help over successive weeks. They are Philip and Sarah Doyne, Julian Lyne-Pirkis and Richard and Georgie Hackett.

I have retained some of the aerial photographs as they give such a good feel for the port or harbour in question. My grateful thanks to Patrick Roach who is responsible for the aerial photography. Most of the other photographs are mine and the rest have been credited accordingly.

I am grateful to Imray and Navionics for their sophisticated and user-friendly digital chart software which has helped greatly with the desk-based research and writing-up phase of the work.

Many readers have taken the trouble to contact the Royal Cruising Club Pilotage Foundation at www.rccpf.org.uk or to email Imray at editor@imray.com with information which is pertinent to the detail in the book. I would like to thank them all for their contributions which have been vital for producing the annual supplements and for updating this new edition. In particular I would like to thanks Charles Nodder for multiple submissions which have been included in this edition. Please keep them coming!

Finally, a big thank you to Jane Russell, as Editor in Chief, for encouraging me throughout the project, and to those at Imray who put this book together.

Nick Chavasse
January 2023

Introduction

OVERVIEW

This third edition of *Atlantic France* covers the coast and off-lying islands between L'Aber Wrac'h and Hendaye, which is over 400 nautical miles of coastline, with more than 100 ports and a similar number of anchorages. It comprises nine distinct areas, loosely based on the French departments. Each area has its own character and is big enough and interesting enough to be a cruising area in its own right.

L'Aber Wrac'h at the west end of the North Brittany coast is often, for British yachts, their first port of call in Brittany on their way from the UK to the Bay of Biscay, or the Golfe de Gascoigne as it is known by the French. There are a dozen main islands off the French coast, excluding the small ones in the Îles de Glénan and the Morbihan, and 20 rivers which may be explored depending on the draught and/or air draught of the boat.

FRANCE – ENTRY PROCEDURES AND PORTS OF ENTRY

The rules and regulations for leaving the UK and for entering France have changed, mainly as a consequence of Brexit. Entry and Exit formalities are still in a state of flux. Cruising yachtsmen and women should make sure they comply with all current regulations before setting sail. RYA provide a good source of updated information; see www.rya.org.uk.

The main considerations when planning a cruise to France are:

- **Pleasure Craft Report Service (sPCR).** The Pleasure Craft Report Service was launched in July 2022. It is a digital pleasure craft report recording all necessary information for both Border Force and HMRC. See www.spcr.homeoffice.gov.uk to access the form. The requirement to complete the sPCR is for Departure and Arrival in the UK.

- **Ports of Entry.** Yachts should report into France at a Port of Entry. Roscoff, Brest and Lorient are the most accessible when cruising to the Atlantic France area from the UK.

- **Q Flag.** You should fly the Q flag on first entering territorial waters. The crew should remain on board until the skipper has completed the necessary customs and immigration formalities.

- **Arriving in / departing from the Schengen Area.** On entering the Schengen area from a non-Schengen country (or when leaving the Schengen area for a non-Schengen country), you should obtain immigration clearance via the port authorities. Passports should be stamped (which may be electronically) on entry into the Schengen area. You will need to ensure they are also stamped on departure otherwise in the eyes of the immigration authorities you may never have left.

- **Limited duration of stay.** Third country nationals (which includes British citizens) can travel to countries in the Schengen area for up to 90 days in any 180-day period. This is a rolling 180-day period.

- **Longer periods of stay.** To stay for longer you will need to meet the entry requirements set out by the French authorities. This could mean applying for a visa and/or work permit. Find out more at www.gov.uk/guidance/check-if-you-need-a-visa-or-permit-for-europe.

Looking NE over Molène outer harbour *Nick Chavasse*

GETTING THERE

Short hops or a long leg?

From the Solent, it is about 210M to Camaret, 260M to Bénodet, 310M to Crouesty and 410M to La Rochelle. In a modern cruising yacht, in good weather, that means about 36 hours to Camaret, less than two days to Bénodet and not much more to Crouesty. Even La Rochelle should take less than three days.

In summer, it is not hard to find a weather window of a couple of days but it is much harder to guarantee any more, at least in the English Channel. Hence on a return trip there is a lot to be said for going as far south as possible as quickly as possible and returning more slowly.

Both the tide and the wind usually make west Brittany and the English Channel easier on the way back. On the other hand, the passage home across North Biscay will usually be against the wind.

The best route

The best route obviously depends on the starting point and personal preference. From the Solent there are essentially two choices: the French route and the English route. The straight-line route is not an option because it cuts diagonally through the traffic separation zone near Alderney.

The shortest route is to head towards Alderney, cross the shipping lanes east of the separation zone and approach the Chenal du Four along the French coast. This has the great attraction of meeting almost no shipping after Alderney and having no tidal gates until the Four. There are also plenty of ports of refuge.

The alternative is to stay north of the separation zone, perhaps with a stop at Dartmouth, and then cross to the Chenal du Four. This is only 20 miles further but will require long hours in the shipping lanes and must take account of the tide gates at Portland and Start Point.

The route via Falmouth is 50 miles further than the Alderney route. It has some tidal advantages and provides the option of going outside Ouessant and Île de Sein. However, from the Solent, it only makes sense if the boat can be delivered to Falmouth in advance of the cruise. The further west the start-point, the freer the prevailing wind is likely to be.

KEEPING THE BOAT IN FRANCE

An increasingly popular option is to keep the boat in a French marina. There are many excellent ones where a boat can be kept or over-wintered. Most are significantly cheaper than UK south coast marinas. There are also an increasing number of dry boatyard facilities where boats can be lifted out of the water and stored ashore for short or long periods of time. They are called port à sec. See www.port-a-sec.org for a discount scheme.

Marina discount schemes

Those who pay annual contracts in certain marinas in the UK or abroad may be entitled to a discount in other marinas. Two such schemes are:
Passeport Escales, www.passeportescales.com and Transeurope, www.transeuropemarinas.com.

Port information online

See www.figaronautisme.meteoconsult.fr. Select menu heading Escales (French) or Stopovers (English). The port information is taken from the French almanac, Bloc Marine. This website gives a good overview of many of the ports covered in *Atlantic France*.

There is a separate scheme for the Morbihan area; see details at www.latitudemorbihan.com.

The Basque ports have a marina group called Euskaquitaine; www.euskaquitaine.com although this group does not have a discount scheme.

Looking SW over visitors' moorings in Doëlan *Nick Chavasse*

TRAVEL

Travel in France is not as difficult as one might imagine. Beware of different timetables during holiday periods and on fête days. The following methods and websites might be useful when planning journeys to and from the region.

Air travel

The regional airports in France are: Brest, Nantes, La Rochelle, Bordeaux, Biarritz and Rennes. Nantes airport is generally the best airport for cheap and frequent flights. It also has good rail connections within France.

Airport information can be found in Reeds; find table in general index under Budget flights.

See websites: www.brittanytourism.com/practical-information/getting-to-brittany/by-plane and other sites such as www.skyscanner.net.

Ferries

Ferry destinations in Brittany are Roscoff and St Malo. However Cherbourg and Caen (Ouistreham) are also practical alternatives. To/from the far south the region of Santander is an option.
www.brittanytourism.com/practical-information/getting-to-brittany/by-ferry

Rail travel

The French rail network is administered by SNCF. The fast, usually inter-city, trains are known as TGV. The regional (local) trains are known as TER. The rail system in generally very efficient.
www.sncf.com/en
www.thetrainline.com/trains/europe

General travel planning in Brittany

It will often be necessary to combine rail and air to get home and the following website is recommended for this purpose. Please note it has nothing to do with either Rome or Rio. Put in your departure point and your destination and view the options.
www.rome2rio.com

Car sharing / car pooling

Bla Bla Car is a relatively new concept in the UK but in France it is widely used. A driver posts details of their journey and invites passengers to join them for a small fee. Visit www.blablacar.co.uk, put in your departure point and destination and follow the instructions. It really works!

TIDES

Tide times

Tide times for Biscay are based on Brest. Those in the Charente and the French Basque ports are based on Pointe de Grave (PdG), which is only about 10 minutes later than Brest at springs and about 20 minutes later at neaps. Brest HW is at about 0600 and 1800 BST at springs and about 1200 and 2359 BST at neaps. Except in the Morbihan and some rivers, local HW is usually within 30 minutes of Brest. Thus, for planning purposes, the whole coast can be assumed to have midday highs at neaps and midday lows at springs.

Unfortunately, the exact differences from Brest vary quite a bit between springs and neaps and in this book have been averaged. French lock-keepers and French tidal atlases use Concarneau, Port Tudy, Port Navalo, St-Nazaire, Les Sables d'Olonne and La Rochelle as additional standard ports. Tide tables for these places are published in French almanacs and are frequently given away free in marinas. It is best to use them where possible, particularly for lock opening times. It is well worthwhile buying a *Bloc Marine Almanac* (which is in French and partially in English) when you arrive in France.

Official tidal predictions for French ports, in this area, are based on UTC +1. This means they are already adjusted to British Summer Time (BST) but need to have an hour added to convert them to French Summer Time (FST). Free tide tables and lock opening times must be checked carefully because they may be in BST, FST or even UTC. In French HW is Pleine mer (PM) or Haute mer (HM) and LW is Basse mer (BM). Springs is Vive-eau (VE) and neaps is Morte-eau (ME).

Tidal heights

All depths and drying heights in this book relate to Lowest Astronomical Tide (LAT) chart datum. Above water rocks, clearances under bridges and the height of lighthouses or hills relate to Mean Level (Same as Mean Sea Level) unless otherwise stated. For clarification on SHOM charts, check the title block under 'Altitudes' for heights.

La Rochelle bridge *Nick Chavasse*

Bridge and power line clearance

There are bridges and power lines throughout the area covered by this book. With a little confidence and some basic maths, it is possible to determine when it is safe to pass underneath these obstacles.

The first point to note is that the clearance heights in this book are given as Mean Level (same as Mean Sea Level). This is because the SHOM charts give the heights in ML (*niveau moyen*). Mean level can be determined, for the purposes of working out air clearance, as the mean (half way) point between HW and LW on any given day. It is believed that SHOM will be migrating to using HAT, but this should be checked in the title block, under the altitude section of the chart.

The figures needed to determine the distance between the sea bed and the bridge are:

Level of Chart Datum
Height of Mean Level
Height of bridge above ML

The figures needed to determine how much distance you need to pass safely under the bridge are:

Keel to masthead height
Safety margins above and below

Next do the sums for the current state of the tide.

Finally apply external factors to your calculation such as the barometric pressure. If the pressure is lower than 1013Mb, expect the water level to be one centimetre higher per Mb drop in pressure. In rivers, the amount of recent rainfall should also be taken into account.

Tidal streams

Tidal streams in Biscay are less intuitive than those in the English Channel. They flow towards and away from the coast as much as they flow along it. They are also unpredictable in direction and significantly influenced by the wind. However, in some places, such as the Raz de Sein or the Teignouse passage, and in most rivers and many harbour mouths they are strong enough to be potentially dangerous. Thus, it is important to take tidal streams seriously.

Tidal stream information is available from many sources. This book provides some simplified tidal charts and there is a summary of key tidal stream data for those ports where it matters. More detail is provided in the tidal stream atlas NP 265 *France West Coast* published by the UK Hydrographic Office and the SHOM tidal atlases, *560-UJA Goulven to Penmarc'h, 558-UJA Penmarc'h to Noirmoutier, 559-UJA St-Nazaire– Royan and 565-UJA Golfe de Gascoigne*. The latter are very detailed and highly recommended. However, note that French tidal atlases for La Rochelle are based on the time of low water not high water.

Tidal coefficients

French tide tables and therefore French harbourmasters use a tidal coefficient to quantify the changing tidal range between springs and neaps. An average tide has a coefficient of 70, mean springs have a coefficient of 95 and mean neaps a coefficient of 45. Knowing the tidal coefficient for a particular tide is useful for gauging the strength of the tidal stream as well as for assessing whether one is likely to be able to use a particular anchorage.

The tidal coefficients for the current year are given in The Cruising Almanac Tide Tables or Reeds. See the Reeds' general index, Tides – Coefficients, to find the relevant page. They are also included in the *Imray Tides Planner* app. Note that tidal-coefficients differ throughout the length of the coast and are based on standard ports; St Malo, Brest and Pte de Grave.

WINDS AND WEATHER

Winds

Biscay is frequently under the influence of either the Azores high or lows passing along the English Channel. This causes the prevailing winds in summer to be west in the northern part and northwest in the southern part. However, other pressure systems are common and changeable Atlantic weather is the norm.

In addition to winds driven by large-scale weather systems, local sea breeze effects are very important. Atlantic France is well supplied with all the features necessary to generate a big sea breeze during the day. As a rule of thumb, a clear sky and a line of fluffy clouds along the line of the coast indicates that a sea breeze is developing and the afternoon wind will blow freshly onto the shore from the southwest, gradually veering to the west. Quiberon Bay and Pertuis d'Antioch (between Île de Ré and Île d'Oléron) are both famous for the strength and complexity of their sea breezes.

There is a reverse phenomenon that is particularly important when anchoring for the night. A land breeze, known by the French as a *brise de terre*, can develop around midnight starting gently and increasing to a fresh breeze from the northeast. This breeze can be particularly strong if it blows down cliffs or along rivers. Île de Groix is a good example. A night breeze blowing down the valleys and rivers in Lorient will blow directly from the northeast into the harbour at Port Tudy with very uncomfortable results.

Whatever the weather

The weather in the southern part of the area is often better than the north. On average, there is less rain, about two hours a day more sunshine, temperatures are about 5°C higher and humidity is 10% lower.

However, when fronts cross southern Brittany or further south they can result in a few days of unsettled weather. One of the attractions of North Biscay as a cruising area is that there is always a protected inland waterway close at hand. The Rade de Brest, Lorient, the Morbihan, the Vilaine, the Charente and the Gironde are all protected and each has interesting towns so it is possible to get away from any unpleasant sea conditions. Further south, however, between the Gironde and the Basque ports there is no port of refuge and a reliable long-range forecast is needed before embarking on the passage.

Visibility

Fog, mist or haze can be frequent in the summer. On average, visibility is less than five miles on one day in five. Real fog, with visibility of less than 0·5M, averages one day in twenty. The coast is so well marked by beacons and towers that navigation in poor visibility is possible, particularly with the help of GPS and radar. However, fog can be particularly unpleasant in narrow tidal waters and rivers.

Swell

Swell is generated by storms and winds of Force 6 and above. With persistent winds of Force 8 or more, large waves are created that can take a few days to die down and will radiate out into areas that were never affected by the strong winds. Hence, storms out in the North Atlantic can bring significant swell to the French Atlantic coast.

A large swell will break heavily on bars and in shallow water and can make some entrances, such as Belon, Etel and the Vilaine, dangerous even in fine weather. If swell enters a narrowing inlet, it tends to increase in height and steepness and funnel up the entrance to make anchorages uncomfortable or even untenable. In open water it can break intermittently and dangerously on rocks that rise from deep water, even if the depth over them is apparently safe.

The northwest and west coasts of Brittany are exposed to swell, particularly in the vicinity of Ouessant and northeast of Le Four. It is a less frequent problem in the Bay of Biscay. However, any anchorages that are open to the Atlantic, such as those on the west and south side of Île de Groix, Belle-Île and Île d'Yeu should only be used in settled weather. French weather forecasts include predictions of the height of the swell (*la houle*) as do a number of weather websites and apps.

Weather forecasts

Biscay is very well served for weather forecasts. The many available sources are summarised in an excellent, 30 page booklet called *Le Guide Marine* from Météo France. This is available free in every port office. It also contains an invaluable lexicon of meteorological terms in French and English.

Navtex forecasts are available from CROSS Corsen on 518kHz (A) and 490kHZ (E). The latter provides more local detail but in French. In the northern part of the area, less detailed forecasts can also be received from Niton on 518kHz (E) and in the southern part from La Coruña on 518KHz (D).

CROSS Corsen and CROSS Etel transmit area forecasts on VHF several times a day. These are detailed and generally accurate. They are in French but, with the aid of the Météo France lexicon mentioned above, even non-French speakers should

Search and rescue

Search and rescue and navigational surveillance are handled by the Centres Régionaux Opérationnels de Surveillance et de Sauvetage (CROSS).

CROSS Corsen covers the coast from Mont-St-Michel to Pointe de Penmarc'h; CROSS Etel from Pointe de Penmarc'h to the Spanish border.

Either station can be contacted on VHF 16 or VHF 70 (DSC). Their telephone numbers are:

CROSS Corsen   02 98 89 31 31

CROSS Etel   02 97 55 35 35

Or in event of a marine emergency call 196, from any phone.

be able to understand them. The times and frequencies vary from place to place and may be found at www.meteofrance.fr/publications/nos-collections/guides-pratiques/guide-marine.

There is also a continuous forecast for shipping on VHF Ch 63. It is broadcast from CROSS Etel in French but the terms used are quite simple and after a little practice, and a basic knowledge of French, one can understand it fairly well. Most marinas display a daily forecast.

Mobile phone coverage is excellent throughout the area and WiFi is commonplace in marinas so that phone and internet forecasts can be used. However WiFi is not generally reliable unless you are in the immediate vicinity of the capitainerie. Mobile phone French weather app is on http://mer.meteoconsult.fr/. Other useful apps and websites are listed at www.rccpf.org.uk/weather-info.

SEAMANSHIP

Biscay harbours

Biscay is a splendid cruising ground for yachts and powerboats of all types. However, smaller marinas and most local harbours are designed around the needs of local boats. These are typically quite small and many dry out on every tide: small fishing boats are ubiquitous and shallow draught sailing boats under 9m are very common. There are plenty of deep-water ports and anchorages that can handle larger boats but a 10m bilge-keeler will certainly get to places that larger boats cannot reach.

At peak time berthing space is scarce so rafting is very common. This may be on a visitors' pontoon or using bow and stern buoys or in a daisy round a central buoy. In all cases, long warps and plenty of fenders are needed. Mooring buoys rarely have a pick-up rope so a threading boat-hook is a great help.

Many former anchorages are now full of local moorings and sometimes it is possible to borrow one rather than anchor. In general, visitors' buoys are a distinctive colour or are labelled with a 'V', 'PL' or the word *Visiteur*. In popular harbours, such as the Morbihan, it is possible to phone the harbourmaster

Fishing boats at Lesconil *Nick Chavasse*

and officially borrow a private buoy. Otherwise it may be necessary to borrow one unofficially. This is always tricky because it is hard to tell whether the mooring is strong enough and whether the owner is about to return. There is no simple advice except to check the ground tackle as well as possible, never leave a boat unattended on a private mooring and be prepared to leave immediately if the owner returns.

Fishing hazards

There are many fishermen's buoys round the coast and sometimes well out to sea. They present a hazard, especially under power at night, and a constant lookout is necessary. The buoys are often laid in pairs, each with a flag. If the pair can be identified, it is advisable not to pass between them.

South of Lorient a different method of fishing is used and a line of very small floats is often run between the larger buoys. It is particularly important not to pass between these buoys.

Much of the area is used for shellfish farming. Mussels are grown on ropes attached to stout stakes driven into the seabed. They are extremely dangerous because the stakes cover at high water. Oysters are grown in metal baskets supported on racks. They also cover at high water and are dangerous. Shellfish beds are usually shown on large-scale charts and are usually marked with buoys or withies. However, the marks are sometimes a bit patchy, particularly in areas that do not get many visitors.

Some fishing harbours do not wish to receive visiting yachtsmen. These harbours have not been covered in this book and should not be visited except in an emergency. With the decline of fishing, attitudes are changing and some of these harbours are becoming more welcoming. If planning to visit a non-yacht harbour, seek local advice.

Wind Farms

A major wind farm consisting of 80 wind turbines has been constructed west of St Nazaire. This constitutes a major hazard to shipping. Others are planned in Quiberon Bay and southwest of Île de Noirmoutier. There are further development zones west of Belle Île and west of Île d'Oléron. For updates go to map.4coffshore.com/offshorewind/

NAVIGATION

The UK Hydrographic Office (UKHO) has announced that it will be phasing out the manufacturing of paper charts with the aim to completely end production by late 2026.

Plans to withdraw the UKHO's portfolio are in response to more marine, naval and leisure users primarily using digital products and services for navigation. This announcement has caused considerable concern amongst the yachting community.

Carrying paper charts is still advised to complement digital charting. They are also useful for passage planning and for briefing crew. Imray and French SHOM continue to produce paper charts and provide excellent coverage of the Atlantic France area.

SHOM charts

See Appendix I, page 352

French SHOM charts are sold in varying scales: Planning charts (1:200,000), passage charts (1:50,000) and large-scale charts. The relevant chart and its scale is given on the information box for each port. In the textboxes, the scale is abbreviated by omitting the thousands; thus 1:50,000 is shown as (50).

The SHOM originals use the same international symbols as British charts and the recent ones have explanatory text in English as well as French. The 'L' series are on good quality thin paper and folded to A4. They are convenient to use, good value and very widely available in chandlers, book stores and even newsagents. They may not be updated by the retailer, so watch out for old stock.

Most navigation will be done using the 1:50,000 series but larger scale charts are necessary for some areas such as the Îles de Glénan and the Morbihan. Beware that a few SHOM charts are in ED50 and not WGS84 datum and positions obtained from a GPS working in WGS84 will need to be converted before being plotted on such a chart.

Imray charts

Imray charts provide an excellent and much cheaper alternative, particularly to supplement a chart plotter. They provide a passage chart, at a scale between 1:77,000 and 1:350,000, plus large-scale plans of most harbours. Another advantage is that all the Imray charts are in WGS84.

Waypoints

Waypoints have been included only as start points for port entry or to assist navigation through a narrow channel. Given the common usage of chart plotters, the long lists of waypoints used in previous editions have now been discarded.

Navigating among rocks

Rocky areas are rarely as bad as they look on the chart. At any moment, many rocks are either below the keel or showing above water; only those in between are dangerous. Suppose a boat with a 2·5m draught (including 0·5m for safety) is entering the Îles de Glénan at half tide on a calm sea. The height of tide will be about 2·9m so all rocks drying more than 2·9m will be visible above the surface. The boat only needs 2·5m so rocks drying 0·4m or less will be safely below the keel. Therefore, only rocks drying between 0·4m and 2·9m are dangerous. In the Îles de Glénan, there are surprisingly few.

In swell or bad weather, even rocks much deeper than the keel of the boat can cause unpleasant or even dangerous seas and are best given a wide berth.

Bearings

All bearings are expressed in degrees true and measured from the boat. Magnetic variation is negligible in 2022.

Lights

The height of lights is given in metres (m), and the range of visibility is given in nautical miles (M). Where a light has sectors, the limits of the sectors are usually shown on the plan.

The distance at which a light may be seen depends on its brightness and its height. Although its loom may be visible from a very long way off, a light itself cannot be seen when it is below the observer's horizon. Tables at which lights of various heights can be seen from different heights of eye are given in most almanacs.

The distance at which a light is visible also depends on the clarity of the atmosphere at the time. A 'nominal' range can be calculated for each light; this is the range its rays will reach if the meteorological visibility is 10M. It is this nominal range (given in *Admiralty List of Lights*) that is quoted in this book. On a clear night it may shine further and on a hazy night less far. Lights with a range of less than 10M will often merge into other lights on the shore.

The general practice is for coloured sectors to indicate dangers and white sectors safe passages. Generally, if a light shows a white safe sector with red and green sectors on each side, the green sector is to starboard and the red to port, at least in the principal channel. This rule is not universal and should be checked for each light. Narrow intensified sectors usually, but not always, fall within the safe width of the channel.

Lights are often 'directional'; that is, they show brightly over a very narrow sector and sometimes faintly outside the sector.

Beacons

In bad weather, the offshore marks on the Atlantic France coast suffer damage that may not be repaired for some months. Beacons and beacon towers can lose their topmarks or even be totally destroyed. In this case, they may be replaced by a small buoy, with the appropriate marking, until they are repaired.

Beacons are commonly painted to conform with the cardinal or lateral buoyage systems and often have the appropriate topmarks. The heads of breakwaters, forming a harbour entrance, are often marked with white paint, and may have a green triangle or red square indicating the side on which to pass them. Bridges often have similar marks to indicate the appropriate channel.

Phare du Plateau du Four 4M W of Le Croisic *Bobby Lawes*

Looking SW from La Roche-Bernard over visitors' pontoon *Nick Chavasse*

ASHORE

Formalities

On arrival at a port, the skipper should report to the capitainerie / bureau du port to book in, pay the marina charges and obtain the code for the toilets and showers.

It is essential to carry on board evidence that VAT has been paid on the vessel, and all yachts visiting France must carry a Certificate of Registry. Either full or small ships registration is acceptable. Documents must be originals and not photocopies. Heavy, on the spot, fines are imposed on defaulters.

All members of the ship's company must carry personal passports which must be stamped, by a customs officer, on arrival and before departing France to comply with the Schengen regulations.

It is not unusual to be boarded by customs even when underway. During a visit ask for *une fiche*; if the officers are satisfied, you will be given one to show that the vessel has been cleared. Should you be approached at a future date, it may only be necessary to show *la fiche* to satisfy the officials.

Every port and marina has its own system for checking in. In most cases, you will be asked to provide details for the boat and the crew, including passport numbers.

Provisions

Before setting out to buy stores it is important to remember that many shops, including some supermarkets, close at 1200LT and do not open again until 1500 or later. (This also applies to many harbour and marina offices.)

It is convenient to think about on-board provisions in three categories. There are foods with a long-shelf life, those items that keep a few days like meat, cheese or fresh vegetables, and those required on a daily basis, like fish and bread. Fresh milk is not always available in France but UHT milk is much more convenient and seems to be more palatable than it used to be, especially in the semi-skimmed form.

Limited provisions only may be taken to France, which is a consequence of Brexit. Major provisions should be purchased from a French supermarket on arrival. However, these wonderful big shops with their wide range of useful long-life provisions have mostly moved to the outskirts of towns, close to the resident population, and are rarely convenient for marinas. Chateaulin and Le Crouesty both have excellent supermarkets close by but in most cases a special expedition will be required.

Larger towns like Audierne, Vannes, Pornic and Rochefort have specialist shops selling cheese, meat or vegetables and will often have a daily covered market. Smaller towns make use of the touring markets. These move to a different village each day and serve the vast temporary population of holidaymakers. Piriac has a market three times a week. In Pornic and Vannes the market stalls are set up in the old winding streets and at La Rochelle and Rochefort the quality of the food on sale is second to none. Where possible market days have been included in the chapters.

Most small holiday villages have bread shops and many have fishmongers selling the local catch. These are often closed from lunchtime until late afternoon and invariably there are long queues just before lunch. When the text refers to 'all shops' it implies at least baker, grocer, butcher and cooked meats.

Websites

Websites have been included in the information box for each port. The larger ports will have their own website and the smaller ports' websites are usually sponsored by the local tourist office or town hall. The idea behind including website details is to provide additional information about local places which is easy to find. Going straight to a suggested URL (website address) should be quicker than using a search facility.

Telephones

Mobile phone coverage is generally very good. Roaming charges vary depending on the network and the contract used. Check with your mobile phone provider before leaving the UK.

Data

Coverage for data varies depending on location, signal strength and provider. It might be more effective to purchase a local SIM. The same applies to tablets. Laptops and tablets can be tethered to mobiles, depending on your network provider's restrictions and a MiFi dongle can also provide a workable solution.

Wifi

Pronounced *wee-fee* in French, is generally available in marinas. However, reception is very variable and is better the closer one is berthed to the capitainerie. In difficult situations most harbourmasters allow laptops to be operated in the harbour office and some offices have a computer for the use of visitors free of charge.

Charges for the use of the system vary widely and increasingly the use of Wifi is included in the marina charge. Wifi is often more reliable in cafés.

Wifi is not nearly as widespread as it is made out. This is due to the popularity of it and the restrictions in bandwidth. As a rule of thumb, it is more effective to use a mobile phone with 3G or 4G for email and to use WiFi for surfing the internet while sitting in the capitainerie or in a café. By adopting this strategy, you will save many hours of frustration trying to get a sufficiently good internet connection.

Water

Water is generally available on marina or pontoon berths. At other places, water may only be available in cans. On a harbour wall, the water supply may be of a size more suitable for a large fishing boat than for a yacht.

If water is not for drinking, it will be labelled '*non potable*'. Water taps rarely have hoses so it is best to carry one, along with a set of threaded adapters. If piped water is available it can be assumed that it is safe to drink, but it should be left to run for a while as there may be stagnant water in the pipes. As dogs often frequent French marinas it is as well to give the tap a good wash before use.

Fuel

Diesel and petrol are available at the waterside in most places. In France, it is illegal to use duty-free diesel for leisure craft and occasionally there will only be a duty-free pump for fishermen.

Marina diesel pumps are often 24-hour self-service, operated by a 'chip and pin' credit card. UK 'chip and pin' cards work usually but not always (in which case it will be necessary to find a marina attendant or a friendly local who can be persuaded to operate the pump for cash).

Yacht clubs

There are yacht clubs and sailing schools in most French harbours; they are invariably hospitable to visitors. Assistance or advice is always given readily, and showers are often available.

Facilities

Not all facilities are listed for every harbour and common sense must be used. 'All shops' in a city like Brest clearly means something different from 'All shops' in a small fishing port. In both cases, it means

Ports of registration

The following letters identify the port of registration of fishing vessels and pleasure boats:

AD	Audierne
AY	Auray
BR	Brest
BX	Bordeaux
CC	Concarneau
CM	Camaret
DZ	Douarnenez
GV	Le Guilvinec
IO	Île d'Oléron
LO	Lorient
LS	Les Sables d'Olonne
MN	Marennes
NA	Nantes
NO	Noirmoutier
SN	Saint Nazaire
VA	Vannes
YE	Île d'Yeu

Fishing boat in Belon, Concarneau *Nick Chavasse*

a good selection of the shops that might be expected in a town of that type. If there is a marina it may be assumed to have water and electricity available on the pontoons, showers and toilets and a displayed weather forecast.

Bicycles

Many long-term cruisers carry bicycles. In places, the best shops and particularly the big supermarkets are beyond easy walking distance. Some marinas have bicycles which can be borrowed free of charge.

All the islands are perfect for cycling. They are usually flat, have lots of cycle tracks and are too big to explore on foot but perfect on a bike. Bike hire is easy and it is usually possible to hire a decent bike. The mainland is slightly less bike-friendly but there are still a great many places that can be explored on a bike but would be too far on foot. Bike hire is possible but often requires a long walk to pick up and return the bike and the quality of bikes is a bit variable.

Visit www.francevelotourisme.com for cycle routes and general information on cycling in France.

Walking

Brittany provides stunning scenery and the national footpath scheme allows you to sample some fabulous walking. In Brittany it is the Grande Randonée (GR) 34, the Breton coastal path, which runs through L'Aber Wrac'h as far south as Quimperlé (west of Lorient). Download a free map from www.brittanytourism.com

The national scheme then has a break before resuming with GR8 known as the south Atlantic coastal trail, from Hourtin Plage (just south of the Gironde entrance) to Sare, in the western Pyrenees. If there is no national route where you are, ask at the local tourist office for information on local walks.

Wine

It would be quite wrong to cruise this part of France without tasting the wine. La Loire is famous for its Muscadet and Sauvignon Blanc and La Gironde, which leads to Bordeaux, for its Cabernet Sauvignon, Merlot and Malbec, amongst others.

HOW TO USE THIS PILOT

There are nine sections in the book, loosely based on the French departments, each containing about 12 ports. The description of each port is set out in a standard form:

Information box

At the start of the chapter is a box containing the key data that a skipper is likely to need. Some abbreviations are used and these are explained below under abbreviations.

Main text

The body of the chapter provides a brief description of the port followed by pilotage notes, suggestions about berthing and anchorages and finally a description of the facilities ashore. The aerial and sea-level photographs are an integral part of the chapter and information is often provided in the captions that is not provided elsewhere in the chapter.

In pilotage information, a draught of 3m or less is assumed and depths greater than this are either not mentioned or described as deep. Where depths or drying heights are given, they are always related to LAT.

Air draught is based on Mean Level and considered to be that of a masted yacht. Motorboats will often be able to go beyond bridges that are described as the limit of navigation.

The side-panels contain personal stories by the author which hopefully add a different perspective and more breadth of information in the book.

There are also some red Warning Boxes which highlight specific dangers worthy of emphasis.

Abbreviations

HW	high water
HW+0230	two and a half hours after HW
HWN	high water at neaps
HWS	high water at springs
kts	knots
LW	low water
LWN	low water at neaps
LWS	low water at springs
m	metres
M	nautical miles

Key to symbols used on plans

 depths in METRES

 rocks with less than 2 metres depth over them

 rock just below or on the surface

 a shoal or reef with the least depth shown

↳ wreck partially above water

⊕ wreck

④ Wk dangerous wreck with depth over it

◎ ◎ eddies

 rock ballasting on a mole or breakwater

above-water rocks

beach

cliffs

⊹ church

☿ mosque

✗ windmill

Ⴧ wind turbine

⌐ chimney

⍟ pine

⍟ trees other than pine

⌗ castle

ruins

houses / buildings

fish farm

⚓ anchorage

⚓ prohibited anchorage

⚓ harbour with yacht berths

⚓ yacht harbour / marina

Ⓥ visitors' berths

visitors' moorings

▲ port of entry

⊖ customs

harbourmaster

☦ water

⚡ electricity

shower

waste pump-out

fuel

travel-hoist

Ⓐ chandlers

tourist information

crane

✉ post office

✈ airport

slipway

nature reserve

⊙ beacon

port hand buoy

starboard hand buoy

mooring buoy

tower

Characteristics

✻ light

white light

red light

green light

sectored light

F fixed

Fl. flash

Fl(2) group flash

Oc. occulting

R red

G green

W white

M miles

s sand

m mud

w weed

r rock

P.A. Position approximate

THE BRETON LANGUAGE

To those unused to Celtic languages, Breton place names seem strange and hard to remember. Many can be translated quite easily and once understood become entirely appropriate and much easier to remember. The wonderfully named Kareg Kreiz, for example, simply means middle rock.

Breton pronunciation is more like English than French, with the final consonants sounded. The letters c'h represent the final sound of Scottish loch or Irish lough (but not English lock); there is indeed a word *loc'h*, meaning a lake or pool; ch is pronounced as sh in shall. The French books and charts do not always distinguish between these, and there may be some errors in this book in consequence. In France, as in England, mobility and the radio / TV are killing regional differences. Thus Raz is now usually pronounced Rah; Penmarc'h, pronounced Penmargh a generation ago, is now often Painmar, and Bénodet has gone from Benodette to Bainoday and collected an accent in the process. The most misleading example is *porz*, which means an open anchorage but is often wrongly changed to the French word *port*.

Breton	English	Breton	English	Breton	English
aber	estuary	ell	rock, shallow	kleuz(iou)	hollow, deep
anaon	the dead	enez	island	koad, goad	wood
al, an, ar	the	er a, an	the	kornog	shoal
arvor	seaside	Breton	English	koz	old
aven	river	fank	mud	kreiz	middle
B (try P)		froud, fred	strong current	kriben	crest
balan, banal	broom	freu	river	Breton	English
bann, benn	hilltop	G (try K)		lan, lann	monastery
barr	summit, top	garo, garv	rough	marc'h	horse
baz	shoal	gavr	goat	melen	yellow
beg	point, cape	glas	green	men	rock
beniget	cut, slit	goban	shallow	mor, vor	sea, seawater
benven, bosven	above-water rock	gromell, gromilli	roaring	nevez	new
		gwenn	white, pure	penn	head, point
bian, bihan	small	hir	long	plou, plo	parish
bili, vili	shingle	hoc'h, houc'h	pig	porz, porzig	anchorage
bir, vir	needle, point	iliz	church	poul	pool, anchorage
bran	crow	izel	shallow	raz	strait, tide race
bras, braz	large	inis	island	roc'h	rock
bre, brenn	small hill	kan(iou), kanal	channel	ros	wooded knoll
breiz	Brittany	karn	cairn	ruz	red
bri, brienn	cliff	kareg	rock	ster	river, inlet
C (try K)		kastel	castle	stiv, stiff	fountain, spring
D (try T)		kazek	mare	teven, tevenneg	cliff, dune
daou	two	kein	shoal	toull	hole, deep *place*
don, doun	deep	kel(ou)	large rock	trez, treaz	sand, beach
dour	water	ker	house, hamlet	V (try B, M)	
du	black	kern	summit, sharp peak	W (try Gw)	
				yoc'h	group of rocks

Looking NE over Molène towards mainland *Nick Chavasse*

I. L'Aber Wrac'h to Le Conquet

The Chenal du Four and the Raz de Sein are two of Europe's nastier tidal races. As a result, many skippers like to pass through this region as quickly as possible. This is a pity because it is a splendid cruising ground with lots of attractive places to visit.

If coming from the UK or Ireland, landfall may be made at L'Aber Wrac'h or, in good weather, at Ouessant. Some of the ports described in this section are more suited to shoal, lifting or bilge keel yachts. Ouessant and Molène are useful to bear in mind if the tide is adverse and the weather is fine. L'Aber-Ildut, with its new marina, should also be considered.

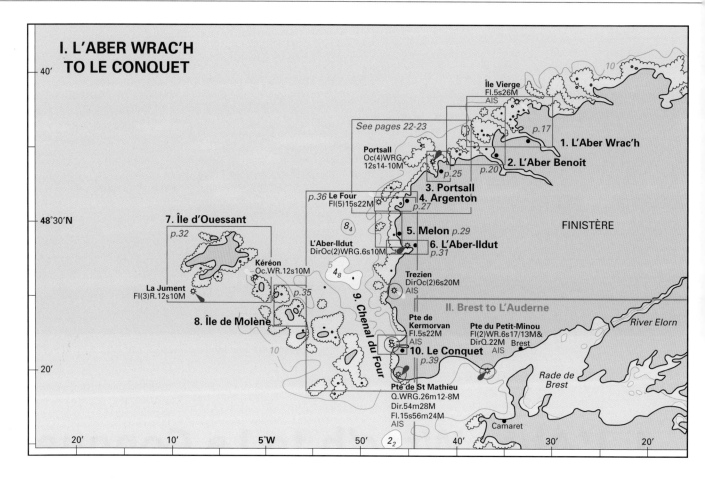

I. L'ABER WRAC'H
TO LE CONQUET

40'

Île Vierge
Fl.5s26M
AIS

See pages 22-23

p.17

1. L'Aber Wrac'h

Portsall
Oc(4)WRG
12s14-10M

2. L'Aber Benoit

p.25

p.20

3. Portsall

p.36 Le Four
Fl(5)15s22M

4. Argenton

p.27

48°30'N

7. Île d'Ouessant

p.32

8₄

5. Melon p.29

6. L'Aber-Ildut

FINISTÈRE

L'Aber-Ildut
DirOc(2)WRG.6s10M

p.31

Kéréon
Oc.WR.12s10M

5

4₈

Trezien
DirOc(2)6s20M
AIS

La Jument
Fl(3)R.12s10M

.0

p.35

II. Brest to L'Auberne

8. Île de Molène

9. Chenal du Four

Pte de
Kermorvan
Fl.5s22M
AIS

Pte du Petit-Minou
Fl(2)WR.6s17/13M&
DirQ.22M Brest
AIS

River Elorn

10

20'

10. Le Conquet

p.39

Rade de
Brest

Pte de St Mathieu
Q.WRG.26m12-8M
Dir.54m28M
Fl.15s56m24M
AIS

Camaret

20'   10'   5°W   50'   2₂   40'   30'   20'

Looking NW over the approaches to L'Aber Wrac'h *Nick Chavasse*

Finistère tidal streams

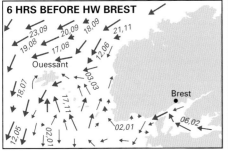

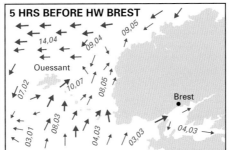

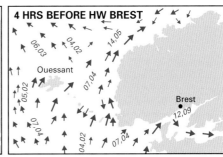

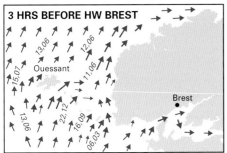

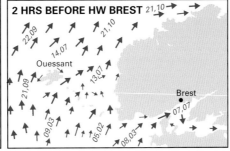

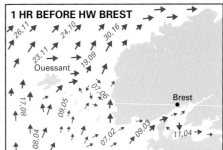

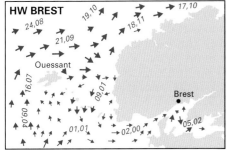

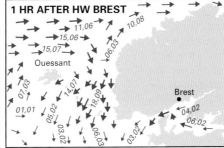

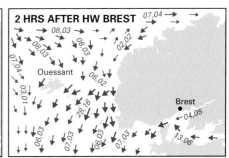

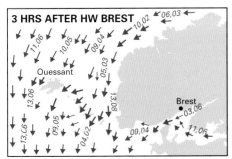

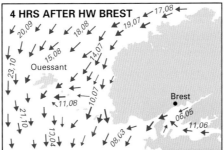

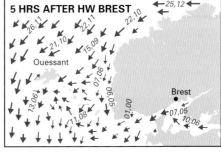

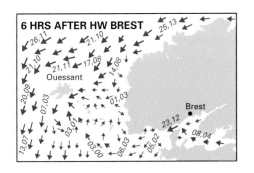

TIDAL STREAMS EXPLANATION

The figures shown against the arrows are the mean rates at neaps and springs in tenths of a knot.

Thus *07,15* - mean neaps rate *0·7* knots, mean springs rate *1·5* knots

1 L'Aber Wrac'h

48°35'·94N 4°33'·64W

Shelter
All weather entry. Excellent shelter in marina. Rather exposed from N and NW on wavebreaker and moorings. The outside of the wavebreaker is untenable in strong north and northwesterly winds. Excellent shelter up river at Paluden, 1·5M

Depth restrictions
2·3m in marina. Beware rocks SE of marina entrance marked by Y buoys and beacons inside and outside the wavebreaker

Night entry
Yes, via Grand Chenal but 5M visibility needed to see Ldg Lts

Tidal information
HW Brest +0030, LW +0037

Mean height of tide (m) L'Aber Wrac'h

HWS	HWN	LWN	LWS
7·7	6·1	2·8	1·0

Tidal streams (off the entrance)
ENE-going stream starts HW Brest -0400
WSW-going stream starts Brest +0200
Rate 3kn at springs 1·5kn at neaps

Berthing
In marina or on mooring buoys outside marina or on buoys up river at Paluden

Facilities
All including fuel berth on Pontoon C but shops 2km uphill in Landéda (Bourg)

Charts
SHOM 7094 (25)
Imray C35

Communications
VHF 09
HM ① 02 98 04 91 62
www.port-aberwrach.com

Good staging post

L'Aber Wrac'h itself is no more than a small village with a large sailing school and a boatyard. But it is on a beautiful estuary and is a useful stop to enable one to get the tide right for going down the Chenal Du Four. The marina is primarily for the locals but there is sufficient space for 70 visitors including the buoys situated just outside the marina entrance. There are bars and restaurants but if stores are needed it is a 2km walk up the hill or bus ride to the village of Landéda.

There is something exciting about L'Aber Wrac'h with its spectacular entrance, which is not difficult but does require concentration, especially the first time. In the summer you will see lots of school children learning to sail. The river enjoys a small and welcoming marina and those on a limited budget may find a mooring opposite the marina or up river at Paludin.

The inside of the breakwater is used for visitors
Nick Chavasse

PILOTAGE

Grand Chenal

By day The easiest approach is by the Grand Chenal which begins 400m southwest of the Libenter west cardinal buoy which marks the extensive Libenter reef. In good visibility the leading marks on Île Wrac'h and at Lanvaon on the hill 1·5M behind Île Wrac'h may be seen on 100° but from Libenter, Lanvaon is 4·5M away. If the leading line cannot be identified, steer on 100° to pass following marks in sequence: Trépied port hand buoy, Grand Pot de Beurre port hand beacon and Petit Pot de Beurre conspicuous BYB east cardinal beacon tower to port. Note that Grand Pot de Beurre is smaller in size than Petit Pot de Beurre which may be confusing. Once past the Petit Pot de Beurre and the Basse de la Croix starboard hand buoy alter course to 128° up the marked channel towards the marina.

Libenter W cardinal buoy
Nick Chavasse

Grand Pot de Beurre *Nick Chavasse*

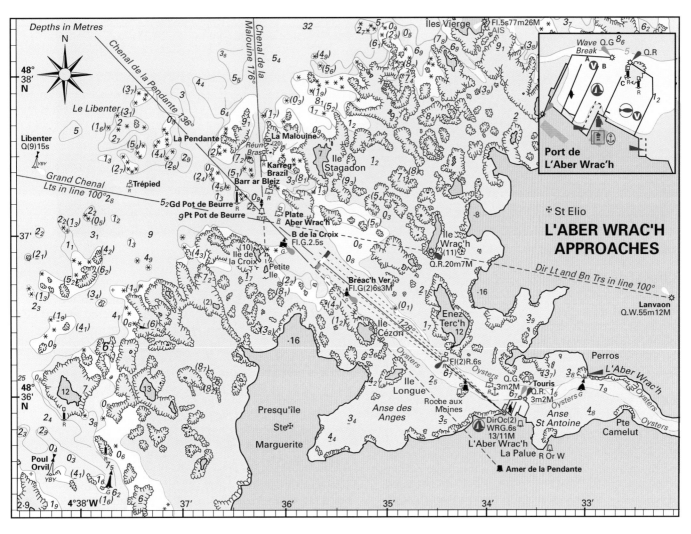

By night After Libenter west cardinal buoy bring Lanvaon F.dir Q.W. in line with Q.R. on Île Wrac'h on leading line 100°. Note that Trépied, Grand Pot de Beurre and Petit Pot de Beurre **are not lit**. Once past Petit Pot de Beurre, steer 128° up the marked and lit channel towards the marina. This is the only navigable channel by night.

Petit Pot de Beurre with white obelisk on Petite Île beyond
Nick Chavasse

Chenal de la Malouine

The alternative approach from the north and east is the Chenal de la Malouine which provides a shortcut of 2–3M. However, it should only be used in daylight and in good conditions and preferably above half-tide. The channel is named after the large rock La Malouine which is left close to port halfway down. Start from a position 1·5M west of Île Vierge and identify the large La Malouine rock with the red port hand tower beacon behind it. Next identify the conspicuous BYB east cardinal tower beacon Petit Pot de Beurre which is the front leading mk and steer 176° towards it when the rear leading mk which is a white obelisk on Petite Île will be seen. There may be a strong cross-tide. Beware of the shallow patch (0·7m) close to starboard of the leading line at the entrance to the channel and the drying rock on the port side a little further on. In any swell seas will be breaking on the starboard side. Once La Malouine Rock and the port hand beacon tower are passed, course should be altered to port to leave two port hand buoys to port and the Petit Pot de Beurre to starboard and the main channel will then be joined. Not suitable for entry by night.

Marina entrance *Nick Chavasse*

Chenal de la Pendante

The third approach channel from the northwest is the Chenal de la Pendante but it is narrow, has a strong set across it and the leading line is difficult to identify from seaward. For a first time it should only be used on departure with a large scale chart, above half-tide and then only in good conditions. Not suitable for entry by night. It will not be described further here.

BERTHS AND ANCHORAGES

Either in the marina or on visitors moorings north of the marina. There is also an anchorage rather exposed to the northwest in 12–17m between Roches aux Moines starboard hand tower beacon and the lifeboat slip but beware oyster beds on either side. Yachts that can take the ground can anchor in the Anse des Anges clear of the oyster beds. Visiting vessels up to 15m moor to the wave-breaker pontoon where there is 2·3m. The inside of the wavebreaker is more sheltered. Inside the marina are pontoon berths in 1m and 2m for vessels up to 12m. Beware of rocks marked by yellow buoys and beacons both inside and outside the western end of the eastern wave-breaker.

The visitors' moorings are in 5–7m and can take vessels up to 18m. The fee charged is 80% of that charged in the marina.

Paluden

There are 4 visitors' moorings 3M further up the river at Paluden which is beautifully sheltered in a blow. There is not much water at LW springs but there is water on the pontoon given sufficient tide. There is a good restaurant overlooking the moorings and it is only about 1·5M to Lannilis where there are plenty of shops. Oysters, mussels and crab may be bought from the wholesale warehouse in Paluden. Anchoring in the river is permitted but beware of the oyster beds.

ASHORE AT L'ABER WRAC'H

There is a boatyard, chandler, bars and restaurants but if stores are required the shops and supermarket are just over a mile up the hill at Landéda. There is a fuel berth at the base of C pontoon and WiFi in the marina. A good bus service to Brest takes you via Lannilis where you sometimes need to change bus. Supermarket, Utile, in Landeda will accept orders by phone and deliver to the marina.

Basic provisions may be bought at the Café du Port in season. Recommended restaurant is Captain ☏ 02 98 04 82 03 which has fabulous views towards the river entrance. There is a lovely walk along the river towards Paluden; part of the coastal path.

Sunset over the approaches to L'Aber Wrac'h looking NW
Nick Chavasse

Looking E across marina and upriver *Nick Chavasse*

Looking NW over the approaches *Nick Chavasse*

2 L'Aber Benoît

48°34'·64N 04°36'·89W

Shelter
Excellent, but do not enter at night, in poor vis, nor in strong WNW winds; best near LW when dangers may be seen. Good shelter at Stellac'h

Depth restrictions
2m as far as St Pabu on South bank

Night entry
Not recommended

Tidal information
HW Brest +0023, LW +0027

Mean height of tide (m) L'Aber Benoît

HWS	HWN	LWN	LWS
7·9	6·3	1·2	3·0

Tidal streams
At Petite Fourche ENE starts HW Brest -5¼
W starts HW Brest +1
Rate 2¾ at springs

Berthing
Many moorings in lower reach, call HM for allocation and possible anchorage up river

Facilities
Minimal, so best to be self-sufficient

Charts
SHOM *7094 (25)*
Imray *C35*

Communications
VHF 09
HM ☏ 06 19 87 75 39
(0830-1230, 1500-1830 Jul-Aug)
www.pays-des-abers.fr

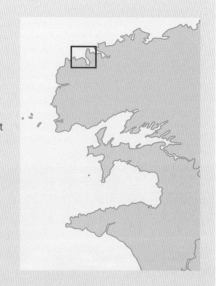

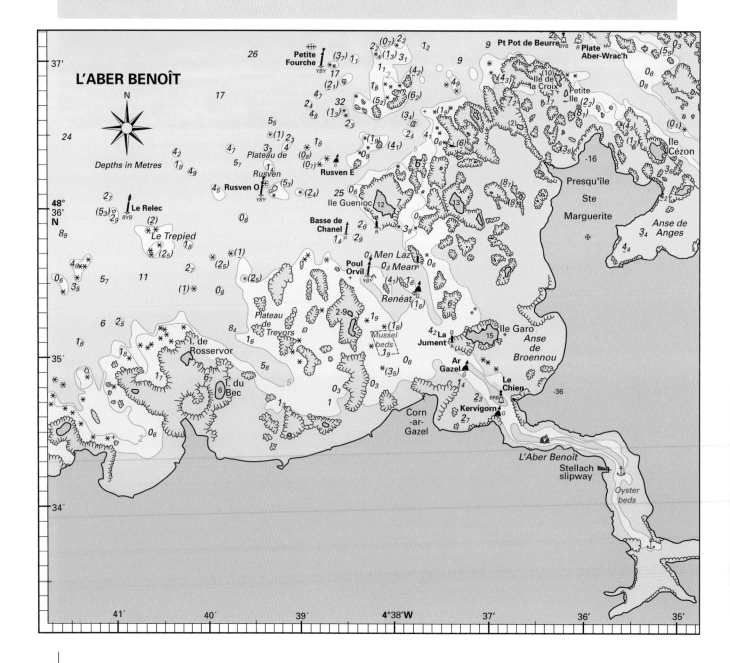

Looking N towards Port du Vil *Nick Chavasse*

Peaceful river valley

L'Aber Benoît is the little sister *aber* (estuary) to L'Aber Wrac'h and has beautiful scenery and lovely beaches. It is unlit and relatively unknown. It does not feature in *Bloc Marine*, the French almanac. If you seek a peaceful night on someone else's buoy or at anchor then L'Aber Benoît is a good choice.

PILOTAGE

L'Aber Benoît approach and entrance

By day From Petite Fourche west cardinal steer 165° for 1·15M to leave Île Guenioc to port, and follow the marked channel into the river, leaving La Jument and the isolated danger mark (Le Chien) to port.

By night The entrance is unlit and therefore not recommended.

La Jument *Nick Chavasse*

Le Chien
Nick Chavasse

BERTHS AND ANCHORAGES

It might be possible to use a private mooring and best to check with the HM in season. Otherwise there may be room to anchor in 1·5m out of the fairway with Stellach being the favourite option. There is more room to anchor further upriver.

⚓ Brenduff

48°33'·69N 4°35'·20W

Charming, sheltered anchorage amongst well spread-out moorings but beware of oyster beds. If you are energetic, you can dinghy upriver to Treglonou on the tide, walk to Lannilis and take the bus to Brest.

ASHORE IN L'ABER BENOÎT

There are no facilities of note in the surrounding hamlets and villages. There are beaches and good walks.

View of Stellach slipway from the moorings *Nick Chavasse*

L'Aber Benoît is a charming uncomplicated river, ideal if you have just crossed the Channel, arrived in L'Aber Wrac'h and want a short trip to placate the crew. There's plenty of scope for a good walk on the GR34 coastal path followed by a barbecue on the beach. Nearest bar/restaurant is Le Charabanc
☎ 02 98 38 09 35.

Île Guenioc is thought to be where British airmen who had been shot down were escorted by the resistance and helped to rendezvous with naval MGBs (Motor Gun Boats) from Devon and Cornwall.

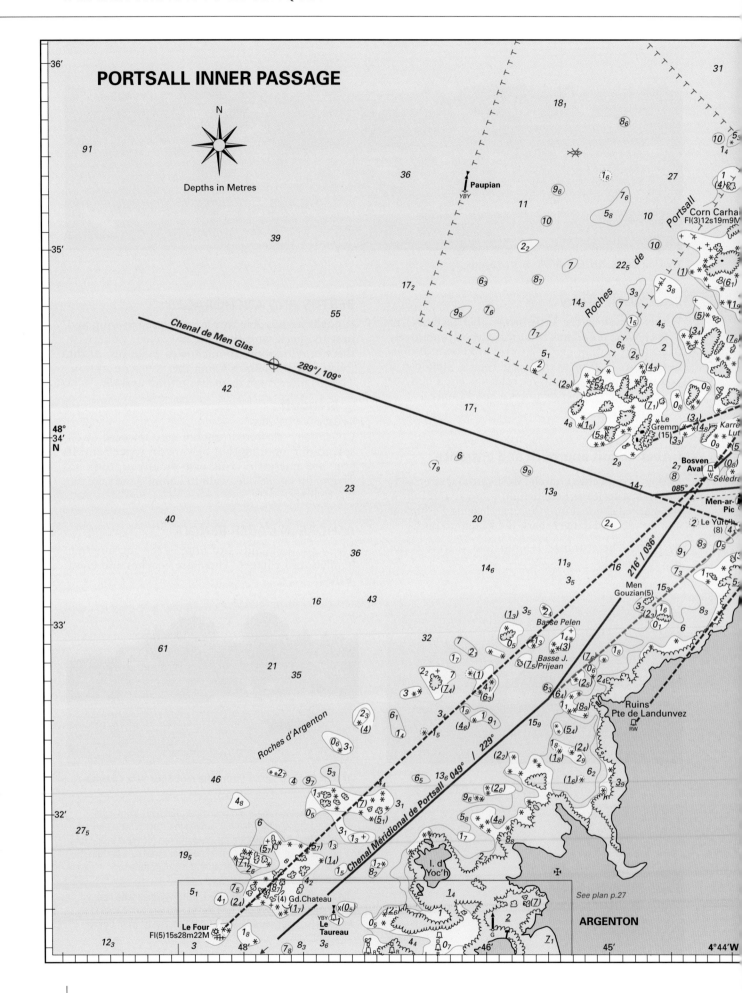

PORTSALL INNER PASSAGE

N

Depths in Metres

91

36

18₁

31

8₆

10 5₃
1₄

36

Paupian
YBY

9₆

1₆

27

1
(4)

35'

11

7₆

5₈

10

Portsall

Corn Carha
Fl(3)12s19m9M

39

55

10

22₅

de

10

Chenal de Men Glas

2₂

7

14₃

Roches

3₃

3₈

289°/109°

17₂

6₃

8₇

1₅

4₅

(5)
(1)

1₉

9₈

7₆

6₅

(3₄)

(7₆)

48°
34'
N

42

17₁

7₇

5₁

2₅

2

(4₃)

(5)

(3₄)

5₃

4₆

0₈

0₉

(7₁)

Le
Gremm
(15)

0₉

(3₄)
(4₆)

Karre
Lut

6

7₉

9₉

4₆

(1₅)

(5₉)

2₉

085°

Bosven
Aval

27

8

0₉

(0₆)

W

Sélédra

23

13₉

14₇

216/036°

Men-ar-
Pic

40

20

2₄

2

Le Yu'ch
(8) (4

36

14₆

11₉

16

9₁

8₃

0₅

3₅

7₃

1

Men
Gouzian(5)

15₃

83

(1₃)

3₅

*2₄

(2₃)

1₆

0₁

6

16

43

Basse Pelen
+
1₄
0₅
*1₃
*(3)

(2₃)

32

7

1₇

*(1)

(7₆)

0₆

1₈

0₅

(2₅)

2₄

2₂
3 **

+ 7
(7₄)

4₁
(6₃)

Basse J.
Prijean
(7₅)

6₃

(6₄)

1₁

(8₉)

Ruins
Pte de Landunvez
RW

2₃

6₁

3₄

1₉

1 9₁
(4₆) 9₃
1₅

15₉

(5₄)

(4)

1₄

0₆ 3₁

*3₁

1₈

(2₄)

2₉

(1₈)

6₂

Roches d'Argenton

*2₇

4 9₇

5₃

6₅

13₆

049°/229°

9₆ **

(2₆)

(1₆)

3₉

46

1₃

(7)

3₁

4₄

(2₆)

5₈

(4₆)

4₈

0₅

(5₁)

Chenal Méridional de Portsall

1₇

8₂

6

3₁ 1₃ +

33'

61

21

35

32'

27₅

19₅

(5₇)

1₃

(1₄)

1₂
8₂

I. d
Yoc'h

1₄

7₅

4₂

See plan p.27

5₁

4₁ (2₄)

(4) Gd.Chateau
x(0₅)

1₇

2

ARGENTON

12₃

Le Four
Fl(5)15s28m22M

3

1₈

48'

(7₈) 8₃ 3₆

Le
Taureau
YBY

0₅

46'

4₄

0₇

G

2

7₁

45'

4°44'W

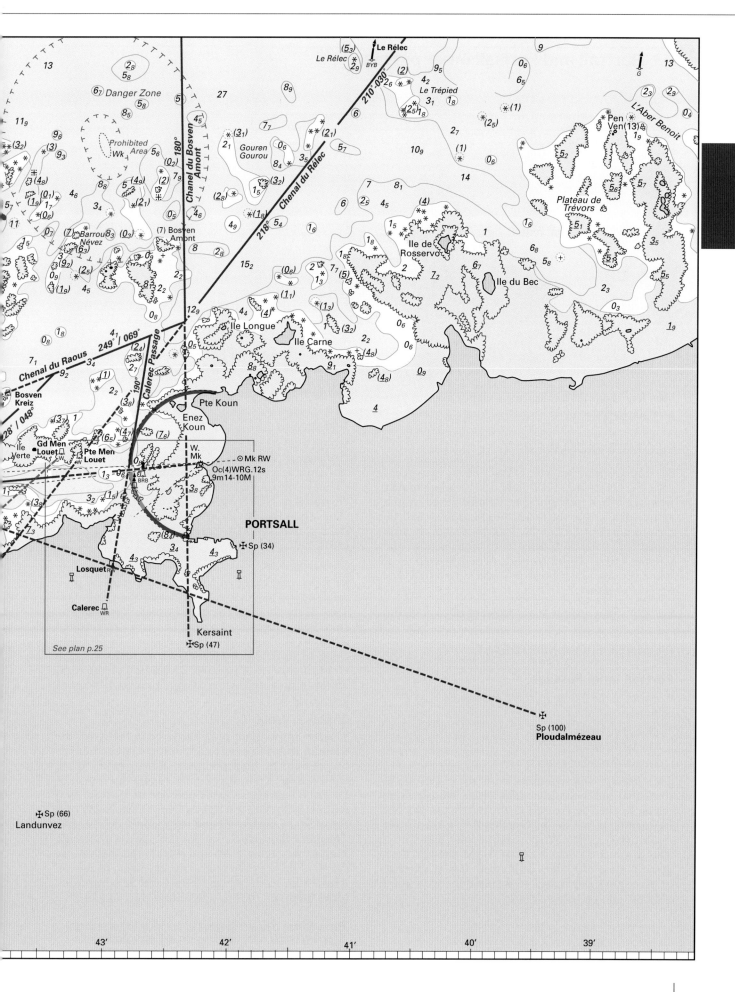

13

(2₈)
5₈

6₇ Danger Zone
5₈

8₅

11₉

9₆
(3) 9₃

*(3₂)

Prohibited
Area 5₆

(0₂)
7₉
(2)

(4₉)
(2)

8₈ 5

4₆
(4₈)
(0₁)
(1₉) 1₇
*(0₆)
5₇ (2₁)

3₄

0₇
(7) Barrou 8₃ (0₃)
Névez
16₃
(9₂)
0₉
(2₅)
(1₉) 4₅

11

(7) Bosven
Amont

0₈ 1₈

Chenal du Raous 4₁ / 069°
(2₄)
249°
7₁
9₂ 3₄

Bosven
Kreiz

Calerec Passage

(1)

2₂

(3₇) 1
(6₅)
(4₇)

Ile
Verte
Gd Men
Louet
Pte Men
Louet
(7₆)

28° / 048°

1₃ 0₆

(3₈)
3₂ (1₅)

7₃

(3₈)

27

4₅

Chanel du Bosven Amont

180°

218°

5

(3₁)
2₁

7₇

Gouren
Gourou
0₆
8₄
3₅

(3₂)

(2₈)

(1₈)

4₉

12₉

15₂

5₄
1₆

(0₆)
1₃

(1₁)

(1₃)

4₄

(4)

Ile Longue

Ile Carne

0₅

8₈

9₁

(4₈)

Chenal du Rélec

210-030

6

5₇

Le Rélec
Le Rélec ※
2₉ BYB

Le Rélec

(5₃)

(2)
2₆

9₅

Le Trépied
3₁
1₈

8₅ 1₈
(2₅)

(2₅)
4₂

(1)

2₇

(1)

10₉

14

7

8₁

6
2₅

4₅

1₈

Ile de
Rosservo

1₅

2

7₁ (5)

2₂

0₆

0₆

(3₂)

1₈

(4₈)

4

7₂

6₇

Ile du Bec

2₃

0₃

9

0₆
6₅

(2)

8₂

9₅

Pen
Ven(13)
1₉

L'Aber Benoît

2₃ (2₉)

0₄

13

G

5₂

Plateau de
Trévors

5₁

5₇

3₅

6₈
5₈

1₆

1

5₅

1₉

Pte Koun

Enez
Koun

W.
Mk

⊖ Mk RW
Oc(4)WRG.12s
9m14-10M

BRB

3₈

PORTSALL

✠ Sp (34)

8₄

3₄

3₄

4₃

4₃

Losquet RW

Calerec
WR

4₃

Kersaint
✠ Sp (47)

See plan p.25

✠
Sp (100)
Ploudalmézeau

✠ Sp (66)
Landunvez

43'   42'   41'   40'   39'

3 Portsall and Portsall inner passage

48°33′70N 04°42′79W

Shelter
Drying harbour with good shelter except in strong north-westerlies

Depth restrictions
Accessible approx 3 hours either side of HW

Night entry
Not recommended

Tidal information
HW Brest +0017, LW +0020

Mean height of tide (m) Portsall

HWS	HWN	LWN	LWS
7·5	5·9	2·7	1·0

Tidal streams
HW Brest -0500 NE-going flood
HW Brest +0130 SW-going ebb

Berthing
Alongside the E side of the jetty where it dries about 4m. 11 drying buoys in the beach area

Facilities
Minimal so best to be self-sufficient. Hypermarket at Ploudalmèzeau 2M

Charts
SHOM *7094 (25)*
Imray *C35*

Communications
VHF 09
HM ① 02 98 45 19 18
mobile 06 75 51 89 80

Quaint drying harbour

With difficult approaches and as a totally drying harbour which is vulnerable to swell, Portsall has been less spoilt than other ports mainly because it is a drying harbour.

PILOTAGE FROM WEST

By day Chenal de Men Glas. From waypoint 48°34′·24N 04°47′·17W Steer 109° leading marks front; Le Yurch rock and rear; Ploudalmezau church spire. Men ar Pic starboard beacon tower will be seen to north of Le Yurc'h. This line leaves the first group of Portsall Rocks with conspicuous Le Gremm (15m) 400m to port. When Bosven Aval white beacon tower bears 070° turn onto 085° for harbour entrance.

By night The entrance is not recommended at night.

PILOTAGE FROM NORTHEAST

Portsall Inner Passage

Consists of the following three interconnecting channels:

> Chenal du Rélec
> Chenal du Raous
> Chenal Meriodional de Portsall

This passage interconnects with six channels, in total, that run within two miles of the shore passing inside Roches de Portsall in the north and Roches d'Argenton in the south. Together they form a short cut between L'Aber Wrac'h and Le Four lighthouse. The distance saving is about 1·5M shorter than going outside of Roches de Portsall. It is an exercise in precision navigation and is best done with good visibility and **up-to-date** charts.

Fast-flowing currents and multiple obstacles require good navigational skills. A chart plotter on the binnacle is an excellent tool when navigating the Portsall Inner Passage. We did this at spring tides and it was exciting!

Tidal streams

Strong tidal streams make the passage navigationally challenging. Avoid wind over tide conditions which can cause severe overfalls west of Île Verte and in the Chenal Méridional de Portsall. Slack water off Portsall is at HW Brest +1 when the W going stream starts to make. If you are heading northeast, then slack water is at HW Brest-6 as the E going flood starts.

Chenal du Rélec

Le Rélec east cardinal should be approached on a track of not less than 210° to avoid the Queyn-an-Treis 1·8m shoal to the north which breaks in any swell below half tide. Leaving Le Rélec east cardinal 200m to starboard, Le Trépied shoal (dries 2·5m) close to port and note the line of rocks Gouren Gourou close to starboard. Leave Île Longue (6m) 300m to port and when abeam alter to 249°on to Chenal du Raous.

Chenal du Raous

The stream will not necessarily be in line with the track in this narrowest part of the passage but the line should be held precisely. When about 500m from Bosven Kreiz alter course to take up transit of La Four lighthouse just open left of Bosven Aval with its white beacon tower. Only towards LW will the rocks be uncovered and the channel clearly seen. The immediate dangers are to starboard with Karreg Luth shoal drying 5·2m and to port the shallows to the W of Île Verte. Note also the extension of Bosven Aval 100m to the south (0·4m) and Seledran rock (dries 0·8m) on the opposite side of the channel.

Note Bosven Kreiz and Bosven Aval are easily confused as they look very similar when travelling at speed. Approaching from the N, Bosven Kreiz is the first and the fatter of the two beacons and has a pole on its top. Bosven Aval is thinner and does not have a pole on its top.

Bosven Kreiz *Nick Chavasse*

Bosven Aval *Nick Chavasse*

Le Taureau W cardinal beacon with Argenton beyond
Nick Chavasse

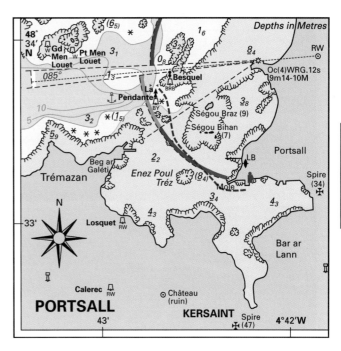

To clear these rocks a minor alteration is required as follows:

When 500m short of Bosven Aval come to port and steer 220° leaving Bosven Aval 120m to starboard.

Chenal Méridional de Portsall

Steer 216° making adjustment as necessary to hold stern transit keeping Bosven Kreiz on a bearing of 036° and just open to the left of Bosven Aval.

When abeam Pointe de Landunvez RW beacon tower alter course to starboard onto 229° and the stern transit will be 049° with Grand Men Louet beacon tower (rear) and the saddle of Le Yurc'h (front) aligned.

This line leads about 0·2M northwest of the prominent Île d'Yoch and about 200m south of Grand Chateau rock (6m) and leaves Le Taureau W Cardinal beacon tower 200m to port. After Le Taureau there is clearer water south of the line. The line then leads into open water about 0·3M south of Le Four lighthouse.

Pointe de Landunvez RW beacon tower at left *Nick Chavasse*

Looking WNW over Portsall harbour with Roches de Portsall in the background. The prominent mark at the top right is Corn Carhai lighthouse. The isolated rock at top left is Le Yurc'h *Peter Carnegie*

BERTHS AND ANCHORAGES

Alongside the east side of the mole where it dries about 4m, but check at the sailing school as fishing boats use it. 11 drying visitors' buoys are available on the beach area. However, grounding and floating off, even with protection of the mole can be uncomfortable and even dangerous. The bottom is hard sand. Anchorage in 5-10m south of two Men Louet beacons or closer in to west of La Pendante in 2-4m.

ASHORE IN PORTSALL

Shops in Bar ar Lann village between Portsall and Kersaint. Hypermarket in Ploudalmèzeau 2M.

Portsall is infamous for the *Amoco Cadiz* disaster which happened on 16 March 1978. The fully loaded, Very Large Crude Carrier (VLCC) suffered steering failure off Roches de Portsall. It foundered on Men Goulven rock (dries 4·9m) 1·5M north of the harbour and broke in two, releasing 1·6 million barrels of oil into the sea. An 18-mile oil slick spread eastwards devastating beaches, harbours and marine life as far as Lezardrieux.

A museum on the quayside at Portsall, 'Ancre An Or' records the event and the heroic struggle of local communities to restore the environment to its natural state.

Looking NW over drying moorings towards Portsall *Nick Chavasse*

4 Argenton

48°31'·35N 04°45'·76W (1·7M E of Le Four lighthouse)

Shelter
Drying harbour with good shelter from N and S but open to the W and subject to swell

Depth restrictions
Good access 3 hours either side of HW

Night entry
Not recommended

Tidal information
HW Brest +0100, LW +0100

Mean height of tide (m) Portsall

HWS	HWN	LWN	LWS
7·3	5·7	2·6	1·0

Tidal streams
HW Brest -0545 ENE
HW Brest +0100 WSW

Anchoring
S of Brividic and the leading line in a pool with about 5m on sand

Facilities
Minimal so best to be self-sufficient. Supermarket at Porspoder 1M

Charts
SHOM *7094 (25)*
Imray *C35*

Communications
HM mobile 06 71 50 29 44
www.nautisme-finistere.com

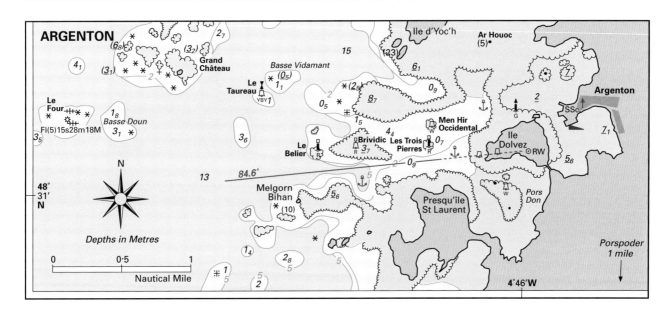

Large, shallow, sandy bay with anchorage

Argenton is a large, shallow, sandy bay that dries out completely at LWS making it a more suitable harbour at neaps. Anchorage is about 0·8M from the drying inner harbour, which makes for a long dinghy ride to this shore.

PILOTAGE

By day From waypoint 48°31'·15N 04°48'·11W, 0·2M southeast of Le Four lighthouse, steer 086° for 1·1M to bring Les Trois Pierres lateral beacon abeam on port side. Proceed to harbour if sufficient water.

By night The entrance is not recommended at night.

Looking N at Les Trois Pierres and Men Hir Occidental beyond
Nick Chavasse

Looking NE towards Argenton with Porz-Don W beacon to port *Nick Chavasse*

BERTHS AND ANCHORAGES

South of Brividic and the leading line in a pool with about 5m on sand. Possible anchorage east of Les Trois Pierres beacon and north of Île Dolvez.

ASHORE IN ARGENTON

Shops in Argenton and supermarket in Porspoder 1M. Restaurants and bars on south side of bay.

Brividic
Nick Chavasse

Above Looking NW towards Melon anchorage with Le Four in distance *Nick Chavasse*

Below Looking E at Melon beach *Nick Chavasse*

5 Melon

48°29'·14N 04°46'·35W (1M N of L'Aber-Ildut)

Shelter
The Anse de Melon is a small drying harbour sheltered from the E and at LW from the W behind Île de Melon

Depth restrictions
Drying inlet

Night entry
Not recommended

Tidal information
As for L'Aber-ildut

Anchoring
2 cables N of Île de Melon in 2-8m depth

Facilities
Minimal, so best to be self-sufficient

Charts
SHOM *7122 (25)*
Imray *C35 (75)*

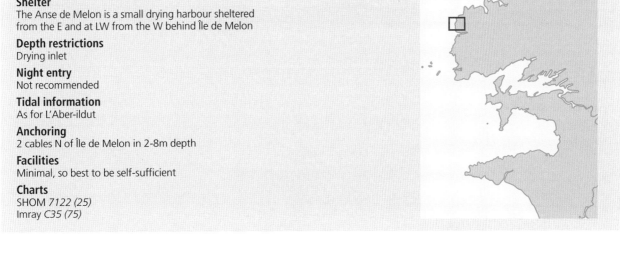

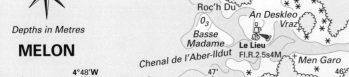

Depths in Metres

MELON

A small drying harbour

The Anse de Melon is a small drying harbour that is little more than an inlet with a beach, but in settled conditions it offers a pleasant anchorage.

PILOTAGE

By day The key to the approach is to identify Le Compère rock about 1M north-northwest of Île de Melon. This dries at 6·6m and is covered at HW springs. From wpt 48°30'·3N 04°47'·82W steer 092° with Le Compere rock in line with La Bougie (the candle) in a position 0·4M southwest of Porspoder village.

When 200m short of Le Compere rock, alter course to 154° until abeam Vervien rock (dries 1·2m). The final approach to the anchorage is made with a bearing of 140° on a ruined coastguard's hut. It is said that providing you can see daylight through both front and back doors you are on the right line!

By night The entrance is not recommended at night.

Looking NW through doors of coastguard's hut
Nick Chavasse

ANCHORAGE

0·2M north of Île de Melon in 2-8m depth. For those drying out, in channel E of Île de Melon towards village. Dries at 5·0m. A second anchor may be required to restrict swing.

6 L'Aber-Ildut

48°28'·24N 04°45'·75W

Shelter
There is good shelter inside the river. The river is fast flowing and there are many fishing boats and local moorings. L'Aber-Ildut is on the north bank

Depth restrictions
2·0m at entrance and 2·4m in river which is dredged

Night entry
Not recommended

Tidal information
HW Brest +0010, LW +0012

Mean height of tide (m) L'Aber-Ildut

HWS	HWN	LWN	LWS
7·3	5·7	2·6	1·0

Tidal streams
In outer approach set strongly N on the flood and S on the ebb, with slack water at about HW and LW Brest

Berthing
Marina and rafting on dumb-bells for <12m. No anchoring inside river. Fuel by fishermen's pontoon

Facilities
Restaurant on quay and basic provisions in village, 800m. Chandlery

Charts
SHOM *7149 (50)*
Imray *C36*

Communications
VHF 09
HM ☏ 02 98 04 04 98 (season)
mobile 06 31 93 58 71
www.lanildut.fr

Looking W at L'Aber-Ildut entrance with marina on right
Benjamin Duval

Southernmost of the three Abers

Famous as the leading seaweed harbour in Europe for unloading algae. 35,000T of seaweed are unloaded on its docks each year, almost half of the national production. The seaweed is burned to ash and used as fertiliser. Visit La Maison de L'Algue next to the Office du Tourisme and the capitainerie.

PILOTAGE

By day Approach on 090° until 200m north of Pierre de L'Aber starboard hand beacon. Steer 083° towards the directional light on conspicuous white gable end of house. Leave Le Lieu about 200m to port and continue until entrance is visible. Entrance marked by Men Tassin port hand beacon and starboard hand beacon. Leave Le Crapaud, a large rounded rock, about 30m to port.

By night Not recommended.

Looking NE over marina and to trots beyond
Benjamin Duval

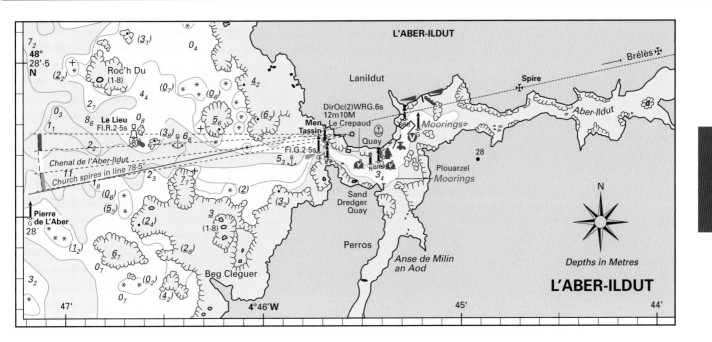

Useful place to be aware of in the event of having to wait for the tide to go through the Chenal du Four, or when awaiting better weather to go to Île de Ouessant.

The bar/restaurant, L'Abri Cotier, ☎ 02 98 36 30 18 is good and has a marvellous view of the river.

Men Tassin at low water *Nick Chavasse*

ASHORE IN L'ABER-ILDUT

Within the confines of the port there is a good bar and restaurant, Harbourmaster's office and a small chandlery.

The village of L'Aber-Ildut is about 800m walk or accessible by dinghy on the tide.

Seaweed collector *Nick Chavasse*

BERTHS AND ANCHORAGES

New marina built in 2019 with visitor berths on outer pontoon. Fuel jetty is just inside the fishing pontoon. There are some trots for visitors southeast of Le Crapaud, just before you reach the first jetty on the port side. There is a second dumb-bell trot, on the port hand side just beyond the second jetty. You may have to raft. Manoeuvre with caution in strong 3kn currents in the river at springs.

In offshore winds and calm conditions anchorage may be found outside and clear of river entrance:

- East of Le Lieu: Le Lieu beacon tower bearing WNW, distant 300m, in least depth of 3·7m
- West of entrance: starboard entry beacon bearing ENE distant 300m, in 3m and sand bottom.

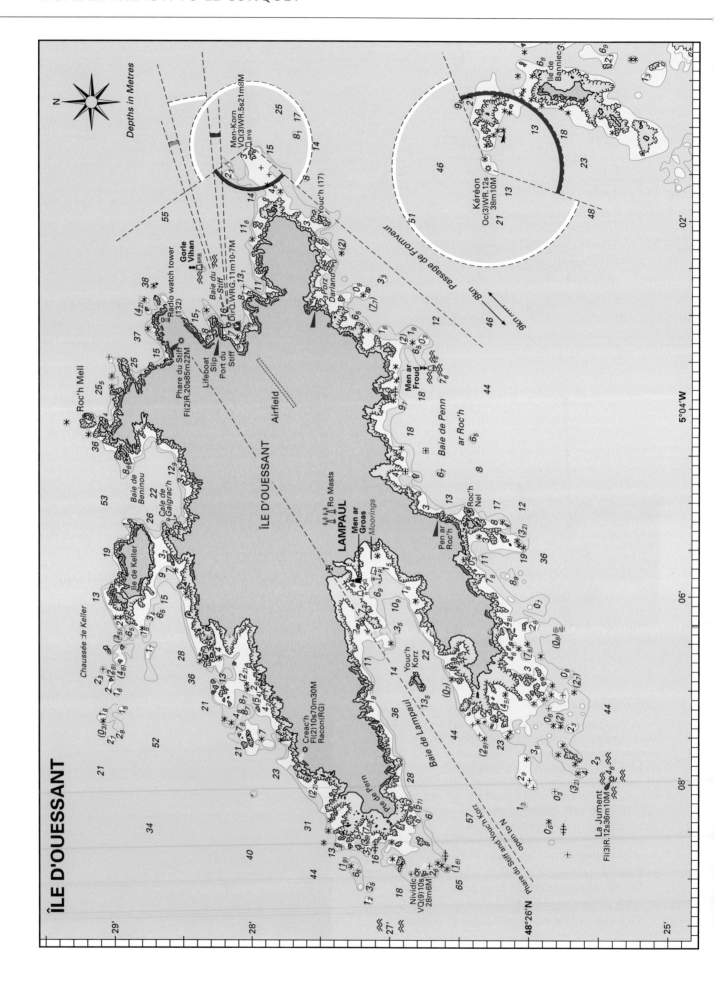

7 Île d'Ouessant (Ushant)

48°26'·64N 05°07'·49W (Baie de Lampaul)

Shelter
Limited shelter at Port du Stiff especially in NE winds and in the prevailing Atlantic swell. Better shelter at Lampaul except in strong SW winds

Depth restrictions
No restriction

Night entry
Not recommended for a first visit

Tidal information
HW Brest +0010, LW +0000

Mean height of tide (m) Baie de Lampoul

HWS	HWN	LWN	LWS
6·9	5·3	2·5	1·0

Tidal streams
At HW Brest the streams are slackish around the island. At mid-ebb the stream in the Passage du Fromveur (south side of island) sets 8kn springs and 3·6kn neaps. Avoid wind over tide, especially at springs, in Passage du Fromveur, where dangerous overfalls form. Note also, there are tidal overfalls, not marked on charts, 1M NW of Nividic

Berthing
Baie du Stiff has 3 white visitors' buoys and little space to anchor. Lampaul is more attractive with 24 free visitors' buoys and plenty of room to anchor in 6-10m

Facilities
Basic provisions in Lampaul from 8 à Huit and Spar Marché. Bike hire in Lampoul and Musée de Phares et Balises at Le Creac'h is well worth a visit.

Charts
SHOM *7149 (50)*
Imray *C36 (80)*

Communications
HM ① 0298488006 (seasonal)
www.brittanytourism.com

Often missed but well worth a visit

Yachtsmen are often in a hurry to sail past Ouessant on their way to southern Brittany, but a visit is well worthwhile. The land is cultivated and the surrounding waters are swept clean of fish and crustaceans. With fierce tidal streams and overfalls, not to mention a vast array of rocks, Ouessant will give the yachtsman cause to plan accordingly.

PILOTAGE

By day Le Stiff. The approach is straightforward leaving Men Korn to port and Gorle Vihan to starboard.

Lampoul. The usual passage is S of La Jument lighthouse and either side of Youc'h Korz (28m high rock). Beware rocks N and NW of La Jument.

By night Not recommended.

BERTHS AND ANCHORAGES

Baie du Stiff

Three white visitors' buoys. Little space to anchor.

Baie Beninou

On the N coast about 3M W of Le Stiff. Surprisingly sheltered from winds NW through S to NE. Useful short-term stop if heading to Lampaul or waiting for tide to avoid overfalls on W coast.

Lampaul

More attractive with 24 free visitors' buoys and plenty of room to anchor in 6-10m. Beware rock less than 50m from closest buoy in NE corner of moorings area.

There are two temporary anchorages on the S coast; Porz Darland 48°26'·46N 05°02'·98W and Baie de Penn ar Roch 48°26'·56N 05°05'·25W.

ASHORE ON OUESSANT

Walking and cycling. The museum of lights and buoys (Musée de Phares et Balises) at Creac'h lighthouse makes an interesting visit.

Looking N at three visitors' moorings with breakwater beyond on right *Nick Chavasse*

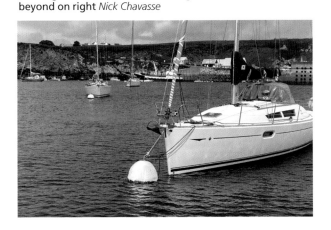

Looking NW with Stiff breakwater on right *Nick Chavasse*

The tides are strong, especially at springs and the overfalls about 1M N of Nividic are serious! The pylons look like lighthouses at first glance. However when built they were linked by a wire to allow resupply to Nividic.

See screengrab of author's experience trying to motor-sail through the overfalls, without hitting the rocks in a F4 wind at springs. It is of note that these overfalls are not mentioned in any other pilot book or almanac. On occasion the speed over ground reading was 2·5kn. with *Wild Bird* being pushed backwards by the currents rather than in a forwards direction.

However, do not be put off, as in the right conditions Ouessant is good news provided you give the overfalls at Nividic a wide berth. There is something rather exciting about exploring the westernmost point of France.

Nividic looking NW towards Creac'h with one of the pylons to the left *Nick Chavasse*

Nividic with pylons looking W *Nick Chavasse*

Lampaul transit open N *Nick Chavasse*

Looking NE at white visitors' moorings with more to right of customs launch *Nick Chavasse*

La Jument *Nick Chavasse*

8 Île Molène

48°24'·07N 04°57'·30W

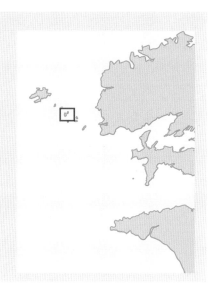

Shelter
Good except in strong north/northeasterly

Depth restrictions
1·2m near lifeboat mooring

Night entry
Not recommended for a first visit

Tidal information
HW Brest +0012, LW +0020

Mean height of tide (m) Île Molène

HWS	HWN	LWN	LWS
7·3	5·8	2·8	1·2

Tidal streams
HW slack is approximately HW Brest -1
LW slack at HW Brest +6

Berthing
12 white visitors' buoys lie west of the lifeboat. Caution as those closest to shore dry with coefficient >90 Anchoring is possible

Facilities
Basic provisions, restaurants and small fish market

Charts
SHOM *7149 (50)*
Imray *C36 (80)*

Communications
HM via Mairie ① 0298073905
www.molene.fr

Remote windswept island with stunning views

The only permanently inhabited island in the Molène archipelago with a story to tell about the fated SS *Drummond Castle*.

PILOTAGE

By day From waypoint 48°26'·22N 4°56'·71W steer 190° for 1·5M, leaving Trois Pierres lighthouse 200m to port, and follow channel between Roche Goulin port hand beacon and Basse Real starboard hand beacon. Then steer 198° for 0·6M to the visitors' buoys near the lifeboat.

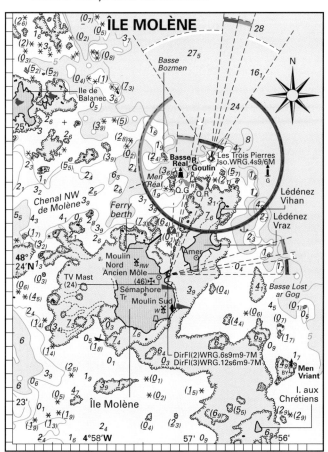

By night Not recommended.

Looking SSE to Molene harbour

Moorings looking towards Les Trois Pierres lighthouse

BERTHS AND ANCHORAGES

12 white visitors' buoys lie north of the lifeboat. Caution at springs as those closest to shore dry with coefficient >90. Anchoring is possible in about 1·2m if able to keep clear of the moorings.

ASHORE IN MOLÈNE

Molène is a lovely stop in fair weather. Basic provisions available, assorted restaurants and a museum dedicated to the loss of SS *Drummond Castle* in 1896. The island is fringed with a fine sandy beach.

On a foggy night in June 1896 the *Drummond Castle* was returning from South Africa when it became wrecked on Les Pierres Vertes, 3M WSW of Molène. Of the 400 persons on board only three were saved. 29 of the passengers are buried in the cemetery at Molène.

L'Archipel Restaurant is reported to do good fresh seafood and is about 100m in from the fish dock.
① 02 98 07 38 56 www.archipelrestaurant.com

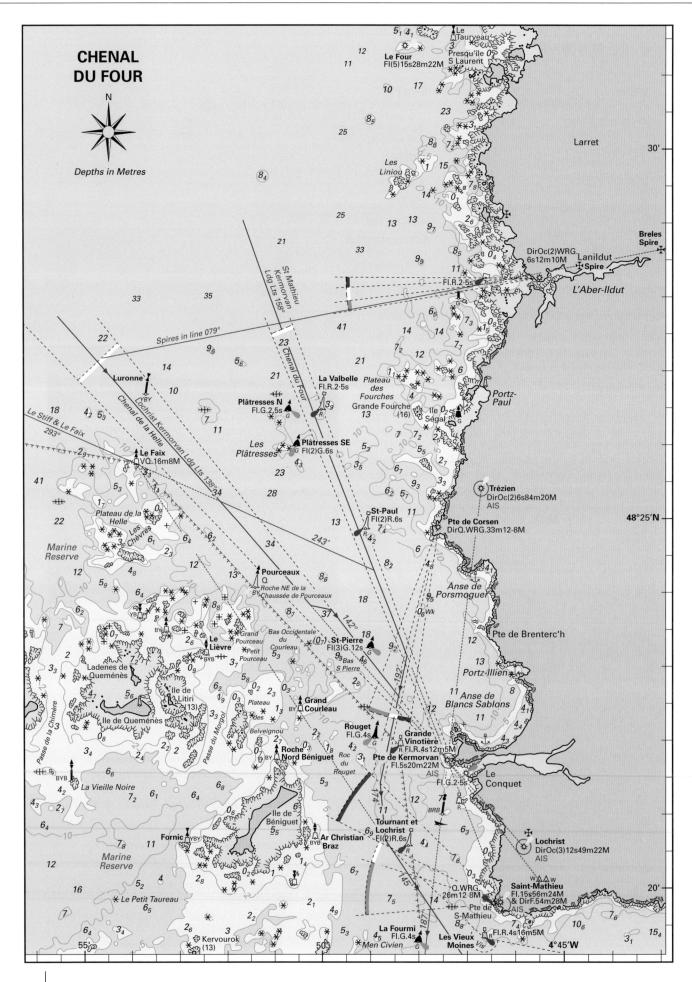

CHENAL DU FOUR

N

Depths in Metres

Le Taureau
Le Four
Fl(5)15s28m22M
Presqu'île
S Laurent

Larret   30'

Les
Liniou

Breles
Spire

DirOc(2)WRG.
6s12m10M
Lanildut
Spire

L'Aber-Ildut

Fl.R.2·5s

St Mathieu
Kermorvan
Ldg Lts 158°

Spires in line 079°

Chenal du Four

Luronne
YBY
Lochrist Kermorvan Ldg Lts 138°

Chenal de la Helle

La Valbelle
Fl.R.2·5s

Plâtresses N
Fl.G.2·5s
G

Plâtresses SE
G Fl(2)G.6s

Les
Plâtresses

Plateau
des
Fourches
Grande Fourche
(16)

Ile
Ségal

Portz-
Paul

Le Stiff & Le Faix
293°

Le Faix
YBY VQ.16m8M

Plateau de la
Helle

Les
Chèvres

Marine
Reserve

Trézien
DirOc(2)6s84m20M
AIS

St-Paul
Fl(2)R.6s
R

Pte de Corsen
DirQ.WRG.33m12-8M

48°25'N

243°

Pourceaux
Q
Roche NE de la
BY Chaussée de Pourceaux

Anse de
Porsmoguer

Pte de Brenterc'h

Wk

Grand
Pourceau
Petit
Pourceau

Le Lièvre
BYB

Bas Occidentale
du
Courleau

St-Pierre
Fl(3)G.12s
G

Bas
S Pierre

192°

Portz-
Illien

Ladenes de
Quéménès

Ile de
Litiri
(13)

Plateau
des

Grand
Courleau
BY

Anse de
Blancs Sablons

Ile de Quéménès

Belveignou

Rouget
Fl.G.4s
G

Grande
Vinotière
R Fl.R.4s12m5M

Roche
Nord Béniguet
BY

Roc
du
Rouget

Pte de Kermorvan
Fl.5s20m22M
AIS

Fl.G.2·5s

Le
Conquet

Passe de la Chimère

La Vieille Noire

174°

BRB
R

Lochrist
DirOc(3)12s49m22M
AIS

Fornic
YBY

Marine
Reserve

Ile de
Béniguet

Ar Christian
BYB Braz

Tournant et
Lochrist
Fl(2)R.6s
R

Q.WRG.
26m12·8M

Saint-Mathieu
Fl.15s56m24M
& DirF.54m28M
AIS

20'

Le Petit Taureau

Pte de
S-Mathieu

Fl.R.4s16m5M

55'   50'

Kervourok
(13)

La Fourmi
Fl.G.4s
G

Men Civien

Les Vieux
Moines
G

4°45'W

15·4

9 Chenal du Four

48°26'·49N 4°50'·36W

Hazards
Strong tide over uneven seabed; complex tidal streams; well-marked rocks and shallow patches; fog

Night passage Well lit

HW time Brest HW

Mean height of tide Le Conquet

HWS	HWN	LWN	LWS
6·8	5·3	2·6	1·1

Tidal stream
Le Four light 48°31'·38N 4°48'·32W
(N end of passage opposite Argenton)
N – starts at Brest HW–0545 (2·2kn)
S – starts at Brest HW (1·6kn)

Tidal stream off Le Conquet
N – starts at Brest HW–0545 (3·4kn)
S – starts at Brest HW–0045 (4·0kn)

Charts
SHOM 7149 (50), 7122 (25)
Imray C36 (80)

Communications
CROSS Corsen VHF 16
Le Conquet VHF 16
CROSS Corsen ☎ 02 98 89 31 31
Le Conquet HM ☎ 02 98 89 16 98
/ 06 30 36 89 56

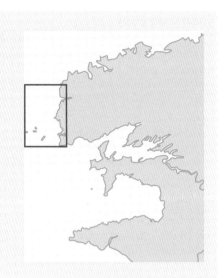

Exposed northwest corner of Brittany

The Chenal du Four is the shortest route between the English Channel and the Biscay ports. It avoids the larger seas and heavy traffic outside Ouessant. The channel is wide and deep and the navigation is not difficult. However, the strong tides and exposure to the Atlantic swell often result in steep seas, and the visibility is sometimes poor.

PILOTAGE

Tidal strategy

Tidal information is quite hard to find. There are two small scale Admiralty tidal atlases which cover the Chenal du Four and the Chenal de la Helle; The Channel (NP250) and France West Coast (NP265). Both Channels and the Raz de Sein are better covered by the large scale French *Atlas de Courants 560-UJA* (2016). Imray's Tides Planner app is also very useful.

The roughest seas occur in the north approaches, not in the Chenal du Four itself. Northerly winds can bring a considerable swell to the area north of Le Four and wind against tide conditions produce steep seas. These reduce as soon as the tide turns. Also, Ouessant and the inner islands provide some shelter from west winds in the Chenal du Four.

Pointe de St Mathieu lighthouse, coastguard station and ruined abbey *Nick Chavasse*

Le Four *Nick Chavasse*

With a fair wind, aim to go through the Four when the tide is favourable. If the wind is ahead, go through the narrow part, off St-Mathieu, at slack water because the stream there runs very hard.

The tide turns at St-Mathieu earlier than it does north of Le Four. Southbound, this is a nuisance because several hours of south stream run to waste. However, south of St-Mathieu the stream is much less strong and will have turned fair by the time the Raz de Sein is reached. Northbound, the tidal lag is a benefit and provides a few extra hours of fair tide.

Navigating in poor visibility requires special care. Once the narrows are reached, it is difficult to turn back. Speed over the ground is likely to be high so the buoys themselves become a hazard. In very bad visibility it may be better to avoid the area altogether.

The Chenal de la Helle is west of the Chenal du Four and is preferable in rough weather.

Chenal du Four

The Chenal du Four is wide and deep. In good weather, it is possible to deviate a long way from the suggested route, providing care is taken to avoid the isolated dangers. In bad weather it is best to stay close to the recommended route.

By day From the northeast keep clear of the rocks and shallows of the Roches de Portsall by passing close to the Grande Basse Portsall west cardinal buoy and then at least 0·25M west of Le Four lighthouse. Then take care to avoid Les Linioux and especially the Plateau des Fourches. Enter the Chenal du Four northeast of Les Plâtresses which are marked by two starboard hand buoys. Valbelle port hand buoy marks the east side of the entrance to the channel. The lighthouses of St-Mathieu and Kermorvan should be in transit, bearing 158°. Continue on this course until Pointe de Corsen bears 012°.

Turn onto 192° and use Pointe de Corsen 012° as a back-bearing to pass between Rouget starboard hand buoy and Grand Vinotière port hand tower beacon. About 0·5M south of Grande Vinotière turn onto 160° to leave Tournon et Lochrist buoy and Les Vieux Moines to port.

Arriving late on the tide, the worst of the foul stream can be avoided by standing into the bay towards the Anse des Blancs Sablons, and the bay south of Le Conquet, but care must be taken to avoid the dangers.

By night From the northeast, the channel is well lit and in good weather the navigation is easy. Steer with Kermorvan and St-Mathieu in transit, bearing 158°. St-Mathieu shows a fixed white directional light in a narrow sector each side of this transit, as well as the flashing light that shows all round.

When Corsen turns white steer in this sector, with the light astern. As soon as the auxiliary light on St-Mathieu becomes red, make good 174°, and enter the red sector of Corsen.

When Tournant et Lochrist buoy is abeam, the auxiliary light on St-Mathieu will turn white and the red light on Les Vieux Moines will open. Make good 145° leaving Les Vieux Moines Fl.R.4s to port and La Fourmi Fl.G.4s to starboard.

Going east or southeast, leave Les Vieux Moines to port.

Chenal de la Helle

By day Bring Kermorvan lighthouse to bear 138°, between the first and second houses from the right of five similar houses forming Le Conquet radio station. In good weather steer on this transit until Corsen lighthouse bears 012°, then make good 192° using Corsen bearing 012° as a stern bearing. Note that Kermorvan/Le Conquet transit leads across the Basse St-Pierre (4·5m) leaving St-Pierre starboard hand buoy to port. In bad weather the shoal can be avoided, by leaving the buoy to starboard.

By night Keep Kermorvan in transit with Lochrist, bearing 138°. To avoid the Basse St-Pierre, if necessary, leave this alignment when Le Stiff light on Ouessant comes in transit with Le Faix, bearing 293°, and make good 113° on this stern transit to join the Four channel.

Northbound, take care not to leave the Lochrist/Kermorvan transit before the unlit Luronne buoy has been passed.

ANCHORAGES

The following anchorages on the mainland are available under suitable conditions:

⚓ Porspaul

48°26'·56N 4°47'·13W

Sheltered from northeast to southeast and slightly sheltered from other directions by the Plateau des Fourches. Porspaul is a drying harbour with an outer anchorage that can be used in fine weather and no swell. The entrance through the Plateau des Fourches requires a large-scale chart.

Identify Grande Fourche, about 1·25M east of La Valbelle, and approach it above half tide from the direction of Valbelle. Avoid the dangers of Plateau des Fourches, which are about 0·25M northwest of Grande Fourche. Pass about 200–300m north of Grande Fourche. Steer towards Basse de Porspaul green beacon tower on 095° and round it by about 200m. Anchor in about 200m east-northeast of the beacon. Boats that can take the ground can dry out in the harbour on firm sand clear of local moorings.

⚓ Anse de Porsmoguer

48°24'·21N 4°46'·77W

Sheltered from north through east, this pretty bay is about 1M south of Pointe de Corsen. There is good holding in sand with depths shoaling from 6m.

The beach is popular for bathing and there is a village, without shops, about 0·5M to the north.

⚓ Anse des Blancs Sablons

48°22'·03N 4°46'·78W

Sheltered from the southeast through southwest, this wide sandy bay is 3M south of Pointe de Corsen. It is free from dangers except off the headlands on each side. The anchorage is anywhere, in from 9m to 1m on a sandy shelving bottom. The bay dries out nearly 0·25M from the shore, except on the west side, where there is 3m close to the rocks off Kermorvan. There is often some swell.

This is a good place to wait out a foul tide. Slip round L'Ilette (the small islet just north of Kermorvan) when the stream becomes fair but watch out for the rock, awash at datum, that lies 200m east of L'Ilette.

⚓ Porz-Illien

48°22'·95N 4°46'·1W

When the wind is from the north or east, better shelter may be found in this little bay in the northeast corner of Anse des Blancs Sablons.

10 Le Conquet

48°21'·60N 04°47'·00W (Harbour entrance)

Shelter
Good except in strong westerlies

Depth restrictions
Visitors buoys not suitable in springs unless draught <1·0m

Night entry
Not recommended for a first visit

Tidal information
HW Brest +0000, LW +0005

Mean height of tide (m) Le Conquet

HWS	HWN	LWN	LWS
6·8	5·3	2·6	1·1

Tidal streams
Beware strong north and south going tides at springs

Facilities
Le Conquet caters mainly for fishing vessels. Short walk up the hill to pleasant town with shopping area. Several good local beaches.

Berthing
Most of the 7 visitors' moorings tend to dry out depending on the coefficient. At neaps and with a 1m draught you might find a buoy

Charts
SHOM *7149 (50)*
Imray *C36 (80)*

Communications
VHF 8, 16
HM ① 02 98 89 18 58
mobile 06 30 36 89 56
www.tourismeleconquet.fr

Fishing village with lots of history

Predominantly focused on fishing but still welcoming. Better suited to shallow draught yachts. The long maritime history here dates back to 1558 when the English sacked the town, leaving behind just eight (English-owned) houses which still stand today.

PILOTAGE

By day Straightforward from Grande Vinotiere, red 8-sided tower, 48°21'·94N 04°48'·42W but beware of strong cross tides which run at 5kn at springs.

By night Not recommended.

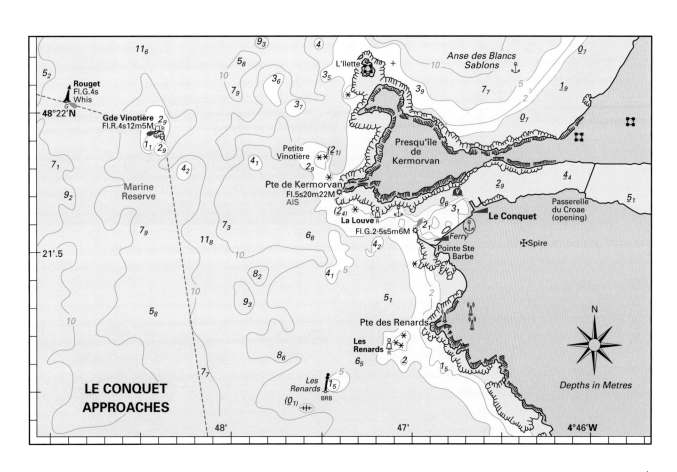

BERTHS AND ANCHORAGES

Moorings are available in the northern part of the old harbour for shoal draught boats. There are seven visitors' buoys to the north of the harbour. There is one visitors' buoy which has 1m and the other six buoys have less. There are four further buoys inside the harbour more suitable for drying out. None of the buoys provide shelter in a westerly.

⚓ Anchorage

48°21'·64N 4°47'·12W

Sheltered from northwest through southeast, there is a good, though often crowded, anchorage in the inlet south of Pointe de Kermorvan. Leave the red La Louve tower to port and go in as far as depth permits.

ASHORE IN LE CONQUET

Picturesque small town with a good selection of shops and eating places. Le Conquet merits the steep uphill climb.

CROSS Corsen, often heard on the VHF is the search and rescue centre for this part of the Atlantic France coastline. The centre is situated at Pointe de Corsen, 8M north of Le Conquet

Looking NE to inner harbour *Nick Chavasse*

Looking W over inner breakwater towards the entrance to Le Conquet *Nick Chavasse*

Looking SW from borrowed mooring *Nick Chavasse*

Morgat from Vieux Port *Nick Chavasse*

II. Brest to Audierne

Brest is a perfect spot in bad weather, either at the excellent Marina du Château in the commercial port or at Moulin Blanc Marina which is handy for a day at the magnificent Oceanopolis aquarium.

However, the Aulne is the real treasure of the Rade de Brest and a trip to Port Launay and Châteaulin will be a high point in any cruise. Outside the Rade, there is excellent sailing round the high cliffs of the Crozon peninsula and the spectacular beaches of Douarnenez bay.

When crossing the Channel, Camaret is a favourite first or last stop. This is subject to current rules and procedures for Entry to France and Ports of Entry. Brest is the nearest Port of Entry. If weather permits, a visit to Île de Sein offers challenging pilotage and an uniquely unspoilt island.

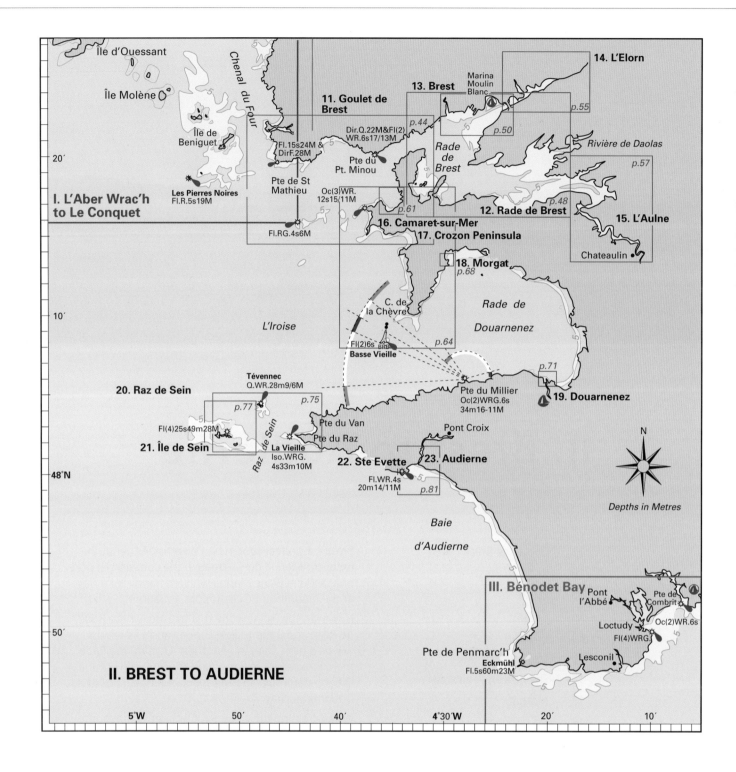

II. BREST TO AUDIERNE

Brest to Audierne tidal streams

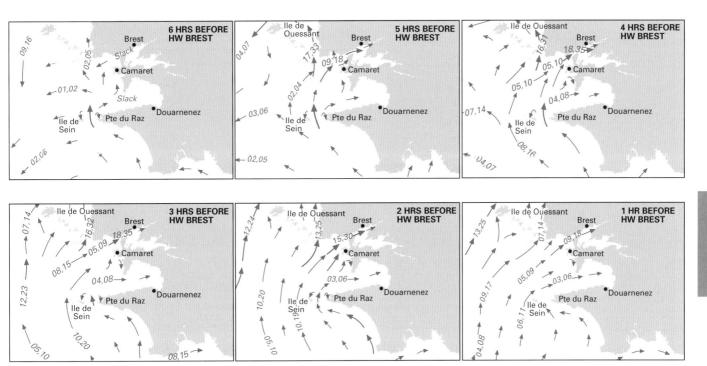

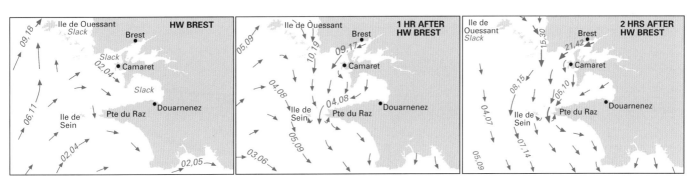

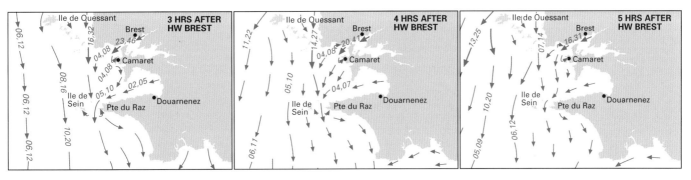

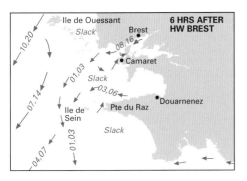

TIDAL STREAMS EXPLANATION

The figures shown against the arrows are the mean rates at neaps and springs in tenths of a knot.

Thus *07,15* - mean neaps rate *0·7* knots, mean springs rate *1·5* knots

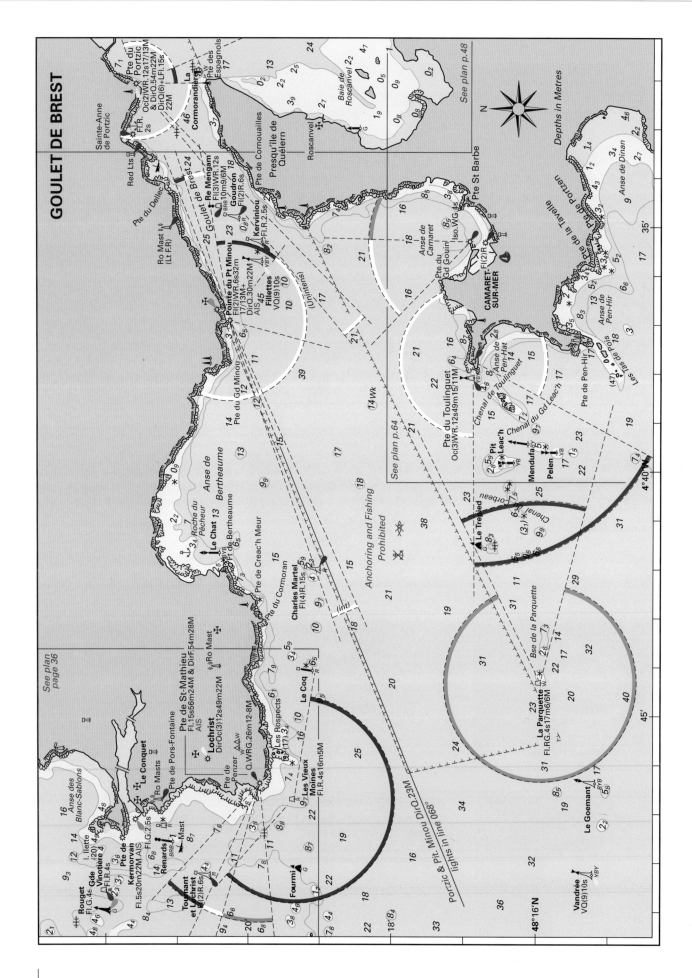

GOULET DE BREST

Pte du Portzic
Oc(2)WR.12s17/13M
& DirQ.54d22M
DirQ(6)+LFl.15s
Fl.R.
2s
La
Cormorandière
Pte des
Espagnols

Sainte-Anne
de Portzic

Baie de
Roscanvel

Depths in Metres

N

Red Lts
Pte du Dellec
Ro Mast
(Lt F.R)

Pte du Minou
Fl(2)WR.6s32m
17/13M+
DirQ.30m22M
AIS 45
Fillettes
VQ(9)10s

Re Mengam
Fl(3)WR.12s
Goudron
Fl(2)R.6s
Kervíniou
Fl.R.2.5s

Goulet de Brest

Pte de Cornouailles

Presqu'île de
Quélern

Roscanvel

Pte St Barbe
Anse de Camaret
Pte de Gd Gouin
Iso.WG.4s
CAMARET-
SUR-MER
Fl(2)R

Pte du Toulinguet
Oc(3)WR.12s49m15/11M

Chenal de Toulinguet

Anse de
Pen-Hat

Anse de Dinan

Pte de la Tavelle

Pte de Penzer

Anse de
Pen-Hir

Les Tas
de Pois

Pte de Pen-Hir

See plan p.48

See plan p.64

Pte du Gd Leac'h

Chenal du Gd Leac'h

Menduff
Pelen

Pit
Leac'h

Le Trépied

Chenal du Corbeau

Bse de la Parquette

La Parquette
Fl.RG.4s17m6/6M

Anse de
Bertheaume

Roche du
Pêcheur
Le Chat
Pte de Bertheaume

Pte de Creac'h Meur

Pte du Cormoran

Charles Martel
Fl(4)R.15s

Anchoring and Fishing
Prohibited

14 Wk

(int)

See plan
page 36

Pte de St-Mathieu
Fl.15s56m24M & DirF.54m28M
AIS
Ro Mast
Lochrist
DirOc(3)12s49m22M
Q.WRG.26m12-8M
Les Rospects

Le Conquet
Le Conquet
Pte de
Kermorvan AIS
Fl.5s20m22M
Ro Masts

Anse des
Blanc-Sablons

Rouget
Fl.G.4s
Gde
Vinotière
Fl.R.4s
Pte de
Kermorvan
Fl.5s20m22M AIS

I. Ilette

Renards
BRB

Tournant
et Lochrist
Fl(2)R.6s

Pte de Pors-Fontaine

Le Coq

Les Vieux
Moines
Fl.R.4s16m5M

Fourmi

Porzic & Pt. Minou DirQ.23M
lights in line 068°

Le Goemant

Vandrée
VQ(9)10s

Le Conquet
Fl.G.2.5s
Mast

48°16'N

ATLANTIC FRANCE

11 Goulet de Brest

48°20′N 4°34′W

Hazards
Strong tide in the narrows; well marked rocks in mid-channel

Night passage Well lit

HW time Brest HW

Mean height of tide (m) Brest

HWS	HWN	LWN	LWS
6·9	5·4	2·6	1·0

Tidal streams Goulet de Brest
NE – Brest HW–0530 to –0030 (3·9kn)
Slack – Brest HW–0030 to +0030
SW – Brest HW+0030 to –0530 (4kn)
South side stream is weaker
Counter current in S side +0530 to –0530

Charts
SHOM 7149
Imray C36

Communications
CROSS Corsen VHF 16, 70 (DSC)
☎ 02 98 89 31 31 or ☎ 112
Le Conquet VHF 16
St-Mathieu ☎ 02 98 89 01 59

Entrance to the Rade de Brest

The Goulet de Brest is the passage between the Avant-Goulet de Brest and the Rade de Brest. At the narrowest point, it is 1M wide and the tide in the narrows is fierce.

There are cliffs on either side but they are steep to. In mid-channel there is a chain of well-marked rocks called Plateau des Fillettes. The navigation is not difficult.

PILOTAGE

Rade de Brest approaches

By day From the Chenal du Four, round Pointe de St-Mathieu and leave Les Vieux Moines port hand tower beacon, Le Coq port hand buoy and Charles Martel port hand buoy all to port. Then pick up the transit for the Goulet which is the twin white towers of Le Petit Minou in line with Pointe du Portzic grey octagonal tower on 068°.

The rocky Plateau des Fillettes is in mid-channel. Fillettes west cardinal marks the west end and Roche Mengam BRB beacon tower, 0·25M to the northeast, marks the east end. A line between them marks the south edge of the north channel.

The plateau extends well south of the line between Fillettes and Roche Mengam and two additional port hand buoys mark the limit of the danger.

Looking SW at Pointe du Petit Minou
©Malfootu / Shutterstock

The south passage is useful if the tide is ebbing because there is a counter-current on the south side of the Goulet in the last hour and a half of the ebb.

When using the south passage, take care to avoid La Cormorandière just off Pointe des Espagnols.

By night From the Chenal du Four or west, round Pointe de St-Mathieu and identify the leading lights (068°) of Le Petit Minou and Portzic and steer on this transit. Once past Charles Martel port hand buoy bear to starboard to pass between Pte du Petit Minou light and Fillettes west cardinal buoy.

Leave Roche Mengam tower to starboard, steer about 070° towards Pénoupèle buoy. Beware that Kerviniou port hand buoy and Goudron port hand buoy are port-hand marks for the southern passage.

Coming from Camaret, steer north to enter the intense white sector of Portzic, occulting light WR.12s54m. Alter to starboard and keep in this sector on about 047° until Roche Mengam beacon tower is abaft the beam to port, then turn onto 065° towards Pénoupèle port hand buoy as above.

ANCHORAGES

⚓ Anse de Bertheaume

48°20'·85N 04°41'·15W

Sheltered from north and west, but exposed to the south and east, this convenient bay is about 3M east of Pointe de St-Mathieu. Fort de Bertheaume, on the southwest corner of the bay, should be given a good berth to avoid Le Chat rocks marked by the east cardinal. These are particularly hazardous when they are covered near HW springs. Anchor in one of the two bays immediately north of Le Chat, going in as far as possible for shelter. Beware pots, particularly when entering at night, between Les Chats east cardinal and Roche du Pecheur. There are some visitors' moorings. Further north and east the bottom is foul with rocks.

⚓ Sainte-Anne de Portzic

48°21'·55N 04°32'·98W

Sheltered from the north and east and with a mole that provides some protection from the west, this is a small local harbour just west of Pte de Portzic. There are no dangers in the approach but there is an isolated rock marked by an isolated danger mark on the east side of the harbour.

The pier is used by survey vessels from the nearby Oceanographic research centre and must not be used by visiting yachts. However, it may be possible to borrow a mooring or to anchor outside the moorings.

The Goulet de Brest looking east.
The Goulet is only 1M wide at its narrowest point, between Pointe de Portzic and Pointe des Espagnols. The Goulet marks the entrance to the Rade de Brest with its many anchorages and rivers and the sprawling city of Brest at the north of the Rade *Patrick Roach*

12 Rade de Brest

48°19'N 4°25'W

Depth restrictions
None in main channel

Prohibited area
Near Île Longue in SW, well marked by yellow buoys

Night passage
Not recommended

HW time Brest HW

Mean height of tide (m) Brest

HWS	HWN	LWN	LWS
6·9	5·4	2·6	1·0

Tidal streams Rade de Brest
Flood – Brest HW–0500 to –0030 (1·5kn)
Slack – Brest HW–0030 to +0030
Ebb – Brest HW+0030 to -0530 (1·0kn)

Flood stream counter-currents
Espagnols 48°20'·73N 04°31'·86W
  Brest HW –0430 to –0030
Armorique 48°19'·63N 04°27'·83W
  Brest HW –0230 to –0030

Berthing
Anchorages

Charts
SHOM *7400*
Imray *C36*

Communications
Roscanvel HM ☎ 06 81 11 18 75

Sheltered sailing area

The Rade de Brest offers very good sailing. It consists of Brest port city, two main rivers, the Elorn and the Aulne, as well as several anchorages in the Rade itself. It has shelter from the Atlantic but is large enough for the wind not to be too disturbed. There are many anchorages for boats that can take the ground and several for deep draught yachts.

Rade de Brest is another mini cruising ground that is often overlooked. Weekenders occupy the anchorages so a mid-week visit may be best to avoid the crowds. There are various anchorages to suit the wind direction, a favourite is Anse de L'Auberlac'h.

PILOTAGE

The restricted areas

There are restricted areas in the south of the Rade where navigation is restricted and anchoring prohibited. In particular, entry is prohibited within 500m of the shore around Île Longue and its military port.

The Naval College south of Pen-ar-Vir, 48°17'·76N 04°24'·88W, has a restricted zone marked by the north cardinal buoys and yellow buoys. Anchoring is not allowed in this area and entry may also be prohibited without warning. Boats may also be refused access to a rectangular area north of the Naval College marked by yellow buoys.

Goulet de Brest to Traverse de l'Hôpital (entry point for River L'Aulne)

By day From the Goulet de Brest steer 120° to Le Renard west cardinal buoy. Leave Île Ronde and the two rectangular concrete dolphins at 48°19'·35N 4°27'·25W 300m to port.

A course of 104° will lead to the outer port hand buoy No.4, about 1M west of the Île du Bindy.

The succeeding channel buoys No. 6 and No. 8 are also red. After No 8 the numbered buoys are closer together and easier to see. Note that port hand buoys are conical although painted red.

By night Night passage is not recommended.

ANCHORAGES

⚓ 1. Roscanvel

48°18'·81N 04°32'·62W

Sheltered from north through west to southeast, the east coast of Presqu'île de Quélern offers good protection. Between Pte des Espagnols and the village of Roscanvel there are several small bays with yacht moorings. There is a welcoming yacht club at Roscanvel, which may loan a mooring on request.

Moorings at Roscanvel *Nick Chavasse*

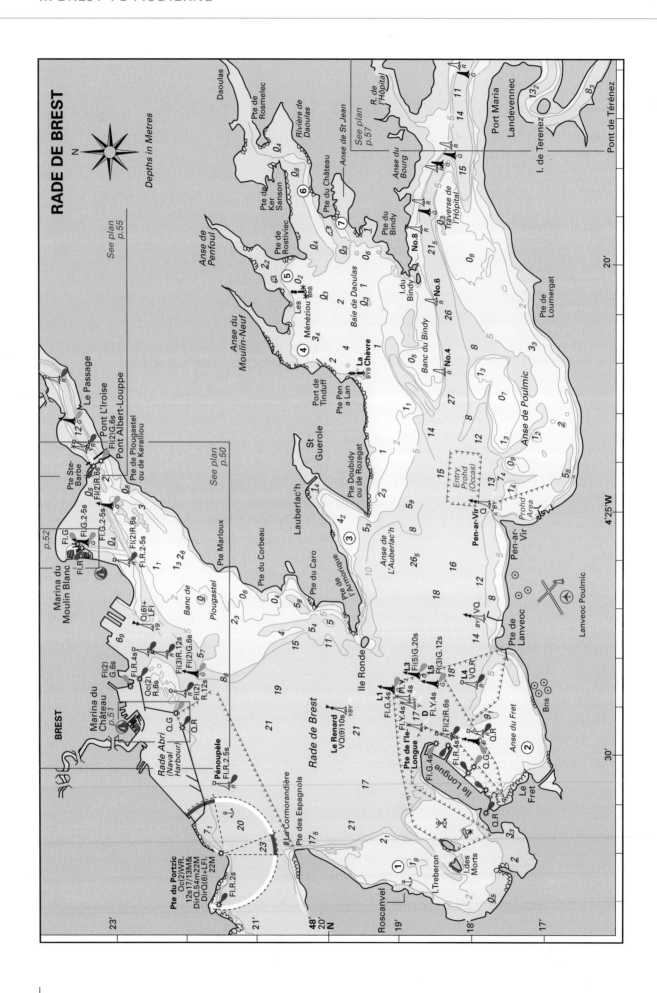

RADE DE BREST

Depths in Metres

Roscanvel is a small holiday village. It has a double slipway, one running out east and the other south. Anchor off the slips clear of the moorings. The east slip dries at LW and there are obstructions outside it. If landing at the south slip towards LW approach from the south and use the inside only.

Watch out for the tidal streams in the Baie de Roscanvel. There is a counter-current on the flood from about Brest HW-3 to HW but no counter-current on the ebb. This means the stream only runs south for a couple of hours after LW.

⚓ 2. Le Fret

48°17'·12N 4°30'·17W

Sheltered from all directions except northeast, the Anse du Fret provides a pleasant anchorage southeast of Île Longue. A course of 215° from Île Ronde will lead into the anchorage clear of the exclusion zone. There is space to anchor with good holding on sand/mud. From the pier, fast ferries go to Brest and occasional buses go to Camaret. The ferry runs in high season but should not be relied upon. Visit www.lebrestoa.com.

⚓ 3. Anse de l'Auberlac'h

48°19'·55N 4°25'·48W

Sheltered from all directions except southwest, the picturesque hamlet of L'Auberlach lies at the head of a bay running northeast from Île Ronde. It is rather crowded with moorings, but there are five white visitors' buoys available from 15 April - 15 October. There may be space to anchor but beyond the pier the bay shoals rapidly.

⚓ 4. Tinduff

48°20'·27N 4°21'·85W

Sheltered from west and north, Tinduff is a small drying harbour on the west side of the shallow Baie de Daoulas, 0·5M to the north of Pointe de Pen a Lan. Keep at least 0·25M from the point to avoid the shoals and La Chèvre rock (dries 4·7m), which is

marked by an east cardinal beacon. There is another rock (drying 4·2m) closer inshore and a third unmarked isolated rock, drying 0·7m, about 300m west-southwest of the beacon. The bay is shallow and can only be entered with sufficient rise of tide but there is a 2m pool off the end of the pier. There are four visitors' buoys, marked with letter 'V' and many moorings but there is room to anchor, with good holding. At neaps, it is possible to go further into the bay where there is better shelter. Keep clear of the fish farm, marked by small, unlit yellow buoys.

⚓ 5. Rivière de Daoulas

48°19'·99N 4°19'·57W

Sheltered from all directions, this shallow river runs into the northeast corner of the Baie de Daoulas. The bay can only be entered with sufficient rise of tide as there is a bar at the entrance. The deepest water is found by keeping Pte du Château on a bearing of 070°. The Pointe is not easy to distinguish against the land but can be identified by the conspicuous large grey shed with houses above and to the right. Almost the entire river is taken up with moorings and there is little space left to anchor. There may be space about 0·75M upriver off the second slip, in 1·8m (mud). The river to Daoulas dries 4·5m.

⚓ 6. Rostiviec

48°20'·53N 4°19'·52W

There are three visitors' moorings. Beware oyster beds to the west and southwest of the slipway.

⚓ 7. Pors Beac'h

48°20'.20N 4°18'.12W

There are four visitors' buoys identified by letter 'V' to be found to west of slipway.

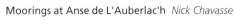
Moorings at Anse de L'Auberlac'h *Nick Chavasse*

13 Brest

48°22'N 4°29'W

Shelter
Excellent in Marina du Château and Moulin Blanc Marinas

Depth restrictions
None at Marina du Château
1·5m in approach to and 1·4m at fuel berth in Moulin Blanc Marina

Night entry
Both marinas well lit

HW time Brest HW

Mean height of tide (m) Brest

HWS	HWN	LWN	LWS
6·9	5·4	2·6	1·0

Berthing
Inside Southern jetty at Marina du Château and on visitors' pontoon and wavebreaker at Moulin Blanc (Northern basin of marina)

Fuel
Pontoon at Marina du Château and S side of Moulin Blanc N basin close to capitainerie

Marina facilities
All services but note that marine services are mainly based on an industrial estate next to Moulin Blanc marina

Charts
SHOM *7400, 7397, 7398*
Imray *C36*

Communications
Marina du Château VHF 09
  ☎ 02 98 33 12 50
Moulin Blanc Marina VHF 09
  ☎ 02 98 02 20 02
www.marinasbrest.fr
Brest port VHF 08, 16
Customs ☎ 02 98 44 35 20
Tourist Office ☎ 02 98 44 24 96

Modern port city with two marinas

Brest is a modern city with a busy port. The Marina du Château is closest to the city centre. It has good facilities and a range of restaurants and cafés on the quay. Marina Moulin Blanc is 3M further east. It is a bus-ride from the city centre and has visitors' berths for vessels up to 30m. There are two large chandlers within walking distance of Moulin Blanc as well as a full range of repair facilities. Both marinas are under the same management.

A spectacular Festival of Sail is held every four years (2024, 2028...). The Oceanopolis, oceanographic centre and aquarium, a major tourist attraction, is next door to Moulin Blanc marina. Transport by bus, train and air is good, making Brest a useful place to change crews.

Brest sounds big and unfriendly but it is not! The city is a good place to stock up before exploring the anchorages in the Rade de Brest and the Rivers Elorn and Aulne. Most of the city was badly bombed by the allies in the Second World War. However, one street, rue St Malo escaped the bombing. It is like an oasis in modern Brest and worth a visit to experience the original architecture.

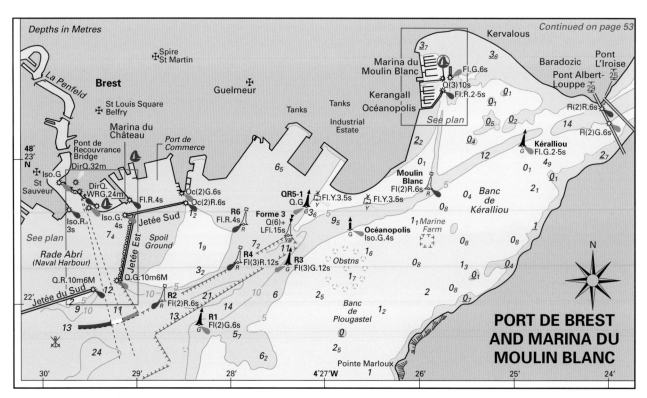

Continued on page 53

PORT DE BREST AND MARINA DU MOULIN BLANC

PILOTAGE – GOULET DE BREST TO MARINA DU CHÂTEAU

See plan on page 48

By day Steer to leave Pénoupèle port hand buoy to port and continue on this east-northeast course to open up the first entrance to the Port de Commerce. Marina du Chateau is located within this area so you need to take the entrance at the right hand end of the very long jetty. Then approach the entrance on a bearing of 344° keeping to the starboard side and keeping a watchful eye open for naval and commercial ships which may be leaving or entering. They must be given right of way. The outer breakwater of the marina will be seen fine on the starboard bow. The marina entrance faces northwest and the outer breakwater end must be rounded to enter the marina. Entry to the naval and commercial parts of the port is prohibited.

By night Steer an east-northeast course from the Goulet de Brest to leave the Pénoupèle port hand buoy to port and continue on this course until the first entrance of the Port de Commerce is opened up and the leading lights will come into line on 344°. The front leading light is a WRG sector light (Dir.Q.WRG.24m.W9M). They lead to the west of the marina entrance when the southern breakwater head can be rounded.

Brest, Marina du Château from south
Capitainerie, Marina du Château

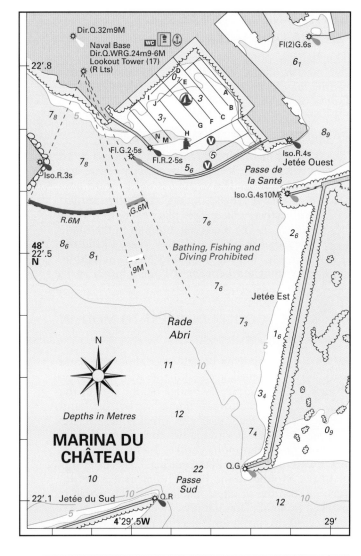

BERTHS AND ANCHORAGES – MARINA DU CHÂTEAU

The visitors' pontoons are in the southern part of the marina along the southern breakwater and rafting may be necessary. There is 5m depth and the largest of yachts can be accommodated.

FACILITIES – MARINA DU CHÂTEAU

The facilities at Marina du Château are good, with several restaurants. It is close to the city centre and good for shopping. The marina closes to short stay visitors for two weeks during the International Maritime Festival which takes place every four years (2024, 2028...). The maritime museum in the castle is worth a visit, with good views overlooking the Rade de Brest. WiFi is good and fuel is available. Sunday morning market near St-Louis Church.

PILOTAGE – GOULET DE BREST TO MOULIN BLANC MARINA

By day From Pointe du Portzic steer about 065° and look for the curved arches of the Albert-Louppe Bridge and the motorway bridge behind it over the River Elorn. In the foreground a line of port hand channel buoys lead past the breakwater of the commercial port. Beyond is the conspicuous white roof of the Océanopolis centre. To its right is the breakwater of Moulin Blanc marina.

Leave Moulin Blanc buoy 200m astern before turning into the dredged marina channel, which is marked by small, lateral buoys.

Proceed up the channel leaving the first entrance to the marina to port and proceed, leaving the MBA east cardinal beacon to port, between the two wavebreakers. The central pier has been extended northwards by a floating breakwater the northern end of which must be rounded to port to reach the visitors' pontoon.

By night Leaving Pénoupèle close to port, steer 065° to follow the buoyed channel to Moulin Blanc buoy. Leave it to port and continue for about 200m before altering to about 005° to locate the lights marking the narrow dredged channel. When MB1 and MB2, the first pair of port and starboard hand buoys have been identified, steer between them on 007° to the marina entrance between floating wavebrakers which have been extended northwards.

BERTHS AND ANCHORAGES –
Moulin Blanc Marina

The visitors' pontoon lies along the southern side of the northern basin. Visiting yachts also berth on both sides of the western floating breakwaters. Yachts with a draught greater than 2m may be berthed on the southern basin's wavebreaker at spring tides.

Brest, Marina du Château becomes very crowded with participating during the International Maritime Festival
Eric Donschachner

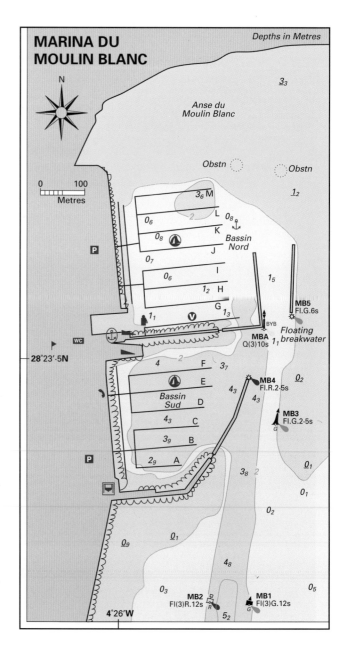

Moulin Blanc marina and Oceanopolis bottom left *Ports de Plaisance de Moulin Blanc et du Château*

FACILITIES – MOULIN BLANC

Carrefour Contact in Rue Aguste Rodin, Brest (☎ 02 98 02 25 91) will do free deliveries to the marinas. Intermarché in Rue de Quimper is 2km uphill walk from Moulin Blanc. There is a regular bus service (Bus No 3) into Brest city centre. The Océanopolis, next to the marina, is a marine scientific centre/aquarium and is distinctive with its white concrete and glass building is shaped in the form of a crab. It has three big aquaria, one of which houses the grey seal collection.

The Conservatoire Botanique National is in the Stang Alar valley one mile north of Moulin Blanc. It is dedicated to the preservation of endangered plant species many of which come from the Brittany peninsula. The gardens cover 40 acres and contain plants native to five continents. Fuel is available.

The Battle of the Atlantic features large in the history of France and particularly in the area covered by this pilot book. When Brest was occupied in 1940, impregnable submarine pens were built for the U-boat fleet, which sank a huge tonnage of Allied merchant shipping in the Battle of the Atlantic, threatening to cut off vital supplies flowing from America to Europe. By 1944, four years of allied bombing had reduced the city, but not the submarine pens, to rubble. The pens in Brest are not open to the public as they are within the prohibited military zone. However, those in St Nazaire, Lorient and Bordeaux are open to the public, so keep sailing south!

Bassin Nord looking NE from the harbour office *Nick Chavasse*

14 L'Elorn

48°23'N 4°24'W

Depth restrictions
Dries above St-Jean
2m to Landerneau at MHWN

Height restriction 25m

Night passage
Lit to St-Jean but not recommended

HW time Brest HW

Mean height of tide (m) Brest
HWS	HWN	LWN	LWS
6·9	5·4	2·6	1·0

Tidal stream Elorn River
Slack – Brest HW–0530 to –0500
Flood – Brest HW–0500 to –0030
Slack – Brest HW–0030 to +0030
Ebb – Brest HW+0030 to –0530

Berthing
Anchorages as far as St Jean
Drying quay at Landerneau

Charts
SHOM *7400 (to St-Jean)*
Imray *C36*

Communications
Lifting bridge ① 06 11 03 31 20

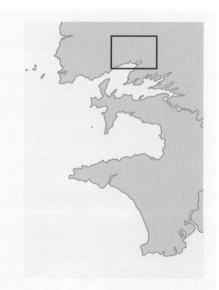

Tidal river to historic town

The Elorn is an attractive tidal river, extending NE from the Rade de Brest, with several peaceful anchorages. At all states of the tide, it is navigable to St-Jean, which is about 6M beyond Moulin Blanc marina. The remainder of the river dries but it is possible to visit the historic town of Landerneau on the tide.

The Elorn leads 8M to the attractive old town of Landerneau. For deep-draught yachts it is navigable at all states of tide as far as St-Jean. Above St-Jean the river dries but is navigable, near high water, for boats drawing up to 2m.

PILOTAGE

Moulin Blanc to Landerneau

By day From Moulin Blanc buoy (*see plan on page 50*), pass under Albert-Louppe Bridge (clearance 29m) and the Pont de l'Iroise motorway bridge (clearance 25m). Follow the channel markers and the deep-water moorings. It is possible to anchor on either side of the river or find a vacant mooring as far up as St-Jean.

Entrance to the River Elorn under the two bridges
Nick Chavasse

At Kerhuon there is a slip, marked by a beacon with an orange top. A wharf marks the eastern end of Kerhuon where the river curves north and then east for the last stretch before St-Jean.

Above St-Jean, rather small and widely spaced green and red buoys and the yacht moorings mark the channel. 3·5M above St-Jean there is a lifting bridge which will be opened on request by telephoning a little while in advance (see number above).

Follow the canal to Landerneau, pass the large sand-barge wharf, and tie up against the wall on the port side before the fixed bridge just above the slip.

By night The Elorn is only lit as far as Anse Saint-Nicolas and night passage is not recommended.

River Elorn *Nick Chavasse*

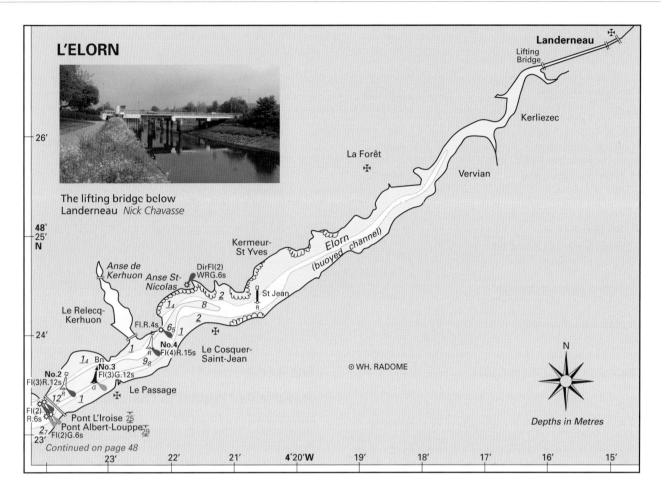

The lifting bridge below
Landerneau *Nick Chavasse*

BERTHS AND ANCHORAGES

Landerneau

Landerneau is attractive and has all the facilities of a fair-sized town. Market days are Tuesdays and Fridays. It is on the Morlaix-Brest railway line.

It may be possible to dry out on the port side against a short length of wall with a slipway and where there are ladders. There is 3m at HW neaps. There is electricity on the quay on the port side and water at the toilet block 100m upstream.

⚓ Le Passage

Although somewhat exposed to the southwest, there is an attractive anchorage about 0·75M above the Albert-Louppe Bridge on the south side of the river near Le Passage. The bottom may be foul so buoy the anchor.

⚓ Kerhuon

Good shelter from all directions can be found in the stretch of river between Anse de Kerhuon and about 0·25M northeast of Saint Jean beacon tower.

⚓ Anse Saint-Nicolas

Anse Saint-Nicolas is better sheltered from the southwest than Le Passage. It is in a bay on the north side of the river, about 1·75M above Albert-Louppe Bridge.

The Elorn is a quiet river away from the hustle and bustle of Brest. You might find a vacant buoy up at St Jean. In the author's experience it is a long way by bicycle from Anse de Kerhuon to Landernau, so the best way to visit the town is by dinghy (or a combination of boat and dinghy). Do not get neaped!

Drying quays at Landerneau *Nick Chavasse*

15 L'Aulne

48°18'N 4°16'W

Depth restrictions
6m to Pte de Térénez
2·5m at MHWN to the Guily Glaz lock
2·7m beyond the lock

Height restrictions
Le Passage power lines 27m above ML

Guily Glaz lock opens
Brest HW -0200 to +0130 (0730 to 2100
    April–September)
(0800 to 1900 October–March)

HW time Brest HW

Mean height of tide (m) Brest

HWS	HWN	LWN	LWS
7·4	5·8	2·9	1·3

Tidal streams Landevennec
Flood – Brest HW–0530 to –0030
Slack – Brest HW–0030 to +0030
Ebb – Brest HW+0030 to –0530

Berthing
Quay at Port Launay
Visitors' pontoon at Châteaulin
Anchorage Port Styvel

Fuel
Châteaulin hypermarket with cans only

Facilities
Water at Port Launay and Châteaulin
Hypermarket at Châteaulin

Charts
SHOM *7400*
Imray *C36*
IGN TOP25 sheet *0518*

Communications
Guily Glaz lock ✆ 02 98 86 03 21
www.brittanytourism.com

Gateway to the Brest Canal

The Aulne is a beautiful, sheltered river which flows into the southeastern corner of the Rade de Brest. It it navigable on the tide to Guily Glaz lock where the Aulne joins the old Nantes-Brest canal. If you lock through at Guily Glaz you can continue to the pretty canal village of Port Launay and the market town of Châteaulin. Perhaps surprisingly, Châteaulin is a good place for provisioning because the visitors' pontoon is very close to a hypermarket.

PILOTAGE

Traverse de l'Hôpital to Châteaulin

Apart from a 6m patch at Traverse de l'Hôpital there is 10m as far as Pont de Térénez. From there to within about a mile of the lock, there is at least 4m at half-tide. In the last mile to the lock, depth is reduced in some places to 2·5m at MHWN. Vessels may enter the lock if the seaward gate is open. In the upper reaches the bottom is generally very soft mud.

The River Aulne with the naval graveyard in the right *Patrick Roach*

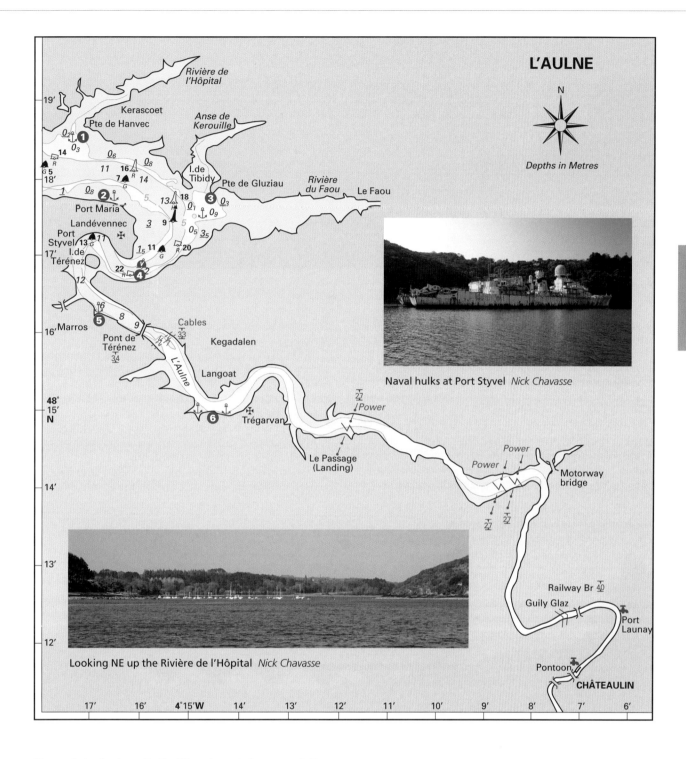

L'AULNE

N

Depths in Metres

19'

Rivière de l'Hôpital

Kerascoet
Pte de Hanvec

Anse de Kerouille

0₂9 **①**

0₃

14
G 5
0₃
0₆
0₈

Rivière du Faou
Le Faou

18'

11
7
R
14
I.de Tibidy
Pte de Gluziau

1
0₈
②
5
13₃
18
③
0₃

Port Maria
0₁
0₉

Landévennec
3
0₉
0₅
3₅

Port Styvel
13 G
1₅
11
20

17'
I.de Térénez

22
R
V
④

12

Naval hulks at Port Styvel *Nick Chavasse*

⑤
6

Marros
8
9

16'

Cables
33

Kegadalen

Pont de Térénez
34

L'Aulne

Langoat

27

Power

48° 15' N

⑥

Trégarvan

Power

Power

Le Passage (Landing)

27
27

Motorway bridge

14'

Railway Br 40

13'

Guily Glaz

Port Launay

12'

Pontoon

CHÂTEAULIN

Looking NE up the Rivière de l'Hôpital *Nick Chavasse*

17'   16'   4°15'W   14'   13'   12'   11'   10'   9'   8'   7'   6'

Beyond the lock at Guily Glaz there is between 2·7m and 3m. The overhead clearance below bridges and power lines is 27m or more.

There is no chart of the river above Pont de Térénez. Sheet *0518 Châteaulin-Douarnenez* in the IGN TOP 25 series of maps is the best alternative and shows the line of deepest water. However, the plan above provides some detail for the passage.

From Traverse de l'Hôpital to Port Styvel there are mud banks on both sides of the river and it is best to keep to the buoyed channel. At Port Styvel

The Aulne river has lots going for it. The naval hulks at Port Styvel make an interesting, if somewhat sad sight. After that the river is full of wildlife and interest. With plenty of places to anchor, there are wonderful walks to be had. The lock at Guily Glaz is fun to go through and the village of Port Launay and the town of Chateaulin are picturesque.

Pont de Térénez *Nick Chavasse*

numerous small warships are laid up in the river and the channel marker buoys end. Continue to the Pont de Térénez and then, keeping to the outside of the bends, continue for 12M to the lock at Guily Glaz. Lock available two hours either side of high water. Inform the harbourmaster the day before. See info box for telephone number. At Trégarvan, about 2M above Pont de Térénez, the river bends north and the banks become lower. With luck you may see kingfishers and egrets in the reed beds. The river passes very close to the dual carriageway just before turning south again. This is the shallowest part of

the trip and the deepest water is close in to the north bank.

At Guily Glaz the flower-covered lock is a surprise after the peace of the river. It evokes an earlier age when barges travelled from Brest to Nantes and pleasure boats from Camaret came up to Port Launay for the day.

Port Launay is 1M above the lock. The village has a long curve of grass-covered quays backed by old houses under high tree-covered hills.

To carry on to Châteaulin, leave Port Launay and pass the hôtel De Bon Accueil on the port side (you

Approaching Guily Glaz lock *Nick Chavasse*

can tie up if you are staying for supper). Opposite the hotel there are two green markers that indicate a rocky patch on the starboard side. Generally, the deepest water from this point to Châteaulin is on the southeast side of the river. Beware rock reported at 48°12'·26N 04°04'·94W. At the town there is a visitors' pontoon on the north bank. Beware the silted shallow water opposite the visitors' pontoon at Châteaulin and another shallow patch a bit further up towards the bridge.

BERTHS AND ANCHORAGES

⚓ 1. Rivière de l'Hôpital
The pretty entrance of this small river lies to the north of the entrance to the Aulne. Since the river dries it can only be visited around HW (*see plan and photo on page 57*).

⚓ 2. Port Maria at Landévennec
Sheltered from the southwest and southeast, Port Maria is a drying jetty. Anchor on the south bank just inside starboard hand buoy No.7 or to the east of the slipway. From here you can walk to the attractive village of Landévennec.

⚓ 3. Rivière du Faou
Upstream of the entrance to the Rivière de l'Hôpital, the Aulne turns south into a large double bend. The mouth of the Rivière du Faou is on the east bank of the curve. The bar dries 0·1m and lies between Île de Tibidy (N of entrance) and the charming little islet of Arun. North-northwest of this islet is a pool with 2·5m. Beyond the pool the river dries but, at springs, it is possible to go up to the substantial village of Le Faou (*see plan on page 57*).

Guily Glaz lock at the start of the old Brest to Nantes canal
Nick Chavasse

Napoleon Bonaparte started to build the canal in 1804 in order to escape the blockade of Brest by using canals to get to Nantes; sadly the canal is no longer continuous.

Port Launay from downstream *Nick Chavasse*

⚓ 4. Rosnoën, Térénez

48°16'·48N 4°16'·8W

There are three visitors' buoys for boats of less than 30' and a further three for boats over 30'. Buoys are marked with letter 'V'. Leave dinghy on pontoon to visit the Brasserie du Bout du Monde. The brewery occupies an old army shelter. Learn about the different stages of brewing and enjoy a tasting. Tours of the brewery are available in season.

⚓ 5. Île de Térénez to Pont de Térénez

There are several, well-sheltered, anchorages between Port Styvel and Pont de Térénez.

The bottom is rocky away from the banks but it is possible to anchor at Port Styvel (buoy the anchor because this used to be a ships' graveyard). The naval hulks are moved occasionally and so there may be more room to anchor at some times than others.

Anchoring may be possible at the mouth of either of the drying creeks southwest of Île de Térénez or on the east side of the river southwest of Île de Térénez. On the starboard side between Port Styvel and Pont de Térénez there are several very small inlets where it may be possible to anchor but buoy the anchor in any of these places as there may have been fish farms in the past.

⚓ 6. Trégarvan

Trégarvan, 2M upstream of Pont de Térénez, provides a reasonable anchorage; there are several moorings and a slip. There is another landing at Le Passage about 2M further up on the starboard hand side. It is also possible to anchor 0·5M west of the jetty at Trégarvan in the first bay towards Pont de Térénez.

Port Launay

Port Launay has a long stone quay that runs alongside the main street. Once it must have been full of barges waiting for the tide but today there is plenty of room for visiting yachts. Lie alongside the quay on the east side. Water and electricity is neatly concealed in the shrubs. There are toilets and showers (key from the town hall), a few basic food shops, a restaurant and a number of cafés.

Châteaulin

Châteaulin has a visitors' pontoon with 2·6m alongside. There is water and one outlet for electricity on the pontoon, basic toilets and showers at the north end of the quay. The shower key is obtainable on deposit from the tourist office in the town. Modest berthing fees are also payable at the tourist office.

Ashore it has a visitor centre dedicated to salmon. It has all the facilities of a medium-sized town with markets on Thursdays. The hypermarket and fuel station is a short walk from the visitors' pontoon.

Châteaulin visitors' pontoon *Nick Chavasse*

16 Camaret-sur-Mer

48°17'N 4°35'

Shelter
Good except in strong easterlies

Depth restrictions
3m in outer harbour
2m shoaling to 1·8m on visitors' pontoon
   in Port du Notic

Night entry Well lit

HW time Brest HW–0010

Mean height of tide (m) Camaret

HWS	HWN	LWN	LWS
6·6	5·1	2·4	1·0

Tidal streams
Weak in the bay

Berthing
Port Vauban and Port du Notic marinas
20 white visitors' moorings (half price) SE of Port Vauban

Fuel
Fishermen's pontoon 24/7 with credit card

Facilities
Chandlers, some repair facilities, many shops, bars and restaurants

Charts
SHOM *7401*
Imray *C36*

Communications
Camaret port VHF 09
Capitainerie ✆ 02 98 27 89 31
www.camaret-sur-mer.com/le-port_0.php

Attractive fishing port with excellent facilities

Just south of the approach to the Goulet de Brest, Camaret is an ideal stopover when sailing direct from England or Ireland and bound north or south through the Raz de Sein and the Chenal du Four. It is an attractive fishing port that has successfully transformed itself into a yachting and tourist centre. There are shops, seafood restaurants, excellent coast path walking, good beaches and some interesting history.

PILOTAGE

See plan on page 44

Camaret approach and entrance

By day From the west, the coast between Pointe de Toulinguet and Pointe de Grand Gouin is steep-to and has no dangers more than 200m from the above-water rocks.

The approach is clear of dangers except for the shallow, rocky bay, close in, between Pointe de Grand Gouin and the green lateral tower beacon, north of Port Vauban. Identify the north mole that extends east from the green lateral tower beacon and steer for the green-topped white light structure at its east end.

Panorama looking NE with town and Port Notic on left, Port Vauban right of centre and fuel pontoon on far right
Nick Chavasse

By night Approach in the white sector of the light on the north mole and round it at a reasonable distance. There are two large fish farms marked by yellow lightbuoys to the northeast and southeast of the outer marina with moorings between the marina and the one in the southeast of the bay. The shore lights usually provide enough illumination to avoid them.

BERTHS

Port Vauban

Visitors with larger boats are expected to use the outer marina which has pontoons connected to the south side of the north mole. This is exposed to the northeast and, in the past, has been uncomfortable or even dangerous in strong winds between north and east. The outside of the wave breaker is for ferries; visitors go inside.

The Port Vauban harbour office is by the old green lighthouse, next to the old Vauban tower (fort) but is frequently not manned. When closed walk to the main harbour office opposite the gangway to the Port du Notic pontoons. Open 0900–1200 and 1500–1900 in season. Showers and toilets are by the Vauban tower as well as at the main harbour office.

Port du Notic

Port du Notic marina has visitors' berths for smaller boats and is in the inner harbour much closer to the town. Depth 1·8m at outer pontoon. Anchoring is forbidden in the inner harbour. The capitainerie and the showers and toilets are on the quay opposite the entrance to the marina. They are better than the ones by the Vauban tower.

Visitors' moorings

In the bay southeast of the north mole there are moorings in 3m or more, including some white ones for visitors. Anchor just west of the fish farm outside the moorings or to the east of the fish farm. Keep clear of the entrance channel. Anchoring is not allowed in the harbour beyond the moorings.

Fishing boat hulks at Port Vauban *Nick Chavasse*

Port du Styvel

This marina, just north of Port du Notic, has no places for visitors.

ASHORE IN CAMARET

Facilities

Camaret has a fuel berth (24h with credit card) at the fishermen's pontoon situated opposite Port Vauban. Chandlers, a shipbuilder, a sailmaker, supermarkets, launderettes, restaurants, bars and a wide variety of leisure shops. There is a bus service to Brest, Line 34, which only runs about twice per day so checking times is critical. In high season, it may be possible to take a bus or taxi to Le Fret and take a fast ferry to Brest. It is more convenient to do a crew change from Marina du Château, Brest.

Leisure

A walk in Camaret is likely to take you along the breakwater to or from Sillon Point, where the Vauban tower stands. The port's rotting fishing boats are much photographed but the more enduring buildings are also interesting. Camaret's church has some fine wooden statues and a collection of votive offerings left by sailors thankful for narrow escapes at sea.

The church with the broken tower is Chapelle Notre-Dame de Rocamadour which has been a place of worship for seafarers over the centuries and is adorned with model ships and other nauticalia.

Above the village are the mysterious standing stones from where, on a fine day, you get wonderful views over the Goulet de Brest.

The rugged Vauban Tower was built just in time to successfully repulse an Anglo-Dutch landing attempt at the end of the 17th century. It is now an interesting maritime museum. There are another two forts near Camaret, one at the Pointe de Toulinguet and the other at Pointe du Grand Gouin. They are not accessible but on a fine day the walking is wonderful and choughs can be seen on the cliffs. No visit would be complete without *moules et frites*.

The memorial to the Battle of the Atlantic overlooking the sea, about 1·5M southwest of the town is a good reminder of the scale of the loss of life when the Allies fought to keep the North Atlantic supply lines open during the Second World War.

There is a very interesting small museum about the Battle of the Atlantic adjacent to the memorial. Check opening times at the tourist office.

17 The Crozon Peninsula

48°15'N 4°38'W

Hazards
Rocks W of Pte du Toulinguet
Rocks S of Cap de la Chèvre
Isolated marked and unmarked rocks
Strong and complex tidal streams

Night passage
Toulinguet is partially lit
S Chèvre is lit

HW time   Brest HW -0015

Mean height of tide (m) Camaret

HWS	HWN	LWN	LWS
6·6	5·1	2·5	1·0

Tidal stream Toulinguet
N – Brest HW–0530 to +0030 (1·7kn)
S – Brest HW+0030 to +0530 (1·7kn)
Slack – Brest HW+0530 to -0530

Tidal stream 5M W Cap de la Chèvre
NE – Brest HW–0530 to -0130 (0·7kn)
Slack – Brest HW–0130 to +0030
SW – Brest HW+0030 to +0330 (0·3kn)
W – Brest HW+0330 to +0530 (0·4kn)
Slack – Brest HW+0530 to -0530

Tidal stream 2M E of Cap de la Chèvre
NE – Brest HW–0530 to -0030 (0·4kn)
Slack – Brest HW–0030 to +0030
SW – Brest HW+0030 to +0530 (0·3kn)
Slack – Brest HW+0530 to -0530

Charts
SHOM *7172, 7121*
Imray *C36*

Communications
www.finisterebrittany.com/crozon-peninsula

Magnificent scenery and interesting navigation

The Crozon peninsula separates the Rade de Brest from the Bay of Douarnenez. Its granite cliffs rise from a relatively modest 50m in the north at Camaret to a more imposing 100m in the south at Cap de la Chèvre. There are many off-lying rocks. Some, like the Rochers du Toulinguet and Les Tas de Pois off Pointe de Penhir, are more than 30m high; others are less spectacular but more dangerous.

Rocks extend west from Pointe du Toulinguet for nearly four miles. There are several passages through them. The Chenal du Toulinguet is the innermost and saves a good many miles when going between the Rade de Brest and the Bay of Douarnenez or the Raz de Sein.

At the southern tip of the Crozon Peninsula several lines of rocks extend like fangs from the Cap de la Chèvre. Careful navigation is required but it is well rewarded by the magnificent scenery.

PILOTAGE

Chenal du Toulinguet

By day The west side of the channel is marked by the Roches du Toulinguet, which rise to 30m. Le Pohen (height 8m) is nearest to the channel and is steep-to. La Louve west cardinal beacon tower marks the east side of the channel.

Keep to the middle of the channel. The depth is at least 4·9m and the channel is 0·25M wide.

By night The passage is partially lit. From the south use Le Toulinguet light and Petit Minou light; from the north use Le Portzic light (*see plans pages 44 and 64*).

Chenal du Petit Leac'h

By day From the southwest, leave Petit Leac'h south cardinal beacon, 48°16'·27N 04°39'·77W to the west and Pelen south cardinal beacon and Basse Mendufa north cardinal buoy to the east.

The channel is 600m wide with a depth of more than 10m. The tide sets strongly.

By night Not recommended.

Looking N at Pointe du Toulinguet and on left
La Louve west cardinal beacon *Nick Chavasse*

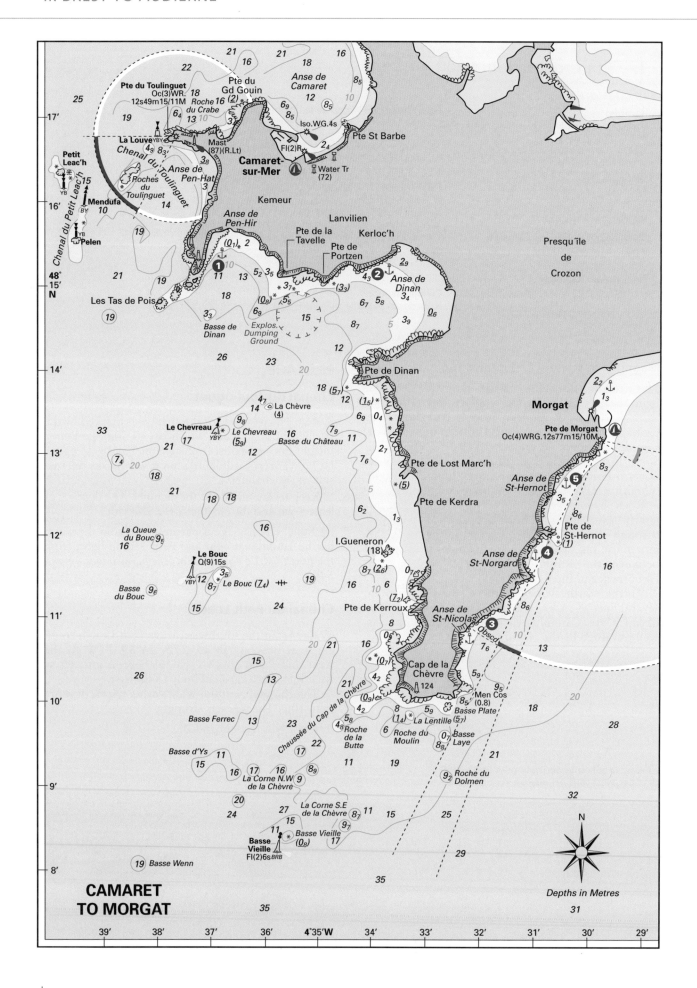

**CAMARET
TO MORGAT**

Depths in Metres

Chenal du Toulinguet and Camaret-sur-Mer looking east. In the foreground the Roches du Toulinguet
rise to 30m and mark the west side of the channel *Patrick Roach*

Les Tas de Pois

Les Tas de Pois are five magnificent rocks extending
out to sea from the Pointe de Pen-Hir. On a calm day
you may feel tempted to pass between them.

Numbering from seaward, the rocks are:

1. Tas de Pois Ouest, height 47m
2. La Fourche, height 10m
3. Le Dentelé, height 35m
4. Le Grand Tas de Pois, height 64m
5. Le Tas de Pois de Terre, height 58m

Looking N, about to pass between Rocks 3 and 4 *Nick Chavasse*

Looking N at Cap de la Chèvre *Nick Chavasse*

Between Rocks 1 and 2, the channel is about 200m wide. There is a rock, drying 0·5m, about 50m northeast of Rock 1 and another drying rock close to Rock 2. Near LW keep to mid-channel, if anything closer to Rock 2.

Between Rocks 2 and 3 the channel is about 100m and clean. Between Rocks 3 and 4 keep closer to Rock 3; there is a rock drying 0·6m close northwest of Rock 4. Between Rocks 4 and 5 passage is only possible near HW as the channel dries almost right across.

Between Rock 5 and the land there is no passage.

Cap de la Chèvre

By day Southbound, pass west of Le Chevreau cardinal. The beacon has been partially destroyed and a west cardinal buoy now marks the rock.

Le Bouc rocks are marked by a west cardinal buoy but the associated shallow patch extends nearly half a mile east of the buoy.

There are dangers up to half a mile offshore around Cap de la Chèvre. At low water, take particular care to avoid Basse Laye 0·4m shallow patch 0·5M south-southeast of the cape.

By night The dangers off Cap de la Chèvre are lit by sectored lights at Pointe du Millier, 48°05'·92N 04°27'·93W and Morgat. See Morgat plan page 68 for details.

ANCHORAGES

1. ⚓ Anse de Pen-Hir (NE of Pointe de Pen-Hir)

Sheltered from all directions except south and southeast but sometimes subject to swell. This snug anchorage is in the sandy Anse de Pen-Hir, just inside Les Tas de Pois. In the centre of the bay, there is a rocky patch just within the 5m line.

2. ⚓ Anse de Dinan

Sheltered from the north and east but exposed to wind or swell from the west and southwest. This wide, shallow bay is 3M east of Les Tas de Pois. Enter from southwest taking care to avoid the rock 400m south of Pointe de la Tavelle and the rock 200m east of Pointe de Portzen. The best anchorage is in the northeast corner of the bay.

3. ⚓ Anse de Saint-Nicolas

48°10'·74N 4°32'·20W

Sheltered from the northwest, this is a rugged but attractive anchorage about 1M north of Cap de la Chèvre on its east side. Approach from the southeast to avoid the dangers of Cap de la Chèvre.

4. ⚓ Anse de Saint-Norgard

48°11'·77N 4°30'·92W

Sheltered from the west and northwest, this rocky bay is about 2M south of Morgat. Approach from the southeast to avoid the drying rocks off Pointe de Saint-Hernot.

5. ⚓ Anse de St Hernot

48°12'·55N 4°30'·31W.

Sheltered from southwest to north.

18 Morgat

48°13′N 4°32′W

Shelter
Reasonable except from N and W
Swell sometimes enters the marina

Depth restrictions
Channel dredged to 1·5m

Night entry
Lit but care is required

HW time
Brest HW –0010

Mean height of tide (m) Morgat

HWS	HWN	LWN	LWS
6·5	5·1	2·5	1·1

Tidal streams
Weak in the bay

Berthing
Marina
Anchorage to N of Morgat buoy in 2m and
40 unmarked visitors' buoys

Fuel Available with credit card 24/7

Facilities In Crozon 1M to N

Charts
SHOM *7172, 7121*
Imray *C36*

Communications
Camaret port VHF Ch 09
Capitainerie ① 02 98 27 01 97
www.morgat.fr

Nineteenth century seaside resort
Morgat is a pretty seaside resort in the northwest corner of Douarnenez Bay.

The marina is not piled and can be uncomfortable but it is well protected by a rocky breakwater and submerged concrete wave breakers (not visible in photo).

Yachts greater than 12m LOA are officially required to use the moorings or anchor but this rule does not appear to be enforced.

Morgat from the south. Note that the submerged wave breaker extending from the end of the curved breakwater is not visible, but is a danger which dries to 0·6m
Patrick Roach

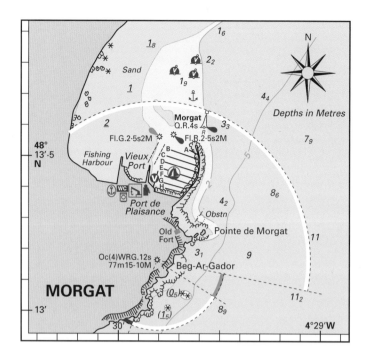

Morgat fuel berth *Nick Chavasse*

PILOTAGE

Morgat approach and entrance

By day Pointe de Morgat is a bold headland with a red and white square tower lighthouse in the trees at the top of the cliff. Two conspicuous above-water rocks at the foot of the headland are steep-to and can be passed within 50m but watch out for the concrete obstruction.

Continue north past the end of the breakwater to Morgat port hand buoy. Leave this to port before entering the harbour between the port and starboard beacons which mark the ends of the submerged wavebreakers. Do not be tempted to cut the corner.

Approaching from Douarnenez itself, or the beautiful beaches in the east of the bay, there is a rocky patch 0·75M south-southwest of Rocher L'Aber and 2M east-southeast of Morgat. It consists of three groups of rocks. The largest is Les Verrès with a partially drying wreck to its northeast. Southwest of Les Verrès is La Pierre Profonde with Le Taureau, the third group, to the north.

By night The dangers south of Cap de la Chèvre can be cleared by keeping in one of the two white sectors of Pointe du Millier light until Pointe de Morgat light turns from red to white. Steer towards Pointe de Morgat light, keeping in the white sector until the 10m depth contour is reached. Turn to run along the coast on a course of about 035° crossing the green sector of Pointe de Morgat light. When Morgat port hand buoy off the harbour entrance (Fl.R.4s) is seen alter course to leave it to port and then into the entrance. Keep a lookout for unlit mooring buoys. There are flashing green and red lights marking the entrance between the wave breakers.

A pleasant walk along a superb beach can be had from Morgat to the town of Crozon. The large hotels developed by Monsieur Peugeot, formerly a bicycle maker but now better known for his cars, are impressive.

Looking SE towards the marina from Morgat *Nick Chavasse*

BERTHS AND ANCHORAGES

Morgat marina and anchorage

Visitors' berth alongside the pontoon with the large 'Visiteurs' sign in the southwest corner of the harbour.

There are many mooring buoys (some of which are for visitors) in the bay north of the harbour. Yachts may anchor in 2m in the bay, clear of the moorings. Anchoring is not permitted in the area enclosed by the breakwater and the wave breakers.

⚓ Île de l'Aber

48°13'·42N 4°25'·81W

Sheltered from the northwest to the northeast, this attractive anchorage behind Île de l'Aber is about 2M east of Morgat.

Coming from Morgat, leave Rocher de l'Aber close to port and turn north-northeast into the anchorage.

Coming from Cap de la Chèvre or Douarnenez, approach from the south to pass east of Les Vèrres and the nearby drying wreck.

ASHORE IN MORGAT

The marina has all the facilities of a substantial marina and fishing port.

Morgat was originally developed by the founder of the Peugeot car company as a place to send his executives for their holidays; consequently there are some fine hotels and villas. There are modest shops, bars and restaurants on the beachfront but the nearest large town is Crozon, which is 1·5M away and a steep climb.

In calm weather it is great fun to take a dinghy trip into the caves at the foot of Pointe de Morgat. The largest cave is like a cathedral and is 100m long and 10m high with brightly coloured walls.

For walkers, the cliff path starts close to the lighthouse and leads all the way to Cap de la Chèvre.

In the summer there is a daily ferry to Ouessant.

Morgat from Vieux Port *Nick Chavasse*

Visitors' pontoon looking E from Vieux port *Nick Chavasse*

19 Douarnenez

48°06'N 4°20'W

Shelter
Good except in strong NW winds when Tréboul visitors' pontoon may be uncomfortable. Good shelter in Port Rhu beyond entry gate

Depth restrictions
1·5m on visitors' pontoon
Port Rhu sill dries 1·1m
3m in Port Rhu

Port Rhu sill gate
Opens HW–0200 Closes HW+0200 when coefficient is >70

Night entry Well lit

HW time
Brest HW –0010

Mean height of tide (m) Douarnenez

HWS	HWN	LWN	LWS
6·6	5·1	2·5	1·0

Tidal streams Weak in the bay

Berthing
Treboul Visitors' pontoon
Port Rhu marina and buoys

Fuel
N side of Tréboul marina

Facilities
Chandlers, repair facilities, good shops and restaurants

Charts
SHOM *7121*
Imray *C36*

Communications
Marina VHF Ch 09
Tréboul ☎ 02 98 60 26 30
Port Rhu ☎ 02 98 60 26 31 (Jul / Aug)
www.mairie-douarnenez.fr
www.tempsfete.com
www.port.de.plaisance@mairie-douarnenez.fr

Fishing port with maritime heritage

Douarnenez, in the sheltered southeast corner of Douarnenez Bay, is really two towns. The River Pouldavid, with Île Tristan at its mouth, splits the fishing port of Douarnenez on the east bank from the beach resort of Tréboul on the west bank.

Visiting yachts use the pontoon at Tréboul near the river entrance or go further upstream. At Port Rhu a barrage with a lock has been built across the river to form a basin. This contains a visitors' pontoon, a large floating maritime museum and a marina for local boats.

PILOTAGE

Douarnenez approach and entrance

By day From Pointe de la Jument (3M west of Douarnenez) there is a safe route clear of the rocky coast by keeping Pointe du Millier lighthouse open of Pointe de la Jument.

Douarnenez is easy to locate from seaward and easy to enter. Île Tristan, with its lighthouse, is in the foreground with Port Neuf north harbour mole east of the island and the Grande Passe and Tréboul marina to the west.

Looking N over Port Rhu towards entrance and Tréboul on left in distance *Nick Chavasse*

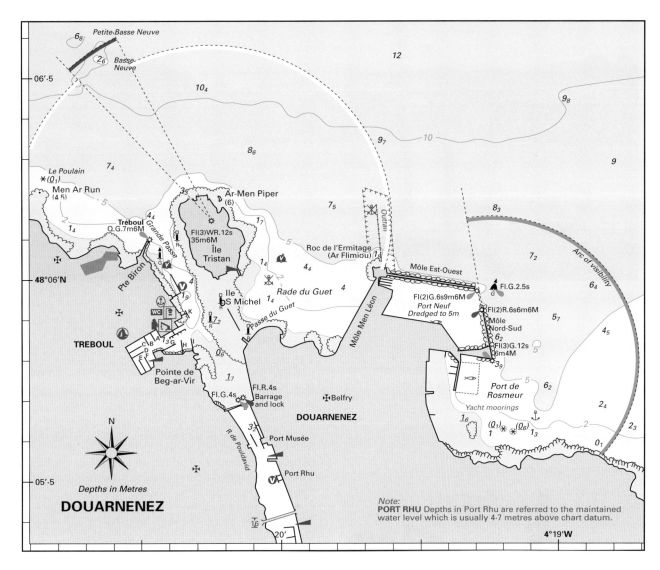

Leave Île Tristan to port to enter the river, or to starboard to continue towards the visitors' moorings in Rade du Guet and and the anchorage in Port de Rosmeur. Douarnenez belfry and Ploaré church at the back of the town form a clearing transit that clears the shallows at Basse Veur and Basse Neuve.

For the visitors' pontoon and moorings in the Grande Passe, or Tréboul Marina, leave Tréboul light to starboard, followed by a starboard hand pillar buoy, beyond which are three visitors' buoys and then the visitors' pontoon.

By night Île Tristan light has a red sector covering Basse Veur and Basse Neuve so keep in the white sector until the inner lights are picked up. For the anchorage at Port de Rosmeur, round the breakwaters a reasonable distance off, keeping a good lookout for the numerous unlit mooring buoys. For the visitors' pontoon in the Grande Passe, or Tréboul Marina, leave Tréboul light to starboard and steer 155° for 1M leaving three unlit visitors' buoys to starboard between Tréboul light and the visitors' pontoon.

BERTHS AND ANCHORAGES

Tréboul

There is a long visitors' pontoon on the west side of the river. There are also three large white mooring buoys in the harbour entrance which may be available by arrangement with the harbour office. These berths are all exposed to the northwest and in rough weather the harbourmaster may be able to arrange a berth elsewhere. Water and electricity on the visitors' pontoons, and toilets and showers are on shore.

Douarnenez visitor's pontoon looking N *Nick Chavasse*

Looking SE towards Port Rhu *Nick Chavasse*

Tréboul basin is dredged to 1·5m. The marina is crowded and no longer has space permanently allocated for visitors. There is not much room to manoeuvre so call by radio or visit the port office before entering the basin. The fuelling pontoon (24 hours with credit card) is just inside the marina on the starboard side.

Looking N through lock into Port Rhu *Nick Chavasse*

Looking N at visitors pontoon in Port Rhu *Nick Chavasse*

Port Rhu

This was once the drying commercial port. In 1992 a barrage was built across the river to create a large wet basin for the Maritime Museum. Additional vessels are housed in the museum building on the east bank. In front of the barrage the bottom dries 1·1m (mud and sand). The lock is open from HW-0200 to HW+0200 when the coefficient is >70 between the hours of 0700 and 2200 in summer. There is a long visitors' pontoon on the port side above the museum area. Water and electricity on pontoon, toilets, showers and laundry on adjacent quay. Before going through the lock a call to the harbour office on VHF Ch 09 is appreciated.

In summer, Port Rhu is the venue for open-air concerts and similar tourist events. A major classic boat rally is held in Douarnenez every two years (see www.tempsfete.com).

Rade du Guet

There are 6 visitors' buoys which are free. Anchoring is now prohibited in the Rade du Guet. Sheltered from west through south to southeast but exposed to swell from the west, this bay lies between Île Tristan and the Môle Men Léon. It has a convenient dinghy landing at the slip in Passe du Guet. It is quieter than Port de Rosmeur.

The Passe du Guet, leading from the visitors' moorings to the river, dries 2·8m, the best water is on the south side near the port hand beacons marking the slip.

Port Neuf fishing harbour

Visitors may not use this harbour.

Looking NE at Passe du Guet *Nick Chavasse*

⚓ Port de Rosmeur

Port de Rosmeur is a well-protected anchorage to the east of Douarnenez. The northwest half of the harbour is for fishing boats and there are many yacht moorings and a fish farm in the remainder of the bay. Anchor in around 5m outside the moorings but buoy the anchor. There is good holding in mud. Inshore the depths vary irregularly and once the 3m line is crossed they shoal quickly in places.

In settled weather at neaps it is possible to anchor just beyond Port de Rosmeur on the west side of Anse du Ris. This is reasonably sheltered from west through south to east.

ASHORE IN DOUARNENEZ

At Tréboul there is a fuel berth, repair facilities, a 6-T fixed crane, 15-T travelift, chandlers, launderette, cafés, restaurants and shops. Market day is Wednesday and Saturday.

Douarnenez has all the usual facilities of a substantial town including a market in Halles de Douarnenez every morning except Sunday. The Maritime Museum in Port Rhu, which has 40 vessels afloat as well as the covered exhibition, is well worth a visit.

ANCHORAGES WEST OF DOUARNENEZ

⚓ Rocher le Coulinec

48°06'·32N 4°21'·05W

Sheltered from the south, there is a fine-weather anchorage off Plage des Sables Blanc about 300m southeast of Rocher le Coulinec, 0·5 west of Grande Passe.

⚓ Porz Péron

48°05'·38N 4°29'·05W

Sheltered from the southwest through south to east, this rocky little bay is about 1·25M west of Pointe de Milier, 5M west of Douarnenez. Approach from the north, leaving the 9m rock Karreg Toull to starboard.

Bureau de Port Douarnenez *Nick Chavasse*

Looking SE over Port Rosmeur with anchorage and moorings beyond *Nick Chavasse*

Douarnenez is special! World famous for its biennial Maritime Festival, which will be held next in 2024 when it will be combined with Brest's Festival of Sail. The place oozes character and history, and warrants staying a night or two. There is normally plenty going on and the port museum (Le Port-Musée), which takes you on a voyage of maritime culture, is definitely worth a visit. A barrage/lock to Port Rhu ensures the river maintains a depth of 3·2m.

20 Raz de Sein

48°03'N 4°46'W

Hazards
Dangerous tide race; unmarked rocks SW of Tévennec, 48°06'·98N 04°56'·11W and W of Pte du Van, 48°03'·98N 04°42'·87W.

Night passage Well lit

HW time
Brest HW+0005

Mean height of tide (m) Île de Sein

HWS	HWN	LWN	LWS
6·1	4·8	2·3	0·9

Tidal stream Raz de Sein
N-going – Brest HW +0545 to –0100
    (Sp 5·2 kn, Np 3·0 kn)
Slack – Brest HW –0100 to –0030
S-going – Brest HW –0030 to +0515
    (Sp 5·5 kn, Np 2·4 kn)

Slack if N bound – Brest HW +0515 to +0545
There are eddies near La Vieille on both streams.

Charts
SHOM *7147, 7423*
Imray *C36*

Communications
Pte du Raz VHF Ch 16
www.brittanytourism.com/accommodation
/restaurants-and-fine-food/restaurants/
le-raz-de-sein

Rocky corner of southwest Brittany

The Raz de Sein is the short passage between the Pointe du Raz on the mainland and the Île de Sein. It has a justifiably bad reputation for fierce tides, rough seas and poor visibility, but under reasonable conditions, it presents no great difficulties.

PILOTAGE

Tidal strategy

Timing is important and when possible, the Raz should be taken at slack water. Even in moderate conditions, with wind and tide, it can be rough. With light winds, neap tides and no swell, it is passable at any time.

The Raz is temperamental and the seas vary considerably but, with strong wind against tide, the overfalls are dangerous.

The Raz de Sein from the north

A yacht leaving the Chenal du Four at the end of the fair tide can punch the tide in the Iroise, where it is weak, and usually arrive at the Raz in time to take advantage of the stream turning south again (see page 43).

By day From the north make for La Vieille lighthouse on 180°, which puts La Vieille midway between Pointe du Van and Tévennec.

When 0·5M off La Vieille, bear to starboard to pass west of La Plate west cardinal yellow and black tower beacon. There may be overfalls west of La Plate but the sea will moderate once it is passed.

Continuing south, keep Pointe du Van in transit with Gorle Greiz, (the large rock between Pointe du Raz and La Vieille), bearing 041°. This leads between the shallow patches Kornog Bras and Masklou Greiz which can be rough in bad weather.

Heading southeast towards Penmarc'h, steer with Tévennec bearing 324° astern, open to the left of La Plate.

By night Make good 180° in the white sector of La Vieille. When Le Chat turns from green to white, steer 215° until the directional flashing light on Tévennec opens. Then steer 150° past La Vieille and Le Chat.

Continuing south use the white sector of La Vieille, on 205°.

Heading southeast towards Penmarc'h use the directional sector of Tévennec until Le Chat turns from green to red, bearing 286°, when you will be clear of the southern dangers.

The Raz de Sein from the northwest

By day Avoid the dangers of Basse Plate, 0·5M to the southwest of Tévennec by keeping La Vieille in transit with the southern limit of the cliffs southeast of the Pointe du Raz, on 112°. When 0·5M off La Vieille alter course to leave La Plate to port.

By night Make good 190° in the white sector of Men Brial light on Île de Sein. When La Vieille turns from red to white, steer 120° until the directional flashing light on Tévennec (Dir.Fl.W.4s) opens. Then proceed as from the north. Basse Plate is 0·5M north of this track.

The Raz de Sein from the south

By day From the south or southeast keep the steep island of Tévennec open to the west of La Plate on a bearing of 327°. Pass La Plate leaving it 0·5M to starboard.

Continuing north, keep the back-bearing on La Vieille between 160° and 200° to clear the dangers off Pte du Van and Tévennec.

Heading northwest, make 295° from La Plate keeping in the middle of the channel between Tévennec and Île de Sein.

By night Keep in the directional Fl.4s sector of Tévennec light until it bears 330° and La Plate bears 110°. A track of 020° will then lead north clear of the Raz. A track of 295° leads northwest between Tévennec and Île de Sein in the white sector of La Vielle.

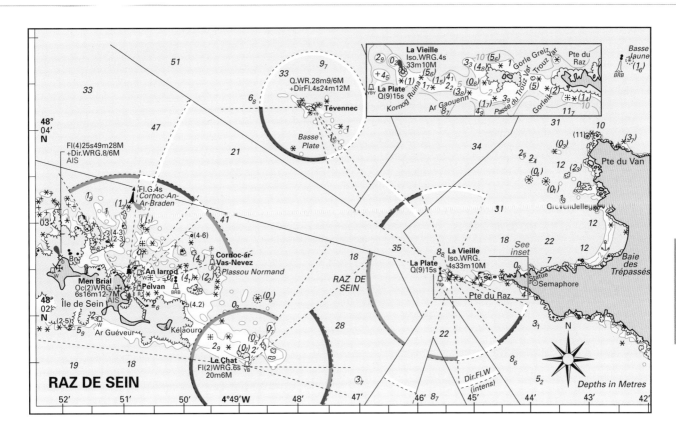

Looking E at La Vieille lighthouse on left, La Plate west cardinal beacon on right and Pte du Raz semaphore in middle beyond *Nick Chavasse*

Looking SW at Tevennec lighthouse *Nick Chavasse*

ANCHORAGES

⚓ Baie des Trépassés

48°02'·87N 4°42'·78W

Sheltered between northeast and southeast but exposed to swell from the west, there is a fair-weather anchorage in the Baie des Trépassés, east-northeast of the Pointe de Raz. To avoid the dangers southwest of Pointe du Van, approach from due west. The bay is sandy and shelving so anchor in the most suitable depth. The best position is either in the centre, facing the valley or in the northeast corner about 200m southeast of Grevendeileg. Expect some swell.

⚓ Port de Brézellec

48°04'·27N 4°39'·72W

Sheltered between west through south to southeast and situated about 5M east of Raz de Sein, this may be a useful anchorage when Baie des Tréspassés is unsuitable due to westerly wind or swell.

21 Île de Sein

48°02'N 4°51'W

Shelter
Fair from S or SW but may be swell

Hazards
Many marked and unmarked rocks

Depth restrictions
1·8m in anchorage

Night entry
Lit but not recommended

HW time Brest HW -0005

Mean height of tide (m) Île de Sein

HWS	HWN	LWN	LWS
6·1	4·8	2·3	0·9

Tidal streams N approach
SE – Brest HW –0300 to +0400
Slack – Brest HW +0430
NW – Brest HW -0500 to -0400

Berthing
Limited room to anchor or dry out in inner harbour

Facilities
Bars and restaurants but very limited shopping

Charts
SHOM *7147, 7423*
Imray *C37*

Communications
Pte du Raz VHF Ch 16
www.mairie-iledesein.com/port.htm

Tiny island surrounded by rocks

Île de Sein is tiny but well worth a visit. The only town, Port de Sein, is a mass of painted houses and narrow streets. The island itself is so low-lying that the sea has occasionally covered it. There are no trees, or even bushes; just old fields surrounded by dry stone walls. However, the real attraction is the ever-present Atlantic and the huge Breton sky.

There are ferries from Audierne/Sainte-Evette all year round and wonderful walks to be had on the island.

Île de Sein is an island of heroes. The entire male population left for England in their fishing boats to join the Free French during the Second World War and their exploits are commemorated in an interesting little museum. When General De Gaulle was first reviewing his troops, a quarter of whom were from the island, he is reported to have said 'Where is this Île de Sein? It seems to be a quarter of France'. Nowadays a large number of the lifeboat men of West Brittany come from the island.

Right **Port de Sein from south. Nerroth Rock is seen top right**
Patrick Roach

Below **Anchorage off slipway** *(see plan page 79)*
Nick Chavasse

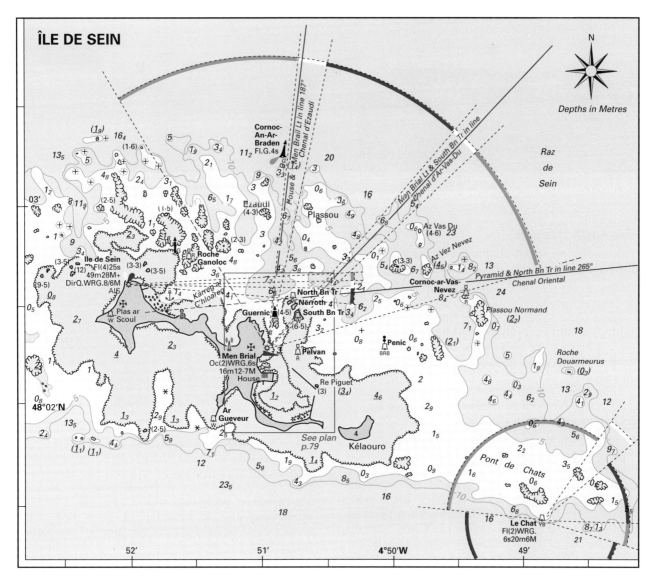

ÎLE DE SEIN

PILOTAGE

Warning A large-scale chart is essential

The navigation is intricate so slack tide at neaps is best for a first visit. Neap tides have the additional benefit of increasing the available anchoring space.

Navigating in the area around Île de Sein is not as difficult as it appears from the chart. The entrance channels are clearly marked. The tidal streams are not nearly as strong as in the Raz. Also the plateau is compact on the northeast and east sides and the fringes are clearly marked.

Identifying Nerroth is the key. It forms the east side of the entrance to the harbour and looks like a flattish, rocky island at low water and three very large flat rocks at high water. Two white masonry beacons on the north and south ends of Nerroth are important day marks.

Looking E at Nerroth North Bn on left and Nerroth S Bn on right *Nick Chavasse*

Looking E at Nerroth north and south beacons *Nick Chavasse*

Looking W at Guernic starboard hand beacon with Men Brial light beyond and house with black stripe to the left *Nick Chavasse*

The north channel

This is the principal channel and the easiest for a stranger.

By day From the north, approach the Cornoc-An-Ar-Braden starboard hand pillar buoy.

Identify the green and white tower of Men Brial lighthouse and beyond it the white house with the vertical black stripe, third from the left by the quay. Keep the black stripe just open left of the lighthouse on 187°.

Continue, keeping within 50m either side of the track until Nerroth is abeam. Continue into the anchorage using the instructions below.

By night Not recommended on a first visit. There must be enough light to make out Nerroth and Guernic starboard hand concrete beacon and tide must be high enough to allow some margin for error.

Enter in the white sector of Men Brial light, bearing 187° and leave Cornoc-An-Ar-Braden starboard hand buoy to starboard. When Nerroth north beacon is abeam follow the instructions below for the entry into the anchorage.

Nerroth to the anchorage

By day With Nerroth north beacon abeam, steer 170° to enter the harbour.

After passing Guernic starboard hand tower beacon steer 180° to avoid a shoal patch.

When Men Brial lighthouse bears 220° alter course to the southwest and aim for the anchorage.

By night Not recommended on a first visit. When Nerroth north beacon is abeam, alter course to 170° and enter the red sector of Men Brial, leaving Guernic starboard hand tower beacon 60m to starboard. When the other white sector of Men Brial is entered, it is safe to steer for the anchorage.

The northeast channel

Coming from the east or northeast this channel is easier than the east channel.

By day Start from about 300m northwest of Ar-Vas-Du rock, 48°02'·90N 04°49'·80W. Approach Nerroth using Men Brial lighthouse in line with the white beacon on the south of Nerroth on 224°.

The beacon on the north end of Nerroth should be left about 100m to port so turn to starboard when it bears 250° to enter the anchorage as described above.

By night Not recommended on a first visit. This channel is covered by a white sector of Men Brial light, but sufficient light is needed for the deviation round Nerroth and into the harbour.

The east channel

By day From the Raz de Sein, keep the Cornoc-ar-Vas-Nevez beacon bearing less than 290° to avoid the rocks to the south.

Start from a position 100m north of the beacon. Approach Nerroth using the north end of Nerroth in line with Plas ar Scoul, the pyramid tower with a fluorescent top, just south of the Île de Sein main lighthouse on 265° (see above). Karreg ar C'hloareg above-water rock and the Cross of Lorraine monument are on virtually the same line. This transit must be held closely because Ar Vas Nevez (dries 5·0m) is close to the north of the line and another rock (dries 1·0m) is close to the south.

Looking S at Cornoc-ar-Vas-Nevez Bn *Nick Chavasse*

Plas ar Scoul tower with fluorescent top *Nick Chavasse*

Cross of Lorraine monument *Nick Chavasse*

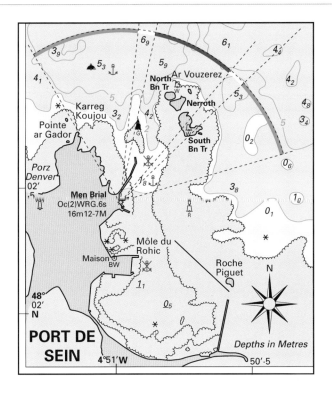

The beacon on the north end of Nerroth should be left about 100m to port and when it is abeam start turning to port to enter the anchorage as described above.

By night Not recommended on a first visit. Pick up the QFl.WRG Directional light from Île de Sein main lighthouse and keep in the white sector on 270° until Neroth is abeam and course can be altered, as in the section above, to the anchorage.

ANCHORAGES

⚓ Port de Sein

Sheltered from the south and west but exposed to the east above half tide, the anchorage is north east of Men Brial in 1·8m. The bottom is mud over rock. Weed can be a problem.

The whole harbour dries near the quays and south of them. The fishing fleet enters the harbour in the evening, and is often there by day. Its position indicates the best water. The round red buoys belong to the fishermen and there is not much room to anchor between them and the slip so it may be necessary to anchor east of them. Permission can sometimes be obtained to use a buoy.

Swell enters if the wind goes into the north and the anchorage would be dangerous in strong winds from any northerly direction.

Yachts that can take the ground may use the inner harbour south of the slips and can find 1·5m in places at LW neaps. The bottom is mainly sand but there are some weed-covered stony patches.

⚓ Île de Sein lighthouse

Sheltered from the south and southwest, this a small bay about 400m east-southeast of Île de Sein lighthouse. Approach it from a point just north of Nerroth. Bring the lighthouse onto 270° and hold this course until due south of Roche Ganaloc red beacon tower at 48°02'·61N 4°51'·57W. Now come round onto 230° and edge in carefully towards the beach as far as draught permits.

ASHORE ON ÎLE DE SEIN

Facilities

Repairs can be arranged and chandlery can be obtained from the fishermen's co-op. There are several small shops, bars and restaurants. Water is scarce but bread is delivered from the mainland.

Yacht drying out in the inner port, looking NE through the entrance *Nick Chavasse*

Anchorage ESE of Île de Sein lighthouse *Nick Chavasse*

22 Sainte-Evette

48°00′N 4°33′W

Shelter
Reasonable except from strong E–SW wind when swell makes it very uncomfortable
Marked wrecks and rocks in approach

Depth restrictions
2·2m patch in approach to moorings

Night entry Well lit

HW time Brest HW –0030

Mean height of tide (m) Audierne

HWS	HWN	LWN	LWS
5·2	4·1	2·0	0·8

Tidal streams
Weak in the bay

Berthing
Visitors' buoys

Facilities
Good facilities in Audierne 1·5M

Charts
SHOM *7147*
Imray *C37*

Communications
Sainte-Evette VHF Ch 9
HM ☏ 02 98 70 00 28

Beach resort with moorings

Sainte-Evette is a small holiday resort situated in the outer approaches to Audierne. It has all-tide access with 20 visitors' buoys. These are well sheltered, except from the east and south. The buoys are rather close together but a few can accommodate 12m LOA maximum.

Sainte Evette is a good stopping place after the fairly long passage from Camaret or further afield.

The visitors' moorings are fine, if a little close together, and there is room to anchor but do use a tripping buoy.

Also a useful spot to wait for the tide before or after going through the Raz de Sein.

Sainte-Evette has few facilities but it is a pleasant walk along the river bank to Audierne.

The moorings at Sainte-Evette looking northeast.
The long breakwater protects the bay from the southwest but not from strong winds from the east or south *Patrick Roach*

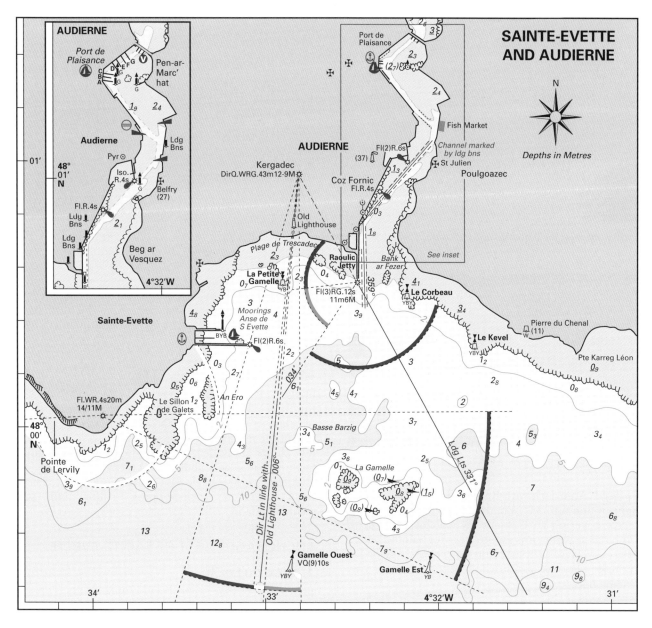

PILOTAGE

Sainte-Evette from the west and south

By day From the Raz de Sein, the entrance to Sainte-Evette is east of Pointe de Lervily and its off-lying rocks and 0·5M west of Gamelle West west cardinal buoy.

Identify two white, red-topped lighthouses to the north of the bay: Kergadec lighthouse is on the skyline and is easy to spot. Below it, the old lighthouse of Trescadec is less easy to locate. Look for it in a gap between the houses. Line up the two lighthouses on 006°. (*See top photo page 83.*)

This will keep you clear of the rocky patches either side of the channel, Le Sillon and An Ero to the west and La Gamelle to the east of the channel. If there is a swell, the seas break on La Gamelle. At low water also note the shoal patch depth 2·2m on the leading line, east of Sainte-Evette breakwater.

For Sainte-Evette moorings, leave the leading line and steer for the mole head when it bears 315°. Take care to avoid the rocks on the north edge of the mole.

By night Enter the narrow white sector of Kergadec quick flashing light (006°). When the light on the Sainte-Evette mole head bears 315° alter course for the Sainte-Evette anchorage.

Sainte-Evette from the southeast

By day From the southeast the channel between La Gamelle to the west and the land to the east is wide and the least depth on the leading line is 2·5m. Gamelle East south cardinal buoy should be left well to port.

The transit is Kergadec lighthouse, white with a red top on the skyline, with the Raoulic Jetty light tower on 331°. When Sainte-Evette breakwater head bears 293° it is safe to steer for the moorings.

Looking NE over the moorings and anchorage towards Audierne entrance *Nick Chavasse*

La Petite Gamelle S Card Bn *Nick Chavasse*

By night Approach with Raoulic light and Kergadec light in line on 331°. Pte de Lervily light has a red sector covering La Gamelle. When this light turns from red to white, it is safe to steer for Sainte-Evette. There is a wreck (dries 1·5m) on the east side of La Gamelle shallow patch about 400m west of the leading line.

BERTHS AND ANCHORAGES

Sainte-Evette moorings and anchorage

The Sainte-Evette moorings are sheltered from west and north by the land and from the southwest by the breakwater. However, some swell enters if there is south in the wind and this may be considerable if the wind is strong. The depths are 2·5m or more north of the end of the mole, decreasing steadily towards the shore. The moorings are tightly packed and not suitable for boats over 12m. Some are not suitable for boats over 10m. A charge is collected for their use.

There may be room to anchor east of the moorings, with less shelter from the south. The holding is not very good and there are a few rocky patches. Buoy the anchor. It is best to tuck in behind the breakwater as far as depth and space allow to get out of the swell, but do not restrict manoeuvring room for the ferries.

The bay contains two hazards. First, the more northerly of the two slips extends a long way and has an inconspicuous east cardinal at its end. Second, there is a rock ledge, La Petite Gamelle marked by a south cardinal beacon, in the northern part of the anchorage. The bay is shallow north of this beacon.

ASHORE IN SAINTE-EVETTE

Dinghy in to the beach next to the ferry slip, or at the little pier in the northwest corner of the bay, which dries at LW. There is a harbour taxi included within the mooring fee. There is a launderette and a few shops at the ferry terminal. Audierne has all facilities and is only about 1·5M away.

A ferry goes to Île de Sein from Sainte-Evette. The ferry takes a rock-hopping route and is recommended.

ANCHORAGES WEST OF SAINTE-EVETTE

⚓ Anse du Loc'h

48°01'·44N 4°38'·29W

Sheltered from all directions except southeast to southwest, this sandy bay is 3M west of Pointe de Lervily. Enter it on 030° to avoid the rocks on the east side.

⚓ Anse du Cabestan

48°00'·56N 4°35'·91W

Sheltered from north through east, this wide sandy bay is 2M west of Audierne. Approach from the southwest to avoid two rocks. Basse du Loc'h (dries 1·9m) between Anse du Loc'h and Anse du Cabestan and Roche de Porz-Tarz at the northwest end of Anse du Cabestan.

ANCHORAGE EAST OF SAINTE-EVETTE

⚓ Pors-Poulhan

47°59'·00N 4°27'·80W

Protected from the northeast, this tiny harbour is 3M southeast of Audierne. The harbour itself is very small and dries but there is an outside anchorage that can be used in settled weather.

23 Audierne

48°01'N 4°32'W

Shelter Good in marina

Hazards
Audierne channel in strong S wind
Marked wrecks and rocks in approach

Depth restrictions
Audierne channel dredged 1m
Marina 2m on pontoons D–G

Night entry
Lit but not recommended

HW time Brest HW-0030

Mean height of tide (m) Audierne

HWS	HWN	LWN	LWS
5·2	4·1	2·0	0·8

Tidal streams
Weak in the bay but strong in the river and
marina

Berthing
Marina

Fuel
Available 24/7 in Poulgoazec

Facilities
Some repair facilities, good shops, market
and restaurants

Charts
SHOM *7147*
Imray *C37*

Communications
Audierne Marina VHF Ch 09, 16
① 02 98 75 04 93
Mob 06 99 23 82 53
www.plaisance.audierne@peche-
    plaisance-cornouaille.fr

Audierne leading line (offset) - old lighthouse with Kergadec behind *Nick Chavasse*

Attractive fishing port with marina

Audierne is an attractive bustling port town popular
with tourists. It is 1M inland, accessed by a dredged
channel (1m) which is subject to silting. The small
marina has some space for visitors on the
hammerheads.

PILOTAGE

Warning The mouth of the Audierne channel is dangerous in
strong south winds.

Audierne approaches

By day Use Sainte-Evette approaches (*see page 81*).
From south or west head for the end of Raoulic Jetty
when it bears 034°.

Pilotage from the end of the jetty is given below.

By night Partially lit but not recommended.

Le Raoulic at the entrance to Audierne *Nick Chavasse*

The dredged channel to Audierne

By day The channel is maintained at between 1m
and 2m but is subject to silting. In the first section it
is narrow and close to the pier and at low water
there is not much room for error so it is best to make
a first visit above half tide. There is a port hand
beacon halfway along the pier and close to it.

There are two leading lines marked with pairs of
red and white chevron boards and they are not easy
to see. The first is on the Raoulic Jetty on 359°. The
second is on 043° with front red/white chevron on
lamp post and rear chevrons on fish market roof.
This second bearing takes one very close to the end
of the Vieux Mole and below half-tide it is better to
follow the junction of the rocks at the base of the
jetty with the sand which can easily be seen.

At the fish market the channel turns on to 303°
and runs along the quays to the marina.

By night Partially lit but not recommended.

Second pair of leading marks with front chevrons on lamp
post and rear on fish market roof *Nick Chavasse*

BERTHS AND ANCHORAGE

Audierne marina

The marina has been extended and there is now some space for visitors on the hammerheads. Pontoons A–C have been dredged 2m on the hammerheads, D–G are reported to have 2m throughout. If possible, avoid F and G because the tide sets across them at 8kn in springs. Beware starboard hand beacon opposite Pontoon D when tide flowing strongly.

ASHORE IN AUDIERNE

Audierne is a pleasant town that has successfully combined fishing with tourism.

There is a shipyard as well as mechanical and electrical engineers. Diesel is available at Poulgoazec. The fuel pontoon is situated on the east bank left of the white fish market building.

The market square and shopping area are close to the pontoons and there is a wide range of shops and restaurants. The showers are next to the harbourmaster's office, on Quai Anatole France, a short walk along the river bank towards the bridge. Market day is Saturday.

Looking W at Audierne marina © SMPPPC

Looking SE along Quai Pelletan *Nick Chavasse*

Looking S over the channel to Audierne © SMPPPC

La Chambre moorings (Îles de Glénan) *Nick Chavasse*

III. Bénodet Bay

Bénodet Bay is classic South Brittany. Bénodet and Loctudy are both delightful and somehow just right for messing about in boats. The Odet river from Bénodet to Quimper is possibly the most attractive river in Biscay and has a number of peaceful anchorages.

The Îles de Glénan, on a sunny day, could be mistaken for the Caribbean. Then there is the fascinating Ville Close at Concarneau, right next to the visitors' pontoon. Those who need a marina, will like the large modern one at Port-La-Forêt.

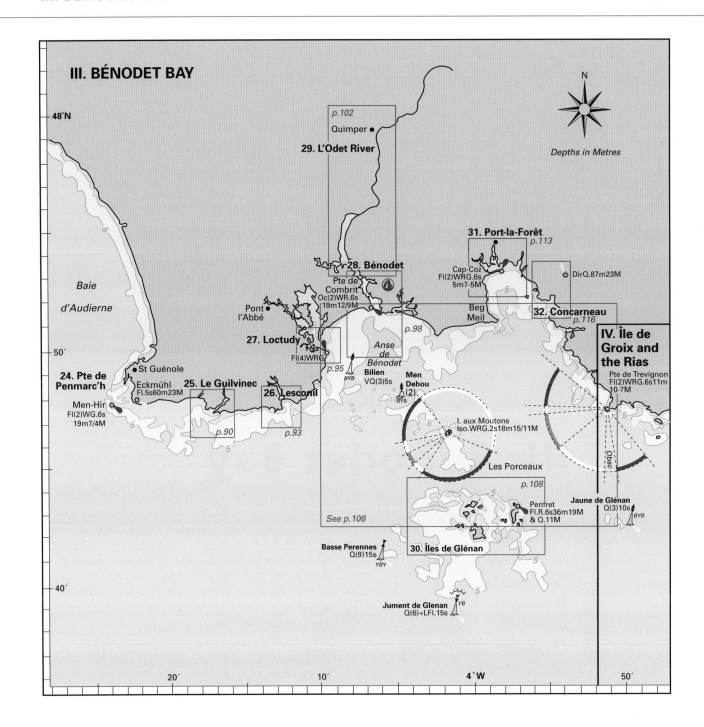

III. BÉNODET BAY

48°N

Baie
d'Audierne

50´

40´

p.102
Quimper •

29. L'Odet River

N

Depths in Metres

31. Port-la-Forêt   *p.113*

28. Bénodet
Cap-Coz
Fl(2)WRG.6s
5m7-5M

Pte de
Combrit
Oc(2)WR.6s
19m12/9M

Beg
Meil

32. Concarneau   *p.116*

Pont
l'Abbé •

27. Loctudy
Fl(4)WRG

p.98

Anse
de
Bénodet

IV. Île de
Groix and
the Rias

p.95

Bilien
VQ(3)5s
BYB

Pte de Trevignon
Fl(2)WRG.6s11m
10-7M

24. Pte de
Penmarc'h

• St Guénole
Eckmühl
Fl.5s60m23M

Men-Hir
Fl(2)WG.6s
19m7/4M

25. Le Guilvinec

Men
Dehou
(2)
BYB

DirQ.87m23M

I. aux Moutons
Iso.WRG.2s18m15/11M

Obsc

26. Lesconil

p.90

p.93

Les Porceaux

p.108

Jaune de Glénan
Q(3)10s
BYB

See p.106

Penfret
Fl.R.6s36m19M
& Q.11M

Basse Perennes
Q(9)15s
YBY

30. Îles de Glénan

Jument de Glenan
Q(6)+LFl.15s
YB

20´   10´   4°W   50´

Bénodet Bay tidal streams

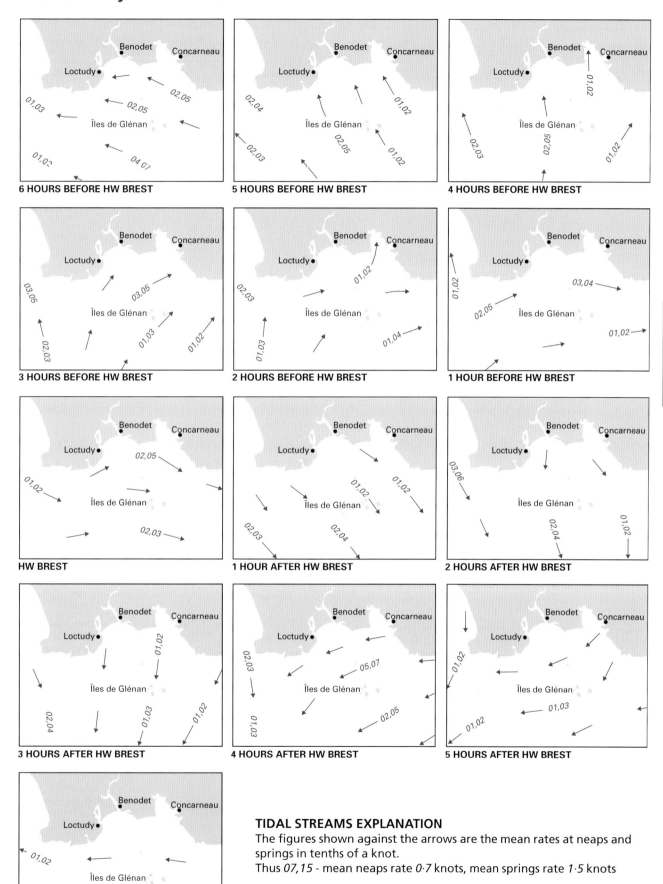

6 HOURS BEFORE HW BREST

5 HOURS BEFORE HW BREST

4 HOURS BEFORE HW BREST

3 HOURS BEFORE HW BREST

2 HOURS BEFORE HW BREST

1 HOUR BEFORE HW BREST

HW BREST

1 HOUR AFTER HW BREST

2 HOURS AFTER HW BREST

3 HOURS AFTER HW BREST

4 HOURS AFTER HW BREST

5 HOURS AFTER HW BREST

6 HOURS AFTER HW BREST

TIDAL STREAMS EXPLANATION
The figures shown against the arrows are the mean rates at neaps and springs in tenths of a knot.
Thus *07,15* - mean neaps rate *0·7* knots, mean springs rate *1·5* knots

24 Pointe de Penmarc'h

47°48'N 4°23'W

Hazards
Well marked rocks
Complex tidal streams that are much affected
   by the wind

Night passage
Well lit

HW time
Brest HW– 00254 neaps, –0030 springs

Mean height of tide (m) Guilvinec

HWS	HWN	LWN	LWS
5·1	4·0	2·0	0.9

Tidal streams Pte de Penmarc'h
SE-going: Brest HW–0230 to +0230 (1·0kn)
NW-going: Brest HW+0230 to –0230 (1·0kn)

St-Guénole
St-Guénole is a commercial fishing port
that does not welcome yachtsmen.
Entry is hazardous except in very good
conditions

Charts
SHOM *7147, 7146*
Imray *C37*

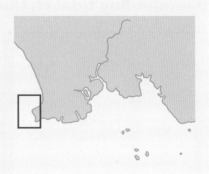

Gateway to the sun

The Pointe de Penmarc'h is a low headland with a very high square prism lighthouse, named Eckmühl after the Prince d'Eckmühl, a heroic marshall in Napoleon's army. Eckmühl lighthouse on the Pointe de Penmarc'h marks the start of South Brittany so passing it eastbound is always a pleasure. In good weather at sunrise or sunset it is a magical place.

Reefs extend in all directions from the headland. These are well marked and, in good weather, it is possible to round close, using the various beacon towers.

PILOTAGE

Rounding Penmarc'h

By day Give Men-Hir Lt Bn a good berth as the reef on which it stands extends over 200m to the west. Otherwise there are no hazards outside the lines joining the buoys. However, there is often a heavy swell in the vicinity of Pointe de Penmarc'h and in these circumstances, or in poor visibility, it is best to stay at least 3M off shore.

By night Use the white sector of Men-Hir to keep clear of the rocks off the Pointe of Penmarc'h. After that the principal buoys are lit although care should be taken to keep well south of the unlit Ar Guisty 47°45'·63N 04°15'·54W, which is south of Le Guilvinec.

Men Hir beacon with Pointe de Penmarc'h beyond, looking E *Nick Chavasse*

25 Le Guilvinec

47°48'N 4°17'W

Shelter Good

Hazards
1·8m shallow patch on leading line

Depth restrictions
3m in harbour

Night entry Well lit

Other restrictions
Total priority to fishing vessels
No entry or exit 1630 1800 due to returning
fishing boats on weekdays

HW time Brest HW−0018

Mean height of tide (m) Guilvinec

HWS	HWN	LWN	LWS
5·2	4·0	2·0	0·9

Berthing
Visitors' pontoons (8 places)

Facilities
As of a busy fishing port

Charts
SHOM 7146, 6646
Imray C37

Communications
HM VHF 09
Pleasure Craft Office
℡ 02 98 58 05 67
mobile 06 63 39 14 47
http://nautisme.meteoconsult.fr/

Colourful fishing port

Le Guilvinec is a commercial fishing port 4M east of Penmarc'h. The harbour is sheltered and the entrance is straightforward, providing care is taken to avoid outlying rocks. Le Guilvinec has recently made an effort to be more welcoming to visitors and there were some plans to extend the facilities to visiting yachtsmen. There is not much room but there are two small visitors' pontoons, one on the northwest side of the harbour and one on the southeast.

It is quite easy to enter the port, where you will find a fine display of colourful fishing boats, but keep your eyes on the chart. The town is lively and there are lots of restaurants. Part of Le Guilvinec's charm is that it is not really equipped to cater for visiting yachtsmen, but plans (as yet unmaterialised) to increase yachting facilities reflect the increasing value of tourism for the local economy.

Entrance to Le Guilvinec *Nick Chavasse*

Looking SW back out of the approaches to Le Guilvinec *Nick Chavasse*

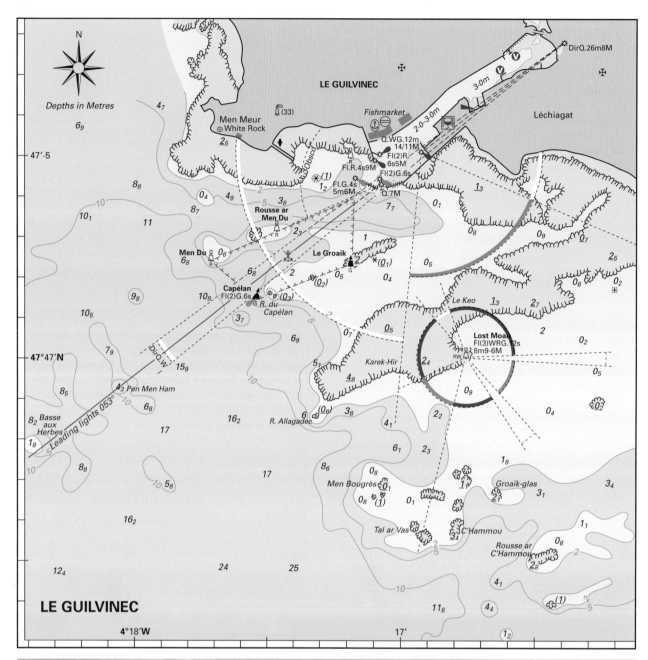

LE GUILVINEC

Looking NE up the river basin at Le Guilvinec towards the red and white leading mark *Nick Chavasse*

Looking NW over visitors' pontoons on both sides of the river *Nick Chavasse*

PILOTAGE

Guilvinec main channel

By day From the west keep well clear of Les Etocs above-water and drying rocks and make for Névez starboard hand buoy, 900m south of Raguen south cardinal tower beacon. Le Guilvinec is difficult to see among all the white houses with grey roofs. Look for the long white fish market, a red-topped lighthouse on the north mole and the massive blue travel-lift. The conspicuous leading marks, two large red cylinders on orange-red columns, will be in transit on 053°.

The leading line crosses a 1·8m shallow patch, Basse aux Herbes. Near low water, especially in rough weather, it is best to move 150m to starboard to avoid this shoal. Follow the leading line and pass between Men Du port hand beacon tower and Capelan starboard hand light buoy, then Rousse ar Men Du port hand beacon tower and Le Groaik starboard hand beacon tower. Enter the harbour between the outer south mole and the north mole head and spur.

From the east leave Basse Spineg south cardinal buoy to starboard to make for the Névez starboard hand buoy and enter as above.

By night The synchronised leading lights are easy to identify. If entering at low water, avoid Basse aux Herbes by keeping 150m to starboard of the leading lights when in the red sector of Locarec light 1·5M to the west-northwest. Stay on the leading line until the south mole light bears 030° distant 200m; it will then be safe to turn to port and head for the harbour entrance.

Guilvinec south channel

By day This route should only be used if the marks can be identified with certainty. Start near waypoint, 47°45'·35N 04°16'·0W, between Ar Guisty south cardinal tower beacon and Spinec south cardinal buoy. Les Fourches rocks 800m northeast of this position never cover. Identify the Men Meur white-painted rock, at the west end of the Guilvinec waterfront, and steer 352° for 1·75M to the Capelan starboard hand lightbuoy and enter as above.

By night Not recommended.

BERTHS AND ANCHORAGES

Le Guilvinec harbour

Le Guilvinec is very busy and visitors must not secure to a quay or a fishing boat except in an emergency.

Yachting facilities have been improved and there are two small visitors' pontoons, one on each side of the harbour.

ASHORE IN LE GUILVINEC

The harbour is packed with brightly painted fishing boats and busy with fishing activity. The main part of town is on the north side of harbour. Water and electricity on the pontoon, toilets and showers on the south side of the harbour. Many seafood restaurants. Market day is Tuesday.

26 Lesconil

47°47'N 4°12'W

Shelter
Good in harbour; anchorage sheltered from W through N to E

Hazards
Do not enter in strong S wind

Depth restrictions
2·5m in approach
1·5m in harbour entrance

Night entry Well lit

HW time Brest HW-0020

Mean height of tide (m) Lesconil

HWS	HWN	LWN	LWS
5·0	4·0	2·0	0·9

Berthing
Visitors pontoon with 19 berths. Three fore-and-aft visitors' moorings in harbour or anchorage outside harbour

Facilities
As of a fishing port

Charts
SHOM *7146, 6646*
Imray *C37*

Communications
HM VHF 09
☎ 06 07 95 80 87
www.plobannalec-lesconil.com

Small fishing port

Lesconil fishing port is less crowded and more attractive than Le Guilvinec. The harbour has very limited room for visiting boats but there is an anchorage outside. Access is easy except in strong southerly winds. The port previously had a poor reputation for welcoming yachtsmen, but is now making real progress. Helpful harbourmaster and solid-looking new visitors' pontoon.

PILOTAGE

Lesconil approach and entrance

By day Identify the Men-ar-Groas light from a position 600m north of Kareg Kreiz east cardinal buoy. Beware Basse Devel, drying 0·9, northwest of Kareg Kreig which should be left 0·25M to port of transit. Men-ar-Groas light has a slender white tower with a green top and is on the east side of the harbour. It is not easy to see but is to the right of a conspicuous black gable end with a large diamond shaped window and to the left of a long grey roof. The belfry of Lesconil church will be just open to the left when the light bears 325°.

Follow 325° passing the white mark on Enizan 400m to starboard and Men-Caës port hand beacon tower to port. Turn to port to enter the harbour between the breakwater lights. There is 1·5m

Entrance to Lesconil *Nick Chavasse*

minimum depth in the entrance and 3m in most of the northern basin. Within the harbour red and green unlit buoys mark the deep water.

By night From Kareg Kreiz east cardinal buoy steer 325° for Men-ar-Groas remaining in the white sector until the entrance opens to port.

Men-ar-Groas
Nick Chavasse

BERTHS AND ANCHORAGE

Lesconil harbour

Visitors are welcome with 22 berths on the visitors' pontoons and three fore-and-aft moorings available. Water and electricity are available. Public toilets on the quay and showers in the Centre Nautic.

⚓ Anse de Lesconil

Sheltered from the west through north to northeast, there is a fair weather anchorage in the Anse de Lesconil immediately to the east of the harbour entrance. Enter from the southwest to avoid the extensive rocks on the east side of the bay.

FACILITIES IN LESCONIL

Fuel is available in cans. There is a launderette, a few modest shops and some bars.

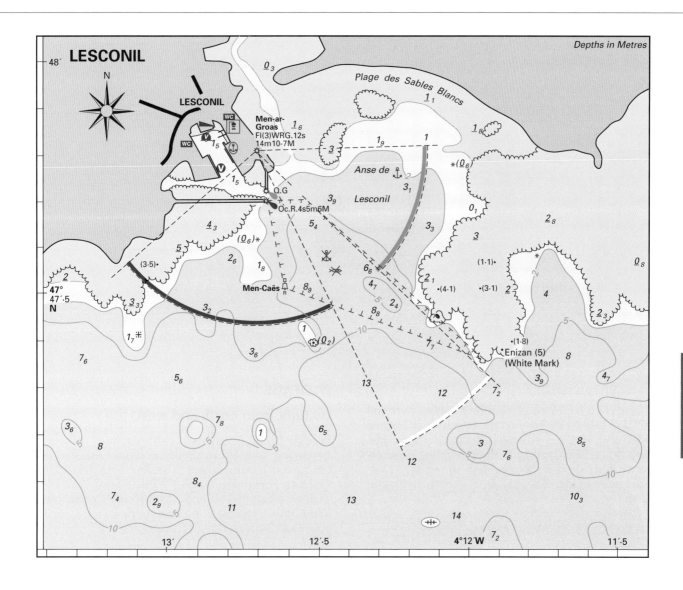

Looking NW at visitors' pontoon from entrance *Nick Chavasse*

27 Loctudy

47°50′N 4°10′W

Shelter
Excellent except in strong ESE

Hazards
Bar and unmarked shallow patches
Strong tide in harbour
Caution when FVs return 1630-1830

Depth restrictions
0.9m in the approach; 1·5m in marina

Night entry Partially lit

HW time Brest HW−0020

Mean height of tide (m) Loctudy

HWS	HWN	LWN	LWS
4.9	3·8	1·8	0·7

Tidal stream Loctudy entrance
Flood – Brest HW −0500 to −0230 (3·0kn)
Slack – Brest HW −0230 to +0230
Ebb – Brest HW +0230 to +0430 (3·0kn)
Slack – Brest HW +0430 to −0500

Berthing
Marina and visitors' buoys

Fuel
Marina wave breaker

Facilities
All facilities

Charts
SHOM *7146, 6649*
Imray *C37*

Communications
Harbourmaster VHF 09
Marina ① 02 98 87 51 36
http://port.loctudy.fr

Pretty Breton estuary

Loctudy is a happy combination of fishing port and yachting centre. Île Tudy on the opposite side of the river is a picture postcard Breton village. The approach is sheltered from the prevailing westerly winds but should be avoided in strong east-southeast winds. The harbour is attractive and secure.

Loctudy Patrick Roach

PILOTAGE

Loctudy from north and west

By day From Bilien east cardinal buoy proceed northwest until Les Perdrix black and white chequered beacon tower is in line with the white Château Durumain on 289°. This transit crosses a shallow patch (1·1m) and leaves Karek Croisic port hand buoy marking it to starboard. Karek Croisic port hand buoy is a small channel marker.

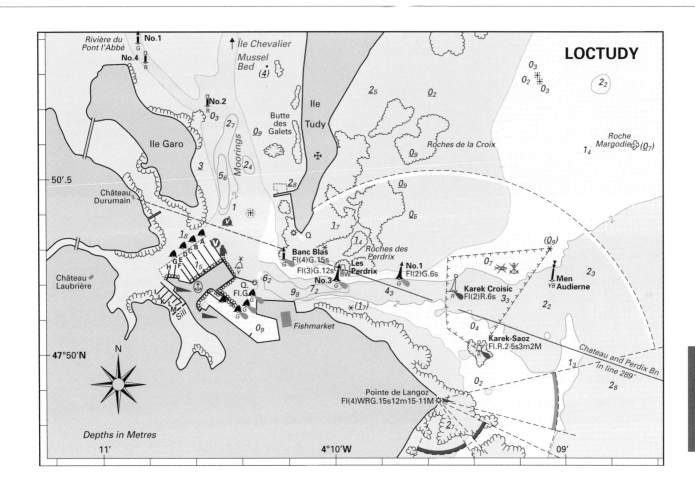

Loctudy from east

By day From the east and southeast leave Île aux Moutons to port and steer northwest, leaving Les Poulains north cardinal beacon tower and Men Dehou east cardinal beacon tower to port. To avoid the shallow patch (depth 2·1m) northwest of Men Dehou, keep Île aux Moutons lighthouse midway between Les Poulains and Men Dehou. Continue to Bilien east cardinal buoy and enter Loctudy as from the north and west.

By night Leave Île aux Moutons light to port and steer north to get into the white sector of Pointe de Langoz light. Stay in the white sector until Bilien east cardinal lightbuoy is abeam to port. Then proceed as above.

Les Perdrix in line with the château in the approach to Loctudy *Nick Chavasse*

Below half-tide leave the transit to pass the port hand buoy correctly. Once you are into the buoyed channel follow it into the river towards the marina.

By night From Bilien east cardinal buoy steer northwest to enter the white sector of Langoz. Follow this until Karek-Saoz port hand light-beacon and Karek Croisic port hand lightbuoy are identified. Leave these to port and then enter the river leaving the two starboard hand lightbuoys to starboard. The approach to the marina is not lit but there are three lit green buoys which lead into the fishing harbour. Note that Les Perdrix beacon tower is no longer lit.

Looking WNW at Les Perdrix beacon tower with No 1 green starboard hand buoy in foreground to right and No 3 green starboard hand buoy to left of tower *Nick Chavasse*

Looking E over marina towards the capitainerie *Nick Chavasse*

Looking north over fuel berth and moorings *Nick Chavasse*

BERTHS AND ANCHORAGES

Loctudy Marina

Visitors should berth on Pontoon A but beware of cross tidal currents. Beware, also, the drying bank to the north of the marina. The channel north of the marina is marked by four green buoys. Larger boats should use the inside of the wave breaker. There are some white visitors' buoys northeast of the marina but check with harbourmaster first. The marina is well managed, modern and has all facilities. It would be a good place to leave a boat.

⚓ Île Chevalier

Sheltered from all directions, there is a useful neap tide anchorage at the southeast end of Île Chevalier (north of Rivière du Pont l'Abbé) but beware of mussel beds on either side.

⚓ Île Tudy

It may be possible to find space to anchor beyond the moorings west of Île Tudy.

Loctudy is a charming place with an excellent chandler, and marine services. It is well worth walking to buy some fish from the shops beside the fishing port's quay. Beware the cross tides in the marina, particularly in a long keel yacht at springs!

ASHORE IN LOCTUDY

Loctudy has a full range of shops, bars and restaurants plus a good vegetable market on Tuesdays and excellent fish shops at the fishing port. Bicycles may be borrowed from the marina office for up to 1 hour. For longer periods, bicycles may be hired from the hut at the top of the ramp opposite Pontoon A. A good day's cycle trip may be enjoyed by going from Loctudy to Pont L'Abbé with a lunch stop in Sainte-Marine, followed by a gentle ride along the coast to Île Tudy and ferry across the river to Loctudy.

Île Tudy is a pretty holiday village. It has only basic facilities but it does have a magnificent beach and good walking. There is a ferry to Île Tudy from May-September.

Rivière de Pont l'Abbé

The channel dries 2m and is reported to have silted further. A visit to Pont l'Abbé is best made by dinghy.

Drying out in Pont L'Abbé *Nick Chavasse*

28 Bénodet and Sainte-Marine

47°53'N 4°07'W

Shelter
Excellent in both marinas

Hazards
Shallow patches in approach
Strong tide in marinas

Night entry
Lit but care required

HW time
Brest HW −0020

Mean height of tide (m) Bénodet

HWS	HWN	LWN	LWS
5·3	4·1	2·1	1·0

Tidal stream
In the marinas, spring rates reach 4 knots

Berthing
Two marinas and visitors' buoys

Fuel
Bénodet marina, base of E pontoon
(beware cross-tide)

Facilities
All facilities

Charts
SHOM *7146, 7249*
Imray *C37*

Communictions
Marinas VHF 9
Penfoul Marina ☏ 02 98 57 05 78
Ste-Marine HM ☏ 02 98 56 38 72
www.benodetport.fr
http://port.combrit-saintemarine.fr/

Major yachting centre in a beautiful river

Bénodet is one of South Brittany's principal yachting centres. There are two marinas, many visitors' buoys, a beautiful river and good facilities ashore. The location, in the centre of the Anse de Bénodet, is a good base for day sailing and there is also the beautiful River Odet to explore. Bénodet gets busy in high season but there is usually space to squeeze in somewhere.

Bénodet looking northwest. Sainte-Marine is on the far bank of the river and the visitors' pontoon is just visible downstream of the marina. Bénodet Marina, on the near side, has two parts. Large boats use the downstream marina and visitors moor on the outer pontoon

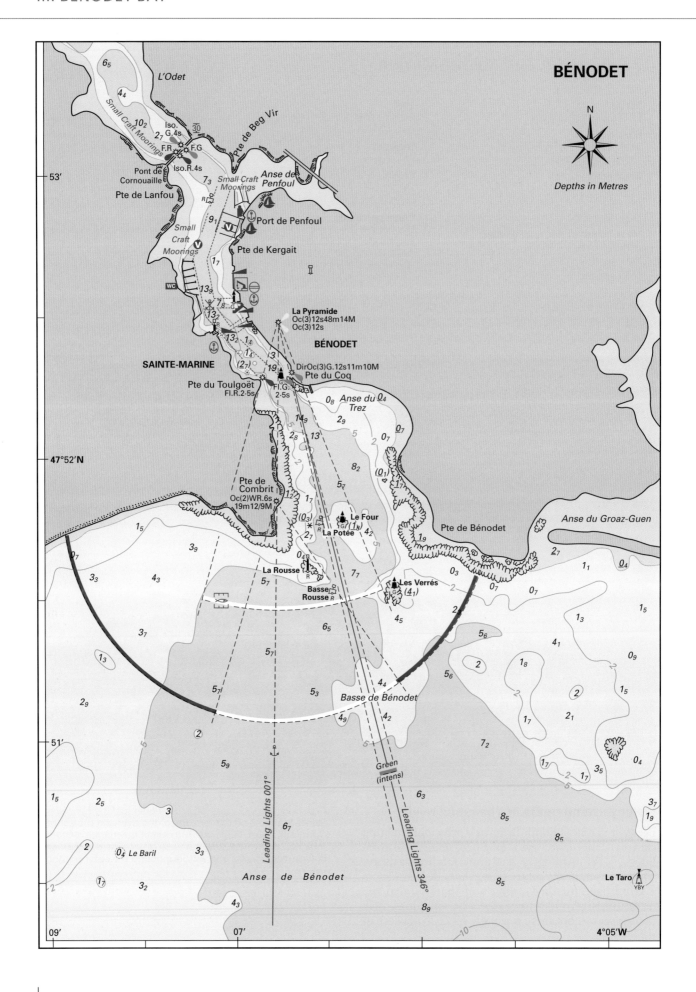

BÉNODET

Depths in Metres

N

L'Odet

Pte de Beg Vir

Pont de Cornouaille

Pte de Lanfou

Iso.G.4s
F.R
F.G
Iso.R.4s

Anse de Penfoul

Small Craft Moorings

Port de Penfoul

Small Craft Moorings

Pte de Kergait

WC

La Pyramide
Oc(3)12s48m14M
Oc(3)12s

BÉNODET

SAINTE-MARINE

DirOc(3)G.12s11m10M
Pte du Coq

Pte du Toulgoët
Fl.R.2·5s

Fl.G.
2·5s

Anse du Trez

Pte de Combrit
Oc(2)WR.6s
19m12/9M

Le Four
La Potée

Pte de Bénodet

Anse du Groaz-Guen

La Rousse

Basse Rousse

Les Verrés
(4₁)

Basse de Bénodet

Leading Lights 001°

Green (intens)

Leading Lights 346°

Anse de Bénodet

Le Baril

Le Taro
YBY

Approaches to Bénodet Pointe de Combrit and Pyramide lighthouse with La Rousse port hand beacon in front looking N
Nick Chavasse

Leading marks with Pyramide lighthouse (rear) open to left of Pte du Coq (front) in entrance to Bénodet *Nick Chavasse*

Bénodet town occupies the east bank of the Odet. It is a busy holiday resort with beaches, hotels, shops, a casino and a large supermarket. Sainte-Marine, on the west bank, is a quiet holiday village with a few shops and restaurants.

PILOTAGE

Bénodet approach from south and southwest

By day There are many hazards between Île aux Moutons and the mainland but they are well marked and the approach is not difficult (*see plans pages 98 and 106*). The usual route, which relies on the buoys, passes between Boulanger south cardinal and Roche Hélou west cardinal, then between Chenal du Bénodet east cardinal and Basse Malvic west cardinal. If the buoys are hard to identify, Pyramide lighthouse at Bénodet (white tower with green top, 47°52'·49N 04°06'·77W) in line with Pte de Combrit Light (white square tower, brown corners and red top) bearing 001° leads safely in from the south. When Les Verrés starboard hand beacon bears 50°, alter course to starboard for the entrance. (*See Entrance page 100.*) The Pyramide/Pte de Combrit transit of 001° ultimately leads onto the shore, not into the river.

In good conditions and with sufficient tide there are several other routes through the shallow patches.

By night Stay outside the lit buoys marking the hazards south of Pte de Penmarc'h. After passing Spinec south cardinal buoy, continue southeast until Île aux Moutons light turns from red to white. Keep within this white sector, until Pte de Combrit and Bénodet Pyramide lights come into line bearing 001°. Turn onto this transit and maintain it watching the Pte de Langoz light; it will change colour as one progresses north. When it changes from green to white bearing 257°, the way is clear to turn to starboard to bring the Bénodet leading lights in line on 346° and enter the river.

Bénodet approach from southeast

By day The easiest entrance is north of Plateau de la Basse Jaune, leaving Les Porceaux, Île aux Moutons, Les Poulains north cardinal tower beacon and Men Dehou east cardinal tower beacon all to port. La Voleuse south cardinal buoy marks the limit of the dangers off Pte de Mousterlin and must be left to starboard. Once past Men Dehou it is safe to turn towards the harbour entrance leaving Le Taro tower west cardinal tower beacon 0·5M to starboard.

Sainte-Marine marina from Bénodet *Nick Chavasse*

By night Approach within or just south of the intensified sector of Île aux Moutons light, leaving Jaune de Glénan east cardinal buoy to port. Continue in this sector until Pte de Langoz light is identified and Trévignon light has turned from white to green bearing more than 051°.

Steer to starboard to get into the white sector of Pte de Langoz light, bearing about 295° and keep within it until Pte de Combrit light opens white bearing 325°. Then steer for this light, crossing the green sector of Pte de Langoz light, and bring the Bénodet leading lights in transit on 346°.

Entrance to the river Odet

By day The leading line is the tower of Pyramide light in transit with Le Coq light (346°). However, the dangers in the entrance are marked and it is not necessary to keep strictly to the transit. Pyramide light is conspicuous, but Le Coq is less easy to identify. It will be seen to the left of the conspicuous grassy bank.

When within 400m of Le Coq, alter to port and steer up the middle of the river. During the season and particularly at weekends the entrance to Bénodet is so busy that speed is limited to 3kn above the Pte de Coq beacon.

By night The leading lights lead clear of all unlit buoys and beacons. When within 400m of Le Coq, turn to port to pass halfway between Le Coq and Pte du Toulgoët flashing red light. Entrance is straightforward, but the river is congested with moorings, and anchoring is prohibited in the channel until well beyond the bridge. Iso.R and Iso.G lights will be seen on the bridge and the shore lights may give some guidance.

BERTHS AND ANCHORAGES

Sainte-Marine visitors' pontoon

Sainte-Marine visitors' pontoon is on the west side of the river 0·25M beyond Pte du Toulgoët. It is a long pontoon where yachts can lie alongside and raft if necessary.

The tidal stream is roughly parallel to the pontoon so, unlike Bénodet marina, manoeuvring in a strong tide is feasible.

Bénodet marina (Port de Penfoul)

Bénodet marina is on the east side of the river about 0·25M beyond Ste-Marine at the entrance to the Anse de Penfoul. There are long outer pontoons that may be used by visitors. One of these pontoons lies across the tide and manoeuvring is difficult except at slack water. Another wavebreaker pontoon lies along the current and manoeuvring alongside it from the outside is less problematic. The current can press a yacht hard against the pontoons so plenty of fenders are needed. Finger berths inside the marina are sometimes available from the harbourmaster. The current inside is less than on the outer pontoons but it is best to enter only at slack water. Short stays are free in the morning for shopping.

Visitors' moorings

Both Bénodet and Sainte-Marine provide river moorings which are usually marked with a V. On the Sainte-Marine side, the harbourmasters buzz around in dorys and will often direct visiting yachts to a free mooring. On the Bénodet side, the harbourmasters are less active and it is necessary to look around for available buoys.

⚓ Anse du Trez

Sheltered from west through north to east, Anse du Trez is an attractive sandy bay just inside the mouth of the Odet on the east side. During the day, the bay is a centre for Optimist and sailboard sailing but it is peaceful at night.

⚓ Plage du Treven

Sheltered from north and west, the long sandy beach west of Pointe de Combrit makes a pleasant lunch-time stop.

ASHORE IN BÉNODET AND STE-MARINE

Facilities in Bénodet

Bénodet has all the facilities of a major yachting centre and holiday resort. Most repairs can be carried out at Bénodet. Chandlery and fuel is available at the Anse de Penfoul marina, but the berth lies across the current so that slack water is the best time to fill up.

There is a full range of shops and a good Carrefour supermarket on the road to Quimper. The attractive footpath along the south side of the Anse de Penfoul is the shortest route to the latter from the Bénodet Marina. Buses run to the rail station in Quimper, making it a convenient place to change crews. There is a regular ferry service from Bénodet to Quimper.

Facilities in Sainte-Marine

Sainte-Marine is a pleasant holiday resort with a small supermarket, a few shops and delightful bars and restaurants.

There is a pleasant walk to Pointe de Combrit from where the energetic can continue along the magnificent three mile Plage du Treven to Île Tudy.

The classic holiday beaches and sea front in Bénodet and Sainte-Marine are classic and particularly pleasant out of high season. The ferry (pedestrians and bikes) from Sainte-Marine across the river to Bénodet operates from April-September.

Looking S along visitors' pontoon toward Sainte-Marine
Nick Chavasse

Looking NW from Bénodet Marina breakwater *Nick Chavasse*

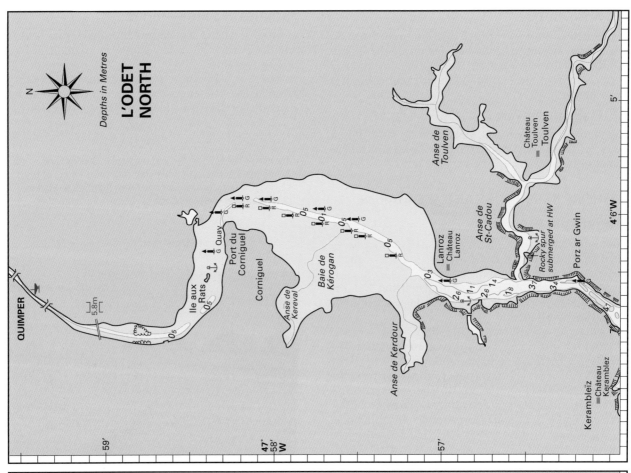

L'ODET NORTH

Depths in Metres

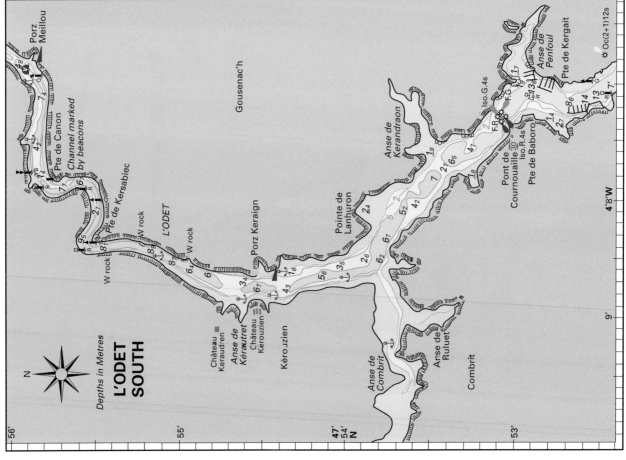

L'ODET SOUTH

Depths in Metres

29 L'Odet

47°53'N 4°07'W

Shelter Excellent

Depth restrictions
2·6m to Lanroz, 0·5m to Quimper

Night passage
Not recommended

HW time Brest HW+0015

Mean height of tide (m) Corniguel

HWS	HWN	LWN	LWS
4.9	3·8	1·6	0·3

Tidal stream
Spring rates can reach 2·5 knots and 4-6kn at Pointe de Kersabiec

Berthing Anchorages

Fuel
Bénodet marina, base of E pontoon

Charts
SHOM *7249*
Imray *C37*

Communications
www.brittanytourism.com

Beautiful river to Quimper

To fully appreciate l'Odet, once north of the Pont de Cornouaille turn off the engine and sail up the river on the tide listening to the birdsong. Appreciate the wonderful scenery but stay alert for ferries plying their trade. Allow sufficient time to find a suitable anchorage and enjoy the sights and sounds of a beautiful river, one of Brittany's best!

Unfortunately there is a bridge (height 5·8m) about 0·5M from the town of Quimper so masted boats must anchor and use a dinghy for the last leg but even without a visit to Quimper, the river is well worth exploring. As far as Lanroz there is plenty of water at all states of the tide and there are several attractive anchorages.

PILOTAGE

Bénodet to Quimper

Leave Bénodet and pass under the Pont de Cornouaille (height 30m). After about 1M the Anse du Combrit opens out on the W side. This is an attractive creek and a pleasant anchorage.

The river then narrows as it runs between steep wooded banks. After about 2M it narrows dramatically and makes a sharp turn to starboard. Port and starboard beacons mark this turn but care should be taken because the shallows extend beyond the starboard mark.

The next stretch is narrow, winding and very attractive. After about 2M there is a little fjord that

Château Kerouzien *Nick Chavasse*

Frank Cowper's *Sailing Tours,* written in 1894, described Château Keraudren as 'a new and rather stuck-up looking château'! *Nick Chavasse*

forms the Anse de St-Cadou (*see Anchorages*). About 0·5M beyond this, at Lanroz, the river opens out quite suddenly into a broad lake from where there is a good view of Quimper.

The route across the lake is well marked by beacons but the river shallows rapidly to a least depth of 0·5m. At the far end of the lake is a sharp turn to port at the commercial jetties of Corniguel used mainly by sand barges.

Above Corniguel the river nearly dries and the beacons are further apart. A bridge (with a clearance of only 5·8m) prevents masted yachts from reaching Quimper, but boats that can take the ground may anchor or borrow a mooring below the bridge and visit Quimper by dinghy. Motor yachts can carry a depth of drying 1·5m up to the first quays in Quimper. The bottom here is hard and rather uneven for drying out.

ANCHORAGES

Anchoring is forbidden near the Pont de Cornouaille, but elsewhere it is possible to anchor anywhere out of the stream. The bottom is rock in the main channel so the holding is poor.

Entrance to Anse St-Cadou *Nick Chavasse*

⚓ Anse de Combrit

Sheltered except from the east, the Anse de Combrit is an inlet on the west side of the Odet about 1M above Pont de Cornouaille. It is possible to go in quite a long way with a large-scale chart.

⚓ Porz Keraign

Sheltered except from due north or due south, this is a small inlet on the east side of the Odet opposite Châteaux Kérouzien. Anchor south of slipway.

⚓ Porz Meilou

Sheltered from all directions, Porz Meilou is on the east side about 0·75M above Pointe du Canon. There is not much of an inlet but there is a shallow area at the edge of the river, marked by a starboard beacon. Tuck in as far as possible to get out of the tide. There are a few visitors' moorings for boats less than 9m.

⚓ Anse de St-Cadou

Sheltered from all directions, this delightful little fjord is on the east side of the Odet about 0·5M before the river widens out at Lanroz. It is hard to spot at first because the entrance is quite narrow. Once identified, keep close to the north bank to avoid the drying rocky plateau on the south side. In this pool a large area has 1m depth and 2m can be found in which to swing on short scope. At the end of the first pool there is a rock with 1m or less, on the inside corner of the sharp turn to the north.

⚓ Lanroz

Sheltered from all directions except north, there is a shallow bay on the west side of the river just south of Lanroz.

⚓ Port du Corniguel

It is possible to anchor just above Corniguel in 1·5m. You may be able to go alongside at Corniguel itself but beware of the sand barges.

ASHORE IN QUIMPER

There are no facilities in the river beyond Bénodet but Quimper has everything. It is the regional capital of West Brittany and is an attractive city with many half-timbered buildings and a fine cathedral. At the heart of the city is an area known as the Quays where flower-decked footbridges criss-cross the Odet.

There is a railway station in Quimper with easy access to Paris, Brest and Nantes. This makes it suitable for crew changeovers. The challenging bit is access by dinghy from l'Odet.

Quimper has three fine museums for those with time to spare. The Fine Arts Museum has one of the best collections of 19th-century Breton art. The Brittany Museum covers regional history and the Museum of the Faience has displays that explain the development of the famous Quimper painted pottery.

Upper reaches of l'Odet *Nick Chavasse*

Heading back down river towards Pont de Cornouaille *Nick Chavasse*

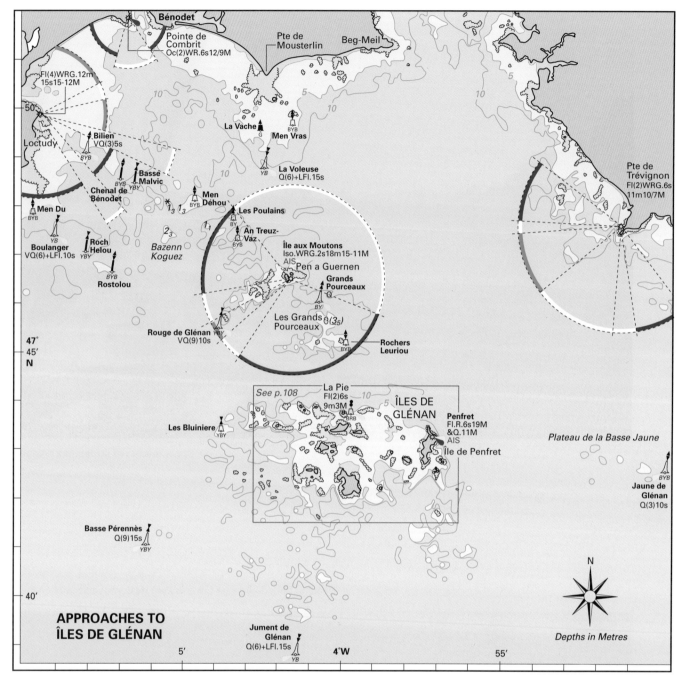

Bénodet

Pointe de Combrit
Oc(2)WR.6s12/9M

Pte de Mousterlin

Beg-Meil

Fl(4)WRG.12m 15s15-12M

50′

Loctudy

Bilien VQ(3)5s
BYB

Basse Malvic
BYB   YBY

Chenal de Bénodet

Men Du
BYB

Boulanger VQ(6)+LFl.10s
YB

Roch Helou
YBY

Rostolou
BYB

La Vache
G

Men Vras
BYB
YB

La Voleuse Q(6)+LFl.15s

1₃   1₃

Men Déhou
BYB

Les Poulains
BY

2₃

Bazenn Koguez

1₁

An Treuz-Vaz
BYB

Île aux Moutons
Iso.WRG.2s18m15-11M
AIS

Pen a Guernen

Grands Pourceaux
Q
BY

Rouge de Glénan VQ(9)10s
YBY

Les Grands Pourceaux

3(3₅)

Rochers Leuriou
BYB

Pte de Trévignon
Fl(2)WRG.6s 11m10/7M

47°
45′
N

La Pie Fl(2)6s 9m3M
BRB

See p.108

ÎLES DE GLÉNAN

Les Bluiniere
YBY

Penfret
Fl.R.6s19M &Q.11M
AIS
Île de Penfret

Plateau de la Basse Jaune

Jaune de Glénan Q(3)10s
BYB

Basse Pérennès Q(9)15s
YBY

N

40′

APPROACHES TO ÎLES DE GLÉNAN

Jument de Glénan Q(6)+LFl.15s
YB

Depths in Metres

5′   4°W   55′

Sunset in La Chambre *Nick Chavasse*

30 Îles de Glénan

47°43′N 3°57′W

Shelter
Limited particularly at high water

Hazards
Many unmarked rocks
Difficult to leave anchorages at night

Depth restrictions
1m or more in most anchorages but much less in some channels

Night entry
Not recommended

HW time
Brest HW –0020

Mean height of tide (m) Île Penfret

HWS	HWN	LWN	LWS
5·0	3.9	1.9	0·8

Tidal stream N approach
Slack – Brest HW–0600 to –0400
E-going – Brest HW–0400 to +0100 (0·5kn)

Slack – Brest HW+0100 to +0300
W-going – Brest HW+0300 to –0600 (0·6kn)

Berthing
Anchorages many of which have visitors' moorings which are charged for in season

Facilities
Boat vendors, restaurant and small shop in season. No water

Charts
SHOM *7146, 6648*
Imray *C37*

Communications
Glénans sailing school VHF 16
www.brittanytourism.com

Beautiful archipelago with a famous sailing school, the Centre Nautique des Glénans (CNG)

Les Îles de Glénan is a beautiful archipelago of small low-lying islands about 12M south-southeast of Bénodet. It has crystal-clear water, white sandy beaches and in good weather is as close to the Caribbean as you can get in South Brittany.

PILOTAGE

Charts

A large-scale chart is strongly recommended, especially SHOM 6648.

Approach from the north via Île aux Moutons

The small uninhabited island of Île aux Moutons, with its unmanned lighthouse, lies 5M southeast of Benodet. In quiet, settled weather, anchoring is possible on the southeast side of the island. Approach from southeast from Grands Porceaux north cardinal, staying well clear of Pen a Guernen, a ledge of drying rocks extending east for 0·25M from the anchorage.

Be brave! You'll need good navigation skills (purchasing a large-scale chart beforehand is a great help) but in settled weather the islands are a delight. Even if the weather deteriorates, Bénodet and Concarneau are not far if you need to make a dash for it. Find an anchorage and enjoy the islands.

Les Îles de Glénan are home to the Centre Nautique des Glénans (CNG). It was founded in 1947 by Hélène and Philipe Viannay, former members of the French Resistance, and is one of the first and largest sailing schools in Europe. The school's main base is on Île Cigogne but their fleets of training boats are in evidence throughout the islands. They are very hospitable to visitors, but obviously that hospitality should not be abused.

Îles de Glénan approaches

By day The main islands are easily distinguished by the conspicuous lighthouse on Île de Penfret at the eastern side of the group and, in the middle, by the stone fort on the southeast side of Île Cigogne which has a tall, partially black-topped concrete tower. The west edge is marked by Bluiniers west cardinal beacon, the south with the Jument de Glenan south cardinal and east by Jaune de Glenan east cardinal.

Looking N at Le Huic disused lighthouse from N side of Île de Drénec *Nick Chavasse*

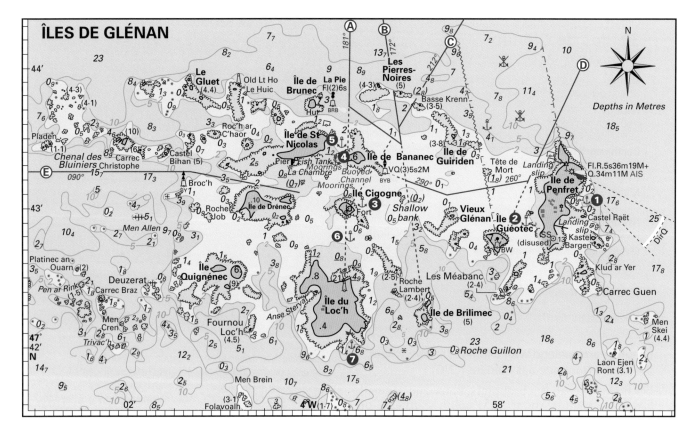

When approaching La Pie isolated danger beacon tower from the north the most conspicuous mark is the disused lighthouse on Le Huic 47°43'·9N 4°00'·69W.

Other useful daymarks are a conspicuous disused factory chimney on Île du Loc'h; some houses on the southeast side of Île de Drénec and the buildings on Île de St-Nicolas.

The easiest entrances are from the north and northeast but take care to avoid Les Porceaux rocks in the north approaches.

Îles de Glénan entrances

In the descriptions of the entrances, note that all routes go to La Chambre anchorage/moorings to the south of Île de St-Nicolas, so appropriate changes must be made for the other anchorages.

By day Entrance routes are shown as lines A to E on the plan opposite.

Northern entrances - A, B and C

These three entrances should be regarded as carrying 1m although a little more water can be found with careful pilotage. B and C should only be attempted in good visibility.

The marks for B and C are four above-water rocks: Les Pierres Noires (4·3, 5m and 2·8m), and Basse Krenn (3·5m).

All these rocks stand on rocky bases and must be distinguished from Île de Guiriden (5·0m) to the southeast, which has a considerable sandy expanse that covers near high water.

A This is the most straightforward of the northern entrances. Identify La Pie and bring the chimney on Île du Loc'h just open to the right-hand side of the Cigogne tower, bearing 181°. Steer this course until inside Les Pierres Noires leaving La Pie isolated danger light beacon tower abeam to starboard. Near low water the chimney dips behind

La Pie in N entrance to Îsles de Glenans
Nick Chavasse

the fort but it is good enough to leave La Pie 100m to starboard.

Except near high water, there is no problem knowing when Les Pierres Noires are passed because a rock that seldom covers marks their southwest extremity. Once La Pie beacon is passed and in transit with the north side of Île de Brunec, steer 140° towards the Pointe de la Balene east cardinal beacon at the east end of Île de Bananec.

B This entrance leaves the two adjacent heads of Les Pierres Noires 50m to port. This is a popular entrance for local boats, but should not be used for a first visit, as Île de Brilimec and Les Pierres Noires must be positively identified and there is a rocky plateau drying 3·2m, 100m to starboard. Follow a course of 172° and when Pointe de la Balene is abeam turn to starboard to join La Chambre channel markers.

East cardinal Pointe de La Balene with Île Cigogne beyond, looking SW *Nick Chavasse*

Looking S at Île du Loc'h chimney *Nick Chavasse*

C This entrance leaves Basse Krenn 100m to port steering on Fort Cigogne tower, bearing 212°. Once Basse Krenn is passed it is possible to bear to port as convenient. The Centre Nautique des Glénans (CNG) use the chimney on Île du Loc'h in transit with the Pointe de la Balene east cardinal beacon southeast of Île de Bananec on 200° for this entrance. Although easy to identify, this transit leaves an outlier of Les Pierres Noires (dries 2·8m) 60m to starboard.

When Pointe de la Balene is abeam turn to starboard to join La Chambre channel markers.

Northeastern entrance - D

D This channel carries 1m with shallow patches of 0·7m very close to the route.

Leave the northern end of Île de Penfret 300m to port and steer 265° toward the stone wall beacon on Île de Guéotec. When Île Cigogne concrete tower bears 265°, alter course onto that bearing. This avoids the shallow patch east of Île Cigogne. Alternatively alter onto 283°, steering for the wind generator on the west end of St-Nicolas. Using either course, leave the Pointe de la Balene east cardinal beacon southeast of Bananec to starboard to enter the buoyed channel to La Chambre.

Looking E towards Penfret lighthouse *Nick Chavasse*

Western entrance - E

E The Chenal des Bluiniers dries 0·5m, but it is safer to regard it as drying 0·8m. If this gives insufficient margin, skirt the north edge of the rocks and enter by La Pie. Visibility of three miles is needed for this channel except towards high water. Coming from the northwest be sure to give Les Bluiniers west cardinal tower beacon at least 200m clearance.

From about 200m south of Les Bluiniers beacon, steer towards Broc'h north cardinal tower beacon keeping Penfret lighthouse open to the north of Broc'h tower beacon, bearing about 090°. Approaching Broc'h tower beacon, leave it 100m to starboard and bring the semaphore station (SS), near the southern point of Île de Penfret, open to the left of Fort Cigogne by the width of the fort (not the tower), bearing 100°. Follow this course until the eastern part of Île de Drénec is abeam to starboard; this island is in two clearly defined parts separated by a sandy strip which covers at HW. Now steer 035° on the summer cottages to the east of the shellfish tank on Île de St Nicolas to enter La Chambre.

For those already familiar with the islands, the transits shown on Admiralty charts may be used, but it is necessary to identify the semaphore mast on Penfret at a distance of 5M as well as the farm buildings on Drénec.

ANCHORAGES

⚓ 1. East of Île de Penfret

47°43'·07N 3°56'·83W

Sheltered from the west but exposed to the NE *brise de terre* (*see page 4*), this anchorage is in the sandy bay south of the hill on which the lighthouse stands. Approach with the middle of the bay bearing 270°. There is a potentially dangerous rock 150m north of Castel Raët, which is the islet in the south of the bay.

There is a large metal mooring buoy on the north side of the bay. However, it is preferable to anchor closer to the beach on sand, taking care to avoid the patches of weed.

South of Castel Raët is another bay with a slip and some CNG moorings. This bay is shallow and unsuitable for anchoring.

⚓ 2. Southwest of Île de Penfret

47°43'·06N 3°57'·93W

Sheltered from the west by Guéotec and from the east by Penfret, there is a good anchorage in 2·5m outside the CNG moorings between Penfret and Guéotec. The tide runs fairly hard.

The easy approach is from the north (route A). An approach from the south is possible but requires intricate pilotage and a large-scale chart.

⚓ 3. East of Île Cigogne

47°43'·20N 3°59'·56W

Anchor in 1m to 1·4m, north of the rocky ledge running southeast from Île Cigogne.

⚓ 4. La Chambre

47°43'·20N 3°59'·56W

This anchorage south of Île de St-Nicolas is the most popular one for visitors, although there are now many moorings. The depths are up to 3m but avoid anchoring in the channel, which is marked by small port and starboard buoys.

A rocky ledge extends 100m along the south shore of Île de St-Nicolas and Île de Bananec. The shoal also extends east of Île de Bananec and Pointe de Balene east cardinal beacon marks its limit. Between the islands there is a sandy ridge with shallow sandy bays (drying 1m) to the north and

Looking west to La Chambre moorings on a quiet day
Nick Chavasse

Looking E across La Chambre with ferry at slipway on left
Nick Chavasse

south. These make excellent anchorages for yachts that can take the ground.

Enter the buoyed channel into La Chambre from a position 100m southwest of Pointe de Balene east cardinal beacon southeast of Île de Bananec. There is a line of visitors' buoys which are the new seabed friendly type and it will be necessary to find one with sufficient water. If La Chambre is full of yachts, it may be necessary to come back out of the La Chambre channel and find an alternative anchorage with sufficient water. Anchoring is permitted outside the channel. At low water depths of less than 1m may be encountered in La Chambre.

Seabed friendly mooring buoy
Nick Chavasse

⚓ 5. North of Île de Bananec

47°43'·94N 3°59'·74W

Open to the north and east at high water, the bay northwest of Bananec and east of St-Nicolas is a popular fair-weather anchorage. The bay shoals from 2m and has a clean sandy bottom so choose a spot outside the moorings according to draught.

⚓ 6. North of Île du Loc'h

47°42'·70N 3°59'·56W

Sheltered from the north by Île Cigogne and from the south by Île du Loc'h, there is a neap anchorage about 400m north of the Île du Loc'h chimney.

⚓ 7. South of Île du Loc'h

47°42'·07N 03°59'·56W

Sheltered from NW to NE. Enter at LW or with large scale chart.

Looking south to anchorage N of Île de Bananec *Nick Chavasse*

ASHORE IN ÎLES DE GLENAN

After mid June, enterprising vendors tour the anchorages each morning with bread, seafood and, occasionally, fresh vegetables. And, again in season, there is a famous restaurant and a creperie on Île St-Nicolas, together with a small shop that occasionally stocks very limited provisions.

Fresh water is in short supply and visitors should not expect to obtain any.

There are a multitude of small islands to be explored but the best activities are on the extraordinarily clear water. The shallow areas between the islands are sometimes just a few inches deep, depending on the tide. Viewed from a dinghy or with a snokelling mask, the underwater gardens just below the surface are quite unique.

Sailing school on W side of Penfret *Nick Chavasse*

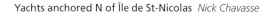
Yachts anchored N of Île de St-Nicolas *Nick Chavasse*

31 Port-la-Forêt

47°54'N 3°58'W

Shelter Excellent in marina

Hazards
Rocks on SW corner and E side of Baie de la Forêt

Depth restrictions
0·6m bar at entrance of channel

Tidal restrictions
Depth restricts entry; channel dredged to 1·2m to marina

Night entry Partially lit

HW time Brest HW–0020

Mean height of tide (m) Concarneau

HWS	HWN	LWN	LWS
5·1	4·0	2·0	0·9

Tidal stream
Weak in the bay, strong in entrance

Berthing
Large modern marina

Fuel
Root of visitors' pontoon, 24/7 credit card

Facilities
All repair facilities and some marina shops. 1M walk to town (La Forêt Fouesnant)

Charts
SHOM *7146, 6650*
Imray *C38*

Communications
Marina VHF 9
☎ 02 98 56 98 45
www.port-la-foret.fr

Port-la-Forêt *Patrick Roach*

Huge marina in sheltered bay

Port-La-Forêt is a large modern marina complex. The facilities are good and the staff helpful so it is a good place to leave a yacht.

Shopping is limited in the marina complex, but there is a pleasant walk over the causeway and footbridge to the town at La Forêt-Fouesnant.

PILOTAGE

Port-La-Forêt approach and entrance

By day In the approach, there are marked dangers off Beg-Meil (*see plans pages 86 and 106*). There are also extensive unmarked dangers west of Concarneau. Many of these rocks never dry but they can be avoided by keeping the slender Le Scoré south cardinal beacon open east of the end of Cap Coz breakwater or, more simply, by keeping well off the east side of the bay.

The entrance to Port-La-Forêt lies to the east of the wooded promontory of Cap Coz. The channel to the marina is dredged to 1·2m below chart datum and is well marked.

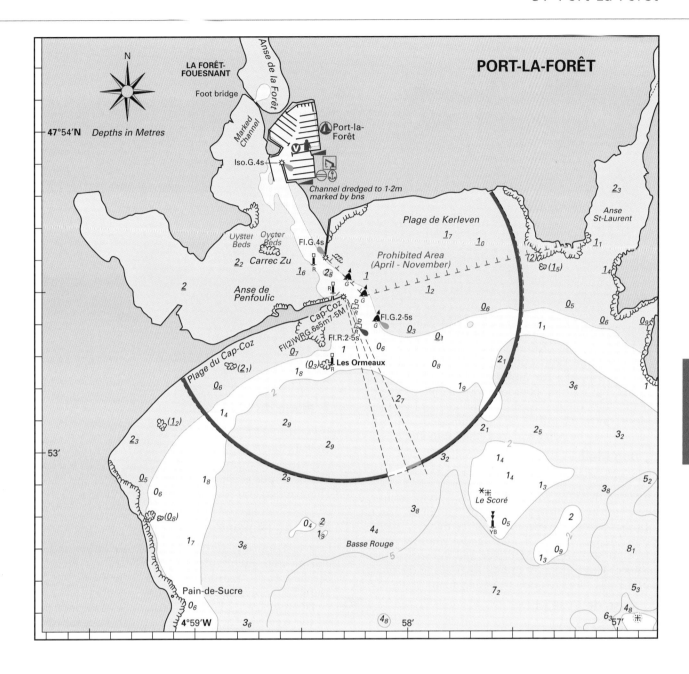

N

LA FORÊT-
FOUESNANT

Foot bridge

Anse de la Forêt

PORT-LA-FORÊT

47°54'N   Depths in Metres

Marked Channel

Port-la-
Forêt

Iso.G.4s

Channel dredged to 1·2m
marked by bns

Plage de Kerleven

Anse
St-Laurent

Uyster
Beds

Oyster
Beds

Fl.G.4s

2₂   Carrec Zu

1₆   2₆

Anse de
Penfoulic

2

Prohibited Area
(April - November)

1₇   1₀

(2)   (1₅)

1₁

1₄

1   G

1₂

0₆

0₅

0₆

0₉

Cap-Coz

G

Fl.G.2·5s

0₃

0₁

1₁

Fl(2)WRG.6s5m7-5M

R

R

Fl.R.2·5s

0₆

0₈

0₇   1

(0₃)   **Les Ormeaux**

Plage du Cap-Coz

(2₁)

1₈

2₇

1₉

2₁

3₆

1

Le Scoré

0₆

1₄

2₉

2₉

3₂

2₁

2₅

3₂

5₂

2₃

(1₂)

1₄

1₄

1₄

1₃

3₈

0₅

0₆

2₉

2

0₅   YB

2

8₁

53'

1₈

(0₈)

0₄   2

1₉

4₄

3₈

1₃

0₉

1₃

1₇

3₆

Basse Rouge

7₂

5₃

4₈

Pain-de-Sucre

0₆

4°59'W   3₆

(4₈)   58'

6₃ 57'

ATLANTIC FRANCE   **113**

Cap Coz at entrance to Port-la-Forêt looking NW   *Nick Chavasse*

Looking N towards the multihull pontoon. The entrance is on the right-hand side past the pontoon *Nick Chavasse*

By night The white sector of Cap Coz light marks the deepest water. The green sector guards a 2·6m shallow patch in the mouth of the bay.

BERTHS AND ANCHORAGES

Port-La-Forêt marina

On the west side of the marina entrance is a long pontoon projecting southward on the east side of which are berths for multihulls. On entering the marina, the visitors' pontoon is immediately ahead, the one with the fuel berth. Secure here and visit the helpful harbour office to be allocated a berth. Bicycles may be borrowed from the capitainerie.

⚓ Beg Meil

47°51'·87N 3°58'·53W

Sheltered from the west, Beg-Meil is a pretty holiday resort in the southwest corner of Baie de la Forêt. Approach from the east to avoid the dangers off the point. Also avoid the Louen Jardin shallow patch (depth 0·8m) off Beg-Meil pier and the rocks close inshore. There are a lot of moorings along the coast but there is room to anchor outside them.

⚓ Anse de St Jean

47°53'·26N 03°57'·04W *(Not shown on plan)*

Sheltered from SW to SE, Anse de St Jean is 2M northwest of Concarneau. Anchor in 2m on sand.

Visitors' pontoon looking W towards entrance, with multihull pontoon beyond *Nick Chavasse*

Beg Meil *Nick Chavasse*

⚓ Plage du Cap Coz

47°52'·81N 3°58'·80W

Well sheltered from northwest and west, the Plage du Cap-Coz is in the northwest corner of Baie de la Forêt. The best spot is usually at the west end of the beach. There are several rocky patches but all close inshore.

ASHORE IN PORT-LA-FORÊT

Port-la-Forêt has all the facilities of a large modern marina and yacht sales centre. There are pleasant beaches nearby. Extrado Yachting ☎ 02 98 56 84 60 is useful for wintering yachts ashore.

The town of La Forêt-Fouesnant lies 1M upstream on the west side of the estuary. It can be reached by dinghy when the tide is up or there is a pleasant walk over the causeway. The lock marked on the charts is now permanently open. There are fairly frequent buses from the port to Quimper and Concarneau. There is a good fish market if you turn left just across the causeway.

32 Concarneau

47°52′N 3°55′W

Shelter Good in marina

Hazards
Rocks on E side of Concarneau bay
Intricate entrance

Depth restrictions
1–5m in marina

Night entry Well lit

HW time Brest HW–0020

Mean height of tide (m) Concarneau

HWS	HWN	LWN	LWS
5·1	4·0	2·0	0·9

Tidal stream
Weak in bay but stronger in entrance

Berthing
Visitors' pontoon (Pontoon D) and
inside floating breakwater

Fuel
South corner of marina, 24/7 with
credit card

Facilities
All facilities

Charts
SHOM *7146, 6650*
Imray *C38*

Communications
Marina VHF 9
① 02 98 97 57 96
www.tourismeconcarneau.fr

Ancient fort and fishing port

The remarkable old town of Concarneau is on an island connected to the mainland by a drawbridge. Secure within massive defensive walls is a labyrinth of beautifully preserved little streets that are packed with tourist shops and restaurants and an excellent museum.

A delightful place with lots of history. A visit to the old town, La Ville Close, with its massive granite ramparts, is vital to appreciate fully the atmosphere.

The indoor fish hall, Les Halles, is one of the best in Brittany and the Festival des Filets Bleus is a lively celebration of the fishing industry held every August.

Entering Concarneau with No.1 starboard beacon to the right and the marina to the left

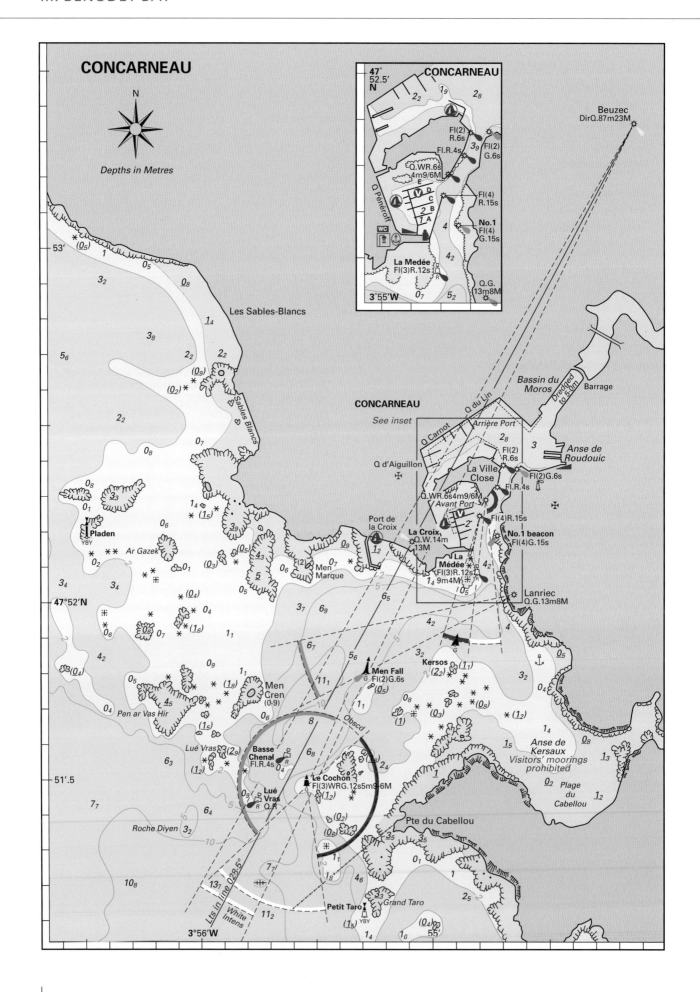

CONCARNEAU

N

Depths in Metres

CONCARNEAU

Les Sables-Blancs

Sables Blancs

CONCARNEAU

See inset

Beuzec
DirQ.87m23M

Bassin du Moros Dredged to 5.0m **Barrage**

Q du Lin

Q Carnot
Arrière Port

Q d'Aiguillon

La Ville Close

Q Péneroff

Fl(2)R.6s

Anse de Roudouic

Fl(2)G.6s

Fl.R.4s

Q.WR.6s4m9/6M
Avant Port

Fl(4)R.15s

La Croix
Q.W.14m 13M

No.1 beacon
Fl(4)G.15s

La Médée
Fl(3)R.12s
1₄ 9m4M

Lanriec
Q.G.13m8M

Pladen
YBY

Ar Gazek

Men Marque

Men Fall
G Fl(2)G.6s

Kersos

Port de la Croix

Men Cren
(0·9)

Pen ar Vas Hir

Obscd

Lué Vras

Anse de Kersaux
Visitors' moorings prohibited

Basse Chenal
Fl.R.4s

Le Cochon
Fl(3)WRG.12s5m9·6M

Lué Vras
Q.R

Plage du Cabellou

Roche Diyen

Pte du Cabellou

Lts in line 028·5°

White Intens

Petit Taro
YBY

Grand Taro

Approaches to Concarneau from Lué Vras port hand buoy with leading line of La Croix lighthouse (front) and Beuzec belfry (rear) *Nick Chavasse*

Le Cochon *Nick Chavasse*

No.1 starboardhand beacon and conspicuous building opposite wavebreaker *Nick Chavasse*

PILOTAGE

Concarneau approach and entrance

By day From any direction, the large buildings on the hill at the back of the town are unmistakable. Steer for a position about half a mile west of the promontory of Pointe de Cabellou.

The official leading line is Beuzec belfry, (co-located with Beuzec Dir Q 87m 23M) on the ridge a mile inland, in transit with La Croix lighthouse, on the seafront, bearing 028°. This works at night but is not clear by day because the lighthouse is hard to spot amongst all the other buildings. Le Cochon starboard hand beacon tower is more easily identified and it is sufficient to pass midway between it and the two port hand buoys on a course of about 030°.

Continue on this course for 600m towards Men Fall starboard hand lightbuoy. Then steer 065° for Lanriec light. This is the end gable of a white house, among many, and is hard to spot. Binoculars may

reveal a black window in the upper half and the name in green under the window. Fortunately, the channel is wide. Simply leave Kersos starboard hand beacon tower 200m to starboard and La Médée port hand beacon tower to port to reach the marina entrance.

By night Approach in the white sector of Le Cochon and bring Beuzec and La Croix lights in transit on 029°. Hold this course past Le Cochon and Men Fall buoy. As Men Fall is passed, Lanriec Q.G light will open. Steer about 070° in the green sector until the Passage de Lanriec light on the Ville Close opens red. Continue to head for Lanriec until the red light turns white. Then alter to about 000° to keep in the white sector, leaving La Médée to port and No. 1 beacon to starboard.

The floodlights, illuminating La Ville Close, give plenty of background light to the marina area. The channel beyond the marina, past La Ville Close, is marked by further red and green lights.

Concarneau marina looking N. Entrance is top right.

BERTHS AND ANCHORAGES

Concarneau visitors' pontoons

Yachts can berth on the inner side of the floating wave breaker and on the visitors' pontoon, directly inside the marina entrance. The visitors' pontoon is Pontoon D and the N side for yachts less than 9m and the S side is for yachts greater than 9m. The wave breaker is claimed to be less disturbed by the wash of passing fishing boats coming from the fishing harbour. Only ferries can use the outside of the wave breaker. Fuel is now available (Aug 2022).

Bicycles may be borrowed from the capitanerie for up to two hours. There is a Carrefour City in the town centre.

⚓ Anse de Kersaux (NE side)

47°51'·84N 3°54'·51W

The main bay at Anse de Kersaux is now prohibited for visitors. However there is a suitable anchorage, outside the prohibited area, on the northeast side of the main bay.

⚓ Baie de Pouldohan

47°50'·81N 3°54'·08W

Sheltered from the east, the Baie of Pouldohan is about 1·5M south of Concarneau. It is surrounded by rocks and best visited in quiet weather at neaps. A large-scale chart is essential.

Start from a position about 1M south of Pointe de Cabellou and enter on 060° between Roche Tudy starboard hand beacon tower and Karek Steir port hand beacon. This route passes over a 2·3m shallow patch.

ASHORE IN CONCARNEAU

There are all the facilities of a sizeable town and busy fishing and leisure port. All repairs can be undertaken. Shops, including a large supermarket, banks, hotels and restaurants are close. Internet café on the quay. The open air market is on Friday mornings.

There is a delightful beach just over a mile northwest of the port. La Ville Close and the Fishing Museum are interesting tourist attractions.

A bus service connects Concarneau to the railway at Quimper and Rosporden.

Old town across drawbridge on right *Peter Bruce*

Concarneau covered food market *Nick Chavasse*

Looking north up River L'Aven *Nick Chavasse*

IV. Île de Groix and the Rias

The mainland opposite Île de Groix has a series of flooded valleys that make interesting and attractive ports. Shallow draught boats can visit Pont Aven, where Gauguin worked, and see the fine art gallery and masses of artists' studios. The Bélon River, home of the famous Bélon oyster, is a pretty river where it is possible to combine peace and quiet with good walking and serious gastronomy.

Lorient is a big city with several marinas. There is plenty to do and a good waterbus for getting about. Etel is famous, or infamous, for having a very dangerous bar. It is necessary to call the pilot for entry instructions, which of course makes entry very easy. Once inside there is a nice town, a spectacular beach and an inland sea not much smaller than the Morbihan.

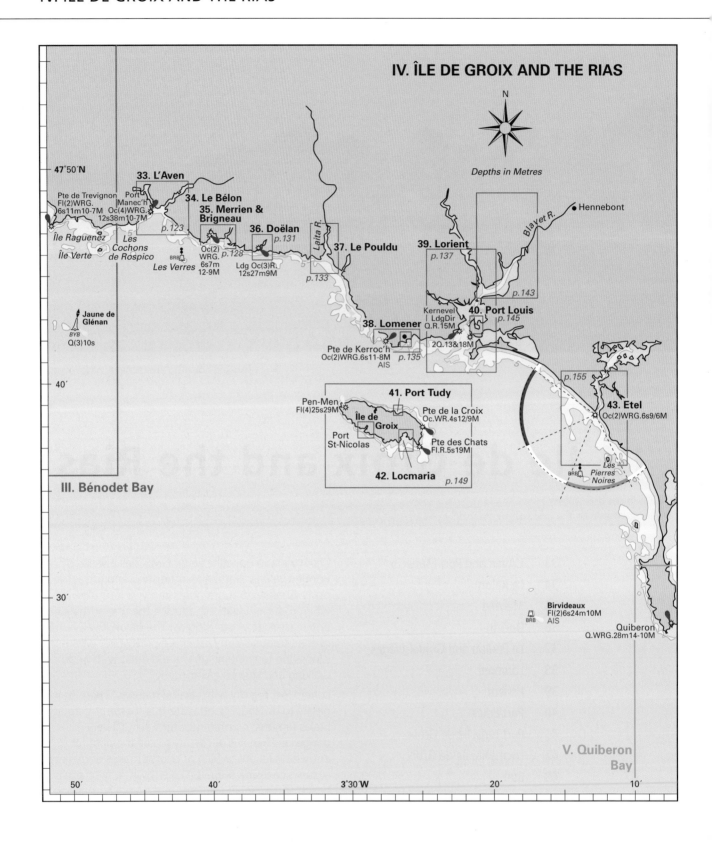

IV. ÎLE DE GROIX AND THE RIAS

N

Depths in Metres

47°50′N

33. L'Aven

Pte de Trevignon
Fl(2)WRG.
6s11m10-7M

Port
Manec'h
Oc(4)WRG.
12s38m10-7M

p.123

34. Le Bélon

35. Merrien & Brigneau

Île Raguenez

Les Cochons de Rospico

Île Verte

Les Verres

BRB

Oc(2)
WRG.
6s7m
12-9M

p.128

36. Doëlan

p.131

Ldg Oc(3)R.
12s27m9M

Laita R.

37. Le Pouldu

p.133

5

Blavet R.

● Hennebont

39. Lorient

p.137

p.143

Jaune de Glénan

BYB

Q(3)10s

Kernevel
LdgDir
Q.R.15M

40. Port Louis

p.145

40′

38. Lomener

Pte de Kerroc'h
Oc(2)WRG.6s11-8M
AIS

2Q.13&18M

p.135

5

p.155

41. Port Tudy

Pen-Men
Fl(4)25s29M

Île de
Groix

Pte de la Croix
Oc.WR.4s12/9M

43. Etel
Oc(2)WRG.6s9/6M

Port
St-Nicolas

Pte des Chats
Fl.R.5s19M

BRB

*Les
Pierres
Noires*

42. Locmaria

p.149

III. Bénodet Bay

30′

Birvideaux
Fl(2)6s24m10M
AIS

BRB

Quiberon
Q.WRG.28m14-10M

V. Quiberon Bay

50′   40′   3°30′W   20′   10′

Île de Groix tidal streams

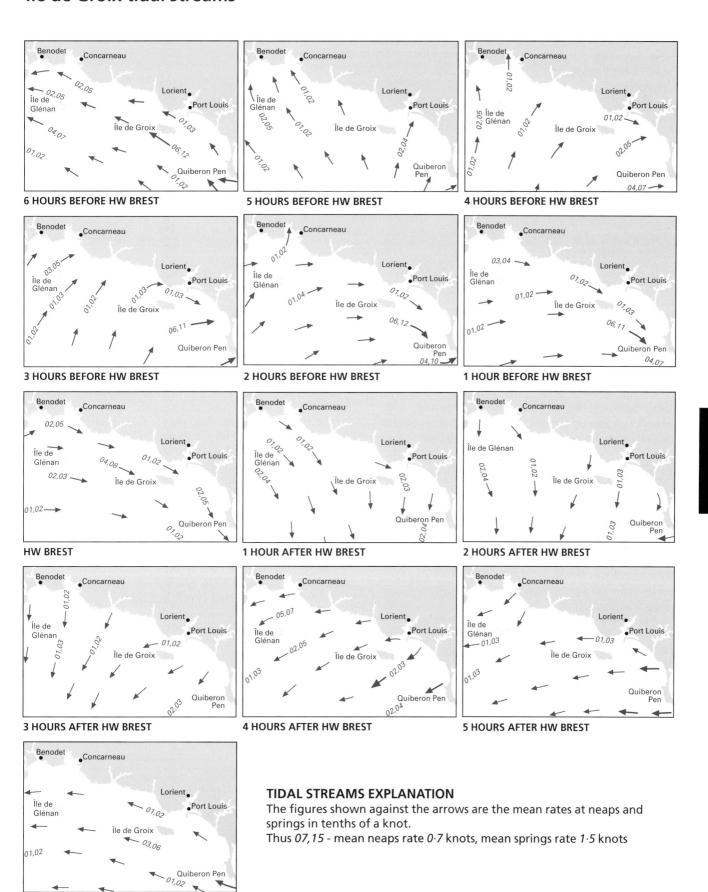

6 HOURS BEFORE HW BREST

5 HOURS BEFORE HW BREST

4 HOURS BEFORE HW BREST

3 HOURS BEFORE HW BREST

2 HOURS BEFORE HW BREST

1 HOUR BEFORE HW BREST

HW BREST

1 HOUR AFTER HW BREST

2 HOURS AFTER HW BREST

3 HOURS AFTER HW BREST

4 HOURS AFTER HW BREST

5 HOURS AFTER HW BREST

6 HOURS AFTER HW BREST

TIDAL STREAMS EXPLANATION
The figures shown against the arrows are the mean rates at neaps and springs in tenths of a knot.
Thus *07,15* - mean neaps rate *0·7* knots, mean springs rate *1·5* knots

33 L'Aven and Port Manec'h

48°47'N 3°44'W

Shelter
Reasonable from SW to NE

Hazards
Unmarked rocks in W approach, bar with dredged channel to 0·6m

Depth restrictions
Visitors' buoys at Port Manec'h 1m.
Bar dredged to 0·6m
River dries 1·5m

Night entry
Well lit to Port Manec'h

HW time
Brest HW–0030

Mean height of tide (m) Concarneau

HWS	HWN	LWN	LWS
5·1	4·0	2·0	0·9

Tidal stream
Weak in bay, strong in the river
3 knots in Rosbraz narrows

Berthing
Visitors' moorings at Port Manec'h and anchorages, drying quays at Rosbraz and Pont Aven

Facilities
Water, a few shops, bars and restaurants

Charts
SHOM *7031, 7138*
Imray *C38*

Communications
HM ① 02 98 06 89 20
mob 06 81 32 70 68
www.toutcommenceenfinistere.com

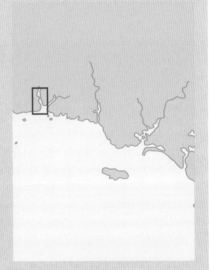

Lovely river scenery to Pont Aven

The Aven is a popular and very pretty river. The holiday resort of Port Manec'h is at its mouth on the west bank. It is a further 7M inland to the picturesque artists' town of Pont Aven.

A quiet anchorage at Port Manec'h is a world away from the busy marinas at Concarneau and Bénodet. A trip up the river by boat or dinghy on the tide is well worthwhile - Pont Aven is a delight.

PILOTAGE

Approach to the River Aven

By day The entrance is easy to locate using the lighthouse at Port Manec'h.

The approach can be made from any direction but take care to avoid the unmarked Les Cochons de Rospico (dries 0·5m) to the west; and Le Cochon (dries 0·8m) 0·4M northwest of Les Verrès isolated danger tower beacon to the east.

The 0·5M passage between Les Verrès and the land, has a least depth of 2·2m. The passage between Île Raguenez and Île Verte is deep but there is a 1m shallow patch south of the channel west of Île Verte.

By night Use either of the white sectors of Port Manec'h light. The red sector covers the dangers of Les Verrès.

The River Aven to Pont Aven

The mouth of the river is shallow and the position of the bar east of Le Roc'h, changes periodically. Within 0·5M of the mouth it dries apart from a few pools.

Enter on a rising tide leaving the Le Roc'h port hand beacon well to port and proceed up the centre of the river. Half a mile up there is an inlet called Anse de Goulet-Riec on the east side. Here the main river deepens and 1·4m or more may be found but with moorings on both sides of the river.

Further on the river shoals to dry 0·6m in places and there is a large drying creek branching off to the west with Château Poulguin on the point. Continuing north, the river narrows between the quays and slips of Kerdruc on the west bank and Rosbraz on the east.

Above Rosbraz the river widens and shoals, but is navigable on the tide or by dinghy a further 2·5M to Pont Aven. The channel is marked by buoys and is easy to follow.

Port Manec'h moorings with visitors' buoys on right
Nick Chavasse

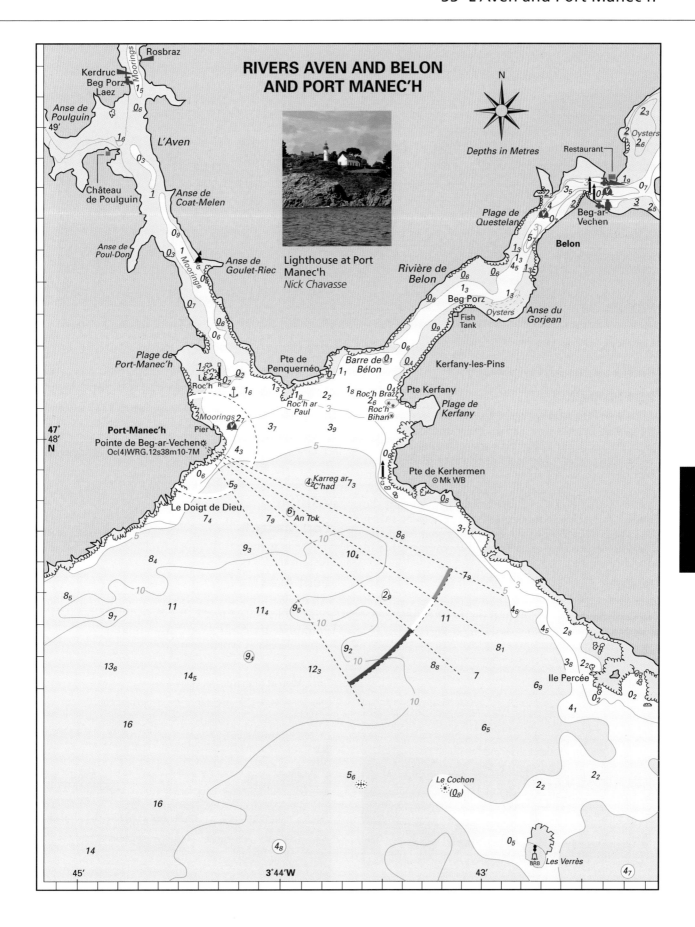

RIVERS AVEN AND BELON AND PORT MANEC'H

Rosbraz

Kerdruc
Beg Porz
Laez

Moorings

1_5

0_6

Anse de
Poulguin
49'

1_6

L'Aven

0_3

Château
de Poulguin

1

Anse de
Coat-Melen

Lighthouse at Port
Manec'h
Nick Chavasse

0_9

Anse de
Poul-Don

0_3

1

Moorings

G

0_7

Anse de
Goulet-Riec

N

Depths in Metres

Restaurant

2_3

2 Oysters 2_6

1_9 0_7

3_5

0_7

4

3 2_5

Plage de
Questelan

Beg-ar-
Vechen

Belon

2

5

1_3

4_5 1_3

Rivière de
Belon

0_6

0_6

1_3

Beg Porz

0_6

0_9

Oysters

1_3

Anse du
Gorjean

Fish
Tank

0_6

0_4

Kerfany-les-Pins

Plage de
Port-Manec'h

1_8 0_2

0_2

Le
Roc'h

1_6

0_7

1_3

1_8

Pte de
Penquernéo

1_1

Barre de
Bélon

0_1

1_8 Roc'h Braz

2_2

Roc'h ar
Paul

3

2_6
Roc'h
Bihan

Pte Kerfany

Plage de
Kerfany

Port-Manec'h

Moorings 2_7

Pier

3_7

3_9

0_6

Pte de Kerhermen
⊙ Mk WB

Pointe de Beg-ar-Vechen ✿
Oc(4)WRG.12s38m10-7M

4_3

G

0_8

5

5_9

Le Doigt de Dieu

4_2 Karreg ar 7_3
C'had

0_6

7_4

7_9

6_1 An Tok

8_6

3_7

5

10

10_4

7_9

5 3

9_3

11_4

9_5

10

2_9

11

4_6

8_4

10

11

9_5

4_5 2_8

8_5

9_7

9_4

9_2

10

8_8

8_1

3_8 2_2

0_2 0_2

13_6

14_5

12_3

7

6_9

Ile Percée

16

4_1

6_5

16

2_2

2_2

14

5_6

Le Cochon
✿
(0_8)

0_5

BRB Les Verrès

4_8

4_7

45'

3°44'W

43'

Kerdruc pontoon on W bank *Nick Chavasse*

BERTHS AND ANCHORAGES

Port Manec'h

The short Port Manec'h breakwater runs north from the point. Behind it is a small quay and slipway. To the east are eight white visitors' mooring buoys in 1·0m but exposed from southwest to southeast through south. Upstream are some fore and aft moorings in 2m depth. They are occasionally available for boats of more than 10m. During the season, all of these moorings are likely to be taken by early afternoon but there may be room to anchor outside them. This anchorage is uncomfortable in onshore winds.

Rosbraz

It is possible to dry out alongside the quays on mud at Kerdruc or on shingle and mud at Rosbraz or to borrow a mooring. No visitors' moorings.

The ebb runs at over 3kn and there is so little space between the moorings that it is difficult for a yacht of over 10m to turn.

Pont Aven

There are drying quays but these tend to be crowded. It is a very attractive quay.

ASHORE

Port Manec'h

There is water on the quay and modest shops and restaurants.

Pont Aven

All the facilities of a tourist town. Gauguin lived and worked here and it is still a magnet for artists and connoisseurs. Pont Aven Museum and Art Gallery are particularly worth visiting.

Rosbraz quay *Nick Chavasse*

Pont Aven at high tide *Nick Chavasse*

34 Le Bélon

47°48′N 3°44′W

Shelter
Good in river

Hazards
Unmarked rocks in E approach
Bar dangerous in strong SW wind

Depth restrictions
Bar dries 0·1m
Visitors' moorings have 3m or more

Night entry
Not recommended

HW time Brest HW −0030

Mean height of tide (m) Concarneau

HWS	HWN	LWN	LWS
5·0	3·9	1·9	0·8

Tidal stream
Weak in bay, moderate in the river

Berthing
Visitors' moorings

Facilities
Excellent seafood

Charts
SHOM *7031, 7138*
Imray *C38*

Communications
Harbourmaster ① 02 98 71 08 65
www.toutcommenceenfinistere.com

Oyster lovers' paradise

Bélon, home of the Bélon oyster, is a must for seafood enthusiasts. It is a pretty, sheltered river with some visitors' buoys. However, in bad southerly weather the bar (Barre de Bélon) is impassable.

PILOTAGE

See plan on page 123

Approach to Le Bélon

By day The outer entrance is identified by a large white day mark with a black vertical stripe on the east side of the entrance at Pointe de Kerhermen. However, this mark was masked by trees in 2021.

The approach can be made from any direction. Be sure to avoid Les Cochons de Rospico (dries 0·5m) to the west; and Le Cochon (dries 0·8m) 0·4M northwest of Les Verrès isolated danger tower beacon to the east. Both are unmarked.

The passage between Les Verrès and the land has a least depth of 2·2m. The passage between Île Raguenez and Île Verte is deep but there is a 1m shallow patch south of the channel west of Île Verte.

By night Not recommended.

Le Bélon looking east.
The village consists of the attractive row of houses on the south bank. The famous restaurant and fish shop, Chez Jacky, is the white building on the opposite bank
Patrick Roach

Le Bélon

It is best to enter the river above half tide. Start from a position midway between the headland at Port Manec'h and Pointe de Kerhermen and enter the river from the southwest. When Pointe Kerfany is abeam to starboard, steer down the middle of the dredged channel on 035° (*see plan page 123*).

Just after Beg Porz, a bar extends from the north bank. The deepest water is on the south side, close to the stakes marking the oyster beds. Half a mile further the river turns to starboard and on the north side of the curve there are three large white metal fore and aft visitors' buoys, suitable for rafting.

Beyond the visitors' moorings is a quay and there are six more fore and aft visitors' moorings for smaller vessels just beyond Chez Jacky's large white restaurant on the north bank. All the moorings are in strong tidal currents but the smaller ones are particularly difficult to pick up when the tide is ebbing strongly as the current is diagonally across the moorings.

The Bélon river winds further inland through steep, wooded valleys. It is well worthwhile exploring up river in a dinghy or else on foot. The GR34 coastal footpath leads for miles around the banks of both the Aven and the Bélon rivers. The TOP25 map of Quimperlé No. 0620 is recommended for those with time to explore further.

Visitors' moorings suitable for rafting *Nick Chavasse*

ASHORE IN BÉLON

Bélon village is on the south bank. There is water, fuel and a public toilet block on the quay and a few bars but no shops. Fish can sometimes be bought from the fishermen at high water. The Plage de Kerfany is a pleasant walk and, in season, has a shop for the campsite. Chez Jacky on the north bank is a famous seafood restaurant that also has a shop selling shellfish. A seafood platter on the terrace over looking the river is highly recommended.

Looking N over dinghy pontoon, visitors' moorings and Chez Jacky restaurant on N bank *Nick Chavasse*

35 Merrien

47°47'N 3°39'W

Shelter
Good in the Merrien river, but visitors'
buoys are exposed.

Hazards
Marked rocks in entrances

Depth restrictions
Approach to Merrien 1m, Brigneau 2·1m
At Merrien the river dries 0·6m except in
    channel
At Brigneau the river dries completely

Night entry
Possible but not recommended

HW time Brest HW –0030

Mean height of tide (m) Port Tudy

HWS	HWN	LWN	LWS
5·1	4·0	2·0	0·9

Tidal stream
Weak in bay, stronger in harbours

Berthing
Anchorages and visitors' buoys at Merrien

Charts
SHOM *7031, 7138*
Imray *C38*

Communications
Bélon HM ℃ 06 25 53 06 65

Attractive drying creek

Merrien, four miles southeast of Port Manec'h, is
delightful, particularly for boats that can take the
ground. There are two fine weather visitors' buoys in
the bay outside. Inside it dries apart from a dredged
channel, 0·5m.

PILOTAGE

Merrien approach and entrance

By day From the west, Merrien is easily identified
0·75M beyond the ruined factory at Brigneau. From
the east, the entrance will open after passing a
headland topped by some white houses with grey
roofs, 1·5M west of Doëlan.

There are marked dangers on both sides of the
entrance. The official transit is the white lighthouse
at the head of the pool with a large grey-roofed
house with a gable on 005°. Unfortunately the
lighthouse is almost obscured by the trees and it is
adequate to line up the grey roof on 005°.

Merrien looking north.
The white light tower is visible just below the building at the
top of the hill on the north bank *Patrick Roach*

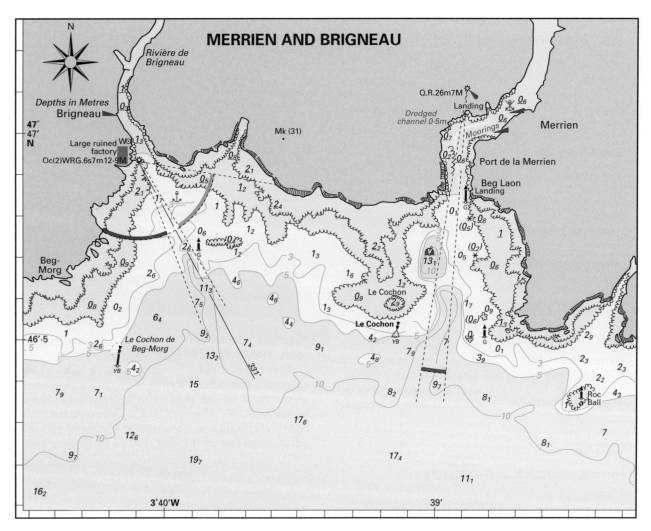

By night Entry to the pool is possible, though not recommended, using the narrow red sector of the light on 005°.

Looking N with Beg Laon starboard-hand lateral beacon and Merrien lighthouse beyond *Nick Chavasse*

BERTHS AND ANCHORAGES

Merrien visitors' buoys

The two visitors' buoys outside are the best place in calm conditions. Merrien Pool inside the entrance is inviting but keep out of the fairway and at least 50m offshore because the sides of the pool are rocky. There are fore and aft moorings for visitors up to about 9m length in depths of about 1m.

Vessels able to take the ground may be able to anchor in the river outside the channel but anchoring is prohibited off Merrien quay because of a submarine cable.

Visitors' moorings at entrance of Merrien river *Nick Chavasse*

Merrien moorings *Nick Chavasse*

ASHORE IN MERRIEN

There is a stone jetty and steps on the starboard side of the entrance at Beg Laon. The jetty is submerged at high water but is marked by a starboard hand beacon. Water is available on the drying quay in the village on the SE side. There are some bars and a restaurant in the village, about 0·5M up the hill.

The GR34 footpath offers wonderful walking either along the coast path or inland on the banks of the river. An evening walk to Brigneau for a meal is pleasant.

BRIGNEAU

Brigneau is completely exposed to the southeast so wind or swell from the south makes it untenable. It is 0·75M west of Merrien and in good weather is an interesting place to visit. It was once a major sardine port but now has a small amount of fishing and a sailing school.

Brigneau approach

By day 331° on the ruined factory chimney.

By night In the white sector of Brigneau Light 329/339°.

The port dries but it is possible to anchor outside the harbour or borrow a mooring. Small boats may be able to use the fore and aft moorings just inside the harbour. Ashore fuel is available and there are two good restaurants and a chandler.

The ruined factory at Brigneau on left above mole on approach
Nick Chavasse

Brigneau entrance which dries *Nick Chavasse*

36 Doëlan

47°46'N 3°36'W

Shelter Exposed to S

Hazards
Marked rocks in entrance.

Depth restrictions
Channel dredged 2·0m

Night entry Lit

HW time Brest HW −0035

Mean height of tide (m) Port Tudy

HWS	HWN	LWN	LWS
5·1	4·0	2·0	0·9

Tidal stream
Little stream in bay or harbour

Berthing
Visitors' moorings and drying quay

Facilities
Bars, restaurants, fish market but no shops

Charts
SHOM *7031, 7138*
Imray *C38*

Communications
Radio VHF 16, 69
HM ① 02 98 71 53 98
www.brittanytourism.com

Small friendly fishing port

The port of Doëlan is larger than the other ports on this stretch of coast but is still very small. There is a small but active fishing fleet and some boats that take the ground at the back of the harbour. It is a pretty place and popular with artists.

PILOTAGE

Doëlan approach and entrance

By day Two lighthouses provide the entry transit on a bearing of 014°. This transit passes a port hand beacon marking Basse la Croix and the starboard hand buoy Le Four.

By night Approach and enter with the leading lights in line on 014°. Coming from the east (direction of Lorient) a vessel can avoid the rocks southeast of Le Pouldu (Les Grand et Petit Cochons) by keeping out of the green sector of the front light, which covers them.

Visitors' fore and aft moorings inside breakwater *Nick Chavasse*

BERTHS

Doëlan visitors' buoys

Visitors may raft to a large white metal buoy with a rail round its edge outside the breakwater on the west side of the entrance. Alternatively, there are 8 fore and aft moorings inside the breakwater which provides more shelter. The fishermen are friendly, and it may be possible to borrow one of their moorings. A boat that can take the ground may be able to borrow a mooring up-harbour.

Doëlan quays

It is possible to dry out at one of the quays. Near the entrance to the harbour there is a landing slip and quay on the west side, a pair of slips forming a V on the east side. Other quays lie further up. Local advice should be obtained before drying out. The inner quay on the west is not suitable as the bottom slopes outwards. The first two quays on the east dry about 1·5m and should be suitable.

ASHORE IN DOËLAN

Water and electricity are available on the quays and there is a fish market on the outer port-side quay, Quay Neuf.

There are bars and restaurants on both sides of the river and a good chandlery but apart from that, the nearest shops are at Clohars Carnoet, 2M inland.

The GR34 footpath is easy to access and can be followed along the rocky coast or inland beside the banks of the river.

Excellent restaurant with lovely view of river: Le Trois Mâts, ☎ 02 98 39 99 72 www.letroismats29.fr.

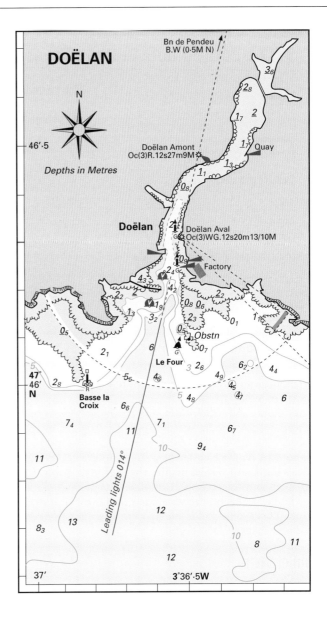

Looking S with visiting yachts on moorings beyond lifeboat
Nick Chavasse

37 Le Pouldu and Guidel-Plages

47°46'N 3°32'W

Shelter
Good in river. Exposed to S in outer anchorage

Hazards
Dangerous bar at entrance. Possibility of being trapped inside

Depth Restrictions
Bar dries 2·2m. 2·0m in marina and parts of river

Night entry Not lit

HW time Brest HW -0020

Mean height of tide (m) Port Tudy

HWS	HWN	LWN	LWS
5·1	4·0	2·0	0·9

Tidal stream
Weak in bay, up to 6kn in river

Berthing
Very small marina. Visitors' buoys and anchorages

Facilities
Bars, restaurants and supermarket. Other shops 1M away

Charts
SHOM *7031, 7138*
Imray *C38*

Communications
Guidel-Plages
HM ① 02 97 05 99 92 or
06 07 18 11 54
www.ports-paysdelorient.fr

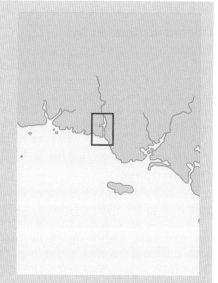

Shifting sands and sluicing tide

The river La Laita is challenging. The entry is difficult and can only be attempted an hour before HW in calm offshore winds and no swell. The sandbanks shift, the tide is very strong at springs and there is not much water over the bar at neaps, however, with a tidal co-efficient of 85 or more there is said to be plenty of water over the bar for a boat drawing 1·5m. Once inside, there is little room for visitors, but the river is attractive.

Le Pouldu is on the west bank and most of it dries out. There is a small marina on the east bank at Guidel-Plages.

PILOTAGE

Approach and entrance to Le Pouldu

Warning The stream in the river runs very hard and except near slack water a yacht going aground will be slewed round uncontrollably and possibly dangerously.

By day The harbour entrance can be identified by the former pilot's house, white with a round tower, situated on the west headland. The final approach is made with the pilot's house bearing 010°.

Looking NE from position N of former pilot's house at breakers on sand bar which dries all the way across. Entrance channel on left hand side *Nick Chavasse*

Entry should only be attempted in calm conditions about an hour before HW. This means there will be no indication of where the channel lies.

It is not possible to give precise directions since the channel moves. The guide-line on the plan is likely to be the best route. The main channel usually follows the west bank. It is marked by the port hand beacon tower at the entrance and by a port hand

Former pilot's house with round tower beyond and to left of Men-Du beacon tower *Nick Chavasse*

beacon pole. The channel then curves to starboard where a second port-hand beacon pole marks the end of a small rocky spit. Except for the stream from the river, this channel dries at LW.

To take the main channel, leave the second beacon pole 40m to port and keep this distance off to avoid a rocky shelf. The river opens out, with a wide shallow bay to starboard, and the protecting breakwater of the marina will be seen ahead on the east bank.

The river is navigable by dinghies at HW up to Quimperlé, but a bridge with 10m clearance two miles from the entrance prevents the passage of masted vessels.

By night Night entry should not be attempted.

BERTHS AND ANCHORAGE

Le Pouldu visitors' buoys

There are two white dumbell visitors' buoys off the marina, where there is sufficient water at neaps, and another further up in the trot moorings where there is more depth. Another option is to continue upriver to find 2m or more for anchoring but the deeper water is very full of moorings. The holding appears to be good in spite of the stream and some weed.

There is a drying sandbank in the middle of the river and there are many small-craft drying moorings on the east side and in the bay downstream.

The Guidel/Le Bas Pouldu marina on the east side is small but there are three visitors' berths, max length 12m and max draught 1·5m.

Guidel-Plages Marina

Guidel-Plages marina is situated on the E bank opposite Le Pouldu. There is room for 8 boats, mainly using the pontoon hammerheads. Maximum length is 13m. There are some moorings outside the marina entrance which could be used by boats up to 12m, depending on tidal range. It is best to telephone the harbour master when arriving at the entrance to the river for guidance on the best route to take in the river. The marina entrance is difficult when the current is fast flowing.

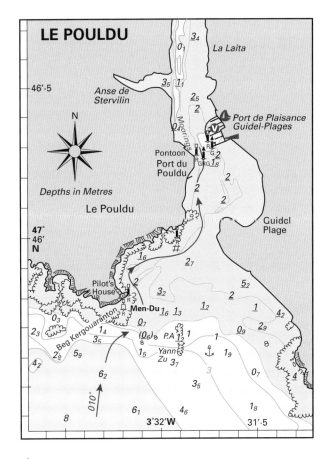

⚓ Outside Le Pouldu

In settled offshore weather an anchorage can be found outside the bar to the east of Yann Zu. The best spot seems to be with the marina bearing 000° as far in as draught permits. The bottom is hard sand.

ASHORE IN LE POULDU

The pontoon on the west bank is for fishermen but there is space to leave a dinghy. There are two hotels close by and the shops of Le Pouldu are 1M along the road.

The harbour office is on the east bank at Guidel/Le Bas Pouldu by the marina. Further south there are restaurants catering for a camping site and there is a large supermarket a short walk round the bay towards the entrance.

Guidel-Plages marina entrance *Nick Chavasse*

38 Loménér

47°42'N 3°26'W

Shelter
Good from NW to NE

Hazards
Marked and unmarked rocks

Depth restrictions
3·0m at breakwater

Night entry Lit

HW time Brest HW −0010

Mean height of tide (m) Port Tudy

HWS	HWN	LWN	LWS
5·1	4·0	2·0	0·9

Tidal stream
Weak in approach and anchorage

Berthing
Anchorages

Facilities
As of a beach resort

Charts
SHOM *7031, 7139*
Imray *C38*

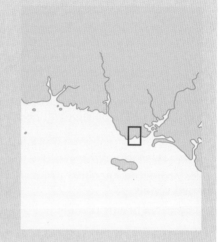

Pleasant seaside resort

The port of Loménér and the adjacent Anse de Stole, form a small harbour on the mainland opposite Île de Groix.

It is open to the south but sheltered from the north and the *brise de terre*. In settled weather, when the effects of the *brise de terre* are most likely to be felt, it can be a better option than Port Tudy on the Île de Groix (*see page 148*).

Loménér has good beaches and all facilities of a small seaside resort.

PILOTAGE

Approach and entrance to Loménér

By day The harbour is easy to identify by a prominent block of flats behind the breakwater.

Enter by keeping the lighthouse with a red top on 357°. Close-in the dangers on the west side are well marked but there are unmarked shallow patches to the west of the leading line further out at Les Trois Pierres (1·2m) and Basse des Chats (0·1m). The dangers on the east are also not well marked and in particular Grasu south cardinal tower beacon should be given a good berth because rocks extend west of it.

By night Enter using the white sector of Anse de Stole light 355°/359°. Beware of the many unlit fishing floats and moorings.

Loménér lighthouse with red top Nick Chavasse

Anse de Stole looking NW with east cardinal beacon pole on left and prominent block of flats on right Nick Chavasse

BERTHS AND ANCHORAGES

⚓ Anse de Stole

Anchor in the Anse de Stole where space and depth permit or borrow a mooring. It is open to the south. The beaches behind the breakwater and in the Anse de Stole are excellent for drying out. There is a landing slip on the spur inside the harbour. Avoid the breakwater wall, as there are vicious rocks at its foot.

⚓ Kerroc'h

47°42'·18N 3°28'·09W

Sheltered from all directions except west when swell can enter near HW, this small harbour is about 4M west of Lorient. Approach from due south steering to pass about 150m west of the west cardinal beacon marking Les Deux Têtes. This is necessary to avoid the unmarked Les Soeurs rocks on the west side of the entrance. Once past the west cardinal, turn to starboard to enter the harbour. Anchor where depth permits or borrow a mooring.

⚓ Le Pérello

47°41'·69N 3°26'·40W

Exposed to wind or swell from the south and southeast, Le Pérello is about 1M east of Kerroc'h. Approach from the south-southeast. The drying rocks on either side of the entrance can be avoided by aligning the elbow of the small slipway on the northeast side of the bay with the seaward-facing gable end of the house behind it on 353°. The house is the one closest to the beach.

There are some moorings but there is also room to anchor.

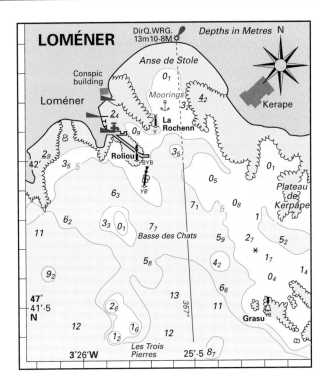

ASHORE IN LOMÉNER

There is water at the root of the quay and shops, bars and restaurants. There is also a large supermarket close to the quay. Shellfish can often be bought direct from local fishermen.

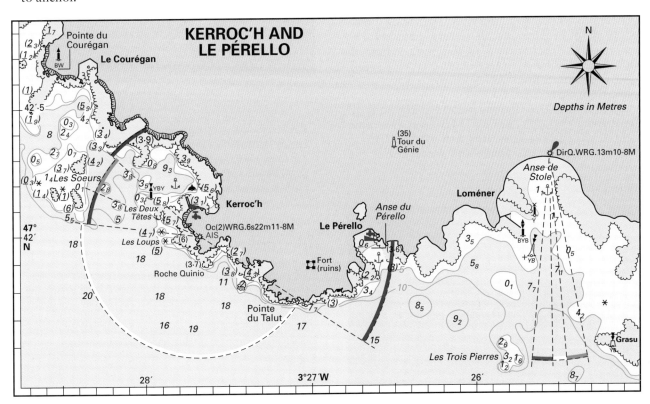

39 Lorient

47°42'N 3°22'W

Shelter
Excellent in marinas

Hazards
Marked rocks in entrance

Depth restrictions None

Night entry Well lit

HW time Brest HW +0010

Mean height of tide (m)

Lorient

HWS	HWN	LWN	LWS
5·1	4·0	2·0	0·9

Hennebont

5·0	3·9	1·8	0·8

Tidal stream in entrance:
Flood – Brest HW–0500 to –0200 (3·5kn)
Slack – Brest HW–0200 to +0200
Ebb – Brest HW+0200 to +0500 (4·0kn)
Slack – Brest HW+0500 to –0500

Berthing
Several marinas

Fuel Kernéval S basin

Facilities All facilities

Charts
SHOM *7031, 7140*
Imray *C38*

Communications
All marinas VHF 9
Lorient Marina ① 02 97 21 10 14
Kernéval ① 02 97 65 48 25
Locmiquélic ① 02 97 33 59 51
Base de Sous-Marin ① 02 97 87 00 46
www.ports-paysdelorient.fr
www.passeportescales.com/fr/port-locmiquelic

Major port with good facilities

Lorient was once an important commercial port, founded in the 17th century as a base for the French East India Company, hence its original name, L'Orient. A naval dockyard followed in the north of the harbour (now closed) and during the Second World War huge concrete submarine pens were built for German U-boats. Today it has the largest fishing fleet in Brittany and seven yacht marinas.

Parts of the harbour are industrial and not very attractive but it is possible to moor in the heart of the city, in a marina near the beach, or to anchor in perfect peace in the beautiful river. The sailing is also good here because Île de Groix protects the approaches. Thus Lorient is an ideal place to hole up in bad weather but warrants a visit even on a sunny day. Communications are excellent so it is a good place to change crews.

The multitude of options in Lorient Harbour all have much to offer. Lorient Marina is the most central with all facilities. It is well worth a trip up the Blavet river to sample the scenery and the wildlife.

Lorient submarine pens Nick Chavasse

Eric Tabarly's *Pen Duicks* at Cité de la Voile *Nick Chavasse*

The recently opened sailing exhibition 'Cité de la Voile Eric Tabarly', situated close to the submarine pens, is interesting and an excellent way to spend a rainy afternoon (www.citevoile-tabarly.com). A trip up the Blavet river provides pleasant scenery and wildlife.

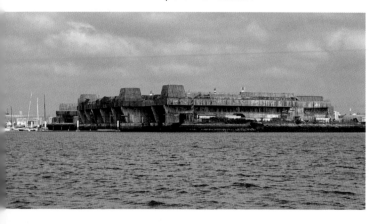

PILOTAGE

Warning Yachts must keep to the edges of channels wherever possible and must keep out of the way of large vessels. In particular they must keep well to the appropriate side of the narrows at the citadel whether or not a large ship is present. Large ship movements are announced on VHF and boats must maintain watch on Ch 16 when underway in the harbour.

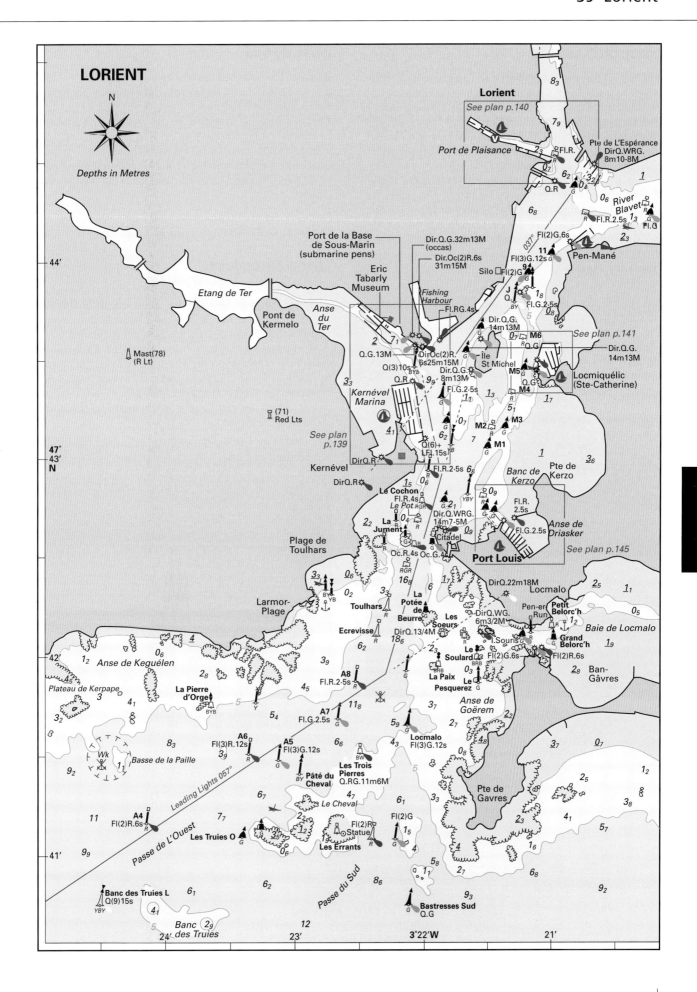

Passe de l'Ouest

By day This channel starts 0·75M south of the conspicuous Grasu south cardinal tower beacon, 47°41'·53N 03°25'·15W. The outer leading line is the red and white tower on Les Soeurs rocks and the red and white banded day mark above the citadel walls (right of a conspicuous church spire) on 057°. The channel is well buoyed.

Soon after passing Les Trois Pierres beacon tower (Black and white horizontal bands), the narrows between La Jument and the citadel will open. The transit is two white towers with green tops on the west side of Île Saint-Michel on 016°. However, the huge white grain silo in the commercial harbour also provides a useful landmark.

By night The intensified sector of the leading lights on 057° covers the channel and all the lateral buoys are lit. Use Les Trois Pierres to identify the position of the turn to port on to 016° with the two directional lights on the west side of Île Saint-Michel in line. This takes one through the narrows marked by the citadel and La Jument.

Passe du Sud

By day This channel starts from a position 0·25M SW of Bastresses Sud starboard hand buoy. Steer for the citadel on 010° and follow the buoys. Leave Les Errants beacon tower (white with black square topmark), Les Errants port hand buoy and the conspicuous Les Trois Pierres (black and white beacon tower) to port. The main channel, the Passe de l'Ouest, is then joined and is well marked to the citadel.

By night Passe du Sud is not recommended at night; use Passe de L'Ouest.

Chenal Secondaire

By day This channel is a bypass for the narrows and is useful to stay out of the main channel during shipping movements. It can only be used above half tide because it passes over Le Cochon (dries 1m).

A red green red can buoy south of La Jument marks the entrance to the channel. Leaving this buoy to starboard, the channel is marked by red and green beacons up to Le Cochon red green red beacon tower, which should be left to starboard as the main channel is re-entered.

By night The Chenal Secondaire is unlit and should not be used at night.

Le Cochon beacon tower *Nick Chavasse*

Entrance to Lorient Harbour with Port Louis citadel on right
Nick Chavasse

Les Trois Pierres white and black special Bn on starboard side of main channel to Lorient
Nick Chavasse

Proceeding up the harbour

By day Once through the narrows, the harbour opens out and navigation is straightforward. Within the harbour, the dangers are marked, and the chart is the best guide.

If bound for Le Port de Lorient (Lorient Marina) or the River Blavet, either the channel to the east or to the west of Île Saint-Michel may be used. Note that there is an unmarked shallow patch, with 0·5m over it, immediately to the east of M5 starboard hand buoy.

By night The usual route up harbour is to the west of Île Saint-Michel although there is often enough background light to see the unlit buoys in the eastern channel. The shallow area, Banc du Turc, south-southwest of Île Saint-Michel is a hazard below half tide, so use the 350° directional leading lights on top of the submarine pens until the middle of the Kernével Marina is abeam to port when the white sector of Pte de L'Espérance light then leads all the way up the harbour on 037°. The light on the end of the jetty at the RoRo terminal can be used to identify the entrance to Lorient (see plan page 140).

The entrance to the Blavet channel is marked by lit port and starboard lateral buoys and the starboard-hand buoys in the lower reaches of the river are also lit. Using these, it is possible to find a temporary anchorage out of the channel.

BERTHS

Kernével Marina

Kernével is on the west of the harbour 0·5M beyond the narrows. It is protected by a line of floating wavebreakers secured to piles. Use the north entrance when looking for a berth. The visitors' pontoon is at the southern end of the north basin. Beware that the current in the marina can cause dificulties when berthing.

The south entrance leads to the fuel pontoon, a slipway for hauling out and scrubbing berths.

Apart from a chandler there are limited facilities nearby but bicycles are available free of charge from the helpful marina staff. Two large supermarkets are situated about a mile northwest round the bay and there is a frequent bus service to Lorient, where workshops and engineers can be found.

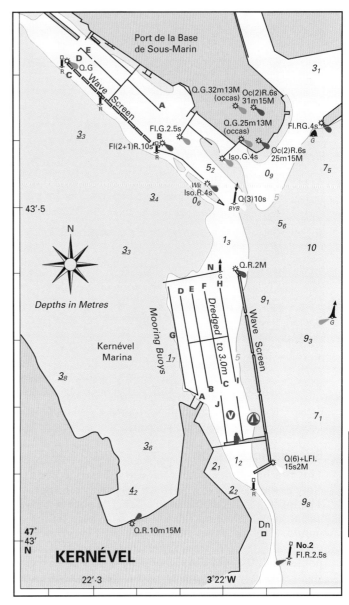

Kernével Marina looking SE with fuel dock on far side approached from the southern entrance
Yvan Zedda

Base de Sous-Marin

This is a brand new marina at the submarine pens close to the 'Cité de la Voile Eric Tabarly' exhibition. The marina is dedicated to professional yachtsmen and women in the Eric Tabarly and Ellen MacArthur mould. Several of the late Eric Tabarly's Pen Duick yachts are berthed here. The casual cruiser will be politely told to find somewhere else unless he has a yacht over 20m long and/or a very deep draught up to 6m and cannot be accommodated elsewhere. Large multihulls will be found a berth.

There are excellent facilities and they are willing to help sort out complex electronic and constructional problems. ☎ 02 97 87 00 46, *mobile* 06 28 56 31 49 or VHF 09 for advice.

The marina also specialises in hosting national and international rallies and in being a 'stop' for passage races.

Le Port de Lorient (Lorient Marina)

The marina is a fully pontooned yacht harbour in pleasant surroundings. At busy times yachts will be met by marina staff in a launch and directed to a pontoon; otherwise tie up on the south side where convenient and arrange a berth with the helpful staff in the capitainerie. Only those planning to stay more than a few days can berth in the wet basin which is entered via a lifting bridge and a lock gate. Entry to and exit from the wet basin is possible for one hour either side of HW at springs, less at neaps.

It is a lively place and has all facilities including a 45-T travel-lift. There are good showers, washing machines and sauna. Bicycles may be borrowed from the capitainerie. Fuel is at Kernével. Covered market seven minutes walk away in Avenue Anatole France. The rail and bus services from Lorient are good. There are frequent ferries to Locmiquélic and Port Louis which run from a pontoon on the north bank of Avant-Port.

Pen-Mané marina

Opposite Lorient, this modern marina at the mouth of the Blavet is attractive and peaceful and under the same management as Locmiquélic (see below). Repair and servicing for both marinas takes place at the yachtyard at Pen-Mané. It is a long way from the shops but there is a waterbus to Lorient.

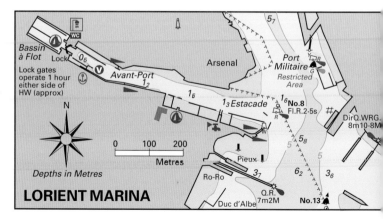

Approach to Lorient Marina *Nick Chavasse*

Lorient marina looking SE with capitainerie in centre *Nick Chavasse*

There are no visitors' berths but a place can usually be found by speaking to the management at Locmiquélic on VHF 09 or ✆ 02 97 33 59 51 (office hours).

Locmiquélic (Ste-Catherine) Marina

Space can normally be found for visitors at this marina, which has all the usual facilities. It is entered from the channel east of Île Saint-Michel. There is a wreck with only 0·4m over it, marked by M5 starboard hand buoy, just south of the marina entrance; boats should pass west of this buoy when the tide is low.

The marina has recently been enclosed with floating breakwaters and the facilities upgraded with a new shower/toilet block and laundry. At night the entrance is lit but, as the channel is unlit, it is easiest for the stranger to approach from north of Île Saint-Michel. There are no dedicated visitors' berths but visitors are welcome. Call the capitainerie on VHF 09 or ✆ 02 97 33 59 51 for a berth (office hours). There is a pump-out facility. Fuel is at Kernével.

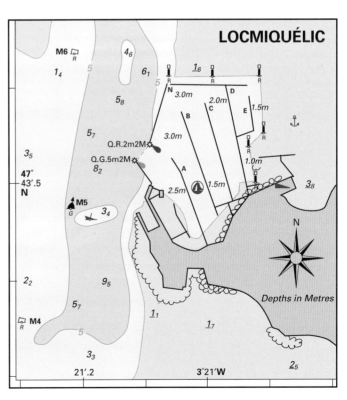

Locquimelic Marina with entrance on right *Nick Chavasse*

There are shops and the usual facilities of a small town about 500m from the marina. Free bicycles available. Frequent waterbus to Lorient where it links with a bus into the town centre.

ANCHORAGES

⚓ The River Blavet and Hennebont

The upper reaches of this little-visited river are most attractive, with an abundance of bird-life. At half tide it is possible to find plenty of water all the way to Hennebont. The two shallowest patches lie just after Pointe de Beger Vil and in the reach before the

power cables after the second road bridge where only 1·5m could be found at LW neaps.

Three bridges cross the river between the entrance and Hennebont. The first two have 22m clearance and the last 21m.

The channel is marked by buoys or beacons to the second road bridge. Above the first bridge at Bonhomme the river narrows and winds a further four miles to Hennebont.

A concrete obstruction, which dries, is reported to lie under the second road bridge, approximately one third of the way out from the left supporting column (heading upriver). When passing under the bridge keep to the centre, or to starboard if proceeding upriver.

Locmiquélic Marina (formerly St-Catherine's) with Pen-Mané at middle right and the entrance to Lorient Marina at the top left of picture *Patrick Roach*

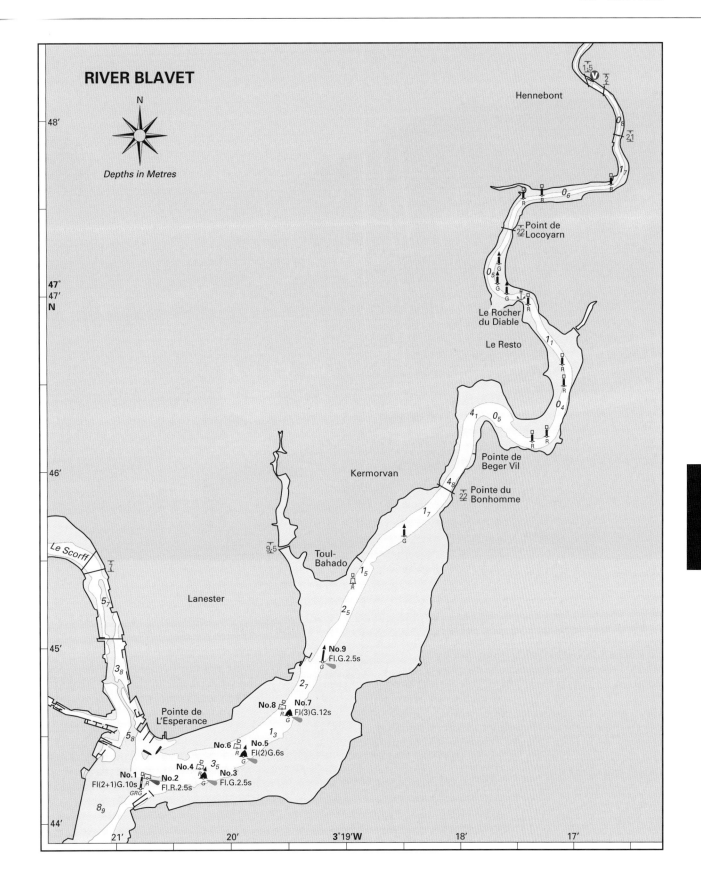

RIVER BLAVET

N

Depths in Metres

Hennebont

Point de Locoyarn

Le Rocher du Diable

Le Resto

Pointe de Beger Vil

Pointe du Bonhomme

Kermorvan

Le Scorff

Lanester

Toul-Bahado

No.9
Fl.G.2.5s

No.8 No.7
Fl(3)G.12s

Pointe de L'Esperance

No.6 No.5
Fl(2)G.6s

No.4

No.1
Fl(2+1)G.10s

No.2
Fl.R.2.5s

No.3
Fl.G.2.5s

Hennebont visitors' pontoon *Nick Chavasse*

There are many possible anchorages on the way to Hennebont. One such anchorage is to be found at Le Rocher du Diable in the pool, 3m by No.10 red lateral beacon. At Hennebont there is a visitors' pontoon on the starboard hand side just before the bridge. The bottom is very soft mud so an overnight stay may be possible. The author spent a comfortable night on Hennebont's visitors' pontoon, at neaps with 1·5m draught. There is also one fore and aft visitors' mooring for yachts less than 10m at the far end of the trot.

Hennebont is a pleasant walled market town with a market in the square on Thursday mornings. There are shops, including a large supermarket, banks and restaurants. Fuel can be obtained from a garage close to the bridge and there is a water tap close to the pontoon. It has good rail connections.

⚓ Larmor-Plage

47°42'·29N 3°22'·74W

Protected from west and north, there is a rather open anchorage on the western side in the approaches to Lorient. Leave the main channel near Toulhars port hand buoy and head towards the two red beacons near Larmor breakwater. It is possible to anchor near the north red beacon. At neaps anchor beyond the beacons towards the Plage de Toulhars. Keep clear of the two cardinal beacons that mark a wreck. A large-scale chart is essential.

40 Port Louis

47°42'N 3°22'W

Shelter
Excellent in marina

Hazards
Intricate entry to Locmalo

Depth restrictions
1·1m in approach to Port Louis
0·2m in approach to Locmalo

Night entry
Partially lit but not recommended

HW time
Brest HW –0010

Mean height of tide (m) Port Louis

HWS	HWN	LWN	LWS
5·1	4·0	2·0	0·9

Tidal streams
Approach as Lorient
4kn in entrance to Locmalo

Berthing
Marina at Port Louis; anchorage at
  Locmalo

Facilities
All facilities; interesting historic town

Charts:
SHOM 7031, 7140
Imray C38

Communications
VHF 9
Port Louis Marina ① 02 97 82 59 55
www.brittanytourism.com

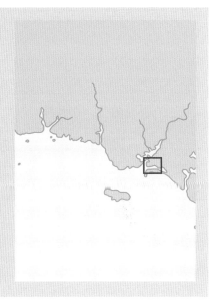

Looking S with entrance to Port Louis to left of the citadel
Nick Chavasse

The other side of Lorient

Port Louis is no distance from Lorient by water but a world away in charm and character. This small tuna port and seaside resort on the eastern side of the main Lorient channel has a magnificent 16th-century citadel with several interesting nautical museums, including an excellent lifeboat museum and one about the Compagnie des Indes.

There is a marina on the north side of the town. To the south, completely protected by the Gâvres peninsula, which gives alternative access to Port Louis, is the delightful bay of Locmalo (*see plan page 137*).

PILOTAGE

(see plan on page 137)

Port Louis entrance

By day Leave the main channel north of the citadel near Le Cochon RGR tower beacon and steer about 100° leaving two starboard hand buoys to starboard. Just beyond the second starboard hand buoy is a starboard hand buoy marking the end of a slip and the beginning of the channel to the marina. Keep close to the starboard side of the channel because the bay shoals quickly.

By night Not recommended.

Port Louis marina entrance *Nick Chavasse*

BERTHS

Port Louis

The visitors' pontoon is the second one in from the entrance. All normal facilities provided. There are also some moorings in the shoaling bay to the east of the citadel, which may be available on application to the yacht club. Marina is dredged to 3m. The nearest fuel and repair facilities are at Kernével.

Looking S at moorings and Citadel beyond *Nick Chavasse*

Port Louis marina *Nick Chavasse*

ASHORE IN PORT LOUIS

There are plenty of shops, bars and restaurants. Port Louis itself is a pleasant and interesting 18th century walled town. Frequent waterbus to Lorient. The citadel contains museums and there are good views of Lorient and Groix from the ramparts.

ANCHORAGES

⚓ Locmalo

47°42'·22N 3°20'·96W

There are moorings off Pen-er-Run, and it may be possible to borrow one. The pool east of the Grand and Petit Belorc'h beacons is clear of moorings and offers good anchorage in up to 4m.

PILOTAGE

Warning A large-scale chart is essential.

Locmalo northwest entrance channel

By day Pass north of La Potée de Beurre starboard hand beacon tower with the north side of Île aux Souris in transit with the end of the ferry slip on the south side of the entrance to the Baie de Locmalo, bearing 112°. Alternatively use La Potée de Beurre in line with Larmor church spire on a back bearing of 278°. On approaching Île aux Souris, with a green light tripod on its western side, alter course to leave the islet to starboard and steer on the north side of the channel. Leave a green buoy to starboard and pass between the red and green beacon towers. The channel then curves northeast towards the jetty at Locmalo.

By night Not recommended.

Locmalo southwest entrance channel

By day Start at the Locmalo starboard hand buoy 0·75M southwest of Île aux Souris and head for Île aux Souris, on a heading of 045°. Once past Le Soulard isolated danger tower beacon alter course to about 000° to pass between Le Cabon reef and Île

aux Souris. Beware that neither the beacon on Le Cabon, nor the light beacon on Île aux Souris mark the extremities of the dangers. Le Pesquerez starboard hand pole beacon astern should be kept just open west of Le Soulard. After Île aux Souris has been passed the channel described above is joined.

By night Partially lit but not recommended.

ASHORE IN LOCMALO

There are shops, banks and restaurants at Port Louis. The best dinghy landing is at Locmalo jetty.

Port Louis looking NW with Kernével Marina on the far side of the channel *Yvan Zedda*

Gâvres Marina

There is a marina at Marina Gâvres, on the south side of the entrance to Petite Mar de Gâvres. It has ten berths for visitors (max length 10m) on a pontoon in 2m but with difficult manoeuvring. ☎ 02 97 65 48 25. There are also four drying moorings available.

⚓ Anse de Goërem

47°41'·67N 3°22'·20W

Sheltered from the east there is a useful bay at the west end of the Gâvres peninsula. Anchor south of La Pesquerez beacon. It is rather exposed for a night anchorage but it is possible to leave at night using the lit Locmalo starboard hand buoy south-southwest of La Paix.

41 Port Tudy, Île de Groix

47°38'N 3°28'W

Shelter
Good except from N or NE

Hazards
Unmarked rocks near leading line to port near entrance
Ferries manoeuvring in harbour

Depth restrictions
2·0m on visitors' moorings and visitors' pontoon
Lock to inner harbour HW ±0200

Night entry Lit

HW time
Brest HW -0015

Mean height of tide (m) Port Tudy

HWS	HWN	LWN	LWS
5·1	4·1	2·1	0·9

Tidal stream in approaches
East – Brest HW–0400 to HW (0·4kn)
Slack – Brest HW to +0200
W – Brest HW +0200 to +0600 (0·4kn)
Slack – Brest HW -0600 to -0400

Berthing
Visitors' buoys and marina

Fuel
SE corner of inner harbour (cans)

Facilities
As of a small port
Blackwater pump-out

Charts
SHOM 7031, 7139
Imray C38

Communications
VHF 9
HM ℡ 02 97 86 54 62
www.groix.fr

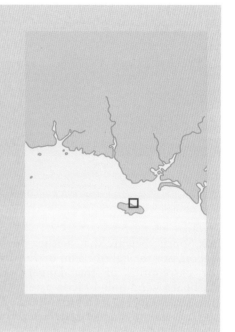

Attractive busy harbour

Port Tudy is an attractive 19th-century tuna port on the north side of Île de Groix. It is now almost entirely devoted to tourism. The outer harbour is rather exposed to the north and northeast, which makes it uncomfortable if the *brise de terre* blows in the early hours of the morning.

It is the only real port on Île de Groix and gets very crowded, particularly at weekends. The large number of tourists and the noisy ferries make Port Tudy lively but rarely peaceful.

For cruising yachtsmen, visiting the islands is part of the fun. Port Tudy is a great little harbour. Note that it's cheaper to pick up a mooring in the outer harbour. It can get busy but well worth exploring Le Bourg, about half a mile up the hill.

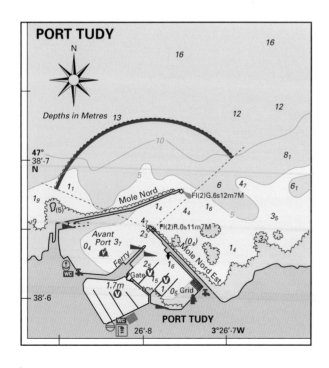

PILOTAGE

Port Tudy approach and entrance

By day The harbour is easily identified and the approach from the west and north is straightforward; there are some mooring buoys and a fish farm off Port Lay, but no other dangers.

From the east and southeast there are some unmarked dangers. The safe transit uses the harbour pierhead lights in line on 217°. This leaves a rock (depth 0·8m) 200m to port. A red beacon marks some other dangers closer inshore.

Enter the port midway between the pierheads, then steer parallel to the north mole to avoid the rocks at the end of the east mole. If a ferry is manoeuvring, stand off as it needs all the room there is.

By night The buoys in the approach are unlit. The east pierhead light is obscured over the dangers to the east of the harbour. It is therefore safe to keep this light showing and just open to the left of the north pierhead light. If they are exactly in transit the rear light is obscured.

BERTHS AND ANCHORAGES

> **Warning** If the NE wind, normally the *brise de terre*, is strong, make sure you have sufficient fenders and warps and that the load on the warps is shared. If this wind blows hard and the harbour is packed with boats, it can make for a challenging night!

Port Tudy outer harbour (Avant Port)

In season yachts entering the harbour will be met by a harbour launch and directed to a berth. In the outer harbour yachts moor fore and aft between the large white mooring buoys, ensuring that there is room for the ferry to manoeuvre. Long warps are necessary and springs are advisable to ensure that spreaders will not foul if the swell gets up. The landing slip is reserved for ferries.

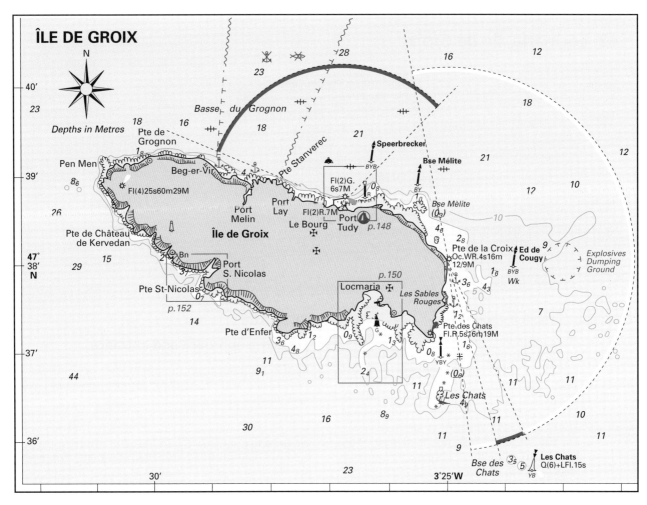

Port Tudy inner harbour

The inner harbour shoals inward but there is plenty of water for most yachts. There are pontoon berths and alongside berths where rafting may be necessary. The inner harbour berths are much more expensive than those in the outer harbour.

Port Tudy wet dock

Entry to the wet dock is possible for two hours either side of HW. If waiting for the gates to open it is better to moor to a pontoon rather than the inner landing slip as there is a stone shelf which protrudes below the top end of the slip near the gates.

Visitors will be directed to a berth in 2–3m. The wet basin is the most crowded part of the harbour; yachts are rafted to the pontoons and it is really only useful for a prolonged stay.

ASHORE IN PORT TUDY

Fuel is available in cans from the depot at the southeast corner of the inner harbour. There is a marine engineer, a hauling-out slip, some chandlery and a launderette on the quay. There are cafés around the harbour and bread may be obtained nearby. All other shops, including a supermarket, are available up the hill in the town, Le Bourg.

Bicycles may be hired to explore this picturesque island and there are frequent ferries to Lorient.

Entrance to Port Tudy *Nick Chavasse*

Looking NE over Avant Port to entrance beyond *Nick Chavasse*

42 Locmaria, Île de Groix

47°37'N 3°26'W

Shelter
Locmaria – open to S

Hazards
Many unmarked rocks

Depth restrictions
1·0m in Loc Maria anchorage

Night entry
Not recommended

HW time
Brest HW –0030

Mean height of tide (m) Port Tudy

HWS	HWN	LWN	LWS
5·1	4·0	2·0	0·9

Tidal stream Pte des Chats
NE – Brest HW–0600 to –0200 (0·5kn)
Slack – Brest HW–0200 to +0100
SW – Brest HW+0100 to +0500 (0·5kn)
Slack – Brest HW+0500 to –0600

Berthing
Moorings and anchorages

Facilities
A few shops and bars, good beach,
nice 1·5M walk to Port Tudy

Charts
SHOM *7031, 7139*
Imray *C38*

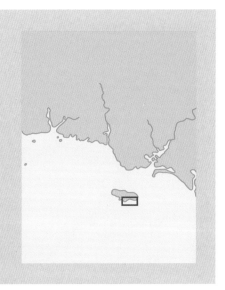

Charming unspoilt harbour

This charming unspoilt little harbour is situated on the south of Île de Groix, 0·75M west of Pointe des Chats (*see plan on p.149*). It is well worth a visit under the right conditions.

The approach is open to the Atlantic, and the anchorage is dangerously exposed to swell or wind with any south in it. However, it is sheltered to a degree from the west through north to east. The harbour dries but outside there is space to moor or anchor in depths of 1m or more.

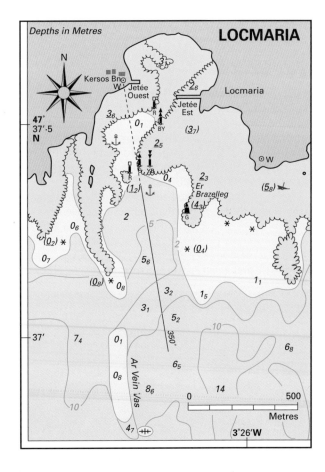

PILOTAGE

Locmaria approach and entrance

By day Coming from the north, east or southeast it will be necessary to make a detour round Les Chats (*see plan on page 149*).

From an initial position S of Les Chats, Locmaria will be seen on the east side of the bay, together with Er Brazelleg starboard hand beacon tower Approach Er Brazelleg on 005° and then steer 312°for 1·6M for the first port and starboard beacons. Then bear to starboard for the pier head, keeping rather closer to the inner port-hand beacon.

By night There are no lights and a night entry should not be attempted.

Kersos Bn white on foreshore to left of trimaran
Nick Chavasse

Kersos beacon

Locmaria harbour looking east *Patrick Roach*

BERTHS AND ANCHORAGES

⚓ Locmaria

The harbour is choked with small-boat moorings and there is no room to anchor and remain afloat. It may be posible to anchor or borrow a mooring buoy laid just outside the harbour in about 1m. There is also a good anchorage just outside the reef, south of the south cardinal beacon, in about 2m. It is not possible to lie alongside the jetty because it may be used for landing.

Locmaria is an attractive white painted village that feels like somewhere much further south. There are shops, a bar and a crêperie and good beaches. It is a pleasant walk of 1·5M to Port Tudy and there are many other walks in the area.

Looking NE from anchorage at moorings in foreground and drying harbour beyond on right *Nick Chavasse*

Kersos beacon

Amer Saint-Nicolas on cliff 0·35M NW from Port St-Nicolas
Nick Chavasse

Port St-Nicolas looking northeast. This magical and
challenging crack in the cliffs has very little swinging room
Patrick Roach

Looking WSW over Rocher de la Vache and Port St-Nicolas
anchorage *Nick Chavasse*

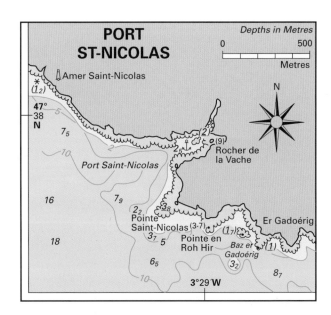

Port-Lay

Open to the north, this very pretty harbour is
believed to be one of the tiniest in Brittany. It is
0·5M west of port Tudy and anchoring is forbidden
but the local sailing school and diving centre has
some mooring buoys which can sometimes be
borrowed.

⚓ Port Saint-Nicolas

Protected from northwest to east and from the *brise
de terre* but wide open to the southwest, this magical
crack in the cliffs is about 1·75M east of Pen Men,
the western point of the island. It can be identified
by a masonry day mark, Amer Saint-Nicolas, 900m
to the west of the cove.

Approach from the southwest and, leaving Pointe
Saint-Nicolas to starboard, steer for the centre of the
cove and anchor in 2m. The bottom is sand with a
lot of rock and weed so it is best to buoy the anchor.
Since there is not much swinging room, it may be
necessary to use two anchors. Alternatively anchor
off in the wider part of the bay.

⚓ Port-Melin and Beg-er-Vir

Open to the north but protected from the south
Port-Melin is a small cove 1M west of Port Tudy and
Beg-er-Vir is the larger bay west of Port-Melin.
Approach from the north at LW taking care to avoid
the rock ledges. Anchor in 2m on sand. A large scale
chart is essential.

⚓ Pointe de la Croix

47°38'·14N 3°24'·87W

Protected from the southwest but otherwise rather
exposed there are a number of possible anchorages
off the beach near Pointe de la Croix.

⚓ Les Sables Rouges

47°37'69N 03°24'93W

Good shelter from W wind. Holding is sand in 2m.

43 Etel

47°39'N 3°13'W

Shelter
Excellent in marina

Hazards
Dangerous shifting bar at entrance

Depth restrictions
0·6m (sometimes much less) on bar
1·5m in marina

Other restrictions
Must call pilot for entry instructions

Night entry
Prohibited

HW time
Brest HW +0005

Mean height of tide (m) Etel

HWS	HWN	LWN	LWS
4·9	4·1	2·2	1·5

Tidal stream in river
Slack – Brest HW–0500 to –0400
Flood – Brest HW–0400 to +0200 (1·5kn)
Ebb – Brest HW+0200 to –0500 (1·3kn)

Berthing
Marina

Facilities
All facilities

Charts
SHOM 7031, 7138
Imray C38

Communications
Radio Semaphore d'Etel VHF 13 and
    Ch 09 for port when over bar
Marina ① 02 97 55 46 62 / 06 83 99 92 39
Semaphore ① 02 97 55 35 59
www.etel-tourisme.com

Delightful river with fierce tides

Etel bar has a bad reputation and should be avoided in strong south or southwest wind or swell. In settled weather it is not a problem.

The bar can shift from day to day so it is necessary to follow VHF directions in French from the pilot. The pilots speak in clear simple French and some English so do not be put off by the language barrier. Follow the instructions given and once inside the river you will wonder what you were worried about.

Once inside, Etel is a delightful place. It has clean blue water, a friendly marina, a pleasant town, spectacular beaches and an inland sea, La Mer d'Etel, almost as big as the Morbihan.

It is unfortunate that the inland sea lies beyond the bridge Pont Lorois, 1M upriver, with an airdraft of 9m. Beware that the current flows strongly near the bridge.

Semaphore station at Etel with the semaphore arrow in the vertical position meaning that entry is permitted. Note the tide running hard past the channel marker
Nick Chavasse

Semaphore station at Etel with the semaphore arrow in the horizontal position which means entry is prohibited *Nick Chavasse*

PILOTAGE

Etel Bar and the semaphore

During the approach it is essential to make contact with the semaphore station and until then to keep at least 0·5M off. The following visual signals are displayed:

- Arrow horizontal: no entry for any vessels
- Black ball: no entry for undecked vessels under 8m length
- Red flag: Not enough water or pilot not on duty.

Once VHF contact has been established, the pilot will give instructions in clear, simple French. If no VHF notify your estimated time of arrival by phone beforehand.

The pilot might also point the arrow right or left depending on the direction he wants the boat to turn, or leave it vertical to signal to maintain present course. (Beware that the vertical position is also the stowed position.)

The harbourmaster recommends crossing the bar between Port Tudy HW–0200 and –0100 (roughly Brest HW–0230 to –0130). Note that the flood stream will still be running strongly.

ETEL APPROACH AND ENTRANCE

By day The position of the deepest water across the bar varies considerably and can change overnight. However, it is usually best to approach with the distinctive 76m red and white radio mast at the back of the town on 020°.

The stream is weak outside the bar, but may reach six knots as the port-hand beacon is passed. Shortly after entering the river continue along the west side, leaving an unlit red beacon to port, a green buoy and beacon to starboard and a final red buoy to port. From there, keep in the centre of the channel where the water is deep.

By night Visitors must not attempt to enter at night.

Etel marina entrance with visitors' pontoon on right of entrance outside the marina and attached to the mole *Nick Chavasse*

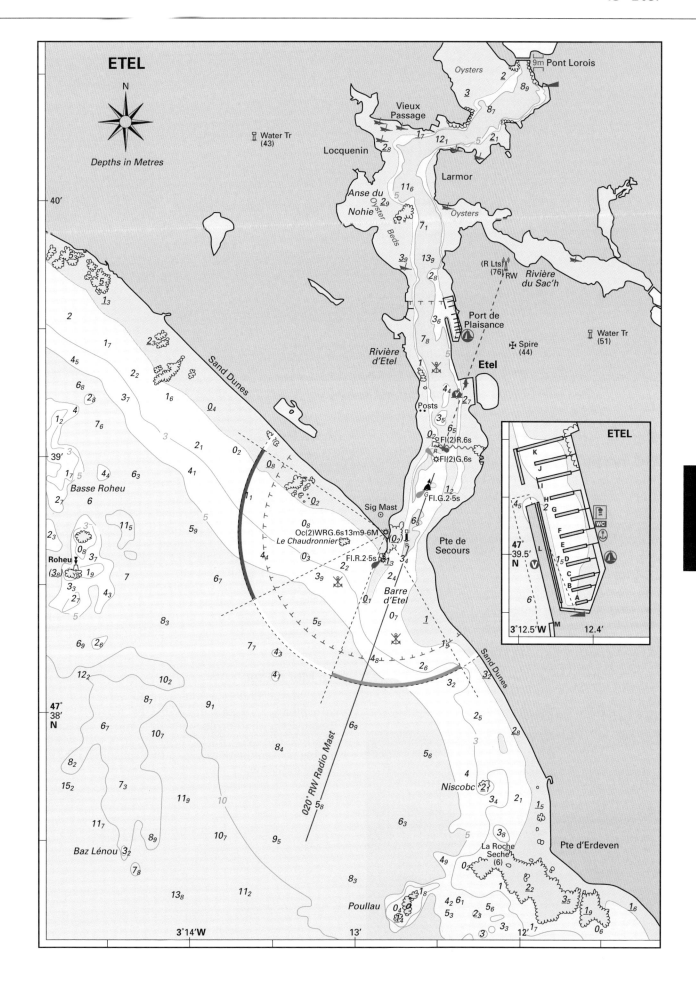

Approaching marina with entrance just aft of lifeboat *Nick Chavasse*

BERTHS AND ANCHORAGES

Etel marina

The marina is on the east bank and has a depth of 1·5m. The visitors' pontoon runs north-south attached to the outside of the mole protecting the entrance to the marina. You may be given a berth inside the marina. Beware that the current is much less strong once inside the marina.

⚓ Etel

Anchoring is no longer permitted in the river due to the large number of moorings and the very strong currents. In addition to the marina, there are six buoys 300m south of the marina adjacent to the Plan d'Eau de Mer, which are available for visitors for boats less than 10m.

Looking NW over marina towards entrance *Nick Chavasse*

ASHORE IN ETEL

There are limited repair facilities and fuel is only available in cans.

Etel is a thriving holiday resort with plenty of shops, bars and restaurants. There is a good supermarket, a fish market next to the marina and a street market on Tuesdays and on Fridays during the season.

The beaches on either side of the river mouth are interesting. They have a particularly rich sand dune flora and are also very popular with male nudists.

The tuna festival is on the second Sunday in August when the town gives itself over to fun and feasting. Bicycles may be borrowed from the capitainerie.

La Mer d'Etel

The Mer d'Etel is a like a small version of the Morbihan. It is not navigable by masted yachts because the road bridge only has 9m clearance and the tide runs very fast. However, it is well worth seeing it from the tourist boat that runs several times a day in season.

Larmor Baden *Nick Chavasse*

V. Quiberon Bay

Quiberon Bay is one of Europe's prime yacht racing centres. There are three large marinas – Haliguen, Trinité and Crouesty – and a dinghy-racing centre at Carnac. In addition, the Morbihan inland sea, which opens into Quiberon Bay, offers yet more good cruising.

It is said that the Morbihan has an island for every day of the year and the tides run so fast they can strip the galvanizing from an anchor chain. Neither statement is true, but there certainly are a lot of islands and the tide does run extremely fast, which makes the pilotage great fun and quite challenging. The Morbihan also has two very attractive medieval towns, Vannes and Auray. Vannes is particularly popular because it has a marina in the heart of town.

The chain of islands that protects Quiberon Bay also offers good cruising. Belle-Île, the 'beautiful island', is the largest with a couple of proper harbours and lots of anchorages; one of these has been described as the most beautiful in all France. The little islands of Houat and Hoëdic are also very attractive and perfect spots to anchor in good weather.

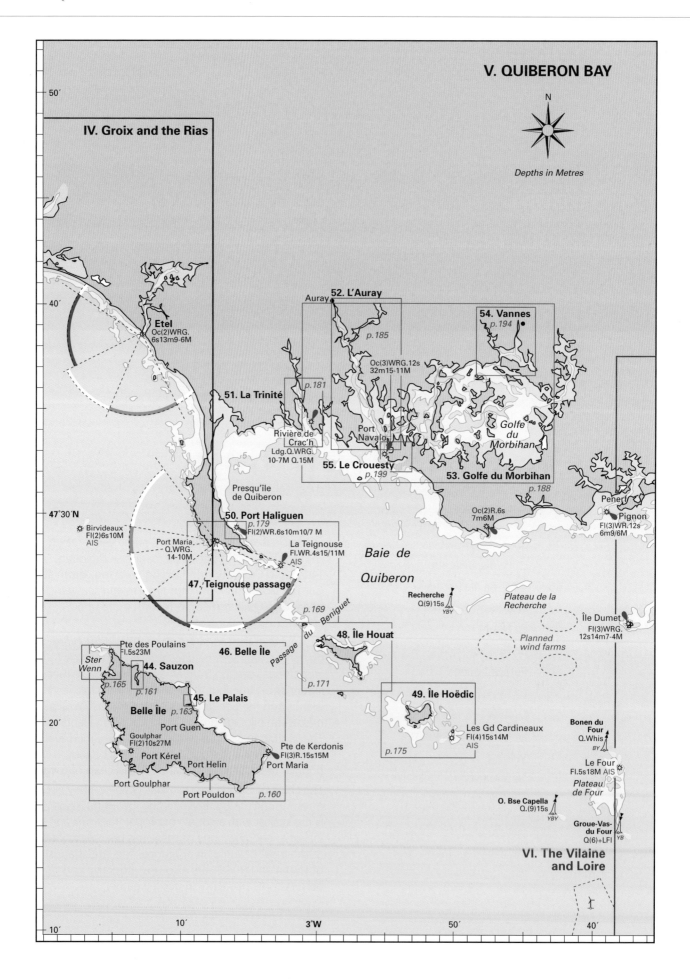

V. QUIBERON BAY

N

Depths in Metres

IV. Groix and the Rias

Etel
Oc(2)WRG.
6s13m9-6M

52. L'Auray

Auray

54. Vannes
p.194

p.185

Oc(3)WRG.12s
32m15-11M

51. La Trinité

p.181

Rivière de
Crac'h
Ldg.Q.WRG.
10-7M Q.15M

Port
Navalo

55. Le Crouesty
p.199

*Golfe
du
Morbihan*

53. Golfe du Morbihan
p.188

Penerf

Pignon
Fl(3)WR.12s
6m9/6M

Presqu'île
de Quiberon

47°30´N

Birvideaux
Fl(2)6s10M
AIS

50. Port Haliguen
p.179
Fl(2)WR.6s10m10/7 M

Oc(2)R.6s
7m6M

Port Maria
Q.WRG.
14-10M

La Teignouse
Fl.WR.4s15/11M
AIS

Baie de

47. Teignouse passage

Quiberon

p.169

Recherche
Q(9)15s
YBY

*Plateau de la
Recherche*

Île Dumet
Fl(3)WRG.
12s14m7-4M

Pte des Poulains
Fl.5s23M

46. Belle Île

48. Île Houat

*Planned
wind farms*

*Ster
Wenn*

44. Sauzon

p.165

p.161

p.171

45. Le Palais *p.163*

49. Île Hoëdic

Bonen du
Four
Q.Whis
BY

Belle Île

Port Guen

Goulphar
Fl(2)10s27M

Port Kérel

Port Helin

Port Goulphar

Port Pouldon

Pte de Kerdonis
Fl(3)R.15s15M

Port Maria

p.160

Les Gd Cardineaux
Fl(4)15s14M
AIS

p.175

Le Four
Fl.5s18M AIS

*Plateau
de Four*

O. Bse Capella
Q.(9)15s
YBY

Groue-Vas-
du Four
Q(6)+LFl
YB

**VI. The Vilaine
and Loire**

Quiberon Bay tidal streams

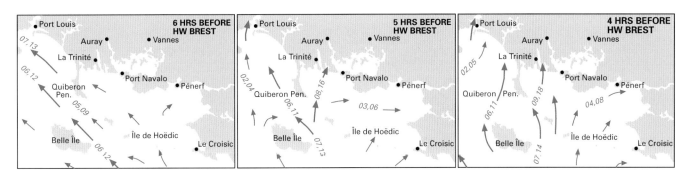

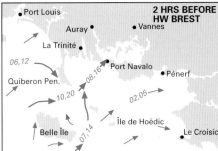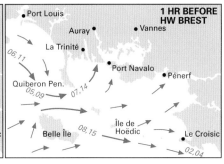

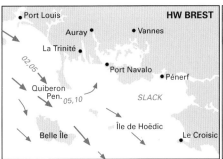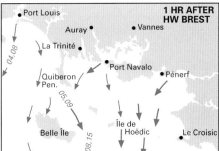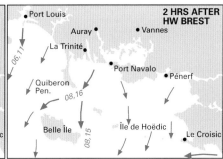

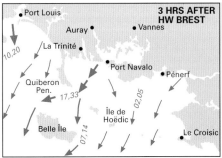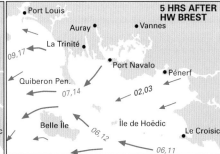

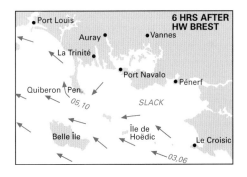

TIDAL STREAMS EXPLANATION
The figures shown against the arrows are the mean rates at neaps and springs in tenths of a knot.
Thus *07,15* - mean neaps rate *0·7* knots, mean springs rate *1·5* knots

44 Sauzon, Belle-Île

47°22'N 3°13'W

Shelter
Reasonable from S to W but exposed to N and vent solaire

Depth restrictions
2·6m on visitors' moorings
1·1m in outer harbour
Inner harbour dries 1·7m

Night entry Lit

HW time Brest HW –0015

Mean height of tide (m) Le Palais

HWS	HWN	LWN	LWS
5·1	4·1	1·9	0·8

Tidal stream Sauzon approaches
SE – Brest HW–0530 to –0130 (0·8kn)
Slack – Brest HW–0130 to +0030

NW – Brest HW+0030 to + 0530 (0·9kn)
Slack – Brest HW+0530 to –0530

Berthing
Visitors' buoys and drying harbour
Anchoring outside

Facilities
Cafés, restaurants, a few shops and bike hire

Charts
SHOM *7032, 7142*
Imray *C38*

Communications
VHF 9
☎ 02 97 31 63 40
www.sauzon.fr/tourisme-découverte/port/

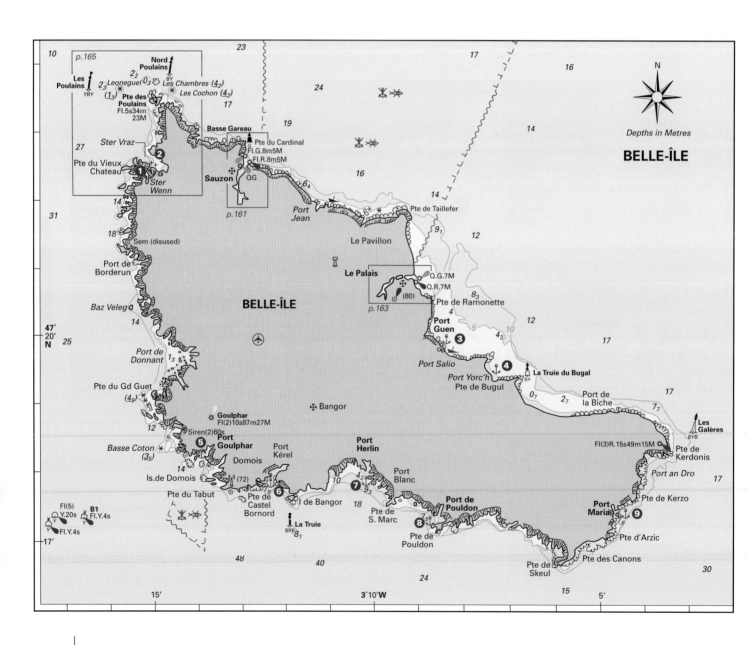

Belle-Île is 10M long and up to 5M wide, which makes it the largest island off the Brittany coast. It has two main harbours at Sauzon and Le Palais (*see page 163*), but there are also many attractive anchorages that can be used as day anchorages or overnight in good weather. The north coast anchorages are well protected from the southwest but mostly open to the north and the *brise de terre*. The south coast is rugged, deeply indented and has a profusion of rocks. There are plenty of opportunities to find an anchorage out of the weather. Some great beaches for a barbecue. Ster-Wenn is a favourite of the French. For anchorage details see *page 165*,

The jewel of Belle-Île

Sauzon is an attractive little harbour on the north coast of Belle-Île. It is well placed for exploring the magnificent northwest coast and not far from Le Palais by bicycle. The harbour is a popular spot with photographers as the sun goes down.

The inner harbour dries but it is well set up for visitors and offers a secure haven for vessels that can take the ground. The outer harbour has a number of visitors' buoys with room for about 40 boats. These are well sheltered from the south and west but exposed to the north and east and the *brise de terre*. There are also about 22 visitors' buoys outside the harbour in Port Belloc, north of the jetty.

PILOTAGE

Warning Anchoring is prohibited between the citadel at Le Palais and the approaches to Sauzon due to cables.

Sauzon approach and entrance

By day The harbour is easy to identify. The Gareau starboard hand beacon tower off the Pointe du Cardinal north of the entrance is distinctive. Low white lighthouses, with red and green tops, mark the ends of the two outer breakwaters. In addition, the taller main lighthouse, also with a green top, can be seen behind the breakwater lights.

The official transit aligns the two green-topped lighthouses on 205°. However, this need not be followed closely.

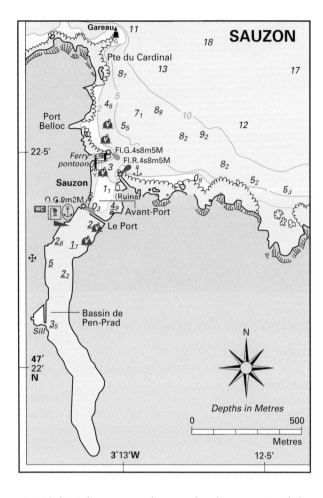

By night The approach uses the day transit of the pier head and main green light in line on 205°. Note that these lights are obscured by the Pointe du Cardinal when approaching from the northwest.

There is very little light from the shore so a powerful spotlight will be necessary to find and pick up a buoy.

The entrance to Sauzon harbour *Nick Chavasse*

Sauzon Harbour looking southwest. The inner visitors' buoys are the two rows of bow and stern moorings on the west side near the ferry berth. The drying harbour, through the gap in the breakwater, has space available for boats that can take the ground *Patrick Roach*

BERTHS AND ANCHORAGES

Outer visitors' buoys

There are 22 white visitors' buoys outside the outer north mole. These are suitable for boats up to 45ft and, with the harbourmaster's permission, it may be possible to use the larger buoys used by vedettes after they have departed for the night. Anchoring on the east side of the entrance is permitted when the mooring buoys are full.

Avant-Port inner visitors' buoys

Between the outer and inner moles on the east side there are some white buoys that are reserved for fishermen. On the west side are two rows of bow and stern moorings for boats up to 12·5m. When the harbour is crowded, up to eight yachts may be rafted between each pair of buoys.

Bassin de Pen-Prad inner harbour

The inner harbour dries to a firm sandy bottom. Boats able to take the ground may moor, secured bow and stern in the lines of red buoys inside the entrance, or anchor further up the harbour. It may also be possible to lie against a wall after consulting the harbourmaster.

Looking S at avant port and Bassin Pen-Brad *Nick Chavasse*

The creek is over 500m long and if there is a crowd near the entrance there is plenty of room higher up for those prepared to dry out for longer each tide.

ASHORE IN SAUZON

There is a tap at the root of the inner west jetty. Showers and toilets are on the west wall of the inner harbour, near the harbourmaster's office. There are hotels, restaurants, bars and food shops. Bicycles and scooters can be hired from a van in the carpark but walkers may prefer to explore the spectacular coast path.

Looking N at Sauzon outer visitors' moorings *Nick Chavasse*

45 Le Palais, Belle-Île

47°21'N 3°09'W

Shelter
Good in harbour, anchorage sheltered from SW

Depth restrictions
3·0m on visitors' moorings
1·7m or more in wet basin

Night entry Lit

HW time
Brest HW–0005 neaps, –0025 springs

Mean height of tide (m) Le Palais

HWS	HWN	LWN	LWS
5·1	4·0	1·9	0·7

Tidal stream Pte de Taillefer
SE – Brest HW–0530 to +0030 (1·1kn)
Slack – Brest HW+0030 to +0130
NW – Brest HW+0130 to –0530 (1·2kn)

Berthing
Visitors' buoys and wet basin
Anchorage outside harbour

Facilities
As for a busy tourist port

Charts
SHOM *7032, 7142*
Imray *C38*

Communications
VHF 9
☎02 97 31 42 90
www.lepalais.fr/Default/52-le-port.html

The capital of Belle-Île

Le Palais is the capital of Belle-Île and a good base for exploring this magnificent island. It is also the site of the citadel, a massive, star-shaped fort built by Vauban in the 18th century. It was thought to be invulnerable but the British took it in 1761. It was restored to France two years later in exchange for Menorca and Novia Scotia. Several Nova Scotian families settled on the island and introduced the potato some years before it became popular on the mainland.

Le Palais is the main ferry port for Belle-Île and it gets very crowded in summer. To add to the fun, the frequent ferries need to maintain quite a high speed while they manoeuvre. They don't have much room, so it is vital for other craft to keep out of their way.

PILOTAGE

Le Palais approach and entrance

By day The citadel is easy to identify and there are no dangers in the approach. Steer for the lighthouse with the green top on the end of the north jetty and keep a sharp lookout for the ferries. They enter and leave at speed and take up most of the channel. In the entrance, keep in the middle of the channel because there are dangers off both pier heads.

By night Steer for the lighthouse, flashing Q.G. and keep a sharp lookout for the unlit buoys near the entrance.

Entrance to Le Palais with Citadel on right *Nick Chavasse*

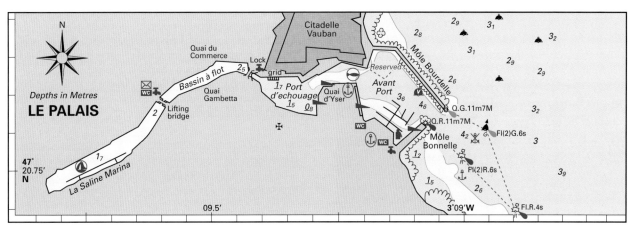

BERTHS AND ANCHORAGES

Avant Port (Outer harbour)

The outer harbour is well sheltered from the south and west. However, strong northeast winds cause seas to break over the breakwater and strong winds from any north or east direction can cause some swell to enter the harbour.

Yachts raft between bow and stern mooring buoys or between buoys and chains suspended from the breakwater wall. Either way, a dinghy is needed to get ashore. The moorings are subject to ferry wash so it is necessary to check that spreaders are clear of adjacent yachts. There are some plastic walk-ashore pontoons in the south corner.

Port d'échouage (Inner harbour)

It is possible to dry out in the inner harbour. Either moor bow to the north wall on either side of the grid, or alongside the quay if a space can be found. The bottom is foul in places so consult the harbourmaster. Note that the white stripes on the harbour walls reserve spaces for fishing boats and that anchoring is forbidden in the harbour.

Bassin à flot and La Saline marina

If it is possible to arrange to arrive close to HW, when the gate is open, it is certainly much more comfortable in the Bassin à Flot but it is more expensive. The gate to Bassin à Flot opens local HW-0130 to HW+0100 between the hours of 0600 and 2200. The opening times vary according to the tidal co-efficient so consult the harbourmaster for exact times. The lifting bridge, which gives access to the marina in Bassin de La Saline, is operated by the harbourmaster when required during the time the gate is open. In the wet dock, yachts raft up to a pontoon in 2·5m or there are finger berths in the marina.

⚓ Anchorage outside

Outside the harbour, anchor to the southeast of the south jetty in 3m, keeping well clear of the fairway. In offshore winds, this is safe and has good holding. Large mooring buoys have been placed east of the

Looking N at walk-ashore pontoons in S corner *Nick Chavasse*

Looking W in Bassin à flot *Nick Chavasse*

Visitors' moorings outside harbour near No 4 port hand *Nick Chavasse*

north pier for the use of local vedettes but, with the harbourmaster's permission, they can be used by visiting yachts after the vedettes have gone in the evening. There are also some smaller visitors' buoys to the south of the harbour entrance.

ASHORE IN LE PALAIS

Water, showers and toilets are available by the harbourmaster's office and in the wet basin. Fuel, by long hose, can be purchased with a card at the root of the south breakwater. There are haul-out facilities, marine and electrical engineers, and chandlery.

Le Palais is a bustling tourist resort with a wide range of restaurants, bars and shops. It is possible to hire bicycles and cars to explore the island.

The Vauban citadel is a museum and has fine views from the belvedere that runs around the central fortifications.

Warning If the wind is a strong northeasterly you will need good fenders properly positioned. Boats are packed in tightly in high season

46 Belle-Île anchorages

47°23′N 3°15′W

Shelter
All southern anchorages exposed to S and W

Night entry Not recommended

HW time Brest HW -0115

Tidal streams
Complex, strong at E and W ends of Belle Isle

Berthing Anchorages

Facilities Limited

Charts
SHOM 7032, 7142
Imray C38

Communications
www.brittanytourism.com
(search 'Belle Île')

Ster-Wenn and Ster-Vraz
(Port du Vieux Château)

'The most beautiful harbour in France'

Ster-Wenn is a beautiful fjord on the northwest coast of Belle-Île, about a mile south of Pointe des Poulains. The anchorage itself is perfectly sheltered except in strong onshore winds but the entrance (or exit) becomes a death trap in bad weather or heavy swell. It has been likened to a lobster pot: easy to get in but hard to get out. However, the French rate it as the most beautiful harbour in France so it is usually crowded. At the first hint of bad weather or swell, it is essential to get out.

The directions and plan should be used with caution because the largest-scale published chart is too small a scale to show much detail. The names Pointe Dangéreuse and Pointe Verticale are unofficial but they are appropriate.

PILOTAGE

Ster-Wenn approach and entrance

By day Coming from the north the dangers off the Pointe des Poulains must be avoided. The completely safe route goes outside Basse Occidentale des Poulains west cardinal. The Port du Vieux Château is divided into two parts: the main inlet, Ster-Vraz, with a smaller inlet, Ster-Wenn, opening up on its south side. Ster-Vraz is 400m wide and 900m long; Ster-Wenn is only 50m wide and 500m long.

The entrance to Ster-Vraz is quite hard to locate because there are several inlets that look similar from seaward but closer-to it is quite distinctive. The north side is encumbered with rocks as much as 300m offshore and should not be approached too closely. However, the south side, shown on the plan as Pointe Verticale, is steep to and forms a cliff that makes identification easy.

Do not cut the corner on the north side of Ster-Vraz but start from a position at least 0·5M offshore and approach on about 120°. Both the tidal stream and the swell will weaken as Stêr-Vraz is entered.

Coming from the south, the cliffs along the southern shore of Ster-Vraz are steep to. However, unless another yacht is entering or leaving, Ster-Vraz will not be seen until it opens up, quite dramatically, to starboard. When it is fully open, alter course sharply to starboard and enter.

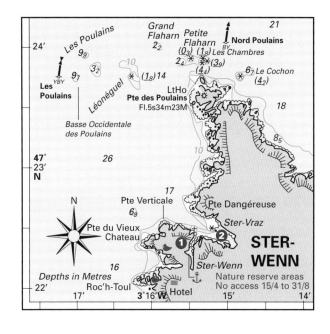

The Port du Vieux Château looking southeast.
The port is divided into two parts: the main inlet Stêr-Vraz, and a smaller inlet, Ster-Wenn *Patrick Roach*

Numbered anchorages are shown on pages 160 and 165

1. ⚓ Ster-Wenn

47°22'·29N 3°15'·23W

Ster-Wenn is deep near the entrance and shoals gradually up to a sandy beach after a small fork. A cable is slung across the inlet to provide moorings for small fishing boats and may be used to prevent swinging in the confined space. Iron rings are set into the rock above the high-water line on the east side. The west side is now a bird sanctuary with access prohibited. There are no rings on the west side. Drop anchor in the middle of the inlet (1·5m or more) and take a stern line ashore to one of the rings or to the cable. The holding is good, but make sure that the anchor is well dug in before going ashore. Do not allow other yachts to raft to you with slack cables and shore lines if you are to survive a *brise de terre* during the night. Also, in the event of a *brise de terre*, check that the anchor is not dragging.

The water is smooth in all winds except northwest. But surge does enter when there is a heavy onshore wind, and the anchorage becomes dangerous.

2. ⚓ Ster-Vraz day anchorage

47°22'·34N 3°15'·00W

If Ster-Wenn is overcrowded, there is a day anchorage further up Ster-Vraz but for use in calm weather only. Keep to starboard and look out for rocks as the beach is approached. Most of the rocks occupy the northern half of the inlet.

ASHORE IN STER-WENN

There is a dinghy landing on the beach and a path leading up the valley to the road. Turn left for the 3M walk to Sauzon or right to visit the Grotte de l'Apothicairerie (0·75M). There is a nature reserve information centre and a café above the cave.

NORTH COAST ANCHORAGES

These anchorages all require a large-scale chart.

3. ⚓ Port Guen and Port Salio

47°19'·84N 3°08'·19W

Protected from the south and west but exposed to the northeast, this bay is 1M east of Le Palais. There arc no dangers in the approach but it is necessary to tuck in well to minimise the swell and ferry wash.

Ster-Wenn anchorage *Bobby Lawes*

Ster-Wenn raft showing lines ashore *Peter Bruce*

Port Salio *Nick Chavasse*

Port Yorc'h *Nick Chavasse*

Port Goulphar with lighthouse in centre *Nick Chavasse*

4. ⚓ Port Yorc'h

47°19'·65N 3°07'·23W

Protected from the west through south to southeast but exposed to the northeast, this bay is 1·5M east of Le Palais. There are a number of local moorings but it is possible to anchor outside them to the west or off the beach.

SOUTH COAST ANCHORAGES

These anchorages all require a large-scale chart.

5. ⚓ Port Goulphar

47°18'·11N 3°13'·72W

Sheltered from the north but completely open to the south, Port Goulphar is a mini-fjord close to Goulphar lighthouse. There are a lot of rocks in the entrance. Approach the bay with Goulphar lighthouse on 015°, which will put it a bit to the right of the hotel on the cliff top. Hold this course through the outer rocks and bear to starboard into the bay. Anchor outside the local moorings. A French cruising guide classifies Port Goulphar as a *mouillage gastronomique* because of the excellent restaurant in the hotel.

6. ⚓ Port Kérel

47°17'·79N 3°12'·22W

Sheltered from the north but completely open to the south, Port Kérel is a very attractive little bay about 1M east of Port Goulphar. Approach from due south starting from a position west of La Truie isolated danger. Locals anchor in the fjords but the easiest spot is off the beach in the northeast part of the bay.

7. ⚓ Port Herlin

47°17'·94N 3°12'·22W

Sheltered from northwest to northeast but completely open to the south, Port Herlin is a fairly wide bay about 1·5M east of Port Kérel. Approach from due south to avoid the rocks on either side of the bay. Anchor almost 0·25M from the shore because of the rocky foreshore.

8. ⚓ Port de Pouldon

47°17'·29N 3°08'·58W

Sheltered from north through east, Port de Pouldon is 2M west of Pointe du Skeul. Approach from the west-southwest and anchor close to the north side of the headland. There are drying rocks just off the north side of the bay.

9. ⚓ Port Maria

47°17'·56N 3°04'·38W

Protected from west to north, Port Maria is an attractive little creek between Pointe de Kerdonis and Pointe du Skeul. The tide can be strong along the ends of Belle-Île so approach with caution from the southeast. Port Maria is quite narrow and it is best to keep in the middle steering 315°. It is possible to leave at night but not to enter.

Port Herlin anchorage *Nick Chavasse*

47 Teignouse Passage

47°26'N 3°06'W

Hazards
Strong tide over uneven seabed
Rough water
Many well-marked rocks

Depth restrictions
The channel is deep

Night entry Well lit

HW time
Brest HW+0015 neaps, −0030 springs

Mean height of tide (m) Le Palais

HWS	HWN	LWN	LWS
5·1	4·1	1·9	0·8

Tidal stream Teignouse passage
NE – Brest HW−0600 to +0030 (1·8kn)
SW – Brest HW+0030 to +0600 (2·1kn)

Charts
SHOM *7032, 7141*
Imray *C38*

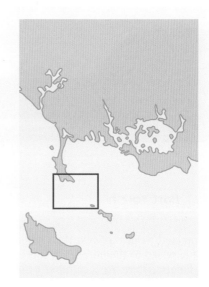

Route through the reefs into Quiberon Bay

There are several passages into Quiberon Bay. The Teignouse is a well-marked big ship passage that can be used by day or night. It is 0·25M wide and there is deep water either side of the marked channel.

The other passages through the Quiberon reefs are described below under Houat and Hoëdic. There are also many shortcuts that can be found using a large-scale chart.

PORT MARIA

This harbour at the southern end of Presqu'île de Quiberon is the ferry port for Belle-Île and yachts are not welcome so it will not be described further here. However, there is an anchorage sheltered in NW-E winds off the beach. Anchor in 3·5m off the beach with the red breakwater light bearing just S of W and distance of about 300m. Port Maria, Quiberon has been chosen to become a new ferry port servicing Belle-Île, Houat and Hoëdic. A railway station is being built to aid connectivity. It is expected that this project will be completed in 2024.

> **Warning** The tides run strongly in the channel and the seabed is very uneven. As a result, surprisingly steep seas build up even with only a moderate wind against the tide. If possible take it at slack water and treat it with great respect if there is any swell running.

Teignouse passage from southwest

By day Bring the white lighthouse on La Teignouse to bear 036°. This line leads south of Goué Vaz Sud south cardinal buoy, which must not be confused with Goué Vas Nord north cardinal buoy, situated 0·5M to the northwest. Steer 036°, leaving Goué Vas Sud south cardinal to port, Basse du Milieu starboard hand buoy to starboard and Goué Vas Est port hand buoy to port.

When this last buoy is abeam alter course to 068°. The official line is St-Gildas, 10M away, on 068°, but it is only necessary to leave Basse Nouvelle port hand buoy to port and northeast Teignouse starboard hand buoy to starboard.

La Teignouse lighthouse *Nick Chavasse*

By night Enter the white sector (033°-039°) of La Teignouse light before Port Maria main light turns from white to green. Steer in this sector between the buoys. When between Basse du Milieu starboard hand and Goué Vas Est port hand alter course to 068° to pass between the Basse Nouvelle port hand buoy and northeast Teignouse starboard hand buoy.

Teignouse passage from east or north

By day Reverse the above courses.

By night Use the white sector of Port Haliguen light to keep off the dangers between Haliguen and La Teignouse light. Then enter the Teignouse Passage between the Basse Nouvelle port hand buoy and NE Teignouse starboard hand buoy. Steer 248° to pass between Basse du Milieu starboard hand buoy and Goué Vas port hand buoy. Steer out on 216° using the white sector of La Teignouse light. When Port Maria main light turns from green to white all dangers are passed.

> **Warning** Beware swimming on the southern tip of Presqu'île de Quiberon, due to strong currents.

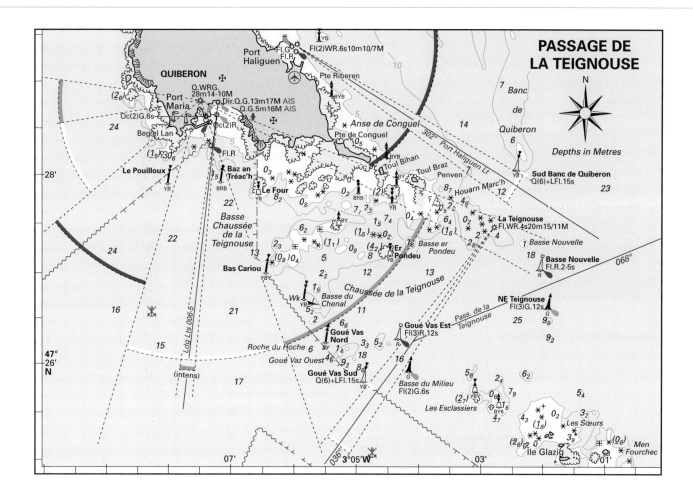

PASSAGE DE LA TEIGNOUSE

Depths in Metres

Port Maria and beach anchorage, and the Teignouse Passage looking southeast.
The passage opens the way to the Morbihan and the Vilaine estuary.
It is bordered on either side by many reefs and the tides run strongly *Patrick Roach*

48 Île Houat

47°23'N 2°58'W

Shelter
Good except from N/NE at Port St Gildas

Hazards
Strong tides and unmarked rocks
Difficult to leave at night

Night entry Only lit to Port St-Gildas

HW time Brest HW –0010

Mean height of tide (m) Île de Houat

HWS	HWN	LWN	LWS
5·1	4·0	1·9	0·7

Tidal stream Beniguet channel
NE – Brest HW–0530 to –0030 (1·5kn)
Slack – Brest HW –0030 to +0030
SW – Brest HW +0030 to +0530 (1·3kn)
Slack – Brest HW+0530 to –0530

Berthing
Dumbell buoys and anchorages

Facilities
Very limited but good beaches,
walking and wild flowers

Charts
SHOM *7032, 7143*
Imray *C38*

Communications
www.mairiedehouat.fr/la-mairie/
   presentation-de-l-ile
☏ 02 97 30 66 42

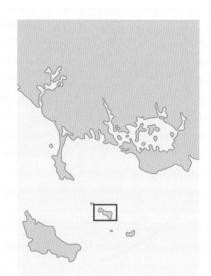

The best beach in Brittany

Houat, pronounced to rhyme with '*that*', is one of the gems of South Brittany. This strangely shaped island is about 2M long and has spectacular beaches, wonderful walking, a profusion of wild flowers and very little else. The small harbour of St-Gildas is generally full of fishing boats and the anchorages are exposed either to the sea breeze or the *brise de terre*. Despite this, Houat is extremely popular and the anchorage off the best beach, Tréac'h-er-Gourhed, can be uncomfortably crowded. However, don't be put off. A visit to Houat in good weather is likely to be the high point of a South Brittany holiday.

Port St-Gildas is named after St-Gildas de Rhuys, a 6th century British missionary who established a monastery close to the entrance of the Golfe du Morbihan and who died on the island (*see more under Le Crouesty*).

Plenty of opportunities to anchor off Houat (Duck) Island. Take account of the prevailing weather and the *brise de terre* to identify the perfect anchorage. Explore the island on foot as it is one of Brittany's gems.

Houat looking southeast.
The harbour and anchorage of Port St-Gildas is shown in the bottom of the picture. The wide curving bay of Tréac'h er Gourhed is at the top left *Patrick Roach*

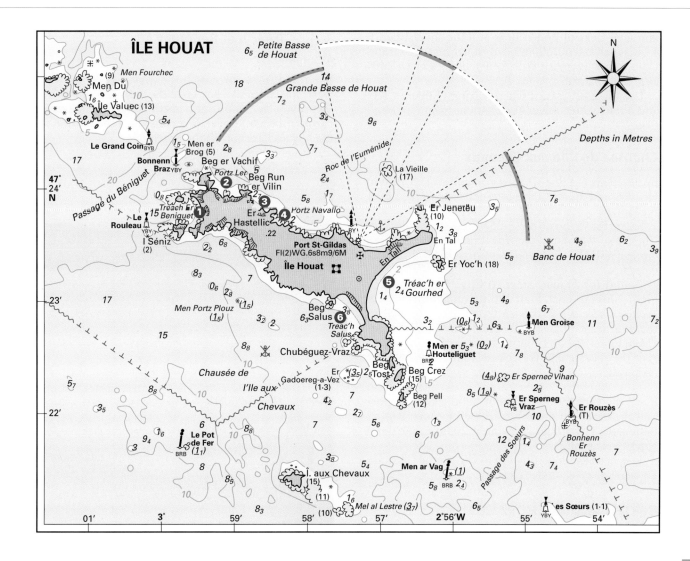

PILOTAGE

Port St-Gildas approach

By day The easiest approach is from the north and east. If possible come down with the ebb stream but, if planning to enter the harbour, do not arrive too near low water because manoeuvring room is much reduced.

From the north steer towards the east end of the island. About 0·6M north-northeast of St-Gildas is a conspicuous rock, La Vieille (17m high), and north-northeast of that is a mussel bed marked by buoys. Once La Vieille is identified it is easy to locate the harbour, which bears 200° from it. Pass either side of the mussel bed. La Vieille is clean to the north and east but to the south the shoals extend about 200m.

La Vieille in the approaches to St-Gildas *Nick Chavasse*

From the east, the outer northeast rock of Houat, Er Jenetëu (16m high), is distinctive. It can be passed at a distance of 100m but there are rocks in the direct line to the harbour so keep well out before turning for St-Gildas.

By night Green sectors of the breakwater light cover La Vieille and the dangers to the east and west of the harbour. Approach in either of the white sectors and anchor off the harbour. The mussel bed is in the green sector of the breakwater light, and the buoys on its north side are lit.

The Béniguet Passage

By day This is an easy daylight passage, immediately to the northwest of Houat. It is the shortest route between Belle-Île and Port St-Gildas or the Vilaine. The strong tide and uneven seabed can cause steep seas in wind against tide conditions so take it close to slack water.

Coming from the southwest, leave Le Rouleau west cardinal beacon tower 600m to starboard and make good 030° to pass between Le Grand Coin east cardinal beacon tower and Bonen Braz west cardinal beacon tower. Keep closer to Le Grand Coin tower and well clear of Bonen Braz and the shoals (depth 1·5m) that extend 600m north-northeast. Le Grand Coin tower in transit with Le Palais citadel on 240° clears these shoals.

Use the 240° transit when leaving Quiberon Bay and alter to 210° when about 400m from Le Grand Coin.

Chausée de L'Île aux Chevaux

By day This is a fine-weather route from Le Palais to Hoëdic, and an attractive alternative to Le Beniguet for Houat.

Steer for a position 0·25M north of Île aux Chevaux, watching out for Pot de Fer isolated danger and the rocks on the north side of Île aux Chevaux.

Bound for Houat, steer to leave Beg Pell (12m high) 200m to port. Don't go too much further out because there is a rock (depth 0·6m) about 0·5M to the southeast of Beg Pell. Then leave the Men er Houteliguet tower 100m to starboard. A detour to visit the spectacular Tréac'h er Gourhed beach may be in order.

Proceeding to Port St-Gildas, cross the bay and leave the rock Er Yoc'h (18m high) 200m to port and the beach on point En Tal well to port. Round Er Jenetëu (10m high), leaving it 200m to port and enter Port St-Gildas.

Instructions for getting to Hoëdic via the Chevaux Passage are given under Hoëdic.

BERTHS AND ANCHORAGES

Port Saint-Gildas

Port St-Gildas is so small that a yacht over 10m is unlikely to find a berth. Moor fore and aft on two dumbbell trots in centre of the harbour or bow-to along breakwater wall. Do not obstruct the access for the ferry. If the harbour is full, anchor in the bay to the east where there are also some visitors' buoys but these are rather close and not suitable for boats over 12m. This anchorage and the visitors' buoys are open to the northeast and the *brise de terre* and suffer from ferry wash.

1. ⚓ Tréac'h er Béniguet

47°23'·79N 2°59'·62W

Sheltered from the east but exposed to south and west, this attractive bay is on the west end of Houat. Approach from a position north of Le Rouleau west cardinal beacon tower. Steer east into the middle of the bay and anchor off the beach.

Tréac'h er Beniguet *Nick Chavasse*

Looking out from Port St Gildas visitors' moorings towards the anchorage *Nick Chavasse*

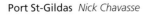

Port St-Gildas *Nick Chavasse*

2. ⚓ Portz Ler

47°24'·02N 2°59'·26W

Sheltered from the south but open to north and east, this bay is at the west end of the north coast. The approach from the north is straightforward. There are two distinct bays and it is important to anchor in one of them and not on the rocks between them. It is easy to leave at night.

3. ⚓ Hastellic

47°23'·89N 2°58'·74W

This bay, sheltered from south and west but open to the north and east, is between Beg Run er Vilin and Er Hastellic. The approach is straightforward from the northeast and it is easy to leave at night.

4. ⚓ Portz Navallo

47°23'·76N 2°58'·42W

Sheltered from south and west but open to the north and east, this bay is just east of Er Hastellic. The approach is simple from the northeast and it is easy to leave at night.

5. ⚓ Tréac'h er Gourhed

47°23'·17N 2°56'·19W

Sheltered from the west but horribly exposed to the *brise de terre*, this bay on the east end of Houat offers one of the finest beaches in South Brittany. It can be approached from the north or east by keeping clear of Er Jenetëu, En Tal and Er Yoc'h or from the southwest using the Chevaux passage. Anchor wherever there is a space. It is important to plan for a night departure because the anchorage is famous for its *brise de terre* pyjama parties, with yachts rolling from beam to beam and dragging all over the place.

6. ⚓ Tréac'h Salus

47°22'·81N 2°57'·50W

Protected from the north and east and the *brise de terre* but exposed to the south and west, this magnificent beach is the other side of the headland from Tréac'h er Gourhed. It can be approached

Portz Ler anchorage *Nick Chavasse*

directly from the southwest but from the north or Tréac'h er Gourhed it is necessary to round the many dangers off southeast Houat. Anchor as close to the beach as draught permits. Shelter is often a little better at the west end but there is a wreck with a doubtful position marked on the chart.

Tréac'h Salus is exposed to the sea breeze and is often less crowded than Tréac'h er Gourhed. It is better protected from the *brise de terre* so is often a better place to spend the night.

ASHORE IN HOUAT

There is water from the public tap in the centre of the pretty village of Saint-Gildas or at the showers on the pier. The shops can supply simple needs, but they are limited. There are some bars, a medical centre, and a post office.

The island is noted for its succession of wild flowers: roses in May, carnations in June, yellow immortelles in July and sand lilies in August. There are wonderful beaches on the north side of En Tal, at Tréac'h er Gourhed in the east, Tréac'h Salus in the southeast and Tréac'h er Beniguet in the west.

Tréac'h er Gourhed *Nick Chavasse*

49 Île Hoëdic

47°20'N 2°52'W

Shelter
Generally good except in N/NE
strong winds

Hazards
Strong tides and unmarked rocks
Difficult to leave at night

Night entry
Only lit to L'Argol

HW time
Brest HW–0020

Mean height of tide (m) Hoëdic

HWS	HWN	LWN	LWS
5·1	4·0	1·9	0·7

Tidal stream Sœurs channel
NE – Brest HW–0530 to –0030 (1·4kn)
Slack – Brest HW–0030 to +0030
SW – Brest HW+0030 to +0530 (1·3kn)
Slack – Brest HW+0530 to –0530

Berthing
Visitors' buoys, pontoon and anchorages

Facilities
Very limited

Charts
SHOM *7032, 7143*
Imray *C38*

Communications
www.hoedic.net/decouvrir-idee-sejour-
  insolite-bretagne/histoire
☏ 02 97 58 30 60
☏ 06 32 83 08 87

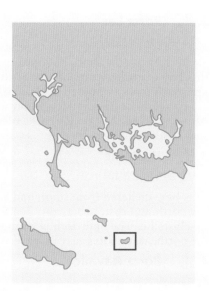

Picture postcard island

Hoëdic is 1M long and 0·5M wide and lies 4M
southeast of Houat. Argol, the main harbour, is on
the north side. It is very small and yachts may prefer
to lie outside. Port de la Croix in the south dries but
in fine weather it is an attractive anchorage.
Wonderful walks across the island with no traffic to
worry about. Worth visiting Hoëdic Fort and the
museum. Some good bars and restaurants.

PILOTAGE

Argol approach from north and east

By day From the north make directly for the island
passing either side of La Chèvre isolated danger.
From Houat, be sure to leave Men Groise east
cardinal beacon and Er Rouzès east cardinal buoy to
starboard. From the east give Beg Lagad a clearance
of at least 400m.

By night Approach in one of the white sectors of the
harbour light. Green sectors cover La Chèvre and
the dangers east and west of the approach.

Argol via the Soeurs Passage

By day Start from a position about 0·3M west of Er
Palaire west cardinal beacon tower. Steer about 015°
to leave Les Soeurs west cardinal beacon tower 200m
to starboard. Avoid Men er Guer and Bonen Bras
shoals by keeping Er Spernec Bras south cardinal
beacon tower open to the left of Men Groise east
cardinal beacon.

Bound for Hoëdic, do not let Les Soeurs west
cardinal beacon tower bear more than 255° until
Pointe du Vieux Château, bearing 175°, hides the
west side of Hoëdic. This is necessary to avoid the
shoals north and west of Point du Vieux-Château.

Bound north, leave Er Rouzès east cardinal buoy
at least 200m to port.

Argol via the Chevaux Passage

By day Start from a position about 0·25M north of
Île aux Chevaux. Steer due east to leave Men er Vag
isolated danger buoy well to starboard. Continue on
the same course, keeping well north of Les Soeurs
west cardinal beacon tower until the Pointe du Vieux
Château, bearing 175°, hides the west side of
Hoëdic. It is then safe to steer for Argol.

Take care to avoid the unmarked rocks and
shallow patch between Les Soeurs west cardinal
beacon tower and the northwest headland of
Hoëdic.

Port de la Croix approaches

A large-scale chart is required.

By day From the north pass outside the Plateau des
Cardinaux and then steer southwest until the
Madavoar south cardinal tower beacon is in line with
the right-hand edge of the fort on 320°. Approach
Port de la Croix on this transit until close to
Madavoar. Then make for a point just south of Men
Cren starboard hand beacon tower. A slight curve to
the north is needed to avoid the rocks southeast of
Men Cren.

With enough rise of tide it is possible to pass
inside the Plateau des Cardinaux. This hazard is a
chain of unmarked drying rocks east of Madavoar.
Those closest to the Madavoar beacon dry 0·8m but
those further out dry 2·3m. If there is enough water
to pass safely over the inner rocks, the outer ones
can be avoided by staying within 400m of Medavoar
beacon.

This shortcut passes close between unmarked
drying rocks east of Madavoar tower.

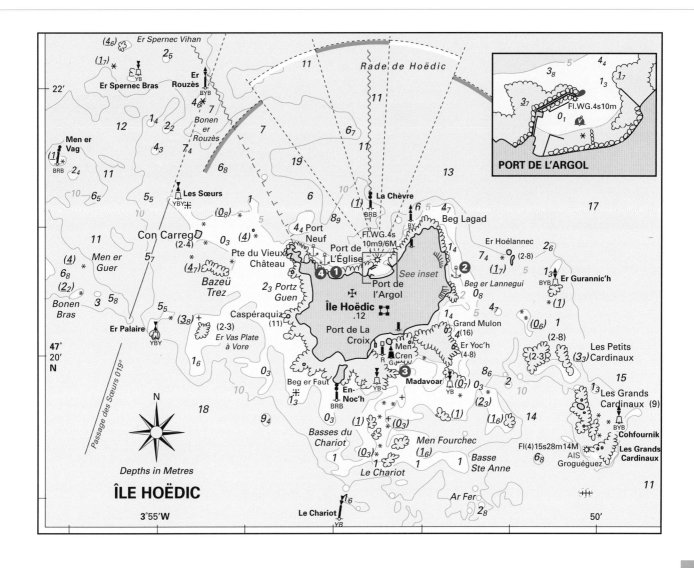

ÎLE HOËDIC

Depths in Metres

3°55'W

47° 20' N

Passage des Sœurs 019°

PORT DE L'ARGOL

Fl.WG.4s10m

Argol harbour looking south with Port de la Croix beyond *Patrick Roach*

Port l'Argol with yachts rafted on visitors' buoys in middle *Nick Chavasse*

BERTHS AND ANCHORAGES

Port de l'Argol

Argol harbour has room for 20 to 30 visiting boats in settled weather. Beware the rocks close to the E pierhead on entry.

In the harbour, there are three visitors' buoys where yachts can raft. This involves attaching a bow line to a large visitors' buoy and boats rafting alongside to form a sunflower effect of boats circled around a buoy. The boats on the innermost one dry out at LW. There may also be room for some yachts bow to the principal breakwater and stern to a buoy at its eastern end. Alternatively, anchor just inside the entrance to port.

It is usually preferable to anchor outside the harbour but be sure to keep clear of the ferries. There is another anchorage further to the west, off the beach near the old lifeboat slip.

⚓ 1. Anchorage off old lifeboat slip

47°20'·62N 2°52'·94W

Sheltered from W-S-E. Beware submarine cable marked by yellow special marks.

⚓ 2. Beg er Lannegui

47°20'·35N 2°51'·67W

Sheltered from northwest to west, there is a secluded anchorage on the east side of Hoëdic just south of Beg er Lannegui. Approach from about 0·5M offshore and anchor on sand, avoiding any patches of weed. It is only possible to stay overnight in perfect conditions. The rock shown as Beg er Lannegi on the northern side of Grand Mulon Bay, on the eastern side of Hoëdic shows at 2·0m of tide, rather than 1·7 shown on chart. Beware uncharted rocky shoal at 47°20'·34N 02°51'·61W. Recorded depth is 0·8m and NOT 2·8m as recorded on most charts.

⚓ 3. Port de la Croix

The harbour dries 1·0m and is often crowded so it is usually necessary to anchor outside. The shelter is good from the northwest to northeast but the anchorage is very exposed to any wind or swell from the south.

Anchor south of Men Cren tower or further in at neaps. Do not go in too close to the shore because there are some short posts set in concrete.

Anchorage 0·3M W of Port de l'Argol off old lifeboat slip *Nick Chavasse*

Visitors moored at end of pontoon and rafted in middle of Port de l'Argol *Nick Chavasse*

Beg er Lannegui anchorage *Nick Chavasse*

Port de la Croix drying harbour on S coast *Nick Chavasse*

⚓ 4. Port de l'Église

47°20'·66N 2°53'·14W

Lovely anchorage with beach but beware submarine cables to north off Port Neuf.

ASHORE ON HOËDIC

Hoëdic has even fewer facilities than Houat but there is a small hotel, a food shop and some bars and crêperies. There is also a primitive shower and toilet block with a fresh-water tap near the harbour. A museum in the fort gives interesting insights into life on the island in the past, including an exhibition of the 1759 Battle of Quiberon Bay, known in France as L'Engagement des Cardinaux.

Port de l'Église *Nick Chavasse*

50 Port Haliguen

47°29'N 3°06'W

Shelter Excellent

Night entry Lit

HW time
Brest HW-0005

Mean height of tide (m) Haliguen

HWS	HWN	LWN	LWS
5·3	4·2	2·0	0·8

Tidal stream Haliguen approaches
NW – Brest HW–0530 to –0230 (0·5kn)
Slack – Brest HW–0230 to +0030
SE – Brest HW+0030 to +0530 (0·6kn)
Slack – Brest HW+0530 to –0530

Berthing Marina

Facilities
Good marina facilities. Shopping is
0·5M away

Charts
SHOM *7032, 7141*
Imray *C39*

Communications
VHF 9
Marina ☎ 02 97 50 20 56
Yacht club ☎ 02 97 29 53 61

Large modern marina on the Quiberon peninsula

Port Haliguen is the marina for Quiberon. It is pleasant with excellent facilities. There is a good beach nearby but Quiberon town and the magnificent Côte Sauvage are on the other side of the peninsula.

Looking N at disused lighthouse, vieux port on its left and port entrance beyond *Nick Chavasse*

Entrance to Port Haliguen *Nick Chavasse*

Looking S with entrance to E basin on left and fuel pontoon straight ahead in W basin *Nick Chavasse*

Looking north over reception pontoon in Bassin Ouest towards entrance *Nick Chavasse*

PILOTAGE

Port Haliguen approach and entrance

By day The approach from the south is easy. Pass midway between La Teignouse lighthouse and the Sud Banc de Quiberon south cardinal buoy on a course of 305°, leaving Port Haliguen south cardinal buoy to starboard.

Enter between the breakwaters and turn to port. The visitors' pontoon runs along the inside of the jetty running north/south from the shore.

By night Approach in one of the white sectors of Port Haliguen Marina light or in the white 246°-252° sector of Port Maria light. Keep a lookout for unlit buoys and avoid the protective spur off the east breakwater head on entering.

BERTHS AND ANCHORAGES

Port Haliguen marina

Anchoring is not permitted in the harbour. Visitors are ususally directed to the east basin following major refurbishment. Floating pontoons for very large yachts may be available in the west basin. If the visitors' berths are full, go to the reception pontoon. It is opposite the fuel pontoon in the west basin.

ASHORE IN PORT HALIGUEN

Port Haliguen has all the facilities of a major marina. There is a fuel pontoon, slip, crane, travel-lift, engineers, and a yacht club. Bread and limited shopping is available in the port. A 15-minute walk along the road to Quiberon finds a large supermarket with fish and oysters on sale outside. Quiberon town is about 1M away. It has all the facilities of a sizeable market town including a good

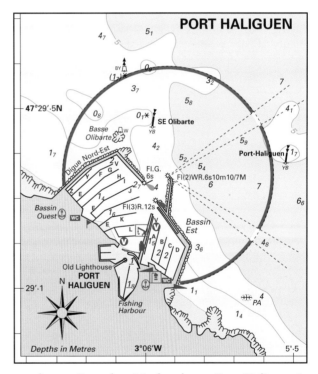

market on Saturday. Market day at Port Haliguen is Wednesday. There are connections by bus, train and plane to all parts. There is a pleasant beach just outside the marina.

⚓ Port d'Orange

47°31'·32N 3°07'·37W

Sheltered from the west but open to the east and the *brise de terre*, Port d'Orange is a small drying harbour 2·25M north of Port Haliguen. Approaching from the south, keep well offshore to avoid the dangers along the east coast of Quiberon. Approach from the southwest and anchor off the pier.

51 La Trinité

47°35'N 3°01'W

Shelter
Excellent except at HW in strong S/SW winds

Hazards
Marked and unmarked rocks on E side
of approach

Night entry Lit but intricate

HW time
Brest HW+0005

Mean height of tide (m) Haliguen

HWS	HWN	LWN	LWS
5·3	4·3	2·1	0·8

Tidal stream
Fairly weak and complex in the bay; up to
3kn in the river

Berthing
Marina

Facilities
All facilities of a major yachting centre
and busy town

Charts
SHOM *7032, 7141*
Imray *C39*

Communications
VHF 9
Marina ① 02 97 55 71 49
www.la-trinite-sur-mer.fr

Major yachting centre

La Trinité is a flourishing oyster river and one of the most important sailing centres in the Bay of Biscay. It is a pleasant place and a perfect base for cruising or racing. The town has excellent sailing facilities and plenty of bars, restaurants and shops.

PILOTAGE

La Trinité approach and entrance

By day La Trinité can be identified by a wooded hill to the west and a lighthouse on the skyline to the east. Approach from the south, steer for the lighthouse until Le Petit Trého port hand buoy is identified. This buoy marks the outer dangers on the west side of the entrance.

From the south or southeast leave the conspicuous island of Méaban and Buissons de Méaban south cardinal buoy to starboard.

The river is entered between Mousker rock (4·5m high), painted white on top and Le Petit Trého port hand buoy. The channel is well marked by buoys.

Approach to the marina at La Trinité *Nick Chavasse*

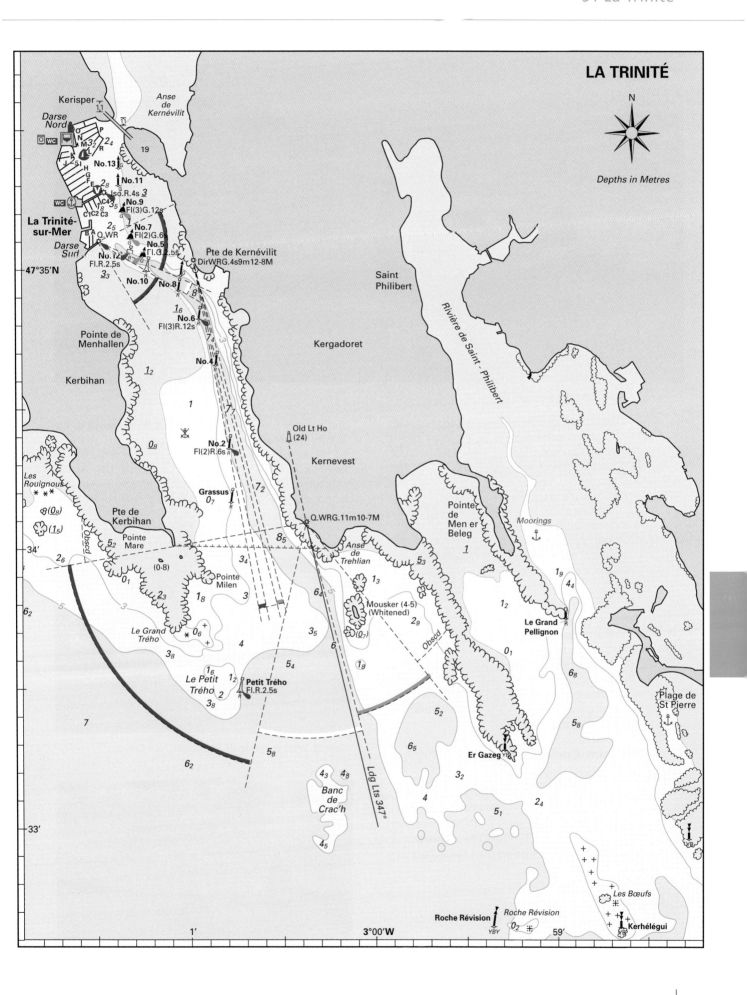

LA TRINITÉ

N

Depths in Metres

Kerisper

Anse de Kernévilit

Darse Nord

WC
O P
N
M 3₂ 2₄
L
K
J 5I H
G
F E 2₈
D
C4 3₅
WC
C1 C2 C3

No.13
No.11
Iso.R.4s 3
No.9
Fl(3)G.12s

La Trinité-sur-Mer

Darse Sud

2₅ 1 No.7 Q.WR Fl(2)G.6s
B A
No.5 Fl.G.2.5s
No.12
Fl.R.2.5s 3₃
No.10 No.8

19

Anse de Kernévilit

Pte de Kernévilit
DirWRG.4s9m12-8M

No.6 1₆
Fl(3)R.12s 7₄

No.4

Saint Philibert

Kergadoret

Rivière de Saint - Philibert

Pointe de Menhallen

Kerbihan

1₂

0₈

1

7₇

No.2
Fl(2)R.6s

Grassus
0₇

Old Lt Ho (24)

Kernevest

Q.WRG.11m10-7M

Les Rouignous
* *
Θ (0₈)
(1₅)

Pte de Kerbihan

Obscd

5₂
2₆ 0₁
(0.8)
2₃
Pointe Mare
Pointe Milen
3₄
1₈ 3

Pointe de Men er Beleg

1

Moorings

5₃
8₅
Anse de Trehlian
1₃

7₂

1₉
4₄

1₂
Le Grand Pellignon

34'

3₅
6₄ 5
Mousker (4·5)
(Whitened)
2₉
(0₇)
Obscd

0₁

6₈

Le Grand Trého
* 0₆
+ +
4
3₈

Plage de St Pierre

5₄
6
1₈

5₂

5₈

Le Petit Trého
1₂ 1₆
Petit Trého
Fl.R.2.5s
3₈ 2

3₅
6₅

Er Gazeg YB

3₂

7

6₂

5₈

Ldg Lts 347°

4

5₁

2₄

4₃ 4₈
Banc de Crac'h

5₂ 6₂ 1'
5 3
6₂

4₅

33'

Roche Révision YBY

Roche Révision
0₂

59'

Les Bœufs

Kerhélégui YB

YB

3°00'W

47°35'N

Looking E across marina *Nick Chavasse*

By night Approach in the white sector of the Q.WRG light on Pointe Kernevest. When Petit Trého port hand comes abeam, steer to port to enter the white sector of the directional light that marks the channel.

Keep in the white sector, Dir.Oc.WRG 4s 9m, up the channel. When the south pier-head light turns from red to white alter to port and stay in the white sector for about 500m. Lit and unlit buoys mark the channel. Follow them to starboard towards the marina breakwater light.

BERTHS AND ANCHORAGES

La Trinité Marina

La Trinité has all the facilities that would be expected of a major yachting centre and small holiday town. Walking distances round the marina are considerable but in season there is a free water-taxi; call on VHF 09, *Service de Rade*. There are bicycles which may be borrowed from the capitainerie.

⚓ Pointe Saint-Colomban

47°33'·79N 3°05'·93W

Moderately sheltered from the north and northeast, there is a pleasant neap anchorage near Saint-Colomban in the northwest corner of Quiberon Bay 3·6M W of entrance to la Trinité. The approach is straightforward. Anchor close west of the Pointe St-Colomban.

⚓ Carnac

47°33'·92N 3°03'·32W

Sheltered from the north but exposed to the southwest and southeast, the dinghy sailing centre and holiday town of Carnac 2M W of entrance to La Trinité has two distinct bays. A rocky spur, marked by a south cardinal beacon, separates them. Approach from the south and watch the depth carefully because the bays shoal quickly. Anchor where depth permits.

Light Q. WRG at Pointe de Kernevest *Nick Chavasse*

Local racing in river entrance *Nick Chavasse*

Carnac anchorage *Nick Chavasse*

Saint-Philbert River moorings *Nick Chavasse*

⚓ Saint-Philbert River

47°33'·76N 2°58'·90W

Sheltered from all directions except south, this unspoilt river just east of Trinité offers a quiet neap anchorage. Start from a position about 0·25M east of Er Gazeg south cardinal beacon and steer north to leave Le Grand Pellignon port hand beacon to port. Beyond that point there are only a few withies and some moorings to indicate the deepest water. You might be able to borrow a mooring. The best spot is on the west side about 0·3M north of Le Grand Pellignon.

⚓ Plage de St Pierre

47°33'·36N 2°58'·38W

Fairweather lunch and swimming anchorage off lovely beach. Eyeball through rocks on entrance.

ASHORE IN LA TRINITÉ

A large and welcoming marina with all facilities. Good place to buy fish from the Halle à Poissons situated behind the capitainerie. Bicycles may be borrowed for the capitainerie. Lovely walk on section of GR 34 or on beach to Pointe de Kerbihan.

The Carnac Alignments

The Quiberon district is famous for a large number of carved menhirs, long mounds, stone circles, passage graves and alignments. This ritual landscape, created between 4000 and 2700 BC, was built by an energetic society that must have been living well above subsistence level. But nobody knows why they were such active builders. The monuments may have been religious, or astronomical or they may simply have been a means of expression.

A visit to the most extensive Alignments at Le Ménec, near Carnac, is highly recommended. The alignments are 1km long with stones in 12 rows laid out between two enclosures.

There is a bus service to Carnac, from which the Alignments can be reached on foot. In season there is a tourist train with audio which goes to the Carnac stones.

Carnac stones *Nick Chavasse*

La Trinité is often described as the home of the racing fraternity and it is where the 1970 Americas Cup entry *France*, is kept. It is thought-provoking to see how the current range of yachts entering the race have evolved.

French entry to the 1970 America's Cup moored at La Trinité *Nick Chavasse*

52 L'Auray

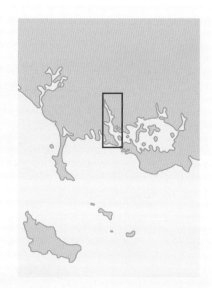

47°35′N 2°57′W

Shelter Reasonable

Depth restrictions
Deep to Le Rocher, 1m beyond

Height restriction
14m under bridge at Auray and 20m at Bono

HW time Port Navalo
Brest HW+0030 neaps, -0005 springs

HW time Auray
Brest HW+0015

Mean height of tide (m) Auray
HWS	HWN	LWN	LWS
4·7	3·6	1·5	0·6

Tidal stream Auray River
Flood – Brest HW–0500 to +0030 (3½ kn)
Ebb – Brest HW +0030 to –0500 (3½ kn)

Berthing
Visitors' moorings and anchorages

Facilities
Boatyard at Port du Parun, shops, cafés and restaurants at several locations

Charts
SHOM *7137*
Imray *C39*

Telephone
Auray HM ☎ 02 97 29 46 39
Le Bono HM ☎ 02 97 57 88 98
Port du Parun ☎ 02 97 57 00 15
www.auray-tourisme.com

Attractive oyster river

The river Auray shares its entrance with the Gulf of Morbihan. It is an oyster river, somewhat less crowded than the rest of the Morbihan. Auray and St Goustan are charming and well worth a visit. Good spot for crew change-overs. Auray was originally a whaling port but by the 16th and 17th centuries it was dealing in grain and wine and had become one of the largest ports in Brittany.

PILOTAGE

See plans on page 185 and pages 188-189

Approach to the Morbihan

Tidal strategy
The tides in the Morbihan entrance are very strong and the final approaches can be rough in wind against tide conditions. Entering the Morbihan is not difficult. However, you do need to be aware of the tidal current at the entrance. In order to reach Auray before the tide starts ebbing, ideally plan to go through the entrance at least 1 hour before local HW. This will give sufficient time as the tide will still be flooding or slack until two hours after HW.

At Auray, the tide stands for quite a long time and then drops very quickly at about half tide. This causes strong currents in the narrows by Le Grand Huernic.

By day From the south, the outer approaches to the Morbihan present no difficulties. Méaban island to the west and the hill of Petit Mont, southwest of Crouesty to the east are both distinctive. Approach leaving Méaban south cardinal buoy and Bagen Hir east cardinal beacon tower to port.

The entrance transit is Petit Veïzit white pyramid in line with Baden Church on 001°. In reasonable visibility, these marks are easy to identify, although Petit Veïzit can be confused with a white sail. The channel is deep. Watch out for the tide because the flood past Port Navalo sweeps first west towards Kerpenhir and then east towards Grégan.

Just inside the entrance, a shallow patch (1·3m depth) extends east of Goëmorent beacon. This is very close to the Petit Veïzit transit so, at low water, it is better to use Grégan south cardinal beacon tower in line with Baden Church on 359° for the final approach. Don't go east of this transit because the tide sets very strongly onto the Grand and Petit Moutons.

River Auray looking north from the narrows at Le Grand Huernic
Patrick Roach

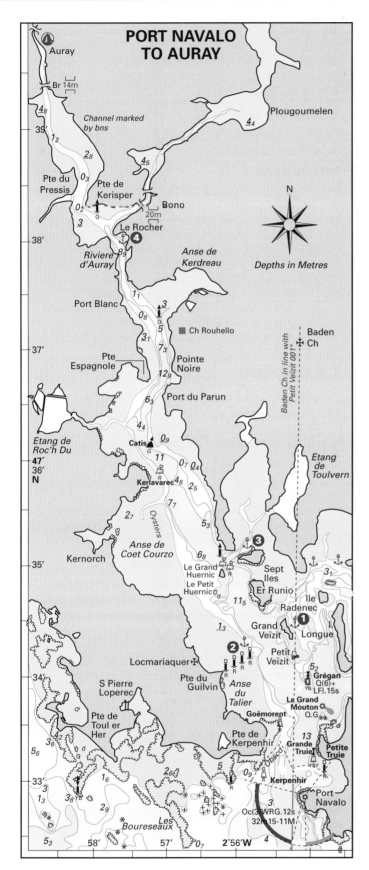

PORT NAVALO TO AURAY

See plan on pages 188-189 for extension east into the Golfe du Morbihan

Looking NE at Petit Veïzit *Nick Chavasse*

Grégan south cardinal tower marks the junction of the River Auray with the Golfe du Morbihan *Nick Chavasse*

By night The river is unlit beyond Grégan tower and night passage is not recommended.

Warning The river is unlit beyond Grégan tower and night passage is not recommended.

THE RIVER AURAY TO AURAY

Pilotage in the river

The strong tides and confusingly large number of islands can make pilotage quite difficult. It is a good idea to mark all courses and their compass bearings on a large-scale chart and to tick off the marks as they are passed.

By day When 0·25M south of Grégan, steer about 330° for Le Grand Huernic island. Leave it to port and continue on the same course past Kerlavarec port hand buoy and Catis starboard hand buoy. Etang de Roc'h Du, west of Catis starboard hand buoy, is kept as a sanctuary and access is prohibited. From Catis starboard hand, steer due north for Pointe Espagnole and, except at high water, do not cut the corner to the port hand beacon beyond the point.

After Pointe Espagnol, it is easy to follow the river through the attractive narrows at Le Rocher to Bono.

Auray bridge *Nick Chavasse*

Beyond Bono the river is shallow and it is only possible to continue to Auray with enough rise of tide. The shallowest patch (depth 0·1m) is just beyond Bono near César port hand buoy, which marks the ruins of an ancient Roman bridge.

Beacons mark the remainder of the river to Auray.

Auray bridge

The height of the bridge just below Auray is 14m above ML but with water level below ML it is possible to get under it with more than 14m of air draught.

The distance from the riverbed to the bridge is 19·3m and there are height gauges on either side of the bridge. Thus by careful calculation, and use of the height gauges, it may be possible to find a combination of depth and height that works. For example at half tide there should be about 3m of water and about 16m of height.

BERTHS AND ANCHORAGES

See plan on p.185

⚓ 1. Grand Veïzit

47°34'·54N 02°55'·21W

Pool (5m) on east side of Grand Veïzit.

⚓ 2. Locmariaquer

47°34'15N 02°56'·41W

This village is on the west side of the river near the entrance. There is a channel to it, with about 1m, marked by port-hand beacons, but it is narrow and used by the ferries. The quay dries 1·5m. Boats can take

Auray bridge tide gauge upstream of bridge *Nick Chavasse*

the ground between the village quay and the *vedette* jetty. Deep-keeled yachts may be able to dry out against the outer side of the jetty. It is possible to anchor off the entrance but it is a long way from the shore.

⚓ 3. Sept Îles

47°35'·09N 02°56'·18W

Small and quiet anchorage. Enter Anse de Baden between mainland and W end of island.

Port de Bono

Bono is an attractive inlet on the east side of the river just above Le Rocher. There are some visitors' buoys in the Auray River opposite the inlet and some in the narrows south of Le Rocher where there is also room for a boat to anchor. In addition there are seven dumbbell moorings, in the Bono creek, just beyond the first bridge (height 20m). The tide runs hard so be careful when arriving or departing.

Bono is a pleasant village with a few shops, bars and restaurants. The hamlet and chapel of St-Avoye, 0·5M on port hand side beyond the second bridge, can be visited by dinghy.

⚓ 4. Le Rocher

47°38'·06N 02°57'·65W

This is an attractive and popular spot. There is room to anchor close to the north end, or it may be possible to borrow a private buoy.

St-Goustan (Auray)

The bridge at Auray is 14m. There are moorings in the middle of the river opposite the quays and for high-masted yachts there are visitors' bow and stern moorings below the bridge. Both have enough water at most tides but a mooring near Le Bono and a visit by dinghy is a good alternative.

As the old bridge in the town is approached, the water shoals rapidly. At springs, the ebb pours violently through this bridge and eddies make the upper end of the mid-stream moorings uncomfortable. The quay should only be used as a temporary berth at high water.

There are various pools you can anchor in just S of the bridge at Auray, particularly at neaps and if prepared to settle in the mud at LW.

ASHORE IN AURAY

At the port, there are a few shops and restaurants and a fish market in the square. The old town of Auray is up the steep hill to the west. The harbour office, on the St Goustan bank, has showers and a dinghy pontoon. Auray has all the facilities of a substantial town, including a marine engineer. Market day is Monday.

The train service is good and Auray station is 1·5M from St-Goustan. There are buses to all parts, including Carnac for the megaliths.

Benjamin Franklin landed at St Goustan from America to negotiate a treaty with France during the American War of Independence.

Looking N approaching Auray N of bridge with air draft of 14m *Nick Chavasse*

Port de Bono dumbbell moorings *Nick Chavasse*

Looking NE at St-Goustan quay and bridge linking Auray with St-Goustan *Nick Chavasse*

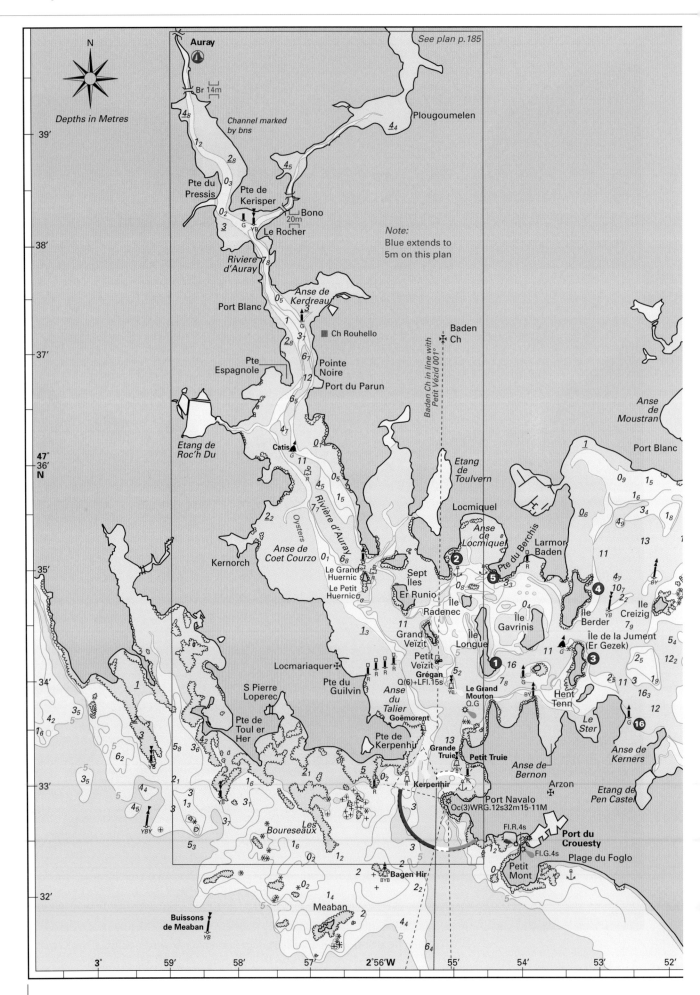

N

Depths in Metres

See plan p.185

Auray

Br 14m

Plougoumelen

4₈

1₂

2₈

4₅

Channel marked
by bns

Note:
Blue extends to
5m on this plan

Pte du
Pressis

0₃

Pte de
Kerisper

Bono

0₂

20m

G   YB

Le Rocher

3

Riviere 7₈
d'Auray

Port Blanc

0₅

Anse de
Kerdreau

3
G

Baden
Ch

Ch Rouhello

Pte
Espagnole

1

3₇

2₈

6₇

Pointe
Noire

Port du Parun

Anse
de
Moustran

12

6₅

Port Blanc

0₉   1₅

Etang de
Roc'h Du

4₇

0₇

Catis
G

11

Etang
de
Toulvern

1

1₆

0₆   3₄   1₈

0₅

4₅

1₅

Locmiquel

4₉

13

Baden Ch in line with
Petit Vézid 001°

Anse
de
Locmiquel

Pte du Berchis
R

Larmor
Baden

11

4₇
10₇
2

Kernorch

2₂

Oysters

Le Grand
Huernic

Anse de
Coet Courzo

0₁

6₈

Sept
Îles

Er Runio

0₈

5₃

2

5

YB

Île
Creizig

Le Petit
Huernic

1₃

Île
Radenec

0₄

Île
Gavrinis

Île
Berder

7₉

Locmariaquer

11
Grand
Veïzit

Île
Longue

11
G

Île de la Jument
(Er Gezek)

5₄

2₅

12₂

S Pierre
Loperec

Pte du
Guilvin

Petit
Veïzit

Grégan
Q(6)+LFl.15s

5₂

1

16

7₈
G

1
Le Grand
Mouton
Q.G

BY

2₅

11   3

1₉

16₃

Hent
Tenn

Le
Ster

12

16

Pte de
Toul er
Her

Anse
du
Talier

Goémorent

Anse de
Kerners

Pte de
Kerpenhir

13
Grande
Truie
YBY

Petit Truie

Anse de
Bernon

Arzon

Etang de
Pen Castel

YB

3₁

0₂
R

Kerpenhir
R

3

Port Navalo
Oc(3)WRG.12s32m15-11M

Les
Boureseaux

1₆

3

Fl.R.4s

Port du
Crouesty

YBY

0₂

1₂

Fl.G.4s

Plage du Foglo

5₃

2

Bagen Hir
BYB

2₂

Petit
Mont

0

Buissons
de Meaban
YB

Meaban

1₄

4₄

6₄

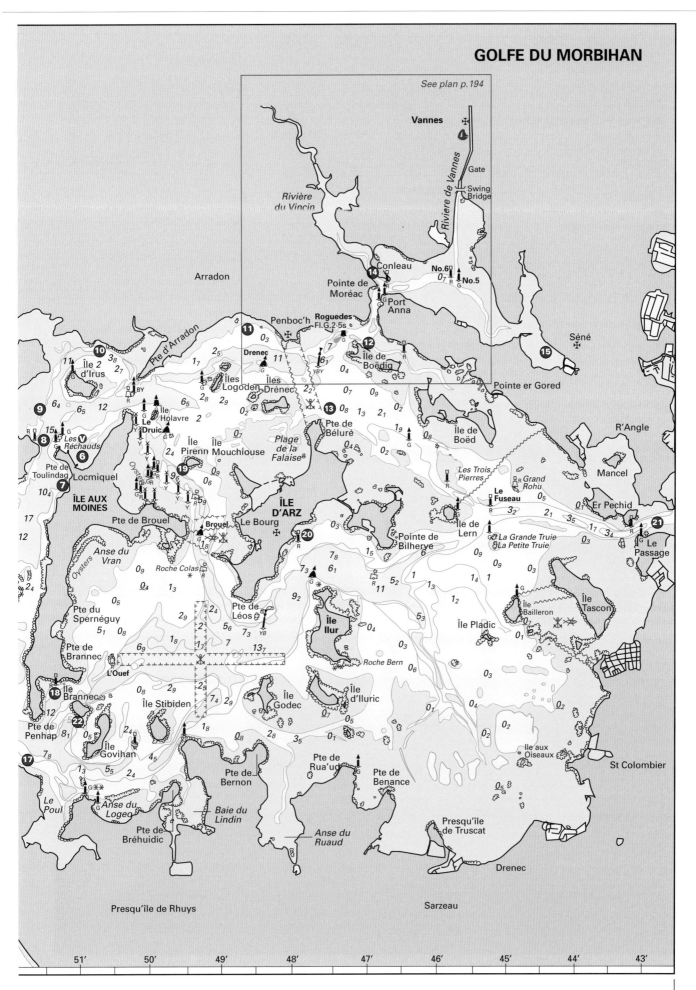

GOLFE DU MORBIHAN

See plan p.194

Vannes

Gate

Swing
Bridge

Rivière du Vincin

Rivière de Vannes

Arradon

Conleau

No.6

No.5

Pointe de
Moréac

Port
Anna

Séné

Penboc'h

Roguedes
Fl.G.2·5s

Pte d'Arradon

Drenec

Île de
Boëdig

Pointe er Gored

Île 2
d'Irus

Îles
Logoden

Îles
Drénec

Île de
Boëd

R'Angle

Le
Druic

Île
Holavre

Pte de
Béluré

Mancel

Les
Réchauds

Île
Pirenn

Île
Mouchiouse

*Plage
de la
Falaise*

Les Trois
Pierres

Grand
Rohu

Er Pechid

Pte de
Toulindag

Locmiquel

ÎLE D'ARZ

Le Bourg

Le
Fuseau

ÎLE AUX
MOINES

Pte de Brouel

Brouel

Pointe de
Bilherye

Île de
Lern

La Grande Truie
La Petite Truie

Le
Passage

*Anse du
Vran*

Roche Colas

Oysters

Pte du
Spernéguy

Pte de
Léos

Île
Ilur

Île Pladic

Île
Bailleron

Île
Tascon

Pte de
Brannec

L'Ouef

Roche Bern

Île
Brannec

Île Stibiden

Île
Godec

Île
d'Iluric

Ile aux
Oiseaux

Pte de
Penhap

Île
Govihan

Pte de
Bernon

Pte de
Rua'uc

Pte de
Benance

St Colombier

Le
Poul

*Anse du
Logeo*

*Baie du
Lindin*

*Anse du
Ruaud*

Presqu'île
de Truscat

Pte de
Bréhuidic

Drenec

Presqu'île de Rhuys

Sarzeau

51'   50'   49'   48'   47'   46'   45'   44'   43'

53 Golfe du Morbihan

47°35′N 2°49′W

Shelter Reasonable

HW time Arradon and Le Logeo
Brest HW+0140

Mean height of tide (m)
Arradon

HWS	HWN	LWN	LWS
3·1	2·4	0·8	0·3

Le Logeo

| 2·9 | 2·3 | 0·6 | 0·2 |

Tidal stream Arradon
Slack – Brest HW–0430 to –0330
Flood – Brest HW–0330 to +0030 (0·5kn)
Slack – Brest HW+0030 to +0230
Ebb – Brest HW+0230 to –0430 (0·7kn)

Berthing
Buoys and anchorages

Facilities
Limited cafés, restaurants and shopping

Charts
SHOM *7137*
Imray *C39*

Telephone
Larmor Baden HM ① 02 97 57 20 86
Port Blanc HM ① 02 97 26 30 57 /
　　06 11 07 56 89
Île Aux Moines HM ① 02 97 26 30 57
Arradon ① 02 97 44 01 23

Sixty islands in an inland sea

The Golfe du Morbihan (*see plan on pages 188–9*) contains about 50 square miles of sheltered water and 60 islands (counting above-water rocks). All but Île aux Moines and Île d'Arz are privately owned and most are uninhabited.

Navigation is not difficult as the islands are easy to identify. There is deep water in the main channels and beacons and buoys mark most of the dangers.

Tidal streams are a major factor. Streams run up to 3-4kn in any narrows. They are fast enough for their direction to be seen on the surface and, except in the entrance where streams run at up to 6kn and to 8kn at springs, tend to follow the channels. There are plenty of counter-currents so it is often possible to make good progress against a foul tide. Nevertheless, the best time for cruising is neaps.

Moorings now fill most of the traditional anchorages so it is often necessary to borrow a buoy rather than anchor. This is easy out of season,

although in season it is best to ensure there is a second buoy nearby in the event of a returning owner. When anchoring, it is important to tuck well in out of the stream and to avoid obstructing the many *vedettes*.

Only the popular places have been described here. Many other anchorages can be found using a large-scale chart.

The Morbihan is a superb cruising ground with hundreds of places to anchor. Some people complain about the increase in the number of moorings in the area but if you look, you will still find plenty of space.

It pays to be a little adventurous if sailing here, given the strength of the streams but if you are cruising in south Brittany, you must visit the Morbihan. It is wonderful!

Large scale chart SHOM 7137 is highly recommended.

Fabulous walks on the GR 34 footpath which covers most of the Gulf.

The Morbihan entrance looking north *Patrick Roach*

Île Longue *Nick Chavasse*

CENTRAL MORBIHAN ANCHORAGES

See plan on pages 188-9

⚓ 1. Île Longue

47°34'·17N 02°54'·44W

There is a northeast-facing bay on the southeast end of this island which is protected from the tide. The bottom shelves rapidly, but there is room to anchor outside the moorings. The island is private and landing not allowed.

⚓ 2. Anse de Locmiquel

47°35'·01N 02°54'·74W

Protected from the north, anchor in 1·7m. Beware of the oyster beds to the north in the bay.

⚓ 3. Île de la Jument

47°34'·10N 02°053'·13W

There is a little bay on the east side. Go in as far as depth allows. Access from the north is easy; access from the south is possible with a large-scale chart.

Île de la Jument *Nick Chavasse*

Le Port, Locmiquel at the north end of Île aux Moines: pontoons and moorings on left *Nick Chavasse*

⚓ 4. Île Berder

47°34'·81N 02°52'·05W

There is a little east-facing bay on the northeast side of Île Berder. Moorings occupy the best spots. There is a very good public walk round the edge of Île Berder, with a low tide causeway and short walk into Larmor Barden, but the tide rises very quickly. The anchorage is good.

Arradon *Nick Chavasse*

⚓ 5. Pointe du Berchis

47°34'·95N 02°54'·45W

Larmor Baden is usually approached from the Vannes channel but it can be approached from the Auray River between Grand Vëizit and Er Runio. Leave Île Radenec to starboard and keep in the north half of the channel because there is a rock and shallow patch northeast of Radenec. Anchor near Pointe de Berchis or borrow a mooring closer to the pier.

⚓ 6. Le Port de l'Île aux Moines

Île aux Moines has a small marina, called Le Port, on the northwest side at Locmiquel. The marina has no designated berths for visitors but there are two pontoons moored off in deeper water with alongside berths for visitors with water and electricity. Beware the drying Réchauds rocks, marked by two beacons, close to the approach to the pontoons and there is also a 0·6m shallow patch, marked by a south cardinal buoy, in the middle of the moorings area. It is therefore best to approach the pontoons south of Les Réchauds from the Vannes channel. A free water taxi operates in season to Le Port and Port Blanc. Ashore there are a few shops, bars and restaurants. Bicycle rental is available.

⚓ 7. Toulindag Anchorage

47°35'·88N 02°51'·21W

Southeast of Pointe de Toulindag in 2m on sand.

⚓ 8. Port Blanc

47°36'·30N 02°51'·56W

There are some visitors' buoys at Port Blanc opposite Pointe de Toulindag. No 23 Bus takes you to Vannes in 24 mins which is a great alternative if you do not have time to make it up the channel to Vannes marina.

⚓ 9. Anse de Moustran

47°36'N 02°51'·43W

Anse de Moustran is the bay just north of Port Blanc. The best spots are occupied by moorings and you might find a comfortable anchorage.

⚓ 10. Pen er Men

47°36'·98N 02°50'·90W

North of Île d'Irus there is room to anchor off the mainland shore, clear of the moorings. This anchorage is excellent in heavy weather. There is a pleasant 30 minute walk to the Arradon waterfront and a good restaurant.

⚓ 11. Arradon

47°36'·82N 02°49'·86W

Rather exposed to the southwest at high water, this popular yachting centre has moorings for visitors but little room to anchor. Pontoon berths available on west side of small pier only. Beware of shallows on east side of pontoon.

⚓ 12. Île de Boëdig

47°37'·07N 02°46'·99W

There is a pleasant, secluded anchorage off the northeast end of the island in the Chenal de Badel. The island is private and landing is not allowed.

⚓ 13. Pointe de Béluré

47°36'·40N 02°47'·39W

On the north tip of Île d'Arz, there is an anchorage east of the green beacon which marks the end of the ferry slip.

⚓ 14. Conleau

47°37'·75N 02°46'·90W

The inlet to the southwest of the peninsula is full of moorings. The best anchorage is in the bight on the port side just before the far end of the narrows. There is a good restaurant.

Île de Boëdig *Nick Chavasse*

⚓ 15. Séné

47°37'19N 02°44'49W

Dry out in traditional harbour at head of inlet.

⚓ 16. Anse de Kerners

47°33'·62N 02°52'·35W

Southwest of Île aux Moines there is a large drying bay. Anchor outside the local boats. Water, showers and provisions are available at the campsite in season.

⚓ 17. Anse de Pen Castel

47°33'·31N 02°51'·87W

Opposite the south tip of Île aux Moines, it is possible to anchor outside the moorings.

⚓ 18. Anse de Penhap

47°33'·79N 02°51'·37W

This is a nice spot in the southeast corner of the Île aux Moines. There is plenty of space to anchor but tuck in well to get out of the stream.

⚓ 19. Île Pirenn

47°35'69N 02°49'51W

There is a quiet anchorage southwest of Île Pirenn but watch out for the oyster beds. It is possible to land at Pointe de Brouel on Île aux Moines.

⚓ 20. Île d'Arz

47°35'32N 02°47'65W

There is an anchorage in the bay on the east side. Anchor outside the moorings and do not go in too far because it shoals quickly. Land at the slipway, marked by a red beacon to visit Le Bourg where there are modest shops.

⚓ 21. Le Passage

47°35'48N 02°42'82W

This is in the extreme east of the Morbihan. It can be difficult to identify and the secret is to first identify Grand Rohu red beacon tower. In the final approach, do not pass too close to the red beacon on the northern shore. It marks the end of a slipway and not the southern extremity of the dangers.

Anchor midstream in the narrows to the north of the island if space can be found among the moorings. Alternatively, in settled weather, anchor east of the narrows. The tide is strong and there may be some silting so check the depth carefully.

⚓ 22. Île Brannec

47°33'·59N 2°51'·03

Good little anchorage in 2m southwest of Île Brannec sheltered in NE wind.

Looking north east at Île Brannec anchorage *Nick Chavasse*

54 Vannes

47°38′N 2°46′W

Shelter
Excellent in Vannes marina

Depth restrictions
Least depth 0·5m in canal and 2·1m in basin

Entry gate and swing bridge
Opens Vannes approx HW ±0230

HW time Port Navalo Brest HW+0015

HW time Vannes Brest HW+0155

Mean height of tide (m)
Port Navalo

HWS	HWN	LWN	LWS
4·9	3·9	1·8	0·7

Vannes

3·2	2·5	0·6	0·2

Tidal stream Grand Mouton
Flood – Brest HW–0430 to +0130 (8kn)
Ebb – Brest HW +0130 to –0430 (9kn)
Times may be 30 minutes later at neaps

Berthing
Marina

Fuel
Cans only. Nearest fuel is at Le Crouesty

Facilities
Most facilities and plenty of cafés, restaurants and shops

Charts
SHOM *7137*
Imray *C39*

Communications
Vannes HM VHF 9
☎ 02 97 01 55 20
www.passeportescales.com/fr/port-vannes

The heart of the Morbihan

Vannes has been the capital of the Morbihan since pre-Roman times. It has an old town with narrow streets and plenty of attractive old buildings but it is also a vibrant modern city with smart shops and excellent transport.

The marina is in a locked basin alongside the old town. It gets rather crowded but as it is completely sheltered the tight packing does not really matter. It is most attractive with wide promenades and open-air cafés. The marina building has excellent showers, laundry and restaurant.

Vannes has something for all the family. Sailing in the Morbihan is exhilarating and a visit to Vannes provides all the excitement of planning access through a tidal gate and swing bridge to gain entry to a port in the centre of town. The town is lively, with plenty to see and do. It is also a good crew changeover place.

PILOTAGE

The Vannes channel to Vannes

Tidal strategy

High water at Vannes is two hours after high water Port Navalo at the entrance to the Golfe du Morbihan. Go through the Morbihan entrance at least half an hour before HW Port Navalo to carry the flood all the way to Vannes.

The entry gate and swing bridge at Vannes

Access to the marina is by day only, no earlier than 0730 hours and no later than 2130 hours. Depending on HW times, the entry gate and the Kerino swing bridge both remain open for free-flow which can last from a minimum of 2·5 hours to a maximum of 4 hours. The basin opening times are

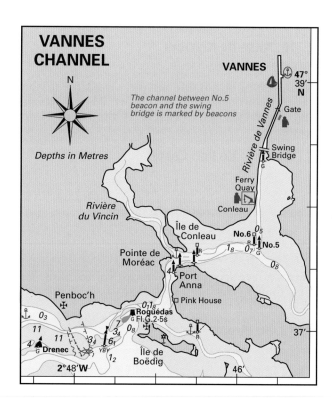

published at: www.passeportescales.com/port-vannes and click on Basin Schedule

Waiting pontoons (partly drying) are situated just north and south of the bridge. There is an intercom to the HM on the south pontoon. The bridgemaster may occasionally speak by loudhailer, which can be disconcerting! The entry gate (not a lock gate) approximately 250m north of the bridge is remotely controlled by the HM. The sill retains 2·1m in the marina.

Pink house on the corner of the channel to Vannes *Nick Chavasse*

Boats need to anticipate their movements for entering and exiting Vannes by being in position and ready to access the bridge and entry gate at the designated opening time. In the event of there being insufficient water, certain openings may be eliminated, to guarantee the safety of the boats in the basin. The depth of the basin is maintained at 2·1m, however, the entry gate has a sill and it is strongly recommended that the depth gauge is checked before accessing the gate.

Boats with a beam >4·2m must call HM on VHF 9 before entering and leaving the port.

The traffic signals at the bridge are:

- 3 fixed red lights – no passage
- 3 fixed green lights – passage permitted
- 3 occulting green lights – proceed only if already underway and the passage is clear.

The traffic signals on the entry gate are:

- 3 fixed red lights – no passage
- 3 fixed green lights – passage permitted

Entry gate displaying green lights on right hand side
Nick Chavasse

Vannes swing bridge and canal *Patrick Roach*

Vannes swing bridge *Nick Chavasse*

Lock gate permanently open N of entry gate *Nick Chavasse*

There are waiting pontoons on both sides of the bridge. In recent years, there has been serious silting in the vicinity of the bridge and dredging has been needed. There is a possibility of being neaped.

Pilotage in the Morbihan

Strong tides and a large number of islands can make pilotage confusing. It is a good idea to mark courses and compass bearings on a large-scale chart and tick off the marks as they are passed.

By day In the entrance, the Grand and Petit Moutons are dangerous because the tide sets directly onto them at up to 8kn. To avoid them, hold the transit until close to Grégan. Then turn sharply to starboard.

The channel passes south of Îles Longue, Gavrinis and Berder before entering a larger area of water west of Île aux Moines. Hold more or less the same course until north of Île Crëizig.

After passing Île Crëizig, turn north to pass through the narrows between Pointe de Toulindag on Île aux Moines and the mainland. Keep towards the east side of the channel to avoid the Banc de Kergonan. Beacons mark the narrows but take care because the stream runs very strongly.

Once through the narrows, pass between the north tip of Île aux Moines and Pointe d'Arradon. Follow the mainland shore north of Îles Logoden and past Roguédas starboard hand beacon. The channel then turns north past a very distinctive pink house on the starboard side. It is important not to cut the corner because there are rocks and a shallow patch on the port hand side between Roguédas and the pink house.

Follow the channel past Port Anna to beacon No. 6, which is the start of the canalised section to Vannes. The channel silts and carries only 0·5m at LAT in the section leading to the swing bridge.

The swing bridge is a short distance past the vedette quay. It is operated from the capitainerie at Vannes, using closed-circuit TV cameras. If the bridge is not open, secure to the waiting pontoon on the starboard side until the bridge opens. Be aware of shallows on starboard side just S of the waiting pontoon.

In season, a marina launch may meet visiting boats and direct them to a berth. Otherwise, moor alongside in front of the marina office on the east side. Rafting may be necessary. A depth of 2·10m is maintained in the marina.

ASHORE IN VANNES

Vannes has limited sailing facilities but excels in most other respects. The marina is adjacent to the medieval old town with its lovely buildings, narrow streets and masses of little shops, bars and restaurants. On Wednesdays and Saturdays there is a colourful street market where entertainers often perform. History buffs will enjoy the fine cathedral and museum and will no doubt walk along the ramparts. The modern shopping area is just beyond the old town.

Vannes is a main rail centre and communications by rail and bus are excellent. Regular bus and train connections to Brest, Rennes and Nantes airports. There are regular ferry services from the gare maritime just S of the Kerino bridge on the W bank. to Conleau, Île aux Moines, Port Navalo, Auray and other points in the Morbihan. Car hire available at the station.

The road tunnel, which had been under construction for many years, is now open. It was thought that the opening of the tunnel might dispense with the need for opening and closing the swing bridge. However, the Kerino swing bridge has been retained for use by pedestrians and bicycles.

Vannes marina (southern section) *Nick Chavasse*

Looking E over marina basin *Nick Chavasse*

55 Le Crouesty

47°32'N 2°55'W

Shelter Excellent

Hazards
Entrance dangerous in strong SW wind

Depth restrictions
Channel dredged 1·8m

Night entry Lit

HW time
Brest HW-0015

Mean height of tide (m) Port Navalo

HWS	HWN	LWN	LWS
5·4	4·3	2·0	0·8

Tidal stream – Crouesty approaches
Slack – Brest HW-0430 to -0330
NW – Brest HW-0330 to +0130 (0·9kn)
SE – Brest HW+0130 to -0430 (1·4kn)

Berthing
Huge marina

Facilities
All facilities

Charts
SHOM *7032, 7141*
Imray *C39*

Communications
VHF 9
Marina ① 02 97 53 73 33
www.rhuys.com

Huge marina on the edge of the Morbihan

Le Crouesty is a huge, six basin marina about 1M outside the entrance to the Morbihan. It has all facilities, plenty of visitors' berths, a good range of marina shops, restaurants and an excellent supermarket. It is an ideal place to stock up before a visit to the Morbihan. There is a good beach but few other tourist attractions.

PILOTAGE

Crouesty approach and entrance

By day From the south, Crouesty can be identified by the hill of Petit Mont and Crouesty lighthouse to the east of Méaban island. Leave Méaban south cardinal buoy to port.

Use the Morbihan entrance transit of Petit Veïzit white pyramid in line with Baden Church on 001° until, just past Petit Mont, the Crouesty channel

Port du Crouesty with Golfe du Morbihan beyond

Le Crouesty entrance with leading marks slighly offset *Nick Chavasse*

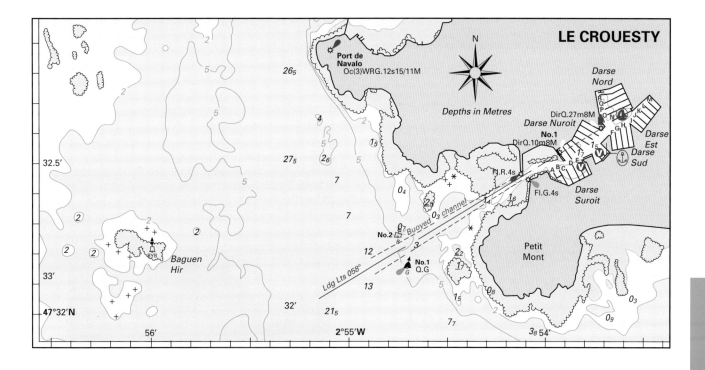

Looking NE over Le Crouesty marina *Nick Chavasse*

buoys are seen to starboard. The leading marks are the lighthouse (rear) in line with a red panel with a vertical white stripe (front) on 058°.

By night Approach in the white sector of Port Navalo light on about 010°. When Crouesty leading lights come in transit on 058°, turn to starboard and follow the transit into the marina.

BERTHS AND ANCHORAGES

Le Crouesty

In season, boats are normally met by a launch and directed to a vacant berth. Otherwise use the visitors' berths in the second basin on the starboard side in front of the capitainerie.

Le Crouesty capitainerie *Nick Chavasse*

⚓ Port Navalo

The bay is full of moorings and it may be possible to borrow one. Otherwise there is a tolerable anchorage in 1·5m off the end of the pier, among the moorings. This spot is exposed to the west and disturbed by the wash from ferries.

⚓ La Plage de Fogeo

47°32'·04N 2°53'·26W

Sheltered from north and east but wide open to wind or swell from the south, this sandy bay is the other side of Petit Mont from Crouesty. Approach from the south to avoid the rocks just east of Petit Mont. Anchor where depth permits. It is easy to move to Crouesty at night but be sure to clear the rocks east and south of Petit Mont.

⚓ Anse de Cornault

47°30'·86N 2°51'·37W

Sheltered from north and east but open to wind and swell from the southwest, this bay is 2M southeast of Petit Mont. Approach from the southwest and anchor where depth permits. It is easy to leave at night but get well offshore before turning for Crouesty as there are several dangers close to shore.

Beware the prohibited anchoring area in the north of the bay. Anchoring is permitted in the south of the bay.

ASHORE IN CROUESTY

The marina has all boating facilities including chandlers, engineers, crane, scrubbing berth, fuel berth, 45-T travel-lift and all repairs. Around the marina are bars, restaurants and a number of shops including a launderette. There is an excellent supermarket and fish market just northwest of the marina. The supermarket is quite a long way round the marina from the visitors' berths so that for a big shop it is worth taking the dinghy across to the north basin where there is a designated victualing pontoon. (There is no access to the supermarket from the fuel berth.) There is a free water taxi across the marina for supermarket shopping (season only).

St-Gildas de Rhuys, a 6th-century British missionary, established a monastery near the entrance to the Morbihan. When St-Gildas died in 570 he was visiting Houat. His body, as he had wished, was placed in a boat and pushed out to sea. Two months later it came ashore at what is now the entrance to Crouesty Marina. A chapel was built at the spot, and it can be seen on the south side of the marina entrance.

St Gildas chapel to the south of the Crouesty entrance *Nick Chavasse*

Port Navalo moorings *Nick Chavasse*

Le Pouliguen *Nick Chavasse*

VI. La Vilaine and La Loire

Brittany is generally considered to end at the Loire but some towns south of the Loire, such as Pornic, consider themselves to be Breton. However, well before the Loire the character of the ports changes and the coastline becomes much softer.

The jewel in this area is the Vilaine which was turned into a huge boating lake when a barrage was built near its mouth. It has 20 miles of non-tidal water, dozens of riverside anchorages and two delightful historic towns, La Roche Bernard and Redon.

South of the Vilaine, the granite hills of Brittany give way to the flat salt country around Guérande. There are several attractive places to stay. Piriac is a pretty holiday town with a new marina; Le Croisic is a fascinating old salt and sardine port that is still surrounded by active salt ponds. La Baule has two marinas for those who need a spectacular beach, some posh shopping and a visit to the casino.

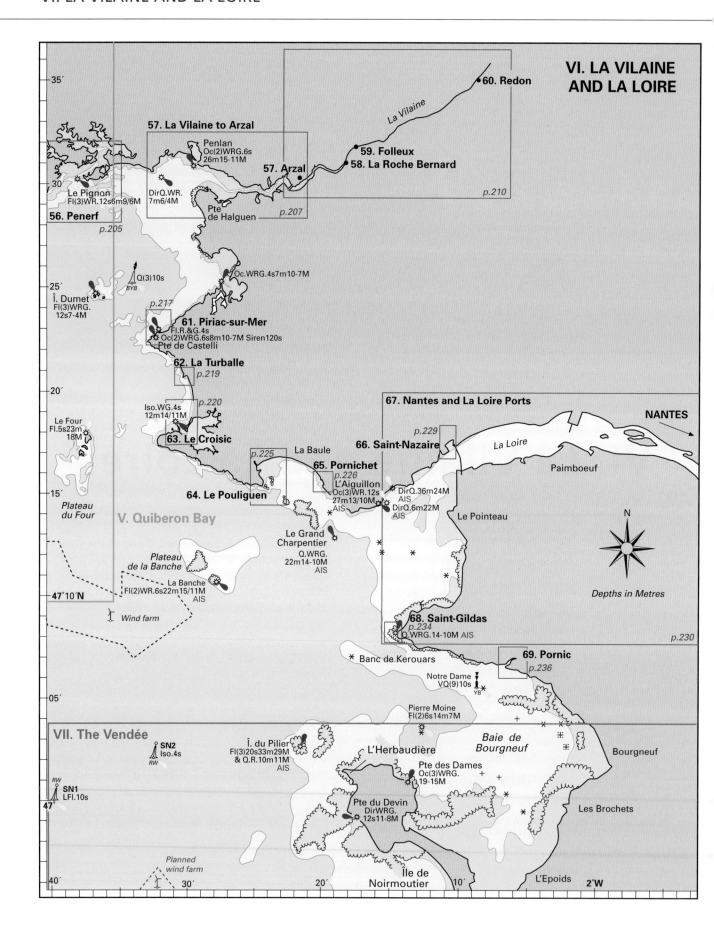

La Loire tidal streams

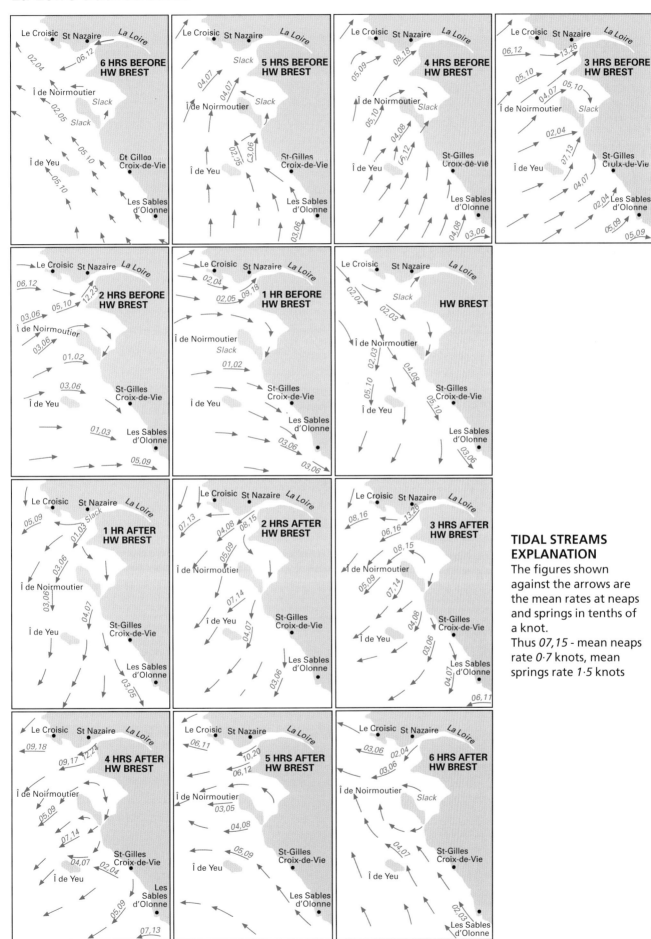

TIDAL STREAMS EXPLANATION

The figures shown against the arrows are the mean rates at neaps and springs in tenths of a knot.

Thus *07,15* - mean neaps rate *0·7* knots, mean springs rate *1·5* knots

56 Pénerf

47°30'N 2°39'W

Shelter
Good except in strong W wind

Hazards
Intricate approach

Depth restrictions
4·5m in E passage
Deep inside

Night entry Lit but not recommended

HW time Brest HW-0005

Mean height of tide (m) Pénerf

HWS	HWN	LWN	LWS
5.4	4·3	2·0	0·7

Tidal stream in passages
3kn when rocks are uncovered, 2kn when rocks are covered

Berthing
New small marina (2022). Visitors' buoy and anchorage

Facilities
Bar, restaurant and a few shops

Charts
SHOM *7033, 7135*
Imray *C39*

Communications
VHF 09
① 02 97 41 20 67
 Mobile 06 30 95 82 79
www.port-penerf-damgan.com

Quiet unspoilt river

The Pénerf is an unspoilt oyster river about 13M east of Le Crouesty and 6M west of the Vilaine. There are many rocky ledges at the entrance that provide good protection but also make the entrance a bit tricky. A first visit should be in good weather close to high water.

The villages of Pénerf and Pen Cadenic are both small, quiet and attractive. They offer excellent oysters but not a great deal else. A small marina has recently been installed just east of the jetty.

PILOTAGE

Historically there were three channels into the River Pénerf. Many of the navigation marks which marked the Western and Central channels have been removed and they are now not used except, on occasion, by local fishermen. The main channel is now the East Passage, Passé de L'Est.

Pénerf E passage (Passé de L'Est)

This passage is deep but very narrow and there are rocky shoals close east of it. Also, the front mark is not easy to see from a distance and trees may hide the back mark. It should not be used in poor visibility.

By day Start from a position near Borénis starboard hand buoy. The transit is the first port hand beacon of the east passage (southeast of Le Pignon) in line with Le Tour du Parc steeple on 354°. Above half-tide it is safe to go in cautiously towards Le Pignon.

Left The River Pénerf looking northeast.
The Port of Pénerf is on the east side of the river near the jetty. The anchorage at Cadenic is 05M further on the west side. The River Pénerf is mostly devoted to oyster farming
Patrick Roach

Below Looking N over the moorings from the slip at Pénerf
Nick Chavasse

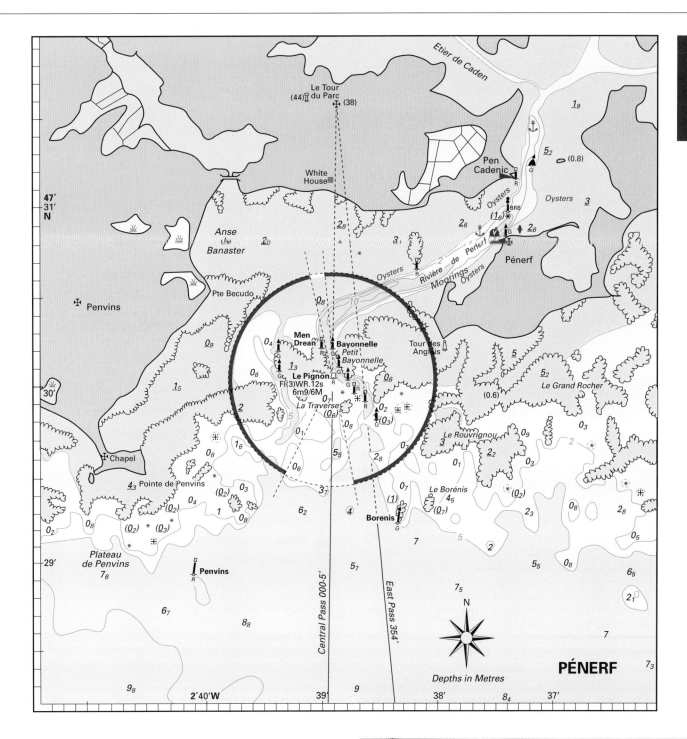

Le Tour (44) du Parc (38)

Etier de Caden

White House

Pen Cadenic

Oysters

Anse Banaster

Rivière de Pénerf

Moorings

Oysters

Pénerf

Pte Becudo

Penvins

Men Drean

Bayonnelle

Petit Bayonnelle

Le Pignon
Fl(3)WR.12s
6m9/6M

La Traverse

Tour des Anglais

Le Grand Rocher

Chapel

Pointe de Penvins

Le Rouvrignou

Le Borénis

Borenis

Penvins

Plateau de Penvins

Central Pass 000·5°

East Pass 354°

PÉNERF

Depths in Metres

However, do not attempt the passage unless the first port hand beacon can be positively identified, particularly if the tide is running strongly.

Leave the Le Pignon port hand beacon fairly close to port. Then steer 340° to leave Bayonnelle and Petit Bayonnelle beacons to starboard and follow one more starboard beacon into the river. At the last beacon, turn onto about 060° and head for the moorings off Pénerf village. On the way there is a red beacon which is in very shallow water.

Approach to Pénerf looking N with
Le Pignon port hand beacon in centre
Nick Chavasse

Looking NE from Pénerf over visitors' mooring and Pen Cadenic anchorage beyond *Nick Chavasse*

BERTHS AND ANCHORAGES

Pénerf

A new marina was installed during 2022. It is situated 75m east of the jetty. It consists of one long pontoon attached to the shore with space for about 8 boats. From April to October there is an additional detached pontoon situated outside the main pontoon suitable for deeper draught yachts. There is one white visitors' buoy just southwest of the isolated danger off the village at Pénerf. All are in a minimum depth of 4m. It may be possible to anchor outside the moorings but beware of oyster beds. This anchorage is quite choppy when wind and tide are opposed.

Cadenic

Cadenic is on the west bank less than 0·5M beyond Pénerf. Leave the isolated danger beacon, just north of Pénerf, to port and aim for the port hand beacon and starboard hand buoy just off Cadenic. There are some fishing boat moorings off the pier and a quiet neap anchorage upstream of the moorings. There is not much room at springs and the holding in deeper water is reported to be poor.

Looking north along new pontoon with detached pontoon beyond behind yacht *Nicholas Bailhache*

ASHORE IN PÉNERF AND CADENIC

Pénerf has shops, bars and two restaurants. Toilets at the lifeboat station and one shower which requires a card for access from the capitainerie. Oysters are sold on the quay. There is also a nice chapel with a couple of traditional model fishing boats as votive offerings.

Cadenic has almost no facilities but, like Pénerf, it is often possible to buy seafood from the fishermen.

⚓ Pointe de St-Jacques

47°28'·97N 2°47'·08W

Sheltered from northwest to northeast, there is a small harbour off the south tip of the Presqu'île de Rhuys, 5M west of Pénerf. Approach from St-Jacques south cardinal and anchor off the pier. A night departure is possible using the pierhead light.

⚓ Anse de Suscinio

47°29'·94N 2°43'·38W

Well protected from the north and northwest but completely open to the south, this wide shallow bay is 3M west of Pénerf entrance. Approach from due south and anchor where depth permits. The ruins of the Château de Suscinio are visible from the anchorage and can be visited.

Canon from *Le Juste* which participated in the Battle of Quiberon Bay 1759. A local man from Pénerf rescued 130 sailors from the ship *Nick Chavasse*

57 La Vilaine to Arzal

47°30′N 2°28′W

Shelter Excellent

Depth restrictions
0·5m over the bar

Night entry Partially lit

Arzal lock
Opens hourly from 0800-2100 (Jul/Aug) and 0800-2000 (rest of year)

HW time Brest HW+0005

Mean height of tide (m) Tréhiguier

HWS	HWN	LWN	LWS
5·5	4·4	2·1	0·7

Tidal stream in the river
Flood 2kn, ebb 3kn in river but much influenced by inland rain

Berthing Two marinas

Fuel W side of Arzal marina

Facilities
Good marina facilities, limited shopping

Charts
SHOM 7033, 7144
Imray C39

Communications
Lock VHF 11
Lock Interactive ☎ 02 97 41 28 39
Marina VHF 9
☎ 02 97 45 02 97
www.passeportecluse.arzal.camoel.com
www.lavilaine.com for lock opening times

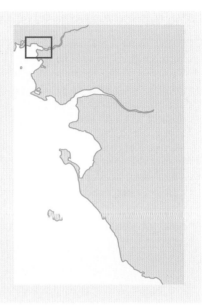

Gateway to the Vilaine

See plan page 210

The Vilaine has a large lock at Arzal through a barrage built to protect the area from flooding and to provide a reservoir of fresh water. It keeps the water level permanently at 3·0m or more. This has created a beautiful, long boating lake with flat water and almost no commercial traffic.

There is a large marina just beyond the lock. It is useful for fuel or repairs and would be a good place to leave a boat but it has little to offer the tourist.

If cruising to the Vilaine for the first time check the depths in the lock, as well as lock opening times, as water depth is shallow when the coefficient is >90. Cruising up the Vilaine river is fun and exciting. La

Roche Bernard is attractive and popular with yachtsmen - some never leave!

In recent summers, due to a lack of rainwater, the lock was used for a reduced number of days per week. Check lock opening times on www.lavilaine.com.

PILOTAGE

The mouth of the Vilaine is shallow and open to the southwest. It can be rough and even dangerous when a strong southwest wind blows against the ebb. The three channels have a bit more depth than the rest of the bay but in good weather, above half tide on the flood, they need not be followed. The Varlingue rock (dries 0·3m) on the east side is dangerous below half tide or in rough weather.

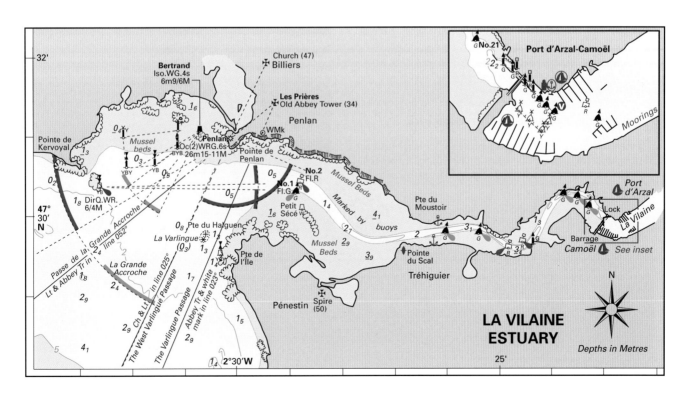

The Grande Accroche Passage

By day Start from a position 0·5M SE of Les Mâts south cardinal buoy. The transit is Penlan lighthouse in line with the Abbaye de Prières on 052°. The Abbaye de Prières is difficult to see due to being partially obscured by trees. In practice it is good enough to steer for Penlan lighthouse, keeping a reasonable distance from Kervoyal tower beacon.

Once Kervoyal tower is due west, steer due east to enter the river between the buoys. A useful transit is Kervoyal tower beacon in line with Tour des Anglais tower beacon (at Pénerf) on 267°.

By night The Grande Accroche is lit by the white sector of Penlan and the narrow white sector of Kervoyal. However, the river is not lit beyond Tréhiguier so night entry is not recommended.

The west Varlingue passage

By day Start towards the east side of the bay with Penlan lighthouse bearing about 025°. The transit is Billiers church in line with Penlan lighthouse on 025°. At low water, it is important to hold it accurately because it passes close to La Varlingue rock (dries 0·3m).

Once Kervoyal tower beacon is due west, steer due east to enter the river between the buoys.

The Varlingue passage

This is the most convenient passage from the south. It is also the deepest and, therefore, the safer passage in bad west and southwest weather, given sufficient water.

By day The official transit is the Abbaye de Prières in line with a small white daymark on 023°. The front mark will be invisible to a stranger. Steer closer to the W cardinal off Pte de Lîlle on the starboard side of the channel to avoid La Valingue (dries 0·3m).

Once Kervoyal tower is due west, or Petit Sécé white tower beacon bears 105° steer due east to enter the river between the buoys.

The Vilaine entrance to the Arzal lock

By day The channel is well buoyed to Tréhiguer. There will be as little as 0·8m or even less in places so take the curves wide and if possible go in or out at high water.

Approaching Arzal lock with waiting pontoon on left
Nick Chavasse

Beyond Tréhiguier there are fewer marks, but the channel is still easy to follow with red and green buoys and the occasional beacon. The approach to the lock is marked with starboard-hand buoys.

The Arzal lock

The lock is on the north side of the river, adjacent to the conspicuous control tower. The lower gates are normally left open so yachts arriving from seaward can wait in the lock. There are two waiting pontoons, one on the port hand side and a shorter one on the starboard hand side, immediately before the lock entrance. The danger area around the dam spillway is marked off by yellow buoys, both above and below the lock. There are mooring buoys above the lock which may be used for waiting.

The lock is worked in daylight hours between 0800 and 2100, during the season and from 0800-2000 for the remainder of the year. The opening times depend on the tide and are displayed at the local marinas, at www.lavilaine.com and in an invaluable booklet available at the lock. The lock may be closed for more than one hour at lunch time or close to low water. Otherwise, it opens on the hour.

Arzal lock showing lifting bridge *Nick Chavasse*

A busy day in the lock *Nick Chavasse*

The lock is big and crowded and, except close to high water, quite turbulent. Moor to the vertical chains and make sure the fenders do not pop out. Also wait until the turbulence has subsided before casting off. Fortunately, the lock-keeper manages the potential chaos with great charm and skill. If possible it is best to avoid times of heavy use such as early on Saturdays, Sunday evenings and early or late on fête days. The lock has been subjected to prolonged periods of closure during the drought in 2022. Check opening times in advance.

BERTHS AND ANCHORAGES

⚓ Tréhiguier

Sheltered from south and east but exposed to west and northwest, there is a visitors' buoy and a convenient anchorage near the entrance on the seaward side of the lock. Anchor outside the moorings in soft mud. Land at the slip.

Port d'Arzal - Camoël

There is a large marina on the north bank above the dam at Arzal and a smaller, quieter one at Camoël on the south side. If using Camoël, check in at Arzal marina.

Facilities at Arzal

Arzal has all the facilities of a major marina complex including fuel, all repairs, 50-T travel-lift, 15-T crane, masting, haul out, laying up outside or under cover. There are bars and restaurants, and two small grocery shops within 2M. The dam has a fish pass which is worth seeing.

Camoël marina on the south side is more peaceful, but has no facilities other than showers and toilets.

Tréhiguier slip in centre
Nick Chavasse

Below
The barrage from southeast with Arzal Marina and large boatyard on the northeast side and Camoël on the southwest
Patrick Roach

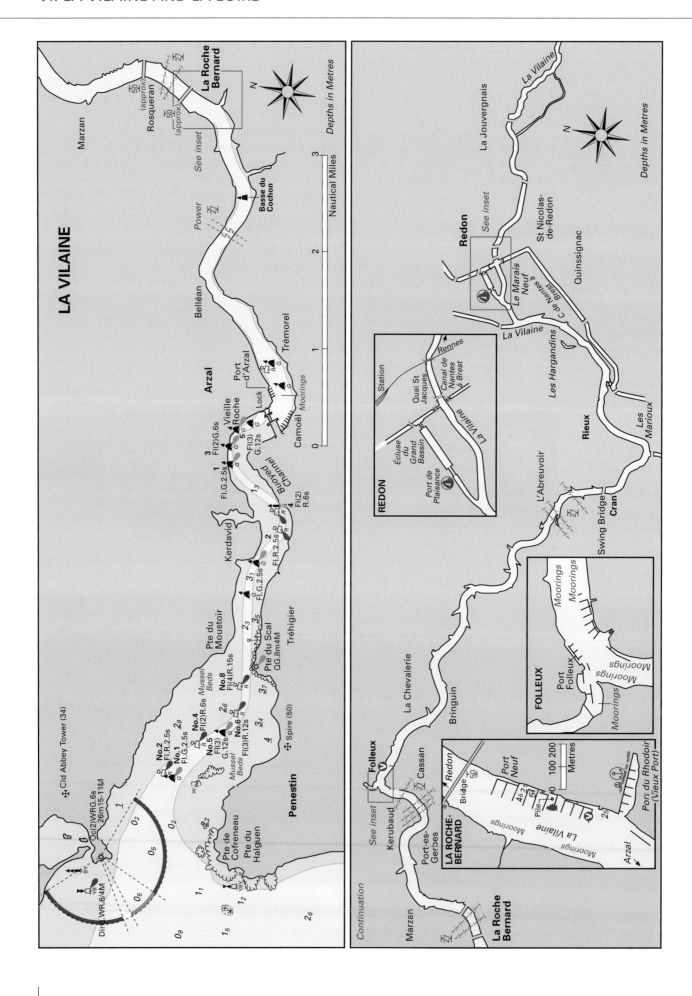

LA VILAINE

Depths in Metres

Marzan

La Roche Bernard

Rosqueran (approx)

50 (approx)

See inset

N

Power

27

Basse du Cochon

Belléan

Trémorel

Arzal

Port d'Arzal

Camoël *Moorings*

Lock

Vieille Roche

Fl(2)G.6s

Fl(3) G.12s

Fl.G.2.5s

Channel Buoyed

Fl(2) R.6s

Fl.R.2.5s

Fl.G.2.5s

Kerdavid

Pte du Moustoir

Mussel Beds

No.8 Fl(4)R.15s

Pte du Scal QG.8m4M

Tréhigier

Spire (50)

Penestin

No.2 Fl.R.2.5s

No.1 Fl.G.2.5s

No.5 Fl(3)

No.4 Fl(2)R.6s

No.6 Fl(3)R.12s

G.12s

Mussel Beds

Pte de Cofreneau

Pte du Halguen

Cld Abbey Tower (34)

Oc(2)WRG.6s 26m15-11M

Dir.Q.WR.6/4M

Nautical Miles

0 1 2 3

REDON

La Vilaine

La Jouvergnais

Redon

See inset

N

St Nicolas-de-Redon

Le Marais Neuf

C de Nantes à Brest

La Vilaine

Quinssignac

Les Hargandins

Rieux

Les Marioux

L'Abreuvoir

Swing Bridge Cran

27

Depths in Metres

REDON (inset)

Station

Rennes

Quai St Jacques

Canal de Nantes à Brest

La Vilaine

Écluse du Grand Bassin

Port de Plaisance

FOLLEUX (inset)

Moorings
Moorings
Port Folleux
Moorings
Moorings

LA ROCHE-BERNARD (inset)

Redon
Bridge
50
Port Neuf
Pile
45
5
Moorings
La Vilaine
Moorings
Arzal
Port du Rhodoir (Vieux Port)
25

0 100 200 Metres

La Chevalerie

Bringuin

Folleux

Cassan

Redon

Port-es-Gerbes

Kerubaud

See inset

27

Marzan

La Roche Bernard

La Roche Bernard

27

Continuation

58 La Roche Bernard

47°31′N 2°19′W

Shelter Excellent

Depth restrictions
3·0m or more beyond Arzal

Night entry Not recommended

HW time
Above Arzal there is no tide

Tidal stream in the river
There is usually a slight stream to seaward. This can be strong after very heavy rain

Berthing
Marinas and visitors' buoys

Facilities
Good marina facilities plus attractive town with shops, cafés and restaurants

Fuel Nearest is at Arzal

Charts
IGN Top25 *1022OT*

Communications
HM ① 02 99 90 62 17
www.passeportescales.com

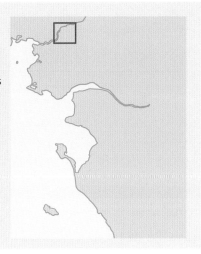

The medieval heart of the Vilaine

The attractive holiday town of La Roche Bernard was once an important river port and boat building centre. Today its quaint medieval streets and houses have been beautifully restored to make it the main tourist destination on the Vilaine. Futher upriver the quiet hamlet of Folleux is a tranquil spot in the middle of the lovely Vilaine countryside.

PILOTAGE

Charts

Beyond the dam, the river is not charted. The section from Arzal to La Roche Bernard is covered by the land map IGN Top25 1022OT (*La Roche Bernard*). However, beyond La Roche Bernard, land maps are less satisfactory and less easy to find. There is deep water to Redon and the dangers are marked. The plan opposite is adequate as a guide but should not be relied upon for navigation.

Arzal to La Roche Bernard

Above the dam most of the river has at least 3·0m so it is only necessary to use common sense and not cut the corners.

From Arzal to La Roche Bernard is about 3·75M. There are overhead cables (27m) about 2M up river from Arzal. The river is very attractive.

BERTHS AND ANCHORAGES

Vieux Port

Le Vieux Port, the old port, is in a small inlet on the south side of La Roche Bernard. Local boats mainly use it but the first pontoon is a reception pontoon. The harbourmaster's office is on the quay.

Port Neuf

Port Neuf is the main marina in the river at La Roche Bernard. The visitors' pontoon is the westernmost one (Pontoon A). If it is full call the marina office. There is an additional visitors' pontoon just south of the entrance to Vieux Port in the Vilaine River which is in position during the season.

Visitors' moorings

There are many moorings in the river and it is usually possible to borrow one.

Approaching La Roche Bernard *Nick Chavasse*

Looking NE up river at Port Neuf   *Nick Chavasse*

ASHORE IN LA ROCHE BERNARD

The marina can carry out most repairs but there is only basic chandlery and no fuel berth. Bread can be delivered to yachts each morning.

Ashore, there are cafés, shops and restaurants to suit every taste. The medieval town is well worth exploring. A map showing a recommended walk through the old streets and alleys is available from the tourist office. The maritime museum has models and reconstructions to show what life by the Vilaine was like. Market day is Thursday.

La Roche Bernard conjures up the delights of cruising. It is a beautiful town on the Vilaine River above the lock at Arzal. Fabulous scenery and wonderful walks. The restaurants are good too and Le Vieux Quartier is recommended ① 02 99 90 61 19.

La Roche Bernard to Folleux

After La Roche Bernard, the river becomes less steep sided but it still winds between wooded hills and is most attractive.

From La Roche Bernard to Folleux is about 4·75M. Just north of La Roche Bernard, the river passes under two road bridges (height 50m approx.) and a power cable with 27m clearance. Just before Folleux another power cable crosses the river, again with with 27m clearance.

Looking SW over 'La Roche' with Vieux Port to left and additional visitors' pontoon beyond   *Nick Chavasse*

Looking out from the inner end of the Vieux Port
Nick Chavasse

Looking NE up river at Port Neuf on right, road bridge and remains of old bridge and second road bridge   *Nick Chavasse*

59 Folleux

47°31'N 2°19'W

Shelter Excellent

Depth restrictions
3·0m or more beyond Arzal

Night entry Not recommended

HW time
Above Arzal there is no tide

Tidal stream in the river
There is usually a slight stream to seaward. This can be strong after very heavy rain

Berthing
Contact marina on VHF 9 to enquire about available berths

Facilities
Two boatyards, chandlery, restaurant, showers and toilets on both banks

Fuel Nearest is at Arzal

Charts
IGN Top25 *1022OT*

Communications
HM ☎ 02 99 91 80 87
www.port-folleux.com

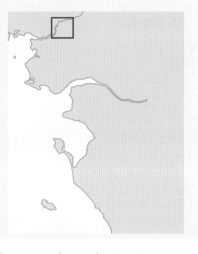

Folleux

A lovely place in the heart of the countryside, Folleux marina is a very sheltered and quiet spot with 400 moorings on pontoons and buoys on both river banks. The capitainerie is situated on the north bank and has responsibility for the moorings on both banks.

There are two boat yards, La Cale de Neptune on the north side and Multi-Nautique on the south side. Both yards have lifting and storage possibilities. Pontoons have water and electricity and can take boats up to 15m and 3m draft.

Folleux is suitable for reasonably priced 12 month contracts and overwintering.

The nearest shops are about 6km in Béganne on the north bank and 6km in Nivillac on the south bank. Electric bicycles are available to borrow. There are some rowing boats which may be borrowed to cross from one bank to the other. There is a restaurant on the north side.

ANCHORAGES IN THE VILAINE

It is possible to anchor almost anywhere in the river outside the navigable channels, except where anchoring is explicitly forbidden. Note that a similar charge to that in the marina will be made for anchoring in the vicinity of La Roche Bernard or Folleux.

Classic river section above La Roche Bernard *Nick Chavasse*

Folleux with capitainerie in centre with solar panels on roof *Nick Chavasse*

60 Redon

47°38'N 2°05'W

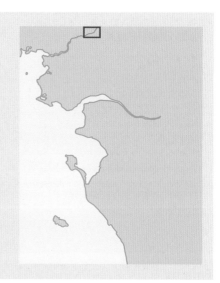

Shelter
Excellent in Redon marina

Depth restrictions
3·0m or more in river beyond Arzal
2·0m in Redon basin

Cran bridge opening (local time)
0930, 1030, 1130, 1400, 1600, 1800 and 1900
1 April to 30 September

Night entry Not recommended

HW time
Above Arzal there is no tide

Stream in the river
There is usually a slight stream to seaward.
This can be strong after very heavy rain

Berthing
Marina at Redon, several riverside
pontoons and anchorages

Facilities
Substantial market town at Redon

Fuel
Diesel at Redon

Communications
Vilaine navigation VHF 10
Redon Marina VHF 9
 ① 02 99 71 22 96,
 mob 07 77 88 23 22
Cran Bridge① 02 99 90 11 31
www.lavilaine.com for Pont de Cran
 opening times
www.redon.fr

Gateway to the canals

Further upriver, Redon is a pleasant market town and major canal port with direct access to the Nantes to Brest canal via a lock at the northeast end of the marina basin. It is 26M from the sea and has a completely different atmosphere from most yacht ports. The town is interlaced with canals and locks, and there are many fine buildings that provide evidence of Redon's important role in Breton history.

PILOTAGE

See plan on page 210

Folleux to Redon

The swing bridge at Cran (closed clearance 5·8m)

Between April and September the swing bridge at Cran opens 0930, 1030, 1130, 1400, 1600, 1800 and 1900. There is a waiting pontoon on the upstream side and a waiting jetty on the downstream side. The bridge does not open for long and it is important to watch the signals and be ready. Two reds means no passage; one red and one green means get ready; and two greens means go. The bridge may also be opened on request given 24h notice www.lavilaine.com..

By day From Folleux to Cran is about 7M. The river winds between fields and wooded hills and is most attractive. A nature reserve with a pontoon will be passed in this section. There are no hazards except two sets of power cables just below Cran with 27m headroom (*see plan page 210*). The speed limit in the river is 5·5knots.

From Cran bridge to Rieux is just under 3M and shortly afterwards the vista widens out for the last 3M to Redon and the river becomes much more like an inland waterway with junctions and signposts.

The marina is in the old sea lock of the Nantes-Brest canal and it is necessary to follow the signposts to the Port du Redon, by taking the port hand stream into the lock on arrival at Redon. The lock gate is permanently open since the barrage at Arzal now maintains the water level.

Cran swing bridge *Nick Chavasse*

Looking NW (downstream) at waiting jetty from Cran bridge *Nick Chavasse*

Port hand stream leading to Redon marina *Nick Chavasse*

Entering the old sea
lock on the way into
the marina
Nick Chavasse

BERTHS AND ANCHORAGES

Rieux

There are two visitors' pontoons, with 4 visitors' berths, in attractive surroundings and fairly deep water 3M upstream from Cran close to the village of Rieux. Pontoons are adjacent to a campsite and there are shops in Rieux (0·5M).

Redon

The marina is through the lock on the port side. Maximum depth is 2·0m but could be less. Canal boats use the starboard side. The visitors' pontoon is situated just outside the lock to the grand basin on the northwest side of the river. The port office is on the starboard hand side on the quay. The fuel berth is on a pontoon on the port hand side of the inlet channel just outside the marina entrance. It is self-service 24/7.

ASHORE IN REDON

Redon is a market town and a major port for canal boats so most yachting requirements can be satisfied. The diesel berth is on the port hand side just outside the entrance to the marina basin.

The town has an excellent covered market (open in the morning on Mondays, Fridays and Saturdays), good shops and restaurants, and an interesting canal

museum. There are some fine 15th to 18th century town houses and a surprisingly large abbey church. For a town that has been sacked repeatedly in its history it has all the appearances of a wealthy past.

There are open air markets every day except Friday and Sunday, a hypermarket a mile away on the road to Nantes and the railway station is within easy walking distance of the marina. It has direct trains to Nantes and along the coast to Vannes and Quimper.

Redon is a good place to leave a boat or over winter. There is an interesting inland waterways museum next to the capitainerie.

Nantes-Brest canal which may be accessed from the Vilaine river in Redon *Nick Chavasse*

Looking NE towards Redon centre *Nick Chavasse*

61 Piriac-sur-Mer

47°23'N 2°33'W *See plan page 202*

Shelter
Good in the marina

Depth restrictions
Sill gives 1·4m on opening. Check gauge on
  entry/exit
The marina has 2m

Night entry Lit

HW time Brest HW−0110

Mean height of tide (m) St-Nazaire

HWS	HWN	LWN	LWS
5.4	4·3	n/a	n/a

Tidal stream in approach
NE – Brest HW−0600 to −0100 (0·7kn)
SW – Brest HW−0100 to −0600 (0·7kn)

Berthing Marina

Fuel On quay

Facilities
Limited repairs; adequate shops, cafés
and restaurants; good market

Charts
SHOM *7033, 7136*
Imray *C39*

Communications
VHF 9
HM ☎ 02 40 23 52 32
www.portpiriacsurmer.fr for sill
  opening hours

Panorama of marina *Capitainerie Piriac-sur-Mer*

Delightful holiday resort

Piriac is a delightful place only 7M south of the
mouth of La Vilaine. It is a small 17th-century town
that has been beautifully renovated as a holiday
resort. The town is full of flowers that make the
cafés and restaurants seem particularly inviting. For
the more adventurous, it is a good base for visiting
the swampy area of Grand Brière for bird-watching
or the medieval town of Guérande, although both
can be reached just as easily from La Baule or
St-Nazaire.

The marina is located in a drying harbour with a
sill and a flap gate.

PILOTAGE

Approach and entrance to Piriac

Piriac flap gate

The sill dries 0·8m and the gate automatically drops
open when the height of tide reaches 2·2m, which
gives 1·4m over the sill. The digital depth gauge
shows the actual depth over the sill. The sill opening
times may be found at www.portpiriacsurmer.fr.

There is no large-scale chart of the approaches but
the channel seems to be deeper than the sill.

However, yachts regularly go aground in the
approach and just outside the marina entrance so
there may be some shallower patches. The deepest
part of the channel is in the middle.

By day From the north, a distinctive belfry on the
seafront identifies Piriac. The approach is rocky so
start from a position 100m northeast of Grand
Norven north cardinal beacon. Steer about 165° and
pass between the green and red beacons to enter the
harbour.

From the south or west, avoid the rocks off Pointe
du Castelli by keeping outside Les Bayonnelles west
cardinal buoy and well outside Rohtrès north
cardinal beacon tower and then approaching Piriac
from the north as above.

The entrance to the marina is to port,
immediately inside the breakwaters. It is only about
15m wide and is marked by two red and two green
beacons. Red lights indicate that the gate is closed;
green lights indicate that it is open.

By night Approach in the white sector of the light on
the inner mole and remain in this sector until past
the breakwater lights.

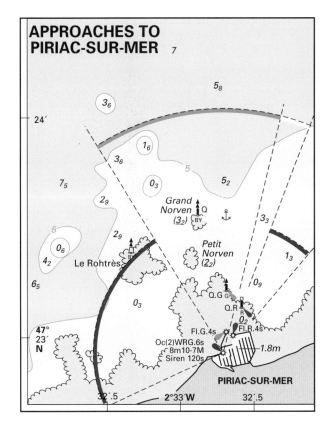

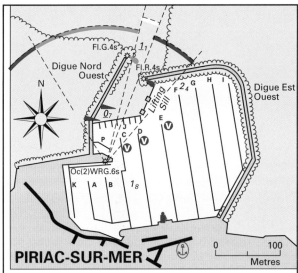

Looking towards entrance from marina at traffic lights and guage showing 2·3m over sill *Nick Chavasse*

BERTHS AND ANCHORAGES

Piriac marina

Visitors are normally met by a launch and allocated a berth. If there is no launch, berth on the visitors' pontoon (pontoon E), which is immediately ahead on entering. If pontoon E is full, try pontoon C.

⚓ Piriac approaches

47°23'·55N 02°32'·72W

In settled weather, there is a temporary anchorage, to wait for the tide, east of the Grand Norven beacon in about 2·5m.

⚓ Pointe du Maresclé

47°28'·16N 2°29'·87W

Protected from the east, this wide bay is just south of the mouth of the Vilaine. Approach from north of west to avoid the dangers near Île de Belair. Anchor 0·5M northeast of Île de Belair where depth permits. A night escape to Piriac or the Vilaine is possible using Penlan light.

⚓ Mesquer

47°25'·44N 2°28'·20W

Sheltered from the east, Mesquer is a little harbour and large drying bay 4M northeast of Piriac. Approach from a position between Basse Normande north cardinal buoy and Laronesse isolated danger beacon and steer about 110° towards Mesquer. Enter the harbour between the red and green beacons. At neaps it is possible to anchor east of the jetty. Boats that can take the ground can go further in for better shelter but beware of shellfish beds.

⚓ Île Dumet

47°24'·77N 2°36'·94W

Slightly sheltered from the southwest, Île Dumet is a bird sanctuary 3M west-northwest of Piriac. There are shallow patches northeast and northwest of the island so approach with the lighthouse on about 215°. Anchor northeast of the lighthouse.

In the 18th century Île Dumet was used by Admiral Hawke as a market garden to provide vegetables for his sailors when they were blockading the French Fleet in the harbours of Quiberon Bay. He was one of the first naval commanders to appreciate the importance of fresh vegetables in preventing disease in men confined on ships for long periods.

ASHORE IN PIRIAC

Piriac has a fuel pontoon and a chandlery but otherwise it has limited harbour facilities. There are marine facilities Rue du Pladreau, 700m from the port; see www.portpiriacsurmer.fr The town is charming. It has a reasonable range of shops and a market on Monday, Wednesday and Saturday. There are many cafés and restaurants.

62 La Turballe

47°21'N 2°31'W

Shelter
Good except from SSW due to swell

Depth restrictions
2·0m in approach
1·5m in marina

Night entry Lit

HW time Brest HW−0010

Mean height of tide (m) Le Croisic

HWS	HWN	LWN	LWS
5.4	4·3	2·0	0·7

Tidal stream in approach
N – Brest HW−0600 to −0100 (0·5kn)
S – Brest HW−0100 to +0400 (0·5kn)
Slack – Brest HW+0400 to −0600

Berthing Marina

Fuel SW harbour wall

Facilities
As for a major fishing port

Charts
SHOM *7033, 7145*
Imray *C39*

Communications
Marina VHF 9 (call before entry)
HM ✆ 02 40 23 41 65 / 06 65 93 03 15
www.peche-plaisance44.com

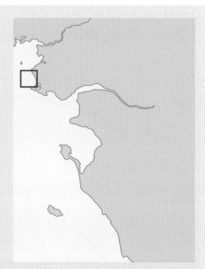

Warning

St Nazaire wind farm

A major wind farm, consisting of 80 wind turbines on the Banc de Guerande is in an area bordered by the following positions:

NW point   47°12'·36N 2°42'·16W

NE point   47°10'·31N 2°30'·40W

SW point   47°10'·51N 2°41'·98W

SE point   47°06'·72N 2°32'·91W

Navigation through the wind farm is permitted for vessels under 25m. See plan p. 202.

For updated information see
www.parc-eolien-en-mer-de-saint-nazaire.fr

Visitors' pontoon is slightly right of a line through the dory
Nick Chavasse

Fishing port with large marina

La Turballe has achieved a good balance as both a working fishing port and a popular beach resort. It is now the leading fishing port in the Loire-Atlantique region.

La Turballe has undergone major refurbishment, extending the mole west of the port and building a smaller mole stretching southwest from the capitainerie towards the outer end of the main mole.

This area will be developed into a reception area (avant-port) during 2023.

There are two harbours. The Basin de Garlahy is locked and totally dedicated to fishing boats. The Port de Plaisance is dredged to provide all tide access; fishing boats use one half and yachts the other half. The visitors' area is quite small so the harbourmaster and his team will help you find a berth.

Approaching La Turballe entrance with extensive works on the western mole under way *Nick Chavasse*

PILOTAGE

La Turballe approach and entrance

Entry restrictions

Entry is not recommended in strong west wind or swell.

The marina gets very crowded in season and it is necessary to call on VHF 9 before entering. When the marina is full, the harbourmaster may broadcast announcements on VHF 9.

By day The long white-walled fish market, the water tower at the back of town and the long beach to the south make La Turballe easy to identify from any direction. However, it must only be approached from the southwest to avoid the rocky shoals to the north.

If approaching from the west, aim for the north end of the beach. Keep towards the west breakwater because rocks extend from the east side. Once past the inner breakwater head, turn sharply to starboard to enter the Port de Plaisance.

By night Night entry is not advised until the refurbishment of the mole is complete and new leading lights are brought into use.

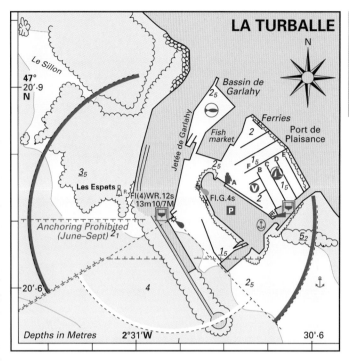

BERTHS AND ANCHORAGES

La Turballe marina

The visitors' pontoons are clearly indicated and are in the southwest part of the marina. Space for berthing and manoeuvring a 12m boat is quite limited and in fact the area designated for visiting boats can become one big raft in season.

⚓ South of La Turballe harbour

In offshore winds there is pleasant anchorage off the long sandy beach to the south of the harbour.

ASHORE IN LA TURBALLE

There is a fuel berth on the south breakwater, a 2·5-T crane, a 40-T and 310-T travel-lift and a slipway. All repairs can be undertaken on yachts. The town is a lively holiday resort with plenty of restaurants, shops and cafés close to the marina.

A magnificent 2M beach is just south of the marina and there is easy access to the salt marshes to see the wildlife.

Looking N over marina *Nick Chavasse*

La Turballe beach adjacent to S of marina *Nick Chavasse*

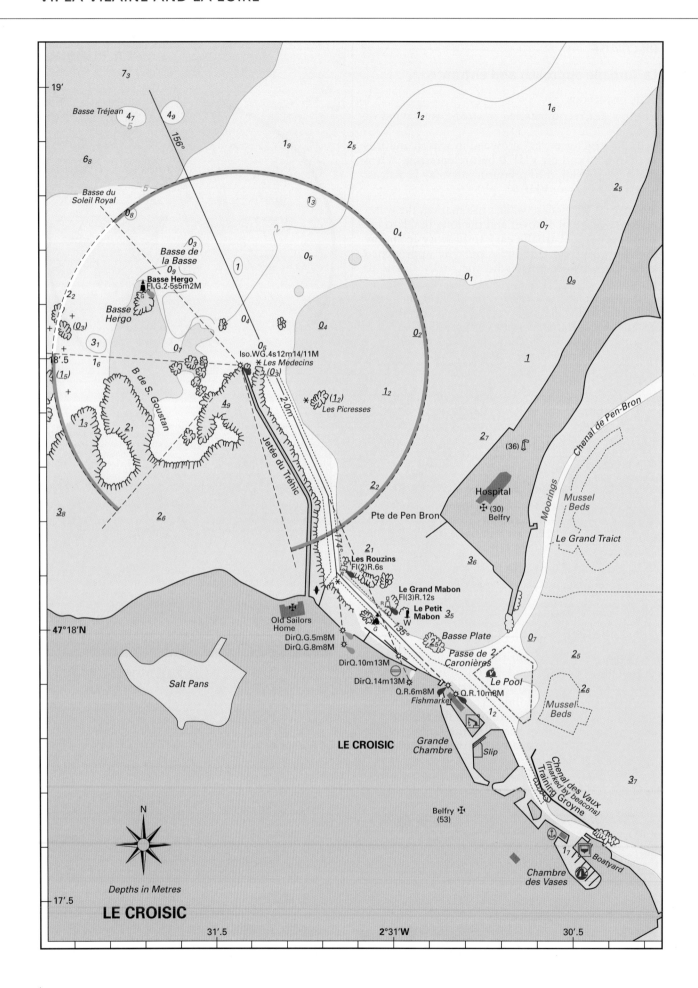

LE CROISIC

LE CROISIC

Depths in Metres

63 Le Croisic

47°18′N 2°31′W

Shelter
Good in drying harbour
Exposed to NW in Le Pool

Depth restrictions
Channel dredged to 2·0m on leading line
Yacht harbour dries 2·0m

Night entry Lit

HW time Brest HW-0010

Mean height of tide (m) Le Croisic

HWS	HWN	LWN	LWS
5·4	4·3	2·0	0·7

Tidal stream in entrance
5kn at half-flood and half-ebb

Berthing
Drying harbour, 1·5m in Le Pool
anchorage

Facilities
As for fishing port and holiday resort

Charts
SHOM *7395, 7145*
Imray *C39*

Communications
Marina VHF 9
① 09 81 12 75 92,
mob 06 65 93 34 05
www.peche-plaisance44.com
www.tourisme-lecroisic.fr

Looking S at belfry on left, tower on old sailors' home in centre and Tréhic light on breakwater head *Nick Chavasse*

Warning
A major wind farm, consisting of 80 wind turbines, has been constructed on the Banc de Guerande. See pages 202 and 218.

Historic salt port

Le Croisic is a fascinating town. It has been important as a salt port since before the middle ages. The salt was very good for fish curing and Le Croisic had a large sardine fishing fleet. Then in the 19th century it became one of the first swimming resorts.

Today it is a thriving tourist resort and an excellent base from which to visit the salt marshes, the beautiful walled town of Guérande, the salt museum at Batz-sur-Mer or the nearby beaches.

The harbour is made up of a curious series of islands with drying basins between them. Fishing boats and sailing boats that can take the ground use these. Boats wishing to remain afloat must anchor or use a mooring outside the harbour in Le Pool.

PILOTAGE

Le Croisic approach and entrance

The best time to access Le Croisic is 2 hours either side of HW. Beware strong cross streams.

By day Start from a position about 0·5M north of Basse Hergo starboard hand beacon tower. This can be approached directly from the northwest. However, coming from the west, particularly at low water, it is necessary to keep at least 1M off shore to avoid the reef between Basse Castouillet west cardinal buoy and Basse Hergo starboard hand beacon tower.

Le Croisic can be identified by a distinctive large belfry in town (not to be confused with the tower on the Old Sailors' home) and a conspicuous hospital at Pen Bron on the east side of the channel. Steer for the town belfry on 156° and pick up the first pair of leading marks which are red squares on white pylons, almost in line with the belfry. Bring them in line on 156° and follow them into the channel. This will leave Basse Hergo starboard hand beacon tower and the Jetée du Trehic to starboard.

Follow the transit to the bend in the breakwater. Then steer 174° to follow the second leading marks, which are yellow squares with a dark green vertical

First pair of leading marks on 156° *Nick Chavasse*

Looking S at second set of leading marks *Nick Chavasse*

Third set of transit marks on 135° *Nick Chavasse*

stripe on green and white pylons. These marks are located in a bay at the root of the breakwater and are not lit during the day. They are difficult to spot and somewhat confusingly are closer than the first set of marks when entering the port.

At Les Rouzins port hand buoy turn onto 135° and the third transit which is a pair of red and white chequered squares on the fish market roof and on the quay in front of the fish market. These are also not lit during the day. This channel is buoyed because it moves.

Hold the transit until close to the fishing quay to avoid Basse Plate, drying 2·5m and when the fishmarket is abeam turn to port to enter Le Pool for a mooring or, for the yacht basin, continue along the channel leaving the port hand stakes marking the training wall about 25m to port. The entrance to the yacht basin is the fifth one on the starboard side.

By night The white sector of Jetée du Tréhic light clears all the distant dangers, including Le Four and Île Dumet. However, it leads onto the rocks nearer to the harbour entrance so make the final approach using the east green sector with the Dir.QW leading lights in line. The three transits are easier to identify by night than by day.

BERTHS AND ANCHORAGES

Le Pool (Le Poul)

Le Pool is a fair size but moorings occupy much of it. There are three orange visitors' buoys. Many of the mooring buoys have very little water at springs. The buoys nearest the sea and on the edge of the channel have the most water. Call the harbourmaster for guidance. Mussel beds cover the drying banks of Le Grand Traict, but the narrow and steep-sided Chenal de Pen-Bron runs up the east side of the peninsula. It contains more moorings. The ebb runs very hard in the Chenal de Pen-Bron and quite hard in Le Pool. The stream is very strong especially at springs and you would not be able to row a dinghy to the quay. Look out for a wind over tide scenario and the mooring knocking the bow and keeping you awake!

Anchoring is prohibited in all areas due to mussel beds.

Port de Plaisance

The Port de Plaisance (drying) is in the Chambre des Vases. Boats that can take the ground can enter and secure bow-to a pontoon with a stern mooring.

⚓ Rade de Croisic

Sheltered from the south and west but horribly exposed to wind or swell from the northwest, there are many anchorages off the beach between La Turballe and Le Croisic.

Looking N at orange visitors' buoy in Le Croisic Pool at LW and Jetée du Tréhic beyond *Nick Chavasse*

Moorings in Le Pool *Nick Chavasse*

ASHORE IN LE CROISIC

Le Croisic is an active fishing and yachting port. There is a 60-T travel-lift and boatyard with haul-out facilities, a marine engineer and good chandlery but no fuel berth.

The town is an attractive, busy holiday resort with a full range of shops, cafés and restaurants. There are good markets on Monday (July and August), Thursday and Saturday. The town is a fascinating place to visit.

Looking SE at moorings in Le Pool *Nick Chavasse*

Port de Plaisance with capitainerie beyond *Nick Chavasse*

64 La Baule and Le Pouliguen

47°16'N 2°25'W

Shelter
Good except in strong S and SE

Depth restrictions
Entrance dries 1·6m
About 1·2m on visitors' pontoon

Night entry Not recommended

HW time Brest HW-0005

Mean height of tide (m) Le Pouliguen

HWS	HWN	LWN	LWS
5.4	4·3	2·0	0·7

Tidal stream in river
4kn at half-flood and half-ebb

Berthing
Marina with visitors' pontoon

Facilities
All marina facilities plus busy and attractive holiday resort

Fuel
By visitors' pontoon

Charts
SHOM *7395, 7145*
Imray *C39*

Communications
Marina VHF 9
☎ 02 40 11 97 97
www.portlabaulelepouliguen.fr

Warning

A major wind farm, consisting of 80 wind turbines, has been constructed on the Banc de Guerande. See pages 202 and 218.

The genteel marina at La Baule

La Baule and Le Pouliguen marina is at the west end of the magnificent 5M beach at La Baule. It is ideally situated for the fashionable resorts of La Baule and Le Pouliguen. There is space for 30 visitors of less than 11·5m length in depths of 1·2m on the visitors' pontoon. A drying entrance adds to the excitement. A waiting buoy, situated off the entrance, is available in season.

Entering La Baule and Le Pouliguen at HW Nick Chavasse

PILOTAGE

Le Pouliguen approach and entrance

Warning The approach dries, the sands shift and it is not very well marked, so enter close to high water. Avoid Le Pouliguen altogether if there is strong wind or swell from the southeast, particularly on the ebb when the seas break in the shallow water.

By day The best approach is from the west between Penchâteau port hand buoy and Les Guérandaises starboard hand buoy. Leave Penchâteau port hand to port and steer 020° to leave Martineau port hand buoy to port. Come round onto about 320° and

The entrance to La Baule and Le Pouliguen towards LW Nick Chavasse

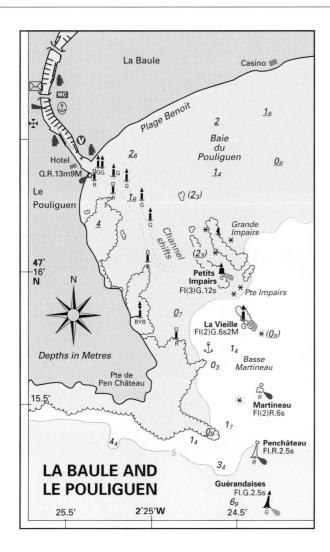

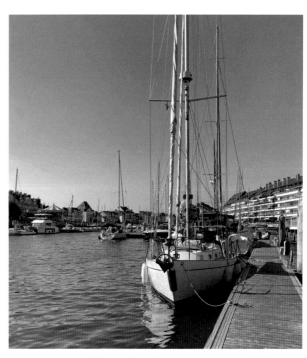

Looking N from visitors' pontoon *Nick Chavasse*

Looking N up harbour towards road bridge from the visitors' berths *Nick Chavasse*

steer for a point just east of the second of the two port hand beacons. This will leave La Vieille starboard hand beacon and Les Petits Impairs starboard hand tower beacon well to starboard.

When the second red beacon is abeam turn to starboard on about 340° and steer for the channel marked by the four starboard and two port beacons. Follow these into the river, if necessary also using the transit of the church spire between the pier heads.

The channel is quite narrow with high sands on either side so caution is needed. Some of the beacons are quite slender and not very conspicuous.

By night There are a few lights but night entry is not recommended. The entry into Pornichet 5M to the east is a well lit alternative.

BERTHS AND ANCHORAGES

La Baule and Le Pouliguen marina

The visitors' pontoon is to starboard near the entrance where there is also a new harbour office and showers in the YC building. The fuel berth is further upstream on the west side. The marina continues upriver and occupies most of the east side of the river as far as the bridge. The marina staff are very helpful.

⚓ Pointe de Penchâteau

If waiting for the tide, there is a temporary anchorage in about 1m some 400m northwest of Basse Martineau buoy.

ASHORE IN LE POULIGUEN

There are all the facilities of a sophisticated yachting centre with a yard, chandlers and engineers close at hand. The yacht club on the east side above the bridge is hospitable to visitors.

Le Pouliguen is a smart holiday resort with a full range of shops, restaurants and cafés. Wonderful beaches.

65 Pornichet

47°16'N 2°21'W

Shelter Excellent

Depth restrictions
2·5m in marina

Night entry Lit

HW time Brest HW-0015

Mean height of tide (m) Pornichet

HWS	HWN	LWN	LWS
5·5	4·4	2·1	0·8

Tidal stream in approach
Streams are weak and irregular

Berthing
Large modern marina

Facilities
All marina facilities, town is 0·5M away

Charts
SHOM *7033, 7145*
Imray *C39*

Communications
Marina VHF 9
② 02 40 61 03 20
www.portdepornichet.fr

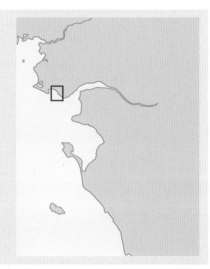

Warning

A major wind farm, consisting of 80 wind turbines, has been constructed on the Banc de Guerande. See pages 202 and 218.

The parking lot at La Baule

Pornichet is a huge modern marina, with room for 1,000 yachts, at the east end of the 5M beach at La Baule. It is a long way from the casino and the fashionable part of La Baule but the marina has easier access and much more room than Le Pouliguen.

PILOTAGE

Pornichet approach and entrance

See plan page 202

By day From the west, pass between Penchâteau port hand buoy and Guérandaises starboard hand buoy (*see plan page 225*). Then steer about 085° for the forest of masts at the east end of La Baule. This route passes close north of a starboard hand buoy.

The marina entrance faces north and the red and green beacons marking the entrance can only be seen on close approach. Pass between the beacons to enter the marina.

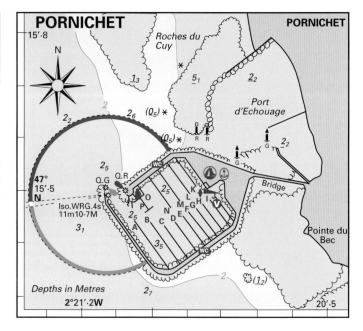

From the south and east, the easy route is the west entrance described above. However, with a large-scale chart, there are some more interesting possibilities. A good approach from the southwest is to enter the reef between the port hand and starboard hand buoys marking Les Evens and Les Troves and approach the marina on 040°. From the east it is possible to enter the reef between the Grand and the Petit Charpentier but this requires a detailed chart as there are several unmarked rocks.

Pornichet marina entrance *Nick Chavasse*

By night Approach from the west using the white sector of Pornichet pierhead light. Watch out for the unlit starboard hand buoy 0·5M east of Penchâteau port hand. The beacons in the entrance are lit.

BERTHS AND ANCHORAGES

Pornichet marina

There are 10 pontoons (A–J) on the south side of the harbour and six (K–P) on the north. The fuel station is on Pontoon P - the first on the port hand side on entry. The heads of most of the pontoons are allocated to visitors. Visitors under 10m can also use the whole of pontoon I and the odd numbered side of pontoon J. All the main berths have a depth of 2·5m. Pontoon O, the second on the port hand side on entry, can take visiting yachts up to 25m.

⚓ Saint-Marc

47°14′22N 02°16′72

Adventurous film buffs may wish to use a large-scale chart to work through the Charpentier reef and visit the pretty holiday resort of Saint-Marc where Jacques Tati made *Monsieur Hulot's Holiday* (worth watching on YouTube!). The anchorage is completely exposed to the south and only suitable as a day anchorage in good weather.

ASHORE IN PORNICHET

Facilities

Pornichet is a well-equipped modern marina. The fuel pontoon is immediately to port on entry and all repairs can be carried out. There is a chandlery, restaurants and cafés in the marina, but no food shops or bakery. There is a 24-T travel-lift.

The marina is about 0·5M from town, across the bridge, which offers all the delights of a fair-sized beach resort. There is a good market on Wednesday and Saturday.

In the late 19th century, holiday resorts developed along many beautiful French beaches, spurred on by the expansion of the railway. La Baule began in this way and has gone on to become the playground of wealthy families with the money to invest in holiday homes. During the 60-year development period architects competed to design something different. A walk along the promenade and back through the side streets is fascinating - every architectural style has been used, from half-timbered cottages to exotic Art Deco designs.

Fuel berth immediately on port hand side after entry
Nick Chavasse

Looking NE over Pornichet marina
Nick Chavasse

Bridge to the town from the marina *Nick Chavasse*

66 Saint-Nazaire

47°16'N 2°12'W

Shelter
Excellent in St-Nazaire basin

Depth restrictions None

Night entry Lit but not recommended

HW time
St-Nazaire Brest HW-0005

Mean height of tide (m) St-Nazaire

HWS	HWN	LWN	LWS
5·8	4·6	2·2	0·8

Tidal stream in Loire approaches
Flood – Brest HW–0600 to HW
Ebb – Brest HW to –0600
Very strong at St-Nazaire at half-flood and half-ebb

Berthing
Alongside in SW corner of commercial dock, Bassin St-Nazaire

Facilities
As for a commercial dock; very limited for cruising yachtsmen

Charts
SHOM *7033, 6797, 7396*
Imray *C39*

Communications
Loire port control and E Lock VHF 14
St-Nazaire Plaisance HM at E Lock
☏ 02 40 45 39 00
www.visit-saint-nazaire.com

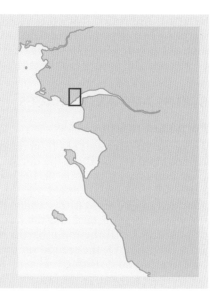

Warning

A major wind farm, consisting of 80 wind turbines, has been constructed on the Banc de Guerande. See pages 202 and 218.

Busy commercial river

Cruising yachtsmen are not encouraged to visit St Nazaire. The reason is that the port is not set up for sea-going visitors. It is very much a commercial dock. However, if you are prepared to accept that there are no facilities, it is possible to moor in the Bassin Saint-Nazaire next to the awe-inspiring submarine pens.

The Loire handles approximately 10% of the French maritime trade and there are often ships being held in the waiting area at the mouth of the river.

Bassin de St-Nazaire showing the east lock entrance and submarine pens opposite *Patrick Roach*

PILOTAGE

La Loire to Saint-Nazaire

See plan page 229

By day The approach is straightforward. The big ship channel is well marked by buoys, but it is not necessary to adhere to it until past Pte de l'Aiguillon as there is plenty of water either side. There are some isolated dangers outside the channel but they are mostly marked. After Pte de l'Aiguillon it is best to keep close to the main channel, although there is generally space to pass outside the buoys if necessary to avoid commercial traffic.

Approach along Chenal de Bonne-Anse leaving the two long breakwaters, which mark the big-ship entrance to the docks, to port. Leave the main channel at this point to pass between the SE Vieux Môle port hand buoy and Sud de la Basse Nazaire south cardinal buoy. Turn to port on about 340° until the east lock, which lies east/west, will open up to port.

The lock (24 hours) opens for exit on the even hours and for entry about 10 minutes later except the times are 10 minutes earlier at 0800 and are at 2300 instead of midnight. The lock is not very user friendly with few accessible rings or methods of securing a yacht. Be ready for the unexpected!

By night The Passe des Charpentiers leading lights close to Pointe de l'Aiguillon are very conspicuous and lit buoys mark the channel. Entry through the lock at night is not recommended.

Entrance to lock Entré Est with lock keeper's office in white building in centre *Nick Chavasse*

BERTHS AND ANCHORAGES

Bassin de Saint-Nazaire

Once through the lock, pass through the swing bridge into the Bassin de St-Nazaire, where yachts berth on the pontoon adjoining the submarine pens. The pontoon by the submarine pens is also used for organised events but it is not secure as the submarine pens can be frequented by petty criminals at night. It is controlled by the town hall and it is managed by the port.

There are few facilities but repairs could probably be arranged. There are no showers or toilets. The town has all facilities and there is a supermarket close to the submarine pens. The submarine museum in the pens (complete with submarine) as well as make-believe tours of shipyards, cruise liners and the world is a paradise for children of *all* ages.

⚓ Trébézy

47°14'·88N 2°15'·33W

Sheltered from west to north, this wide, attractive bay is just north of the Phare de l'Aiguillon. Approach from the southeast and anchor where depth permits outside the moorings. There are several more anchorages in the bays between Trébézy and Saint-Nazaire.

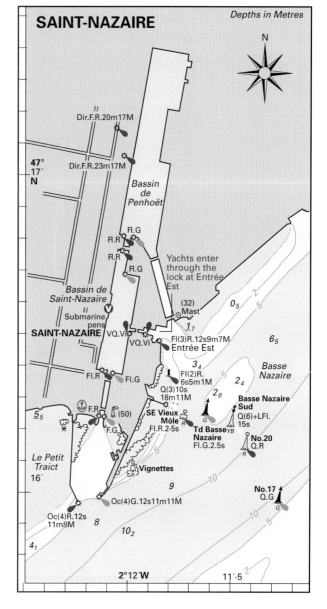

The Louis Joubert Forme Écluse, to the E of Bassin de Saint-Nazaire, was the scene of a courageous action by the Royal Navy and Royal Marines during the Second World War, when the destroyer *HMS Campbeltown* was rammed into the lock gates and detonated to prevent the use of the submarine pens. This was the only dry dock on the Atlantic coast of Europe big enough to take the German battleship *Tirpitz*.

Visitors' pontoon on W side of Bassin de Saint-Nazaire
Nick Chavasse

St Nazaire office du tourisme occupying a small proportion of one submarine pen
Nick Chavasse

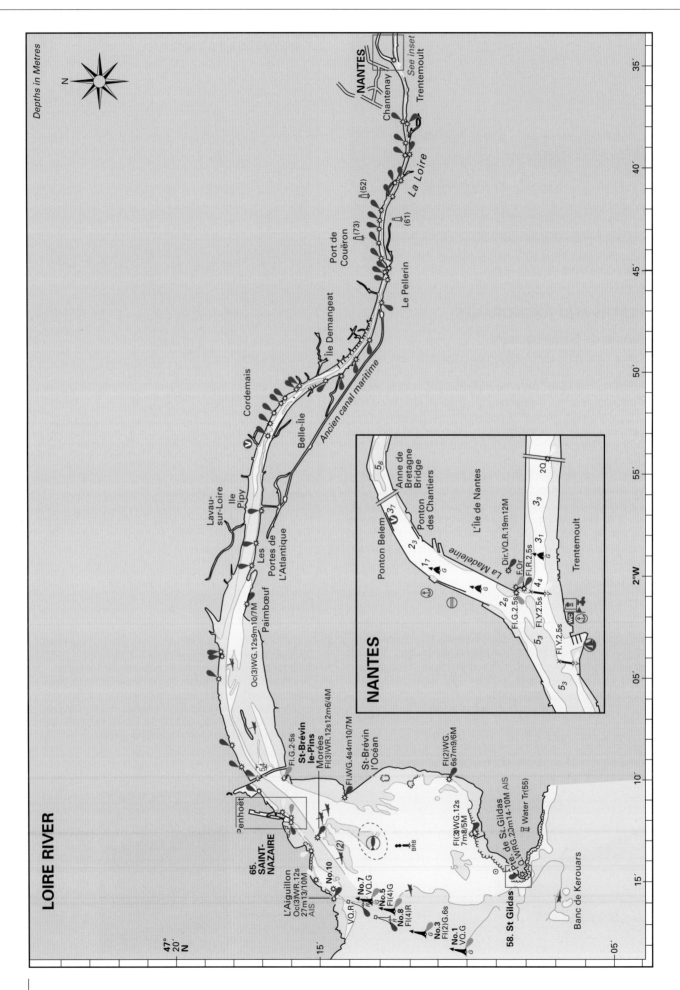

LOIRE RIVER

Depths in Metres

N

47°
20'
N

L'Aiguillon
Oc(3)WR.12s
27m13/10M
AIS

No.10

65.
SAINT-
NAZAIRE

Penhoët

No.7
VQ.G

No.5
Fl(4)G

No.8
Fl(4)R

No.3
Fl(2)G.6s

No.1
VQ.G

VQ.R

54

Fl.G.2.5s

St-Brévin
le-Pins

Morées
Fl(3)WR.12s12m6/4M

Fl.WG.4s4m10/7M

St-Brévin
l'Océan

Fl(2)WG.
6s7m9/6M

Fl(3)WG.12s
7m8/5M

BRB

58. St Gildas
Pte. de St.Gildas
Q.WRG.22m14-10M AIS

Water Tr(55)

Banc de Kerouars

Oc(3)WG.12s9m10/7M

Paimbœuf

Les
Portes de
L'Atlantique

Île
Pipy

Lavau-
sur-Loire

Cordemais

Belle-Île

Ancien canal maritime

Île Demangeat

Port de
Couëron

Le Pellerin

(73)

(61)

(52)

La Loire

NANTES

Chantenay
Trentemoult

See inset

05'

10'

15'

05'

10'

15'

20'

25'

30'

35'

2°W

40'

45'

50'

55'

NANTES

Ponton Belem

Anne de
Bretagne Bridge

Ponton
des Chantiers

La Madeleine

L'île de Nantes

Dir.VQ.R.19m12M

F.Or.

Fl.R.2.5s

Trentemoult

Fl.G.2.5s

Fl.Y.2.5s

Fl.Y.2.5s

5_6

3_7

2_3

1_7

2_6

3_1

4_4

5_3

3_3

3_3

$2Q$

5_3

67 Nantes and La Loire ports

47°12′N 01°33′W

Shelter
Excellent in St-Nazaire basin

Depth restrictions
2m in Nantes near the bridge

Night entry Lit but not recommended

HW time Nantes Brest HW+0115

Mean height of tide (m) St-Gildas

HWS	HWN	IWN	IWS
6·3	5·1	1·8	0·9

Tidal stream approach
Flood – Brest HW–0600 to HW
Ebb – Brest HW to –0600
Very strong at St-Nazaire at half-flood and half-ebb

Berthing Ponton Belem

Facilities
Water, electricity, showers and toilets on pontoon; substantial city

Charts
SHOM 7396
Imray C39

Communications
VHF 9
Ponton Belem, Nantes
Ⓣ 02 40 37 04 62
Nantes Gestion Equipement (NGE) for
access code Ⓣ 02 40 37 04 62
Les Portes de L'Atlantique
Ⓣ 02 40 27 10 10
Cordemais Ⓣ 02 40 57 73 95
Couëron Ⓣ 02 40 37 04 62
www.en.nantes.fr/
www.portasec-cordemais.com
www.ville-coueron.fr
www.placedeport.fr/services.
phpcoueron

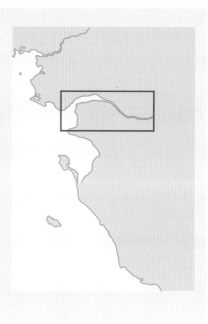

Warning

A major wind farm, consisting of 80 wind turbines, has been constructed on the Banc de Guerande. See pages 202 and 218.

Commercial river

There are several ports which have facilities to lift boats in the Loire, for technical repairs or winter dry berthing. Cordemais, is an example which is a safe and quiet place to leave a boat. It is also well connected to UK, with low cost flights via Nantes airport.

Paimbœuf light *Nick Chavasse*

PILOTAGE

St-Nazaire to Nantes

Tidal strategy

Leave Saint-Nazaire an hour before low water Nantes and expect to carry a fair tide all the way to Nantes, although there are places such as Cordemais, about half way to Nantes, where you can stop. Heading down river, leave Nantes about an hour before high water Nantes and expect to encounter some foul tide as LW St-Nazaire is less than five hours after HW Nantes.

By day The channel from St-Nazaire to Nantes is well marked. The river is wide and deep, until Paimbœuf, with starboard hand white tower with green top. A significant sea can build up west of Paimbœuf. Further upstream there can still be a considerable chop in strong winds. The passage is interesting but not particularly attractive. It is mainly undulating near Saint-Nazaire and then low-lying marshland.

By night Lit but not recommended.

Pont de St Nazaire looking SE *Nick Chavasse*

Les Ports de L'Atlantique *Nick Chavasse*

BERTHS

Les Portes de L'Atlantique

47°17'·13N 01°59'·85W

Les Portes de L'Atlantique, a *port á sec*, is 7M from the Atlantic, and 1·5M east of Paimbœuf. Dry berthing facility with all-tide access to waiting pontoon (2·8m at LW) prior to lifting boat. Boat lifting dock 7·5m wide by 25m long and 50-T travel-lift. Suitable for repairs and winter storage. Visitors welcome to stay on pontoon. Fuel available 24/7.

Cordemais

47°16'·9N 001°52'·7W

Half-way between St Nazaire and Nantes, Cordemais, a lovely quiet harbour hidden away up a tributary of the Loire, is a good place to stop. It is a safe and quiet place to leave the boat, where repairs can be done. Well connected to UK with low cost flights via Nantes' airport which is approximately 32km distant.

Enter the Cordemais arm by turning to port at the west cardinal, 47°16'·92N 01°53'·88W. You will see several very high chimneys which is the power station at Cordemais, well before you reach the west cardinal. Access is possible from HW-3 to HW+3.

Chimneys at Cordemais power station with house on a tower folly and west cardinal marking entrance to Cordemais *Nick Chavasse*

Visitors' moorings in Cordemais *Nick Chavasse*

Couëron entrance with church as landmark *Nick Chavasse*

There is a mid-river all-tide pontoon with three visitors' places, and a very reasonably priced drying pontoon. It is possible to safely leave a boat here for a week or two. Water and electricity at all berths. Bar/lunch time restaurant at the harbour and bakery, grocery store, ATM and post office in the village 500m. There are buses and trains which run direct from Cordemais to Nantes.

Boats up to 15m, 15 T and 2·2m draught may be hauled out at Loire Nautic Services (LNS). Boats are taken with a trailer behind a tractor. Also suitable for catamarans up to 7·5m beam. Approx 250 berths with water and electricity included. All kinds of repairs possible and small chandler at LNS. Sailmakers and engine mechanics available on demand.

Couëron

04°12′56N 01°43′78W

Couëron is 6M from Nantes and is situated at the mouth of the small Darau Channel. The entrance is marked by two spars and is accessible for two hours either side of HW. Three visitor berths in drying harbour, pontoon mooring and max draught of 1·2m.

Ponton Belem, Nantes

Ponton Belem has replaced Ponton Anne de Bretagne, Ponton Des Chantiers, Ponton D'Aiguillon and Trentemoult Marina as the visitors' berths in Nantes. It is situated on the north side of the Madeleine branch of the Loire, immediately below the Anne de Bretagne bridge. It has water, electricity, showers and toilets on the pontoon. There is a minimum depth of 3–4m and it is immediately adjacent to the pretty city. Telephone Nantes Gestion Equipement (NGE) for the access code to the pontoon gate. (*See port facts box on page 231 for NGE contact details.*) Trentemoult marina is silted up and no longer accepts visitors. Ponton Belem changed ownership in 2021 and is expected to be refurbished by 2023.

Looking E over Ponton Belem towards city centre
Nick Chavasse

Nantes, Ponton Belem *Nick Chavasse*

68 Saint-Gildas

47°08′N 2°15′W

Shelter
Good from S, reasonable from W but exposed to N

Depth restrictions
1·5m on moorings

Night entry Lit

HW time
Brest HW–0045 neaps, +0025 springs

Mean height of tide (m) St-Gildas

HWS	HWN	LWN	LWS
5·6	4·4	2·1	0·8

Tidal stream approach
E – Brest HW–0600 to HW (1·0kn)
W – Brest HW to –0600 (1·3kn)

Berthing
Dry out on anchor

Facilities
Limited facilities

Charts
SHOM *7395*
Imray *C40*

Communications
HM VHF 9
☎ 02 40 21 60 07

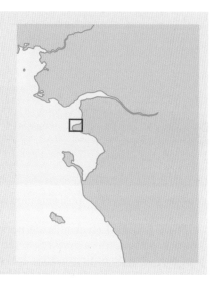

Small port and anchorage

Saint-Gildas is a small harbour (also known as the Anse du Boucau) on the north side of Pointe de Saint-Gildas, which is on the south side of the mouth of the Loire (*see plan on page 230*).

PILOTAGE

St-Gildas approach and entrance

By day From the north or northwest identify St-Gildas lighthouse and the large white tide gauge near the end of the jetty. Steer for the lighthouse, just right of the tide gauge, on 177°. L'Ilot port hand beacon, just north of the harbour, marks a dangerous rock (dries 1·7m). A starboard hand beacon marks the end of the jetty and in summer there is also a lit starboard hand buoy.

From the south, avoid the Banc de Kerouars, give Pointe de St-Gildas a wide berth and then follow the north entrance.

By night The white sector of Pointe de St-Gildas light leads into the harbour and the breakwater end is lit.

BERTHS AND ANCHORAGES

⚓ Anse du Boucau

This is a crowded, holiday-resort mooring field with numerous numbered buoys for small fishing boats. Anchor outside the moorings or dry out on the sandy

beach at the head of the harbour. You might be able to borrow a mooring. The bay is sheltered from the south but exposed to the west at HW springs and completely open to the north and northeast.

ASHORE IN SAINT-GILDAS

There is a tap at the dinghy pontoon and the usual facilities of a small holiday village. Basic provisions at Préfailles 1·6km to the east.

Looking SE at moorings in St Gildas and Anse de Boucau on left
Nick Chavasse

69 Pornic

47°06'N 2°07'W

Shelter
Very good in marina

Depth restrictions
Old harbour dries from entrance
1·0m in approach to marina
Marina dredged 2·0m but silts

Night entry Lit

HW time Brest HW–0010

Mean height of tide (m) Pornic

HWS	HWN	LWN	LWS
5·8	4·6	2·2	0·8

Tidal stream approach
E – Brest HW–0600 to HW (1·0kn)
W – Brest HW to –0600 (1·0kn)

Berthing Large marina

Facilities
All marina facilities, 0·75M to smart
holiday resort

Charts
SHOM *7395, 7394*
Imray *C40*

Communications
HM VHF 9
℡ 02 40 82 05 40
www.passeportescales.com
www.ot-pornic.fr

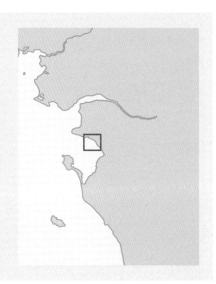

Attractive town with large marina

Pornic is an attractive seaside resort within easy reach of Nantes. It has a delightfully southern feel, with elegant holiday villas set in large gardens. There are numerous pine trees growing near the marina.

The modern, well-managed marina has excellent road, rail and air communications. It is a pleasant 500m walk to town past the old drying harbour and Bluebeard's castle. There is a good beach next to the marina.

PILOTAGE

Pornic approach and entrance

Warning Do not attempt to enter the marina with a draught of >2m with a coefficient of >75 two hours either side of LW. The approach can also be dangerous in strong SW–SE winds at LW.

By day From the north, round Pointe de Saint-Gildas at least 0·6M off. The long marina wall is distinctive.

From the southwest avoid the well-marked dangers close to the northwest of Noirmoutier and the dangers off Île du Pilier that extend 1M to seaward of the lighthouse (*see plan page 202*).

From the west, the Banc de Kerouars is a hazard. The unmarked shallow patches are dangerous in rough weather or below half tide.

The marina entrance is at the southeast corner and is not visible in the approach. Steer for the port hand and starboard hand 200m southeast of the entrance and be ready to turn sharply to port between the red and green beacons. Once inside keep clear of the south wall, which is lined with submerged rocks. The east breakwater head is also foul. Pornic entrance silts so assume a depth of 1·0m.

By night Approach in the white sector of Pornic light, which clears the Banc de Kerouars and Notre Dame rock. Steer between the lit port hand and starboard hand channel marks 200m southeast of the entrance and then enter the marina between the entrance lights.

Looking SW across marina Nick Chavasse

Entrance to Pornic with visitors' pontoon first main pontoon on right *Nick Chavasse*

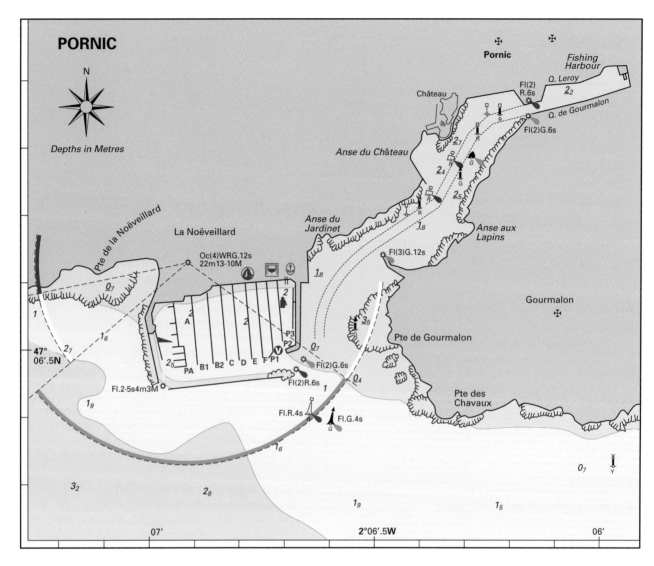

BERTHS AND ANCHORAGES

Pornic marina

The reception berth in the marina is directly ahead on entering and clearly marked. Facilities include a 40-T travel-lift, dry-berthing, sailmaker, mechanic, electronics and riggers.

Drying harbour

Visitors are discouraged from using the old drying harbour. The channel (dries 1·7m) is marked by buoys and beacons. Night entry not recommended.

Looking N to drying old harbour *Nick Chavasse*

ASHORE IN PORNIC

Pornic has all the facilities of a major marina and the marina staff are particularly helpful. The fuel dock is at the base of the narrow first aisle and rather awkward for a 12m yacht.

On the north side of the marina there are cafés, restaurants and chandlers. It is a very pleasant 10-minute walk along the riverbank to the town, where there are shops and restaurants and a market on Thursday and Sunday. Pornic is one hour by taxi to Nantes Airport for crew changes.

A walk from the marina beside the estuary passes the fine 11th-century château and the old harbour. In town there is a maze of winding streets that fill with stalls on market day.

Pornic, like La Baule, was developed in the 19th century after the railway arrived. Known as the Jade coast, the area gets its name from the attractive green pine trees that can be found here.

Entrance to Port de la Meule *Nick Chavasse*

VII. The Vendée

South of the Loire, the two lovely islands of Noirmoutier and Yeu are well worth visiting. The former is flat and sandy with lots of salt ponds. If the tides are not suitable for crossing the Gois Causeway which links Île de Noirmoutier with the mainland, hire bicycles to see it for yourselves. Île d'Yeu is rocky with good walking, a modern marina and the best tuna steaks in France.

On the mainland are the attractive fishing port and beach resort of St-Gilles and France's premier yachting port, Les Sables d'Olonne. It is at the latter that the Vendée Globe round-the-world race, the pinnacle of single-handed racing, starts and finishes every four years.

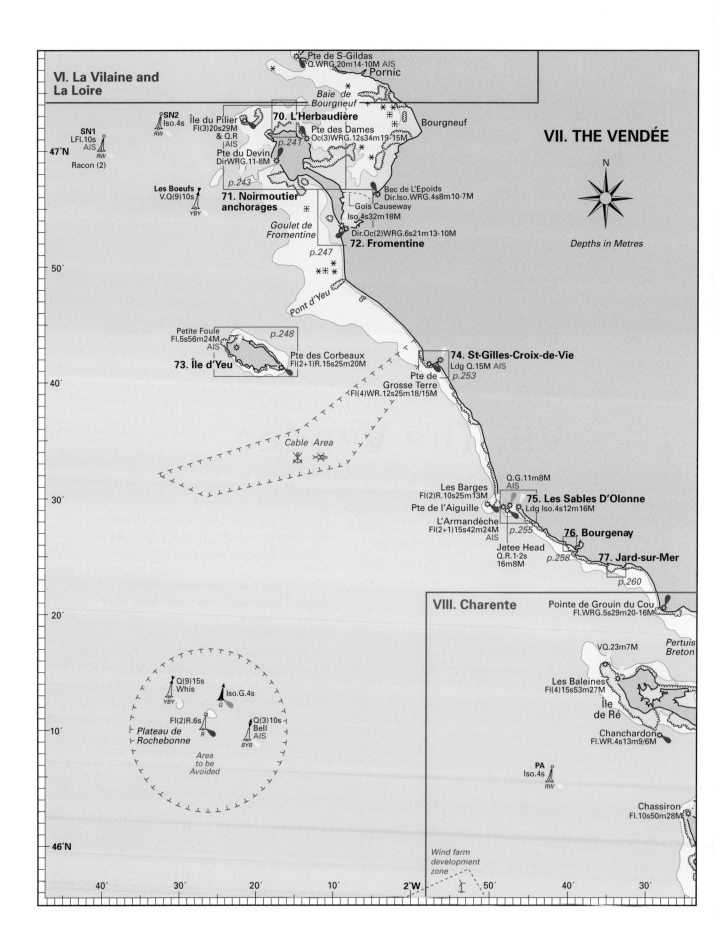

VI. La Vilaine and
La Loire

Pte de S-Gildas
Q.WRG.20m14-10M AIS
Pornic

Baie de
Bourgneuf

SN2
Iso.4s
RW

Île du Pilier
Fl(3)20s29M
& Q.R
AIS

70. L'Herbaudière

Bourgneuf

VII. THE VENDÉE

SN1
LFl.10s
AIS
RW

47°N

Racon (2)

Pte des Dames
Oc(3)WRG.12s34m19-15M

p.241

Pte du Devin
DirWRG.11-8M

N

Les Boeufs
V.Q(9)10s

p.243

71. Noirmoutier
anchorages

Bec de L'Epoids
Dir.Iso.WRG.4s8m10-7M

Gois Causeway
Iso.4s32m18M

YBY

Depths in Metres

Goulet de
Fromentine

Dir.Oc(2)WRG.6s21m13-10M

72. Fromentine

50'

p.247

Pont d'Yeu

Petite Foule
Fl.5s56m24M
AIS

p.248

74. St-Gilles-Croix-de-Vie
Ldg Q.15M AIS

73. Île d'Yeu

Pte des Corbeaux
Fl(2+1)R.15s25m20M

p.253

40'

Pte de
Grosse Terre
Fl(4)WR.12s25m18/15M

Cable Area

Q.G.11m8M
AIS

30'

Les Barges
Fl(2)R.10s25m13M

75. Les Sables D'Olonne
Ldg Iso.4s12m16M

Pte de l'Aiguille

L'Armandèche
Fl(2+1)15s42m24M
AIS

76. Bourgenay

p.255

Jetee Head
Q.R.1-2s
16m8M

77. Jard-sur-Mer

p.258

p.260

VIII. Charente

Pointe de Grouin du Cou
Fl.WRG.5s29m20-16M

20'

VQ.23m7M

Pertuis
Breton

Q(9)15s
Whis
YBY

Iso.G.4s
G

Les Baleines
Fl(4)15s53m27M

Île
de Ré

Fl(2)R.6s
R

Q(3)10s
Bell
AIS
BYB

10'

Plateau de
Rochebonne

Chanchardon
Fl.WR.4s13m9/6M

Area
to be
Avoided

PA
Iso.4s
RW

Chassiron
Fl.10s50m28M

46°N

Wind farm
development
zone

40'   30'   20'   10'   2°W   50'   40'   30'

Vendée tidal streams

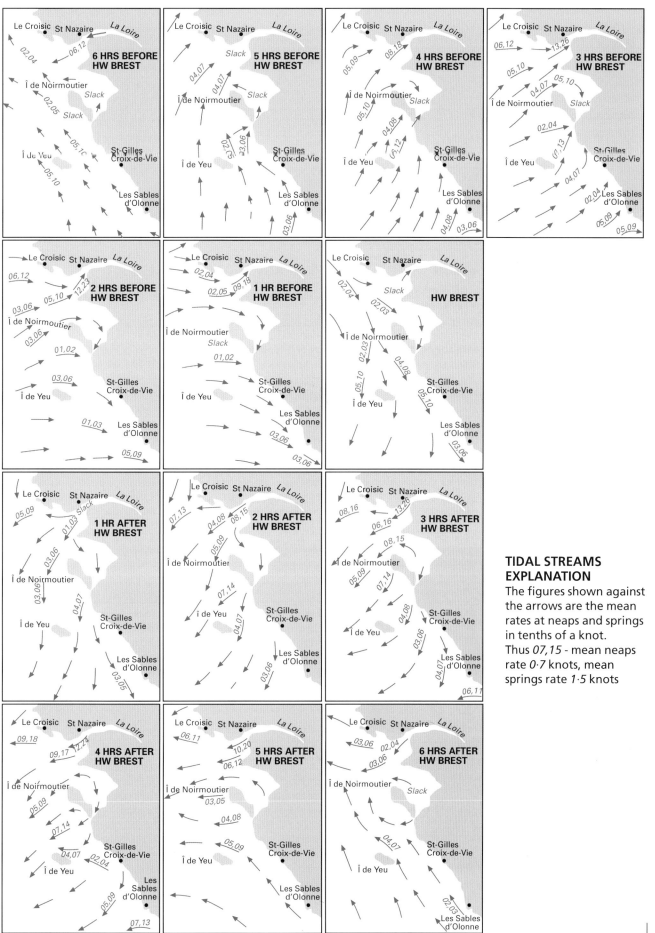

TIDAL STREAMS EXPLANATION

The figures shown against the arrows are the mean rates at neaps and springs in tenths of a knot.

Thus *07,15* - mean neaps rate *0·7* knots, mean springs rate *1·5* knots

70 L'Herbaudière, Île de Noirmoutier

47°02′N 2°18′W

Shelter
Good except from N and NE

Depth restrictions
Entrance dredged 1·2m
Marina 1·5m to 2·5m

Night entry Lit

HW time Brest HW–0010

Mean height of tide (m) L'Herbaudière

HWS	HWN	LWN	LWS
5·5	4·4	2·1	0·8

Tidal stream in approach
ESE – Brest HW–0600 to HW (1·9 kn)
WNW – Brest HW to –0600 (1·6 kn)

Berthing
Raft on visitors' pontoon

Facilities
All facilities

Charts
SHOM *7395, 7394*
Imray *C40*

Communications
HM VHF 9
① 02 51 39 05 05
www.ville-noirmoutier.co.uk

The main port on Île de Noirmoutier

Île de Noirmoutier is well worth exploring. It is about 10M long by 3M wide, mostly flat and sandy, with much of the north part given over to salt ponds. A road bridge (24m) at the southern tip and Le Gois tidal causeway link the island with the mainland. Le Gois is 2·5M north of the southern tip of the island (*see plan page 247*). Bicycles are a perfect way to get about and can be hired in L'Herbaudière.

L'Herbaudière is the only all-tide port on Île de Noirmoutier. Not to be confused with Noirmoutier-en-l'Île, a busy drying port covered on page 244. It is shared between fishing boats and yachtsmen and has a pleasant down-to-earth atmosphere. Yachts over 14m may not be accepted 15 July–15 August due to space limitations.

PILOTAGE *See also plan on page 243*

L'Herbaudière approach and entrance

By day From the north, L'Herbaudière can be identified by a 40m radio mast to the west and the stone breakwater.

Start from a position about 0·5M west of Basse du Martroger north cardinal tower beacon but do not approach the beacon from due north because there are several shallow patches. From this position, steer for the harbour on 188° keeping the breakwaters just open. The last 0·25M is marked by buoys and beacons and, if visibility is poor, the leading lights are switched on. Beware the rock awash at LAT on the east side, port hand side on entering, approximately opposite the halfway distance between No.1 and No.3 starboard hand buoys and quite close to the leading line.

The harbour entrance faces east so it is necessary to round the west breakwater and turn fairly sharply to starboard.

From the southwest, use the Chenal de la Grise. Start south of Passe de la Grise south cardinal buoy. Then steer 058° towards Basse de Martroger north cardinal tower beacon. About 0·45M before Matroger, when the harbour bears 188°, turn onto this course and enter the harbour as described above. Note that the tide runs very strongly in the Passe de la Grise.

By night From north, approach in either of the two north white sectors of Basse du Martroger light. Then use the white sector of L'Herbaudière breakwater light on 188°. Identify the leading lights on 188° and follow this transit into the harbour, leaving the red and green lit buoys to port and starboard. As by day beware the rock awash at LAT on the east side of the near approach.

From the south, through the Chenal de la Grise, use the white sector of Basse du Martroger light, bearing between 055° and 060°. When the breakwater head light turns white, steer 188° and proceed as above.

L'Herbaudière from the west *Patrick Roach*

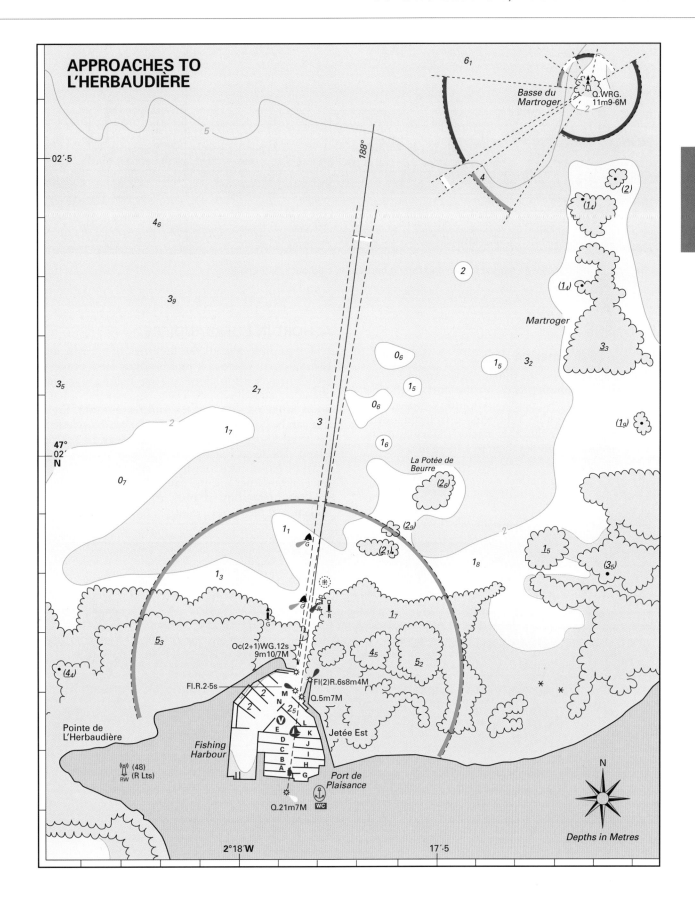

APPROACHES TO
L'HERBAUDIÈRE

188°

6_1

Basse du
Martroger

Q.WRG.
11m9-6M

4

(2)

(1_4)

4_6

2

3_9

(1_4)

Martroger

3_5

0_6

1_5

3_2

$\underline{3}_3$

2_7

1_5

0_6

2

1_7

3

1_6

(1_9)

**47°
02′
N**

La Potée de
Beurre

0_7

(2_6)

1_1

(2_9)

1_3

(2_1)

1_5

1_8

(3_5)

1_7

5_3

$\underline{4}_5$

5_2

(4_4)

Oc(2+1)WG.12s
9m10/7M

Fl.R.2·5s

Fl(2)R.6s8m4M

Q.5m7M

Pointe de
L'Herbaudière

2

2_5

M
N
V
E   K
D   J
C   I
B   H
A   G

Jetée Est

Fishing
Harbour

$\binom{(\!(\ )\!)}{RW}$ (48) (R Lts)

Port de
Plaisance

Q.21m7M

WC

N

Depths in Metres

2°18′W

17′·5

L'Herbaudière entrance with marina to port and fishing harbour to starboard *Nick Chavasse*

BERTHS

L'Herbaudière marina

Visitors' berth is on the outside of pontoon F, past the first two hammerheads on the port hand side after entering. These berths are a little exposed and may be uncomfortable if the wind is from the north or northeast. The harbourmaster's dory usually meets visitors and guides them to a berth in season.

ASHORE IN L'HERBAUDIÈRE

L'Herbaudière has all the facilities of a yacht and fishing port. There is a fuel berth, a 30-T crane, a 140-T travel-lift located in the fishing harbour, chandlers and all repairs. The town is small but has a good range of shops, cafés and restaurants. Fresh fish can be bought from the fish market. Bicycles can be hired and provide an excellent way to see the island. The local beaches, the saltpans and the main town of Noirmoutier-en-Île are all worth visiting. If time and tide permit, the causeway to the mainland is also interesting, if only to see the scale and diligence of the *pêche à pied*.

L'Herbaudière visitors' berths on right *Nick Chavasse*

71 Île de Noirmoutier anchorages

47°01′N 2°13′W

Depth restrictions
Noirmoutier-en-L'Île dries 2·6m
Bois de la Chaise (Pointe des Dames) about 1.0m
Port Morin harbour 0·9m

Night entry
Lit to Bois de la Chaise and Port Morin

HW time
Brest HW–0010

Mean height of tide (m) L'Herbaudière
HWS	HWN	LWN	LWS
5·5	4·4	2·1	0·8

Facilities
Noirmoutier-en-L'Île has good shops,
Bois de la Chaise has a few shops, Port
Morin only has a good beach and a
seasonal shop

Charts
SHOM 7394

Communications
Noirmoutier HM ☎ 02 51 26 03 36 /
06 27 04 03 91
Port de Morin ☎ 02 51 35 81 26
www.vendee-tourism.co.uk

⚓ Bois de la Chaise, Pointe des Dames

Attractive anchorage with some visitor moorings

Sheltered from west and south and to some extent from north and east, this attractive anchorage is on the northeast corner of the island, near Pointe des Dames.

PILOTAGE

Bois de la Chaise approach and entrance

By day From the northwest, keep outside Banc de la Blanche north cardinal buoy and Basse des Pères east cardinal buoy. Then steer 150° for La Chaise safe water buoy. The headland is steep and tree covered and only the lighthouse top is visible.

From L'Herbaudière, stay inside Banc de la Blanche using a back-bearing of the red and white radio tower in line with Martroger tower on 215° until Basse de Pères is abeam to starboard, then follow the above track.

By night Approach in the white sector of Pointe de Dames light.

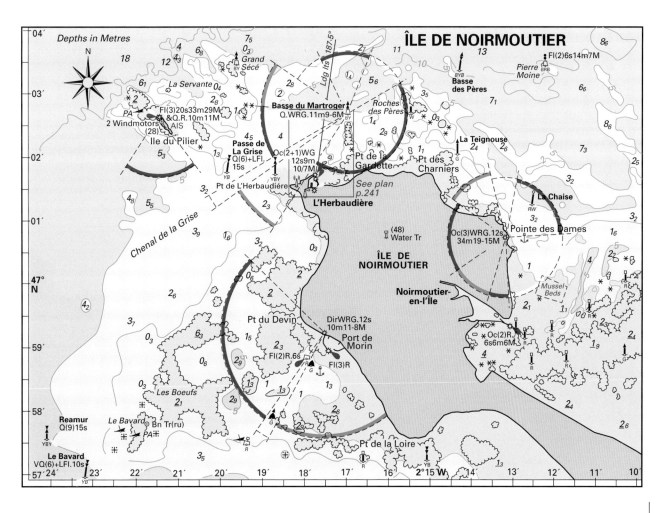

Approach to Noirmoutier-en-l'Île *Nick Chavasse*

Looking NE to jetty off Pointe des Dames and anchorage *Nick Chavasse*

BERTHS AND ANCHORAGES

This is a popular holiday beach and sailing school base with a large number of small craft moorings for the summer visitors. There is room to anchor and there are five red mooring buoys for visitors. Call the HM to see if others are available.

There are a few shops and restaurants in Bois de la Chaise but Noirmoutier-en-l'Île is only 1·6km away. There is a big campsite with a shop just to the south.

Noirmoutier-en-l'Île

Busy drying port

Noirmoutier-en-l'Île is a nice place but best visited by bicycle. It dries 2·6m leaving steeply sloping, unstable mud. Rafting is normally necessary and rafted boats may tip and cross masts, or fall outwards into the scoured channel.

PILOTAGE

Noirmoutier-en-l'Île approach and entrance

By day From the Bois de la Chaise anchorage, keep about 400m offshore, inside the mussel bed. There is a line of green beacons along the shore. Continue into the entrance and up the marked channel to town. The best water at the entrance is on the south side near the training wall.

BERTHS AND ANCHORAGES

Moor to the first quay on the starboard side, just before the crane. Further up, the quays are shallower. The mud is very soft so, with luck, a fin keel may sink in, leaving the boat upright.

ASHORE IN NOIRMOUTIER-EN-L'ÎLE

Noirmoutier-en-l'Île, a pleasant market town, has all facilities and a special holiday feel. Markets are held Monday, Tuesday, Friday and Sunday, in season.

Moored in soft mud at Noirmoutier-en-l'Île *Nick Chavasse*

Port de Morin from the southwest *Patrick Roach*

Port de Morin

Shallow harbour and anchorage

This drying harbour is on the west of the island. There are pontoons but it is really a place for locals and holidaymakers to keep their shallow-draught boats during the season. Good shelter in all winds except southeast and south. There is a pool outside the harbour where deep draught yachts can anchor in good weather.

PILOTAGE

Port de Morin approach and entrance

By day Steer 032° towards the lighthouse at the root of the north breakwater close to a large white reservoir. First there is a port hand lightbuoy and then a starboard hand buoy about 0·6M apart. The route crosses a shallow patch (dries 1·3m), with deeper water to starboard.

The entrance channel is marked by a red and a green buoy. Pass between them then steer for the end of the breakwater.

BERTHS AND ANCHORAGE

The capitainerie may be contacted on VHF 09.

Berth on the south side of the first pontoon inside the entrance. Most of the harbour dries to mud. There is 0·9m depth at LW springs. Maximum length allowed is 12m. Water and electricity on the pontoon.

Anchor in the pool to the southeast of the inner red and green buoys. Visitors' berths may be found on the E side of the first pontoon to starboard when entering.

ASHORE IN PORT DE MORIN

There are very few facilities apart from a magnificent beach, a 5-T mobile crane and a seasonal shop.

The island is dotted with salt marshes and evaporating ponds in which the salt crystalizes under the sun. There are about 80 establishments on the island, producing 800T of salt each year. The salt is renowned for its mineral content and can be easily found for sale in local shops- why not buy some to take home and cook with? Walk along the bank of the channel from Noirmoutier-en-Île to Le Fort Larron to see several salt flats.

Noirmoutier-en-Île salt flats *Nick Chavasse*

72 Fromentine

46°54'N 2°10'W

Shelter Fairly exposed

Hazards
Shifting bar with very strong tides

Depth restrictions
Bar dries 1·5m

Night entry
Lit but not recommended

HW time Brest HW–0015

Mean height of tide (m) Fromentine

HWS	HWN	LWN	LWS
5·2	4·1	1·8	1·9

Tidal stream in entrance
Flood – Brest HW–0600 to –0130 (5kn)
Ebb – Brest HW–0100 to +0530 (8kn)

Tidal Stream at Le Goéland Starboard Bn
S – Brest HW–0500 to –0030 (2kn)
N – Brest HW+0030 to +0600 (1·5kn)

Berthing
Anchorage

Facilities
All facilities of a small holiday resort

Charts
SHOM *7394*
Imray *C40*

Communications
HM ① 02 51 39 05 05

Small resort with challenging access

The Goulet de Fromentine is the passage between the south end of Île de Noirmoutier and the mainland. The streams are very strong, the sand bar shifts and the anchorage is uncomfortable. Although Fromentine is a pleasant holiday resort, a visit is probably not worth the effort.

PILOTAGE

Tidal strategy
The tide ebbs for eight hours and floods for four and the streams, particularly on the ebb, are very strong. Only attempt to enter in the last hours of the flood and do not attempt to enter if there is strong southwest wind or swell.

Fromentine approach and entrance

By day The Goulet can be identified by a conspicuous water tower on Île de Noirmoutier and Notre-Dame-de-Monts lighthouse in Fromentine. Start well offshore at L'Aigle south cardinal buoy and steer 050° for Fromentine fairway buoy. Be prepared for some south stream. From the landfall buoy, follow the channel buoys to the red and white tower beacons that mark the entrance. Passing between the beacons, the channel deepens and a starboard hand buoy indicates the course to the navigation arch of the bridge (clearance 24m). After the bridge, a port hand buoy marks the channel to Fromentine pier. North of this buoy are two wrecks, exposed at LW.

BERTHS AND ANCHORAGES

⚓ Fromentine and Pointe de la Fosse

Depending on draught, anchor off the jetty on the Noirmoutier side at Pte de la Fosse, with less tidal stream, or just west of the Fromentine ferry jetty and just east of the cable area. The streams in the fairway are very strong, about 5kn, but they moderate towards the shore. Anchor as far in as draught and tide allow.

Owing to the strength of the tide it is said to be unwise to leave a yacht unattended while at anchor, and this would certainly be true at the top of springs. If going in to the Pte de la Fosse side, beware of the wrecks just north of the channel; they lie between the first and second red buoys after the bridge, so turn in either before the first red buoy or after the second. It is not practical to row across the stream to Fromentine in the dinghy.

ASHORE IN FROMENTINE

Water can be obtained from the ferry jetty. Fromentine is a small holiday resort with typical facilities, including a ferry to Île d'Yeu. Berthing at the ferry pier is not permitted.

Looking E at Fromentine bridge *Nick Chavasse*

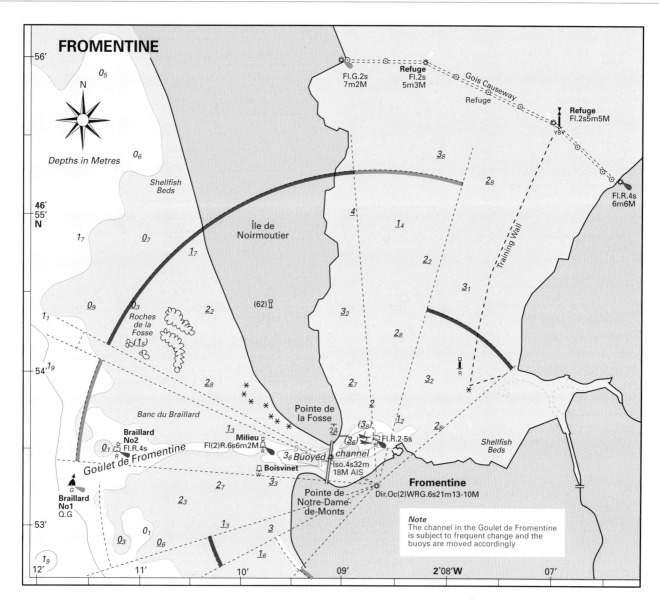

FROMENTINE

N

Depths in Metres

56'

0₅

0₆

Shellfish Beds

46° 55' N

1₇   0₇

Île de Noirmoutier

1₇

0₉   0₃

Roches de la Fosse
(1₅)

2₂

(62)

54'   1₉

1₁

2₈

Banc du Braillard

1₃

Braillard No2
Fl.R.4s

Milieu
Fl(2)R.6s6m2M

3₆ *Buoyed channel*

Boisvinet

Braillard No1
Q.G

0₁

2₇   3₃

53'   0₁

0₃   0₆

1₃   3

2₃

1₉

1₆

Fl.G.2s 7m2M

Refuge Fl.2s 5m3M

Gois Causeway

Refuge

Refuge Fl.2s5m5M
YBV

Fl.R.4s 6m6M

3₈

2₈

4

1₄

2₂

3₁

3₂

2₈

3₂

Training Wall

R

Pointe de la Fosse

2₇

2₄

(3₈)

(3₆)   Fl.R.2·5s

Iso.4s32m 18M AIS

2

1₂   2₈

Shellfish Beds

Pointe de Notre-Dame-de-Monts

Fromentine Dir.Oc(2)WRG.6s21m13-10M

Note
The channel in the Goulet de Fromentine is subject to frequent change and the buoys are moved accordingly

12'   11'   10'   09'   **2°08'W**   07'

THE GOIS CAUSEWAY

Warning The adventurous may wish to use the Goulet de Fromentine as a shortcut to Pornic or L'Herbaudière by crossing the causeway 2M north of Fromentine. The combination of very shallow water and very strong tides make this passage unsafe for deep draught yachts.

The author crossed the causeway in *Wild Bird*, a Bowman 40 with draft of 1·5m in Sep 2021 at HW springs to prove it can be done! See photographic evidence.

The passage is 7M long from Fromentine pier to Le Goéland starboard hand beacon and the Gois Causeway dries 3m. There is said to be more than 1·5m over the causeway 2hrs before HW at springs and less than 1.0m at HW neaps. The causeway is about 30m wide with a 10m wide cobbled road on top. South of the causeway it dries 3·2m in places. There are three refuges on the causeway for pedestrians who get caught by the tide. The usual crossing point is between the middle and easternmost refuges but the best place is sometimes marked (starboard-hand marks on the west side, porthand marks on the east). An up-to-date large scale chart is essential to identify the deepest water and the position of shellfish beds.

Looking W at markers on Gois Causeway from boat crossing it at HW springs *Nick Chavasse*

Looking W from refuge tower at causeway at LW *Nick Chavasse*

73 Île d'Yeu

46°44'N 2°21'W

Shelter
Good in marina

Hazards
Entrance dangerous in strong N and
E winds

Depth restrictions
Entrance 1·1m, marina 1·5m to 2·5m

Night entry Lit

HW time
Brest HW–0010

Mean height of tide (m) Port-Joinville

HWS	HWN	LWN	LWS
5.0	4.0	1·9	0·4

Berthing Marina

Fuel
At entrance to marina

Facilities
All facilities

Charts
SHOM *7410*
Imray *C40*

Communications
HM VHF 9
☎ 02 51 58 38 11
www.ile-yeu.fr

Attractive island with a busy tuna port

Île d'Yeu is a delightful island and a perfect size to
cycle around in a day. There are neolithic remains, a
ruined castle perched precariously on the south coast
and open to visitors, and a lighthouse to climb. Port-
Joinville is the only safe harbour and is an excellent
base from which to explore. The marina is modern
and welcoming. The town is an active fishing and
ferry port with lots of shops, cafés and restaurants;
the fishmonger alone makes the visit worthwhile.

Warning Do not risk running aground as it would block ferry
movements.

PILOTAGE

Port-Joinville approach and entrance

By day Port-Joinville is easy to locate from seaward
and steering 224° for the conspicuous water tower
behind the town leads straight into the harbour.

Enter the harbour leaving the northwest
breakwater head 50m to starboard. After passing
the old lighthouse bear to port and round the inner
end of the breakwater to enter the marina. Do not
stray to starboard in the outer harbour because the
southwest corner is very shallow and beware that
the ferry may be manoeuvring inside.

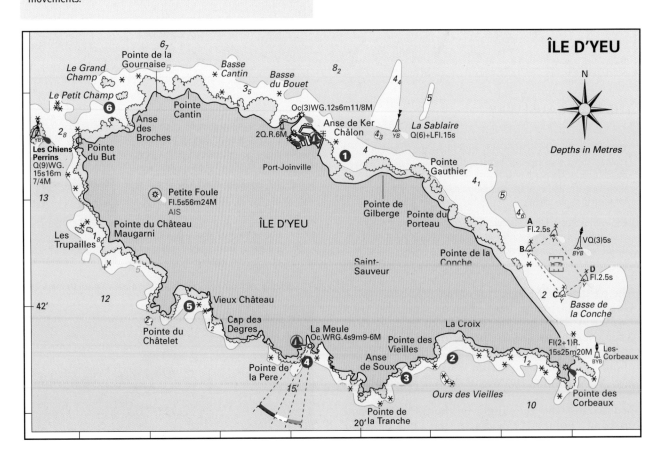

Port-Joinville old lighthouse is half way along the northwest breakwater and harbour entrance is beyond on the left
Nick Chavasse

By night Approach in either of the white sectors of the northwest breakwater light and enter the harbour with the leading lights in line on 219°. Remember to avoid the drying patch in the southwest corner of the outer harbour.

BERTHS AND ANCHORAGES

Port-Joinville Marina

Visiting boats berth in the marina according to size. To reach the reception pontoon follow the inside of the breakwater and turn to starboard at the end of Pontoon B in front of the harbourmaster's office. At busy times, visiting yachts are met by a launch and directed to a vacant berth.

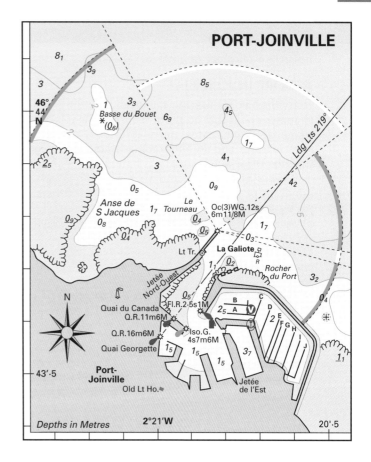

Looking SE from capitainerie to marina *Nick Chavasse*

Fuel jetty on right inside entrance *Nick Chavasse*

Typical Île d'Yeu street *Nick Chavasse*

ASHORE IN JOINVILLE

Joinville has all marine facilities including a big chandler and a fuel berth. In the town there is a full range of shops, cafés and restaurants, two good supermarkets and an outstanding fishmonger selling the tuna for which the island is famous.

Bicycle hire is easy and very popular with the hundreds of visitors. Those who enjoy walking may prefer to visit the magnificent south coast on foot because the footpath and bicycle path are mostly separate and the latter is a bit of a racetrack. Cars can also be hired and the island is just about large enough to make this worthwhile. Maps are available from the harbourmaster's office.

There is a regular ferry service to Fromentine and, in summer, to St-Gilles-Croix-de-Vie.

Marshal Pétain, head of the collaborationist Vichy government from 1940 to 1944, was imprisoned in Joinville from 1945 to 1951.

ANCHORAGES AROUND ÎLE D'YEU

⚓ 1. Anse de Ker Châlon

Sheltered from south and west but exposed to the north, there is a convenient bay 0·5M southeast of Joinville harbour. There are rocky outcrops on either side and some rocks close inshore so it is best to anchor quite well out.

⚓ 2. Anse des Vieilles

46°41'·53N 2°18'·70W

Sheltered from the north, this attractive sandy bay is just over 1M east of Port de la Meule. It should be approached from the southeast to avoid the Ours des Vieilles reef that extends nearly 0·5M southeast of Pointe des Vieilles. Anchor in about 3m in the centre of the bay.

Anse de Ker Châlon *Nick Chavasse*

Anse de Vieilles *Nick Chavasse*

⚓ 3. Anse des Soux

46°41'·37N 02°19'·33W

Sheltered from SW-N-NNE approx 1·5M east of La Meule. Popular beach and pretty cove for swimming.

Anse des Soux *Nick Chavasse*

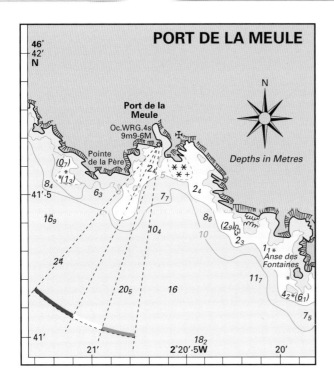

Vieux Château anchorage looking W towards the Cross
Nick Chavasse

Vieux Château *Nick Chavasse*

⚓ 4. Port de la Meule

The tiny picturesque harbour dries, but in settled offshore winds it is possible to anchor in the entrance, though some swell enters even in northeast winds. The bottom is rocky and there is little swinging room, so two anchors are necessary.

There is not really room in the harbour for a boat to dry out but it might be possible with advice from the local fishermen. There are some buoys off Port de la Meule but moorings may be light. The entrance is lit but night entry is not recommended.

Approach to Port de la Meule *Nick Chavasse*

Looking inside NW Port de la Meule near to HW *Nick Chavasse*

⚓ 5. Vieux Château

46°41′N 02°22′49W

Sheltered from W-N-E, approx. 1·5M west of La Meule, a delightful little anchorage. Large scale chart or good chart plotter needed to avoid Les Ours in the middle of the bay and sundry other rocks on the periphery.

⚓ 6. Anse des Broches

46°43′89N 02°23′54W

Sheltered from southwest through south to east, this fair-weather anchorage is on the northwest coast of Île d'Yeu.

Approach with the Petite Foule lighthouse, main lighthouse inland, east of aerodrome bearing 145°. There are drying and above-water rocks on both sides of the bay but this approach passes well clear of them. When Les Chiens Perrins west cardinal beacon tower bears about 225° turn to port onto 125° and go in as far as depth and draught allow. Anchor on sand, with Petite Foule bearing about 155° and Les Chiens Perrins west cardinal about 250°.

74 St-Gilles-Croix-de-Vie

46°41′N 1°56′W

Shelter Good in marina

Hazards
Entrance dangerous in strong SW wind or swell

Depth restrictions
Entrance channel dredged to 1·5m but silts to
    0·8m at breakwater head
Marina and reception pontoon 1·5m

Night entry Lit

HW time Brest HW−0010

Mean height of tide (m) St-Gilles

HWS	HWN	LWN	LWS
5·1	4·1	2.0	0·7

Tidal streams
Weak in the bay but 6kn on ebb in harbour,
much affected by rain

Berthing
Marina and visitors' buoys

Fuel
Next to the visitors' berth

Facilities
All facilities

Charts
SHOM *7402*
Imray *C40*

Communications
HM VHF 9
☏ 02 51 55 30 83
www.vendee-guide.co.uk

Fishing port and beach resort

St-Gilles and Croix-de-Vie are two towns on opposite sides of the Vie River, approximately 14M east of Île d'Yeu. St-Gilles, on the south, is a beach resort whereas Croix-de-Vie is an important fishing port and sizeable town. The river separating them has a fishing harbour and a large marina. The combination of resort and bustling river gives the place a very pleasant atmosphere.

PILOTAGE

St-Gilles approach and entrance

Warning The entrance is shallow and exposed to winds from the southwest; the ebb runs at up to 6kn. Entry is therefore dangerous in strong wind against tide conditions. Even in moderate conditions it is better to enter and leave on the last of the flood.

By day The entrance can be located by the low rocky headland of Grosse Terre, to the north, and the high lighthouse of Croix-de-Vie. On closer approach, Pilours island can be seen in front of the harbour entrance and the red-topped leading lighthouses.

With the leading lighthouses in line on 043° the approach should preferably be made shortly before

Entrance channel to St-Gilles-Croix-de-Vie. The red topped lighthouse and red on white tower is the leading line on 043°
Nick Chavasse

high water because the strong currents at mid-tide, particularly the ebb, make manoeuvring difficult. This leaves Pilours south cardinal to port and leads between the breakwater heads into the buoyed channel. The stream runs very hard and the buoys should be given good clearance as they are moored on the high ground beside the channel.

After a 90° turn to starboard, the channel passes the fishing-boat basins to reach the marina. The reception berth lies at the far end, beyond the fuel berth and round the bend to port. There is not much room to manoeuvre near the pontoon. Beware of the shallow water marked by green buoys and the strong stream. Departure should be made before high water, as the strong ebb quickly raises a sea at the entrance.

By night The entrance is well lit. Get the leading lights in line before passing Pilours south cardinal buoy. Once the southeast breakwater head is reached, follow the lit channel buoys. Unless conditions are ideal, borrow a vacant berth in the main part of the marina rather than attempt to berth on the visitors' pontoon in the dark.

BERTHS

St-Gilles Marina

The visitors' pontoon, Pontoon 8, is often crowded and a berthing master may direct yachts, particularly those over 10m, to a vacant berth in the main part of the marina so it is worth calling on VHF 09 on the way in. There are some drying visitors' buoys to south of marina but check depth at LW.

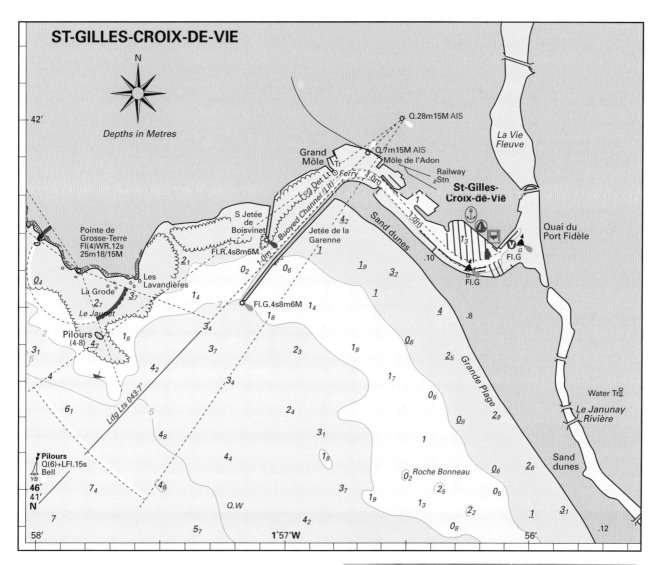

ST-GILLES-CROIX-DE-VIE

N

Depths in Metres

42'

Pointe de Grosse-Terre
Fl(4)WR.12s
25m18/15M

La Grode

Le Jaunet

Les Lavandières

Pilours
(4·8)

S Jetée de Boisvinet
Fl.R.4s8m6M

Jetée de la Garenne

Buoyed Channel (Lit)

Grand Môle
Tr

Ferry

Q.28m15M AIS

Q.7m15M AIS
Môle de l'Adon

Railway Stn

St-Gilles-Croix-de-Vie

Quai du Port Fidèle

Fl.G

Fl.G

La Vie Fleuve

Sand dunes

Grande Plage

Fl.G.4s8m6M

Ldg Lts 043·7°

Pilours
Q(6)+LFl.15s
Bell
YB

Roche Bonneau

Q.W

Water Tr

Le Janunay Rivière

Sand dunes

46°
41'
N

58'   1°57'W   56'

ASHORE IN ST-GILLES

The marina has all facilities including a fuel berth near the visitors' pontoon. St-Gilles and Croix-de-Vie have a full range of cafés, restaurants and shops with a good supermarket over the bridge in St-Gilles. There are connections by rail to Nantes.

Right Welcome pontoon is furthest up stream on port-hand side *Nick Chavasse*

Below St-Gilles Marina

75 Les Sables d'Olonne

46°30′N 1°48′W

Shelter Good in marina

Hazards
Entrance rough in strong SW wind or swell, particularly on the ebb

Depth restrictions
Entrance 1·1m
Visitors' berths 2.0m in Port Olona and 1·5m in Quai Garnier

Night entry Well lit

HW time Brest HW–0010

Mean height of tide (m) Sables

HWS	HWN	LWN	LWS
5·2	4·2	2.0	0·7

Tidal streams
Weak in the bay but 2·5kn on ebb in harbour

Berthing Marinas

Facilities All facilities

Charts
SHOM *7402, 7403, 7411*
Imray *C40*

Communications
Both Marinas VHF 9
Port Control VHF 12
Port Olona Marina ☎ 02 51 32 51 16
Quai Garnier Marina ☎ 02 51 96 43 34
www.vendee-guide.co.uk

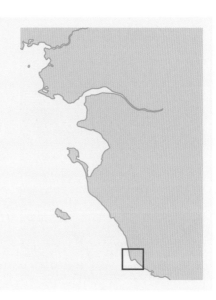

Premier yachting port

Les Sables d'Olonne is a sophisticated resort on the east side of the river. It has a casino, shops, restaurants and a splendid beach. The fishing port with its market and cafés is just behind the beach.

Port Olona, the large modern marina, is on the west side above the town of La Chaume. Ferries run continuously between the two towns and the walk from the marina to La Chaume is about 0·5M. The marina is the home of the Vendée Globe yacht race and has every facility. La Chaume has cafés, shops on the river front and a market.

Quai Garnier Marina is on the south side of the west part of the Port de Pêche. It is run by the Chamber of Commerce and can accommodate larger yachts. The marina office, showers and laundry are all on a pontoon. It is convenient for the shops, restaurants and beach of Sables d'Olonne.

Les Sables d'Olonne from the south showing the two marinas. Quai Garnier is on the left-hand side of the near basin, Port Olona is in the far basin *Patrick Roach*

PILOTAGE

Les Sables d'Olonne approach and entrance

> **Warning** Entry under sail is prohibited.
>
> The approach can be very rough and even dangerous in strong southeast, south or southwest winds, especially if there is any swell. Avoid entering or leaving in these conditions. In bad weather, the southeast approach is reported to be safer.

By day Les Sables d'Olonne can be identified by two large blocks of flats and the tall L'Armandèche lighthouse. The harbour entrance has a conspicuous red-topped white lighthouse at the end of the west breakwater, while the green-topped lighthouse on the east breakwater is less easy to spot.

From the southeast, use the transit of the green-topped breakwater light with the crenellated, white-topped, La Chaume lighthouse on 320°. This leaves all the shoals to port and the water is deep until within 400m of the harbour entrance. This approach should always be used in bad weather.

From the north or northwest, start close to La Petite Barge south cardinal buoy and make good 100° to leave Nouch Sud south cardinal buoy to port. Turn onto 033° and then identify the leading line which is between the belfry and two blocks of flats. Turn again to port and follow the leading line on 320°. The front light is above a red board on the beach. They are permanently lit.

After passing the end of the west breakwater, alter to starboard to bring the red panels in transit on 328°. Above half tide the dangers are covered and the transit need not be followed precisely.

By night The harbour is well lit. Follow the leading lights on 320° until the west breakwater light is abeam to port. Then turn to starboard to get the leading lights into line on 328°.

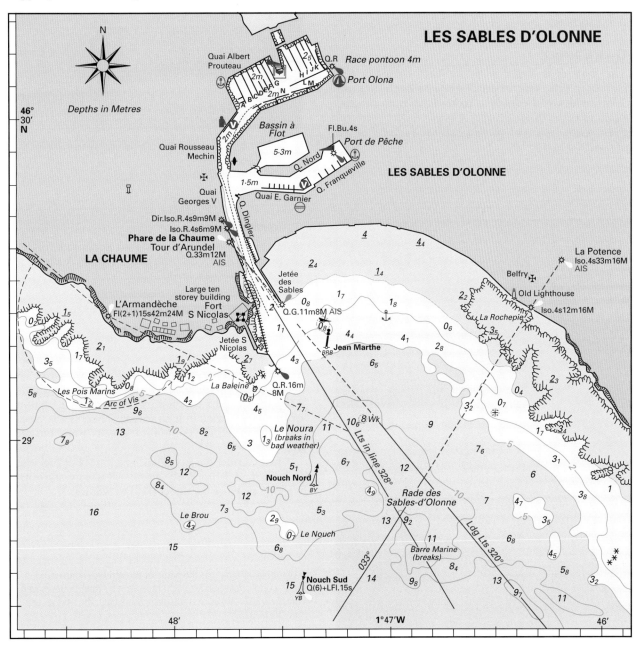

Entering Les Sables d'Olonne past Jeteé des Sables *Nick Chavasse*

BERTHS

Port Olona

The reception pontoon is on the port side just before the fuel berth and the marina basin. The ebb runs hard here. Visitors must secure to the pontoon and visit the capitainerie to be allocated a berth. The nearer pontoons are in 2m and the further ones in 2·5m and 4m.

Quai Garnier

The marina is situated in the first basin on the starboard side. Visitors are berthed on Pontoon A (in 1·7m) which is the furthest from the entrance to the basin near the floating office. Larger yachts berth on the outside. Visitors should call on VHF 09 to be allocated a berth.

Looking NE at Bureau de Port Olona with marina beyond
Nick Chavasse

Looking E at Quai Garnier marina *Nick Chavasse*

Looking W from Quai Garnier capitainerie with marina beyond *Nick Chavasse*

⚓ Town Beach

In settled conditions there is an anchorage off the beach to the east of the entrance channel. Anchor east of Jean Marthe beacon in 2-5m.

ASHORE IN LES SABLES D'OLONNE

Port Olona has all facilities including a 28-T travel-lift, two slips and all repair facilities. The fuel berth is near the reception pontoon and there are some shops, cafés and restaurants in the marina complex. The shops of La Chaume are nearby and the delights of Les Sables can be reached by ferry from La Chaume or from the marina in high season. There is a large car park and excellent communications by train, bus and air.

Quai Garnier has good basic facilities but fuel must be obtained from Port Olona. Railway station is walking distance for direct train to Nantes.

Les Sables d'Olonne is the home of the Vendée Globe round-the-world single-handed yacht race. Won by Yannick Bosthaven in 2020/2021. The race is run every four years. The next race is in 2024/2025.

76 Bourgenay

46°26'N 1°41'W

Shelter Good in marina

Hazards
Entrance dangerous in moderate SW wind or swell

Depth restrictions
Entrance 1·0m
Visitors' berths 1·5m to 2·0m

Night entry Lit

HW time Brest HW-0010

Mean height of tide (m) Sables

HWS	HWN	LWN	LWS
5·2	4·2	2·0	0·7

Tidal streams in approaches
SE – Brest HW-0530 to +0030 (0·9kn)
Slack – Brest HW +0030 to +0130
NW – Brest HW+0130 to –0530 (1·3kn)

Berthing
Marina

Fuel
S breakwater

Facilities
All marina facilities

Charts
SHOM *7403*
Imray *C41*

Communications
HM VHF 9
① 02 51 22 20 36
www.vendee-guide.co.uk/port-bourgenay

Modern marina and holiday complex

Bourgenay is a large, artificial yacht harbour and marina village about 6M southeast of Les Sables d'Olonne. The nearest town of Talmont-Saint-Hilaire is 3·2km inland. There is a beach to the south, oyster farms on the Payré River and pinewoods and marshes to explore.

Bourgenay is conveniently placed on passage to and from Île de Ré or La Rochelle and is a popular port of call for rallies.

PILOTAGE

Bourgenay approach and entrance

> **Warning** Entry should not be attempted in strong west or southwest winds. Even in moderate winds there will be confused water in the entrance. However, once inside, there is good shelter.

By day Bourgenay is identified by the sandy beach at the mouth of the Payré River to the south and the white roofs of the two marina buildings.

Locate the landfall buoy 1M southwest of the marina. The leading marks on 040° are green panels with the rear one on a tall white column. This column can be seen easily and it is sufficient to keep

Entrance with leading marks to left of starboard hand beacon
Nick Chavasse

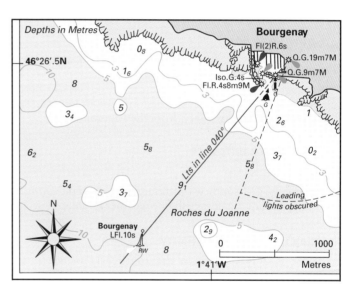

this on 040° at the low point between the two white roofs until the front mark is seen on the breakwater.

On close approach leave a green buoy and a green beacon to starboard; then make a 90° turn to port followed by a 90° turn to starboard to enter the marina. Fluorescent red and white chevrons indicate this latter turn.

By night Follow the leading lights until the entrance is reached. The breakwater heads are lit but the green buoy and beacon are not.

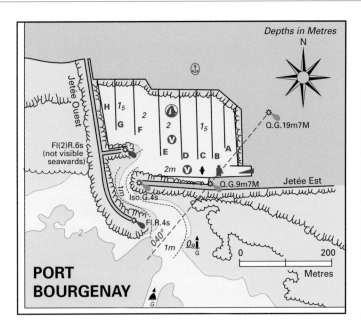

PORT
BOURGENAY

Looking NW across marina towards capitainerie
Nick Chavasse

BERTHS

Bourgenay Marina

The visitors' pontoon is on the south side of the marina along the south breakwater. Visiting yachts should secure to it unless met by a marina launch and shown to a berth. There are 30 berths for visitors; maximum length 20m. Bicycles may be borrowed from the capitainerie.

⚓ Le Payré entrance

46°25'47N 01°39'47W

Anchorage 1M southeast of Bourgenay, sheltered from N-E-SE, pleasant anchorage in fine weather in 2m.

ASHORE IN BOURGENAY

There is a fuel berth in the southeast corner of the marina, a grid, a slip, a 20-T travel-lift, a chandlery and engineers. There are cafés, a few small shops and bicycle hire in the marina complex. Up the hill at La Croisée about 500m, is a supermarket, baker, two restaurants and a post office. The nearest town is two miles away in Talmont-St-Hilaire.

Looking W along visitors' pontoon towards entrance
Nick Chavasse

Bourgenay
marina looking
north
Patrick Roach

77 Jard-sur-Mer

46°24'N 1°35'W

Shelter Good in marina

Hazards
Entrance dangerous in strong SW wind or swell

Depth restrictions
Entrance dries, access HW±0200

Night entry Not recommended

HW time Brest HW−0010

Mean height of tide (m) Sables

HWS	HWN	LWN	LWS
5·2	4·2	2.0	0·7

Tidal streams in approaches
SE – Brest HW−0530 to +0030 (1.0kn)
Slack – Brest HW+0030 to +0130
NW – Brest HW+0130 to −0530 (1·4kn)

Berthing Drying harbour

Facilities Limited

Charts
SHOM *7403*
Imray *C41*

Communications
HM VHF 9
℡ 02 51 33 90 61
www.francethisway.com/places/jard-sur-
mer.php

Small drying harbour

Jard-sur-Mer is a small drying harbour that lies about 10M north of the tip of Île de Ré. It is a pleasant spot for those with shallow draught or who can take the ground. The village of Jard-sur-Mer has reasonable facilities and there are good beaches nearby.

In offshore weather at neaps a deeper draught yacht could find a pleasant day anchorage off the harbour.

PILOTAGE

Jard-sur-Mer approach and entrance

By day Jard is easy to identify as it is the only town on this stretch of coast and the blue roofs of the harbour office and nearby apartment blocks are visible from 3M offshore. However, there are off-lying dangers so it is best to identify the unlit starboard hand marker buoy, 46°23'·73N 01°34'·86W, that marks the start of the entry channel.

From this buoy, it should be possible to identify two white beacons set in the sand dunes on 036°. Follow this transit towards the shore. The course appears to be quite a long way east of the harbour. This is necessary to avoid a shallow patch (dries 1·0m) southeast of the harbour.

Once the harbour opens, turn to port to enter. The transit is two red boards with a white stripe on 293° but it is sufficient to follow the line of the breakwater. There are also some beacons to indicate the deepest water.

By night
Entry at night is not advisable as the harbour is unlit.

Looking SW towards entrance with three pontoons on right
Nick Chavasse

Capitainerie situated at top of welcome pontoon at Jard-sur-Mer *Nick Chavasse*

BERTHS AND ANCHORAGES

Jard-sur-Mer harbour

The pontoon extending 75m from the capitainerie and the southwest side of it is reserved for visitors. Alongside and 5m out from the pontoon a minimum depth of 1·2m at LW is maintained. But the fairway channel to this pontoon dries. Boats that can take the ground may dry out alongside the little quay on the outer breakwater, or borrow a mooring. It is also possible to anchor clear of the moorings but bow and stern anchors should be used and legs are obligatory.

⚓ Outside the harbour

Deep-keeled yachts can anchor outside in settled weather. The best spot is just south of where the two leading lines cross at neaps or further out at springs. This spot is untenable in any wind or swell from the west and it would be difficult to leave at night.

ASHORE IN JARD-SUR-MER

Water and electricity on the pontoon, showers, toilets and laundry at the capitainerie. There are cafés and restaurants round the harbour and modest shops and a bank in the village about 1km away. There are good beaches nearby.

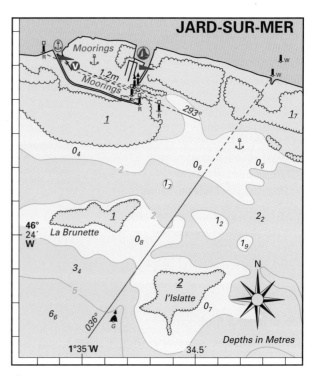

JARD-SUR-MER

Depths in Metres

⚓ Anse de Maupas, La Tranche-sur-Mer

This is a drying anchorage 2M to the east of Pointe du Grouin du Cou, off La Tranche-sur-Mer. Enter on a bearing of 335° on the end of the jetty used by tourist launches from St-Martin. The line starts about 0·5M east of the easternmost of two south cardinal buoys marking a shoal south of the jetty. Pick up one of the orange mooring buoys to the east of the jetty. It may be possible to remain afloat at neaps but the anchorage is exposed in winds from southwest to southeast and a swell comes around the point in westerlies.

Looking SE through the entrance to the Jard-sur-Mer anchorage beyond at LW *Nick Chavasse*

La Tranche-sur-Mer jetty *Nick Chavasse*

The Ré Bridge *Nick Chavasse*

VIII. Charente

The Charente feels like the real south. There are sunflowers everywhere and the crew start complaining about sunburn and heatstroke instead of frostbite and mildew.

The area is centred on the two holiday islands of Île d'Oléron and Île de Ré. Both have north coast harbours that make good bases for biking and walking. On the mainland, the historic city of La Rochelle is a must and a trip up the River Charente to Rochefort is likely to be the high point of a cruise in this area. Both La Rochelle and Rochefort have good marinas.

The more adventurous can take the canal to Marans and visit the marshes of the Marais Poitevin or perhaps visit the River Seudre to see industrial scale oyster farming around Marennes. The oysters themselves can be sampled almost anywhere.

It requires careful planning, but it is possible to go under the Pont de L'Île d'Oléron to visit Marennes and then continue on south via the Pertuis de Maumusson and into La Gironde for Bordeaux.

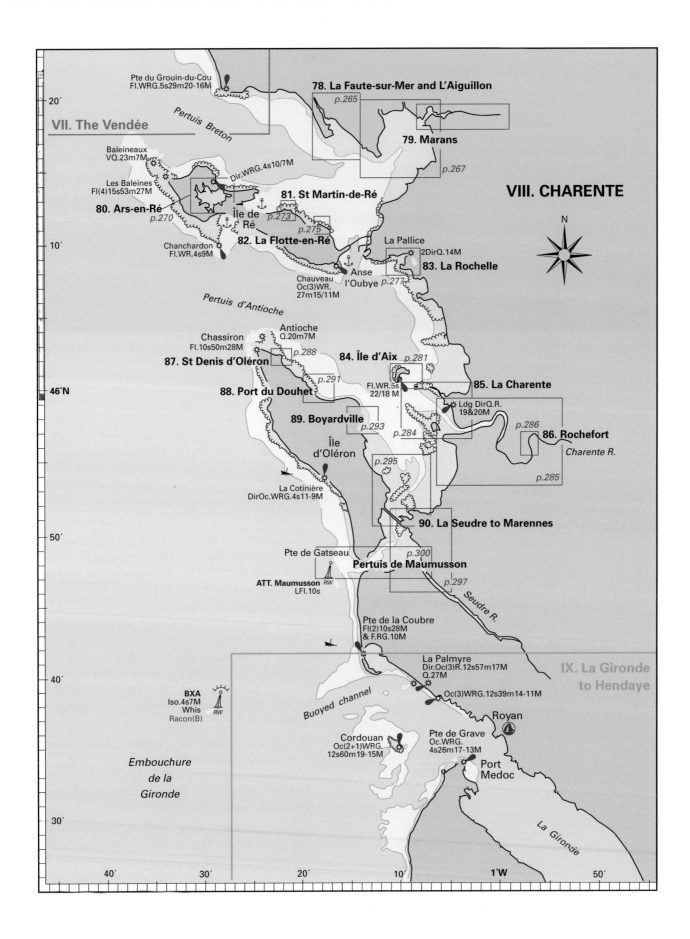

Charente tidal streams

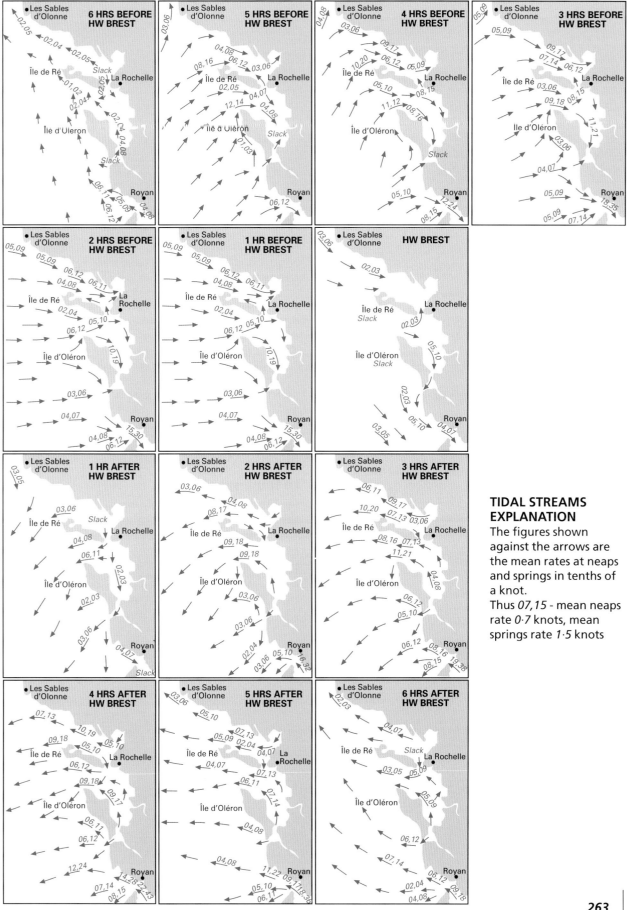

TIDAL STREAMS EXPLANATION
The figures shown against the arrows are the mean rates at neaps and springs in tenths of a knot.
Thus *07,15* - mean neaps rate *0·7* knots, mean springs rate *1·5* knots

78 La Faute-sur-Mer and l'Aiguillon

46°16'N 1°16'W

Shelter
Fair weather only

Hazards
Timber and steel piles of mussel beds extend into channel

Depth restrictions
Approach dries 2·0m or more

Night entry Not recommended

HW time at St-Martin
Pointe de Grave HW-0015

Mean height of tide (m) St-Martin

HWS	HWN	LWN	LWS
6.0	4·9	2·4	0·9

Tidal stream in approach
Flood – PdG HW-0530 to -0030 (1·3kn)
Slack – PdG HW-0030 to +0030
Ebb – PdG HW +0030 to +0530 (1·0kn)
Slack – PdG HW+0530 to -0530
1·5kn in river

Berthing
Drying jetty, moorings and anchorage

Facilities Limited

Charts
SHOM 7404
Imray C41

Mud and mussels

Le Lay river to La-Faute-sur-Mer and L'Aiguillon is a major oysterage. The entrance dries 2·0m and at low water there is just a vast expanse of mud and salt grass.

A surprising number of yachts are based in Le Lay but a visitor will almost certainly have to take the ground in very soft mud, probably a long way from any facilities.

PILOTAGE

L'Aiguillon and La Faute-sur-Mer approach and entrance

Warning Much of the shore is devoted to the culture of mussels. These are grown on substantial timber piles that cover at HW and are very dangerous. Some of the piles have steel tops. Yellow buoys or withies usually mark the mussel beds.

There is also a large rectangular mussel farm, 3x1M in area, in the middle of the Pertuis Breton. It is marked by four large cardinal lightbuoys, one at each corner and a large yellow lightbuoy in the middle of each of the long sides.

By day Approach only when the tide is well up. Start from a position about 0·3M west of Le Lay south cardinal. Head for the transformer, adjacent to a conspicuous barn, on a track of 035°. This course passes between No.1 and No.2 buoys.

After No.2 buoy, the channel swings steadily to port between oyster and mussel beds, until the river opens up and the distant town of L'Aiguillon, with the prominent water tower of Bel Air, can be seen ahead. From there, beacons mark the channel.

At Banc des Marsouins, the channel splits. Both channels are very narrow but the north one is preferred. The river then turns sharply to starboard and runs northwest to La Faute-sur-Mar and L'Aiguillon.

BERTHS AND ANCHORAGES

La Faute-sur-Mer

On the west bank about two-thirds of the way up to the bridge, is a landing slip marked by two posts with orange tops. Just upstream of the slip is the Yacht Club jetty (drying), where visitors may secure.

L'Aiguillon

Continuing up to L'Aiguillon, the river is full of fishing boat moorings and wooden jetties line the east bank. It may be possible to anchor or borrow a

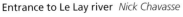
Entrance to Le Lay river *Nick Chavasse*

Unmarked mussel bed piles *Nick Chavasse*

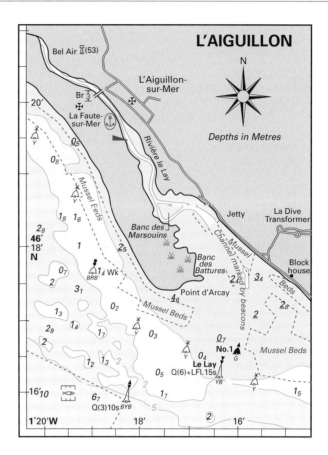

mooring in the pool below the bridge at L'Aiguillon. Depths are uncertain due to silting and the river can almost dry on any tide. Moorings are generally for shallow-draught fishing boats.

ASHORE IN L'AIGUILLON AND LA FAUTE-SUR-MER

There is a boat-yard and slipway but no fuel at L'Aiguillon. There are shops, cafés and restaurants in both L'Aiguillon and La Faute and a good beach at La Faute. There are markets in La Faute on Thursday and Sunday and in L'Aiguillon on Tuesday and Friday.

L'Aiguillon mud berths *Nick Chavasse*

La Faute-sur-Mer visitors' pontoon *Nick Chavasse*

79 Marans

46°17′N 1°10′W

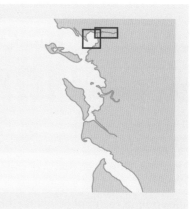

Shelter Good in Marans

Hazards
Shallow approach with strong streams; can be rough

Depth restrictions
Approach 0·2m
2·0m in canal to Marans

Brault lock times
Entry – Brault HW
Exit – Brault HW –0100

Night entry Not recommended

HW time at Brault lock
HW La Rochelle +0020

Mean height of tide (m) St-Martin

HWS	HWN	LWN	LWS
6·0	4·9	2·4	0·9

Tidal stream in approach
Flood – PdG HW–0530 to –0030 (1·3kn)
Slack – PdG HW–0030 to +0030
Ebb – PdG HW +0030 to +0530 (1.0kn)
Slack – PdG HW+0530 to –0530

Berthing Visitors' pontoon

Facilities All facilities

Charts
SHOM *7404*
Imray *C41*

Communications
Lock ① 06 64 49 29 60
　　VHF 72
HM ① 05 46 01 02 99,
　　mob 06 25 79 16 35
Lock times ① 06 64 49 29 60
www.port-marans.fr

Gateway to the Marais Poitevin

The Marais Poitevin is a huge marshland conservation area that extends from the sea to Niort. The coastal part, west of Marans, has been drained to form the 'dry marsh' of flat fields and salt marsh. The 'wet marsh' extends from Marans to Niort and is a mass of canals that wind through the lush landscape.

In the 1920s and '30s a very large proportion of French cereal exports passed through Marans and many disused silos remain close to the harbour.

The 9M passage up the river, La Sèvre Niortaise, to Marans provides a wonderful opportunity to see the rich birdlife of the 'dry marsh'. In Marans, it is possible to hire a canal boat to visit the 'wet marsh'. Marans is a pleasant market town where visiting boats are completely sheltered in an old canal.

PILOTAGE

Marans approach and entrance

Warning Much of the shore is devoted to the culture of mussels. These are grown on substantial timber piles, some of which are steel tipped, that cover at HW and are very dangerous. Yellow buoys or withies usually mark the mussel beds.

If approaching from west, beware of the large rectangular mussel farm in the middle of the Pertuis Breton. See page 264 under La Faute-sur-Mer and L'Aiguillon.

Tidal strategy

Telephone the lock-keeper in good time to advise him of your arrival. The lock opens for entry at local HW, which is approximately 20 minutes after La Rochelle HW. The lifting bridge is 0·5M before the lock and about 5·5M from ATT. de l'Aiguillon safe water mark, so it is best to start well before La Rochelle HW and wait at the bridge. The tide will still be flooding quite strongly.

By day Start at ATT. de l'Aiguillon SWM. Make good 035° for the second SWM. Try to hold the track accurately to avoid the mussel beds on either side. At the second SWM, follow the beacons on about 025° towards the starboard hand beacon on Port du Pavé jetty. The channel shifts and buoys are moved accordingly.

Looking E at lifting bridge, 0·5M west of Brault lock, with traffic lights showing red on right *Nick Chavasse*

Rafting in lock with swing bridge at E end of lock
Nick Chavasse

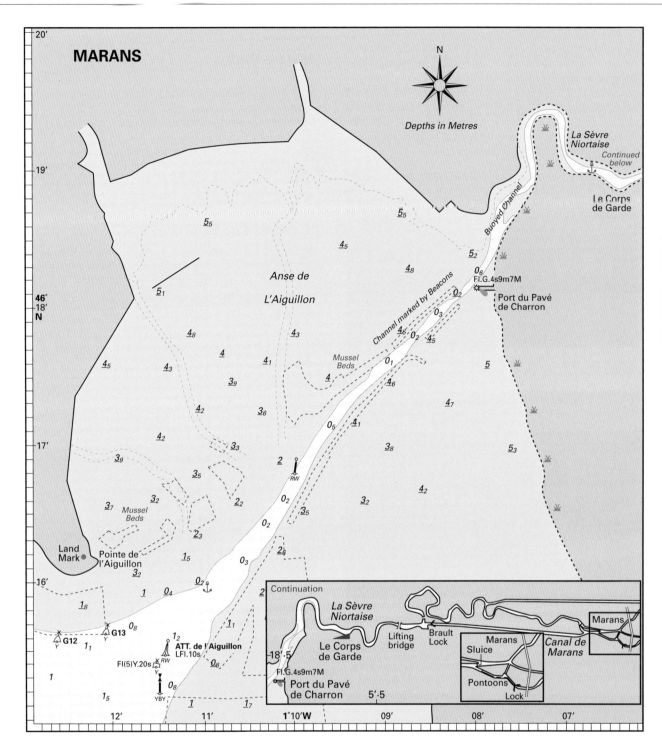

MARANS

Beyond Port du Pavé, the river is constrained by banks. The plan indicates the deepest water but in general, stay in the middle but watch out for buoys that mark shoals on the bends.

The lifting bridge is about 3M beyond Port de Pavé. There are two waiting buoys on the starboard side before the bridge. Do not lie to these on a falling tide with a strong west wind because they are very close to shallow water.

The lock-keeper operates the bridge using CCTV cameras to observe the road and river traffic. It is best to book the lock 24h in advance. If boats are waiting, the bridge is opened so they can enter the lock at local HW. On the way back, remember that the departure opening is one hour before local HW.

Port du Pavé *Nick Chavasse*

The lock is enormous with gently sloping banks and a short pontoon on the port-hand side that can be used while the lock is operated. A swing road bridge, at the upper end of the lock, gives access to the Marans canal; this attractive tree-lined canal runs straight for about 3M to Marans. Towards the end, it appears to come to a dead end, but the channel to Marans opens up to starboard, through a pair of permanently open lock gates.

Marans canal *Nick Chavasse*

Visitors' pontoon in Marans marina *Nick Chavasse*

BERTHS AND ANCHORAGES

Marans Marina

Secure to new visitors' pontoon on the starboard side at the commencement of the mooring area or find a berth in the new pontoon section with catways about 200m before reaching the capitainerie, against the quay. Depth is about 2·5m. At the entrance to the marina just beyond the waiting pontoon there is a foot bridge which is opened by the harbourmaster, and on request, at arrival and departure times in conjunction with opening times for Brault lock.

⚓ Anse de L'Aiguillon

Sheltered from northwest to northeast, it is possible to anchor between the two red and white buoys. Go as far towards the second as depth permits.

⚓ Le Corps de Garde

Sufficient water to stay afloat at LW can usually be found in the region of Le Corps de Garde. This can be useful if locking out of Marans in the late afternoon.

ASHORE IN MARANS

Marans has all marina facilities and is a popular place to over-winter. However, fuel is only available in cans from the garage by the supermarket.

The town has a good range of shops, cafés and restaurants. There is a covered market and an excellent supermarket on the main road out of town. Markets are held on Tuesday and Sunday.

Hire boats for the Marais Poitevin are found at the end of the marina, beyond the road bridge. The Marais Poiterin is made up of 112,000 hectares of intertwined canals. The wet marsh is also known as the Green Venice.

Waiting pontoon on right and sliding footbridge at entrance to Marans marina *Nick Chavasse*

View of Marans towards town centre *Nick Chavasse*

80 Ars-en-Ré, Île de Ré

46°13'N 1°30'W

Shelter
Good in either marina

Hazards
Shifting very shallow approach. Easy to get neaped

Depth restrictions
Channel dries 3·4m
Marinas have 1·5m or more

Night entry Lit but not recommended

HW time Pointe de Grave
HW-0015

Mean height of tide (m) St-Martin

HWS	HWN	LWN	LWS
6.0	4·9	2·4	0·9

Tidal stream in approach
Slack – PdG HW–0030 to +0030
W – PdG HW+0030 to +0530 (1·2kn)
E – PdG HW+0530 to –0030 (1·3kn)

Berthing Two marinas

Facilities Marina facilities plus small town

Charts
SHOM *7404, 7412*
Imray *C41*

Communications
VHF 9
HM Port de la Criée ① 05 46 29 25 10
HM Port de la Prée ① 05 46 29 08 52
www.portlarochelle.com/en/surroundingports

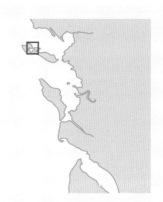

Île de Ré

Île de Ré conjures up magical thoughts and for many it is a paradise. The famous bridge linking the island to the mainland was only built in 1988. It has a very mild climate and wonderful beaches on the southern side of the island. All kinds of water sports are on offer and miles of cycle paths are ready to be explored. There are three main options for cruising yachtsmen: Ars-en-Ré, St-Martin-de-Ré and La Flotte-en-Ré.

Large drying natural harbour

Le Fier d'Ars is the large drying bay through which a channel leads to Ars-en-Ré. It is well sheltered and, despite only having access near HW, the two marinas with gates have become the principal sailing centre for the island. Interesting entrance channel which dries leading to the northernmost port on Île de Ré. Numerous whitewashed houses with traditional green shutters. Impressive church with black topped spire. The village is small but Ars-en-Ré is an excellent base for exploring the island by bicycle.

Looking W up channel towards Ars-en-Ré and Bassin de la Criée on right. The distinctive black topped spire of Ars church on 231° is easier to see than the official leading marks on 232° *Nick Chavasse*

Entrance with entry gate to Bassin de la Criée with waiting pontoon on left *Nick Chavasse*

PILOTAGE

Ars-en-Ré approach and entrance

Warning The very shallow bar in the final approach (dries 3·4m) makes it extremely easy to get neaped. Occasionally the sluices are opened at LW to scour the channel. This is seldom done in season but when it occurs, access to the harbour is restricted.

By day The easiest approach is to start from a position close north of Les Islattes north cardinal beacon tower. This is about 1M east of Pointe du Grouin.

Steer 268° towards the first starboard hand lightbuoy. Le Banc du Bûcheron tends to move south, so do not go too close to the starboard hand channel buoys and beacons as they may be off the line.

At the red beacon 0·2M east of Pointe du Fier turn to port and steer 231° for the black-topped Ars church spire. The official leading marks on 232° are not easy to see by day.

Les Islattes N cardinal beacon tower
Nick Chavasse

Le Fier d'Ars at low water *Nick Chavasse*

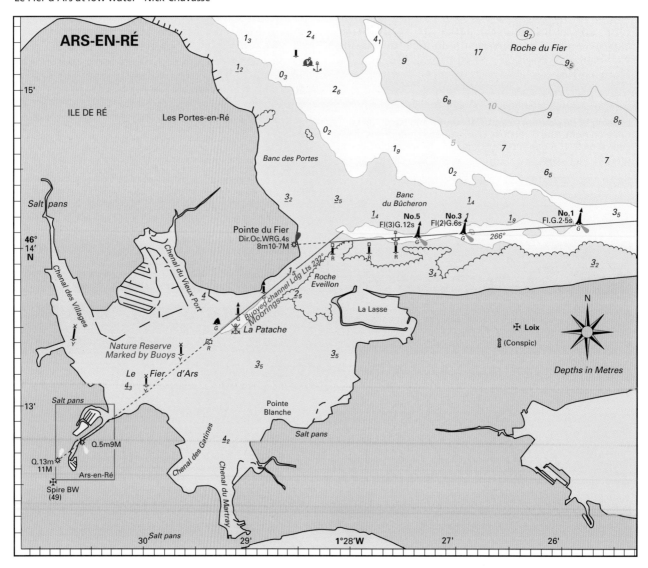

If proceeding to the harbour, follow the buoyed channel, which dries 3·4m.

By night (*See plan*) Both transits are lit but night entry is not recommended for a first visit.

BERTHS AND ANCHORAGES

Bassin de la Criée

This is the outer locked marina and the gate opens local HW±0300. Time of access will depend on draught and height of tide. The height of tide over the sill is shown on boards inside and outside the gate. Maximum draught 2·0m.

It is close to the excellent daily market. It is quieter than Basin de la Prée and is probably the best and most comfortable base for exploring Île de Ré by bicycle. Visitors berth on the pontoon on the port side with larger yachts longer than 10m furthest from the entrance.

Bassin de la Prée

This is the inner harbour at Ars-en-Ré. It is in the centre of the attractive village and has a visitors' pontoon against the wall on the starboard side. The sill dries 2·9m and the time of access will depend on draught and the height of tide. Gate open approximately 2·5hours either side of HW. There are drying berths immediately outside the gates to La Prée but they are mainly used by fishing boats. Maximum draught 1·8m.

⚓ Les Portes-en-Ré

46°15'·20N 01°28'45W

Sheltered from the southwest, there are visitors' buoys and an anchorage east of Les Portes-en-Ré.

⚓ Pointe du Fier

46°13'·59N 01°29'37W

Sheltered except from the northeast, there are some drying moorings just west of the channel south of Pointe du Fier. Anchoring is not allowed. There is an anchorage further out in a pool in the channel, 200m west of No.5 starboard hand buoy, however it is rather exposed and cannot be recommended.

ASHORE IN ARS-EN-RÉ

Ars-en-Ré has all the facilities of a small fishing, yachting and holiday town. There are basic marina facilities. The small town is attractive and has shops, restaurants, cafés and, most important, bicycle hire. There is an excellent market every day during the season.

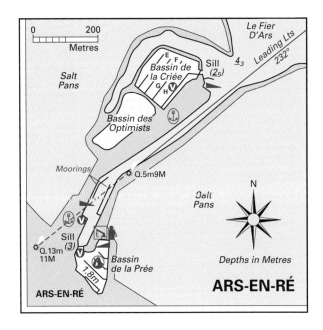

Bassin de la Criée visitors' pontoon, first on left after entry
Nick Chavasse

Channel leading from Bassin de la Prée towards the sea
Nick Chavasse

81 Saint-Martin-de-Ré, Île de Ré

46°12′N 1°22′W

Shelter
Good in Bassin à Flot

Depth restrictions
Entrance dries 1·5m
Wet dock has 3m

Other restrictions
Wet dock gets very crowded in season

Night entry Lit

HW time
PdG HW−0015

Mean height of tide (m) St-Martin

HWS	HWN	LWN	LWS
6.0	4·9	2·4	0·9

Tidal stream in approach
Slack – PdG HW−0030 to +0030
W – PdG HW+0030 to +0530 (1·2kn)
E – PdG HW+0530 to −0030 (1·3kn)

Berthing
Drying harbour and wet dock

Facilities
All facilities in a very attractive town

Charts
SHOM *7404, 7412*
Imray *C41*

Communications
VHF 9
HM ① 05 46 09 26 69
www.saint-martin-de-re.fr and follow
    bureau du port > Ecluse du port for
    lock times

Attractive historic port

Saint-Martin, on the north coast of Île de Ré, is one of the most attractive harbours in west France and a magnet for visitors. It is crowded in season but the lively atmosphere is part of its appeal. The yachts lie afloat in the heart of the town, with smart shops, cafés and restaurants nearby. Energetic crew members can explore the Vauban fortifications or hire bicycles to tour the island. It was from the prison here that convicts used to be shipped out to the penal settlements in French Guiana.

Saint-Martin has such a good reputation, it would be criminal to sail on by. Accessed via a lock gate, you will soon make friends with your neighbour. The town is lively and there is plenty to do.

PILOTAGE

Saint-Martin approach and entrance

By day The entrance dries 1·5m so entry is only possible at neaps from local HW−0200 to +0130; a bit more at springs. Beware of rocks to the east marked by Pte de Couronneau north cardinal mark.

The harbour and Vauban fortifications are distinctive. Start from a position about 1M away, with the harbour bearing 200°. Then approach with the square church tower in line with the green-topped pierhead marker at the end of the Grand Mole on 201°. Try to follow the transit accurately and particularly avoid drifting off course to the east by ensuring that the large, red-topped lighthouse is to the left of the church tower.

Saint-Martin-de-Ré looking northeast.
When entering the harbour, leave the wave breaker close to port and the mole head very close to starboard. Wait alongside the pontoon in the harbour for the lock to open. Once inside visitors raft on the W side of the basin *Patrick Roach*

On arrival at the harbour, leave the wave breaker close to port and the mole head very close to starboard. The waiting pontoon in the outer harbour is to starboard and, beyond that, the channel to the dock gates is also to starboard.

Approaching from the east, keep well to the north of the north cardinal beacon on the Couronneau rocks and do not confuse the citadel, to the east, with St-Martin itself.

By night Approach in the white sector of St-Martin light bearing 200°. On close approach alter to starboard to bring the mole light onto 195° and enter leaving the light, marking the northwest end of the wave breaker, close to port and the mole light close to starboard.

Entrance to St-Martin-de-Ré *Nick Chavasse*

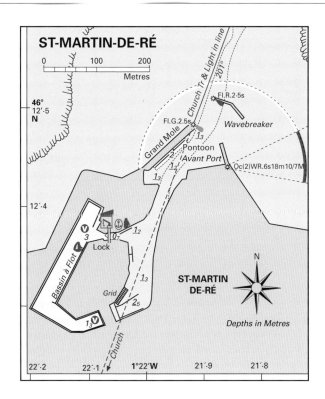

ST-MARTIN-DE-RÉ

BERTHS AND ANCHORAGES

Outer harbour

There is a long waiting pontoon along the Grand Môle dredged to 2m along its length. This is initially dredged 16m wide to allow boats to raft alongside the pontoon, but it quickly silts up with soft mud, into which the keels of deep-draught yachts sink. In northerly winds a swell enters round the wave breaker, causing the pontoon to pitch.

Drying harbour

There are quays on the east side that dry 1·5m. Vessels should not berth along the inner half of the west quay because there is a large grid.

Wet dock

The wet dock gates are opened about HW−0300 to +0230, less at neaps, between 0600 to 2300. Exact times are posted at the harbourmaster's office and

other harbours in the area. The lock opening times are also availiable at www.saint-martin-de-re.fr/ (see info box). The harbour staff take details as you enter.

To get a place inside, it is usually necessary to arrive early and wait in the outer harbour for the dock. Once inside, berth as directed. There is not much room and larger yachts are likely to be rafted alongside opposite the gate.

Rade de Saint-Martin

There are four white visitors' buoys off the entrance but they are subject to swell and tide. It is possible to anchor nearby in the bay just west of the harbour (*see plan page 262*).

ASHORE IN SAINT-MARTIN

The harbour has all facilities including a fuel berth on the starboard side just before the entry gate to the bassin à flot. The town is a sophisticated holiday resort with a good range of shops, cafés and restaurants. There is a market every day in the season.

Looking SW across wet dock at boats rafted *Nick Chavasse*

Looking S towards St-Martin-de-Ré centre *Julian Lyne-Pirkis*

Lock gate and swing bridge into Saint-Martin harbour with yachts leaving *Nick Chavasse*

82 La-Flotte-en-Ré, Île de Ré

46°11'N 1°19'W

Shelter
La Flotte, good except from N

Depth restrictions
La Flotte-en-Ré dries

Night entry La Flotte-en-Ré is lit

HW time PdG HW -0015

Mean height of tide (m) St-Martin

HWS	HWN	LWN	LWS
6.0	4·9	2·4	0·9

Tidal stream in approach
E – PdG HW–0530 to –0130 (0·9kn)
Slack – PdG –0130 to +0030
W – PdG HW+0030 to +0530 (0·9kn)
Slack – PdG HW +0530 to –0530

Berthing
Anchorages and drying harbour

Facilities Limited

Charts
SHOM *7404*
Imray *C41*

Communications
VHF 9
La Flotte HM ☎ 05 46 09 67 66
      06 20 66 85 76 (mobile)
www.laflotte.fr

Attractive drying harbour

The drying harbour of La Flotte, 2M southeast of St-Martin, was once a fishing port, famous for its lobsters, shrimps and sole. Today it is a quiet, attractive leisure port with narrow streets, white painted houses and a beautiful church. The inner harbour is well sheltered so for shallow-draught boats and boats that can take the ground, La Flotte provides a good alternative to the bustle of St-Martin. The outer harbour is exposed to the east and

The attractive curved wall of the drying harbour at La-Flotte-en-Ré *Patrick Roach*

northeast and for deep keel yachts there are two visitors' berths which are dredged at the beginning of each season and where deep-keeled yachts are supposed to be able to lie afloat in a hole but the hole is reported to silt up with very soft mud quite soon after dredging.

PILOTAGE

La-Flotte-en-Ré approach and entrance

By day La Flotte is easy to identify by the curved breakwater with the green-topped lighthouse on the end but the approach requires care. The channel through the sand dries 2.0m. On both sides are ledges of rock, and oyster beds marked by yellow beacons.

Start from a position about 1M offshore and steer 215° for the lighthouse on the end of the breakwater. A moiré fringe indicator on a post to the left of the lighthouse will be visible day and night. This ingenious device displays vertical black and orange stripes on the correct course of 215° but, on incorrect courses, it changes to one or more arrowheads pointing in the direction to steer.

To enter the harbour, leave the breakwater head to starboard and steer for the narrow entrance between the jetty heads.

By night Approach on 215° in the white sector of the breakwater light.

BERTHS AND ANCHORAGES

Visitors' moorings

Deep-draught yachts can anchor or use the five white mooring buoys some 0·75M offshore north of the harbour in 2m.

Outer harbour

Visitors may use the outer sides of the hammerheads of the second and third pontoons (F and E) in from the outer breakwater head but only on the hammerhead of Pontoon E will there be any chance

Looking SW at visitors' moorings on hammerheads
Nick Chavasse

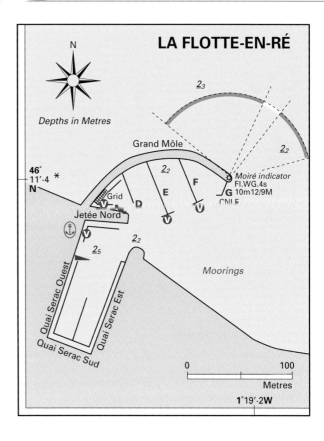

of staying afloat in a keeled yacht. A small section of Pontoon E is dredged to 2m. The outermost Pontoon G is reserved for rescue craft etc. Maximum LOA is 10m. The harbour regularly silts up but is occasionally dredged. There is a better chance of staying afloat during neaps.

Inner harbour

The inner harbour dries 2·5m. Pontoons for local boats are installed in the inner half of the basin. Space for visitors is limited but they may take the ground at the pontoon on the inner side of the Jetée Nord.

ASHORE IN LA FLOTTE

Water and electricity on the pontoons, showers and toilets ashore. There is a chandler and shops, cafés and restaurants in town. Markets are held every day. Fuel at St-Martin-de-Ré.

⚓ Anse du Martray (south coast)

46°11'·56N 1°28'·02W   *See plan page 262*

Sheltered in light northwest to northeast wind, Anse du Martray is a sandy bay on the west end of the south coast. Start from a position 0·5M east of Chanchardon octagonal black-topped white tower.

Steer 350° past the white mooring buoy into the bay. There are reefs less than 0·5M either side of the approach so it is important to hold the course fairly accurately. Anchor where depth permits but note that a deep-draught yacht will not be able to get very close to the beach. It is possible to land at the sea wall and walk to Ars-en-Ré through the salt pans or along the coast road to Martray.

⚓ Anse l'Oubye

46°9'·59N 1°15'·21W   *See plan page 262*

Sheltered from the west, there is a wide bay at the east end of Île de Ré, between Pointe de Chauveau and the bridge. Approach from the southeast and anchor in 2m on sand and mud or pick up one of the five free visitors' buoys.

La Flotte-en-Ré harbour entrance showing lighthouse and moiré indicator   *Nick Chavasse*

83 La Rochelle

46°09′N 1°10′W

Shelter Good

Depth restrictions
Approach old port 0·5m; Approach to Minimes 0·5m; Depth in old port 1·0m in very soft mud; Depth in Minimes 2·0m; Le Bassin des Yachts 3·0m, sill 1·2m

Night entry Well lit

HW time PdG HW +0005

Mean height of tide (m) La Rochelle

HWS	HWN	LWN	LWS
6.0	4·9	2·4	0·9

Tidal stream in approach: Pointe de Grave
E – PdG HW–0530 to –0030 (1·9kn)
Slack PdG HW –0030 to +0030
W PdG HW+0030 to –0530 (2·3kn)

Berthing
Huge marina and old port

Facilities All facilities

Charts
SHOM *7404, 7413*
Imray *C41*

Communications
Port des Minimes VHF 9 (24H)
    ☎ 05 46 44 41 20
La Rochelle VHF 9
    HM ☎ 05 46 41 32 05,
    mob 06 03 54 00 57
Lock ☎ mob 06 16 46 60 26
www.portlarochelle.com
www.francethisway.com/places/a/la-
    rochelle-charente-maritime.php

Fascinating historic city

La Rochelle has something for everyone. Elegant shops housed in some of France's finest historical arcaded buildings; a variety of museums; an ancient fortified port; dozens of cafés and restaurants as well as the best food market on this coast. In summer, street entertainers and musicians perform on the waterfront.

La Rochelle is so lively that wherever you moor expect to hear the sounds of music and of people enjoying themselves.

If you want a large marina, then Minimes is the way to go. However, you must follow the channel into the old part of the town and go between the two towers into the old port, if only to take in the view. If there is room, stay the night and enjoy the town's atmosphere.

Visitors' pontoon in Port Vieux is dead ahead on entry. L'Eglise St-Sauveur in centre of towers
Nick Chavasse

PILOTAGE

La Rochelle via the Ré bridge

By day The navigable part of the Ré bridge is clearly marked by buoys and on the pillars. The clearance is 30m. One arch is used for south-going boats and another for north-bound. After passing under the bridge, leave the outer breakwaters of the commercial harbour and the fishing harbour to port. Then follow the coastline, about 0·5M off, until the Tour Richelieu is sighted.

The final approach is the same as from the west or south. However, be sure to keep to the leading line for the final approach because there is a shallow patch just west of Tour Richelieu. The channel carries a minimum depth of 0·7m as far as Tour Richlieu and 0·5m into the Vieux Port.

By night The navigable section of the bridge, the commercial harbour and the fishing harbour are all well lit. However, the shortcut inside Plateau du Lavardin is not lit.

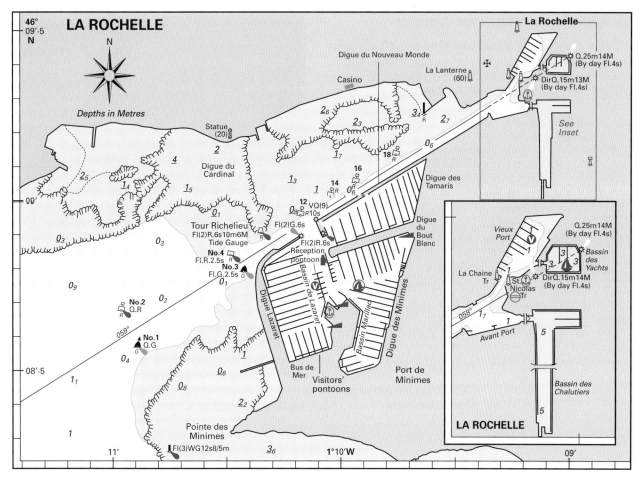

46°
09'·5
N

LA ROCHELLE

N

Depths in Metres

Digue du Nouveau Monde

Casino

La Lanterne
(60)

La Rochelle

Q.25m14M
(By day Fl.4s)

DirQ.15m13M
(By day Fl.4s)

See Inset

Statue
(20)

2₆

2₃

3₄
R

2₇

0₆

2

₂₅

1₄

1₅

1₃

1

18
R

16
R

14
R

Digue des
Tamaris

Digue du Cardinal

0₁

Tour Richelieu
Fl(2)R.6s10m6M
Tide Gauge

Fl(2)G.6s

12 VQ(9)
0₈ R10s

Fl(2)R.6s
Reception
pontoon

Digue du
Bout
Blanc

0₃

0₃

0₉

0₂

0₁

Digue Lazaret

Bassin de Lazaret

Bassin Marillac

Digue des Minimes

No.4
Fl.R.2.5s

No.3
Fl.G.2.5s

No.2
Q.R

No.1
Q.G

059°

0₄

1₁

1

1

0₆

0₈

2₂

Bus de
Mer

Visitors'
pontoons

Port de
Minimes

Pointe des
Minimes

Fl(3)WG12s8/5m

3₆

1°10'W

08'·5

11'

**Vieux
Port**

Q.25m14M
(By day Fl.4s)

La Chaine
Tr

St.
Nicolas
Tr

1

3
3

3

Bassin
des
Yachts

DirQ.15m14M
(By day Fl.4s)

058°

1₇

1

Avant Port

5

Bassin des
Chalutiers

5

LA ROCHELLE

09'

Looking south at the Ré bridge *Nick Chavasse*

La Rochelle approach with Tour Richelieu on left, Vieux Port towers in centre and entrance to Minimes marina on right
Nick Chavasse

La Rochelle from the west or south

By day Start from a position between Chauveau south cardinal buoy and Roche du Sud west cardinal buoy. Steer 059° towards the distinctive red Tour Richelieu and the two famous stone towers. The transit is two lighthouses in line on 059°. The front one is striped red and white; the rear one is white with a green top. They are very distinctive because they show bright white lights by day (Fl.4s) but these are quickly obscured when off the transit. Follow the transit to Tour Richelieu. Follow the buoyed channel for the Vieux Port or Bassin des Yachts continuing past Port des Minimes.

Port des Minimes is just past Tour Richelieu to starboard. The entrance is buoyed but be sure not to cut the corner; go all the way to the west cardinal buoy before turning into the channel.

By night The leading lights on 059° make a night entrance very easy. However, note that north of the transit the stone towers may obscure the lights.

To enter Port des Minimes marina, turn to starboard 200m past Tour Richelieu. The west cardinal buoy is lit at the entrance to Minimes, as is the starboard lateral beacon on the head of Digue Lazaret. The second port hand lateral beacon at the head of Digue de Nouveau Monde is also lit.

BERTHS AND ANCHORAGES

Port des Minimes

Port des Minimes is a 5,000-berth marina about 1M from the centre of La Rochelle. It has 2m depth. The reception pontoon is situated straight ahead on entry to the marina. Tie up at reception to be allocated a berth or contact marina staff on VHF 09 (24 hours).

Minimes welcome pontoon on right with cabin on end of pontoon and capitainerie tower beyond. Fuel pontoon is at bottom left

Looking NW at capitainerie and W section of Port des Minimes *Nick Chavasse*

In season there is a sub-office, which will take payment for marina fees, on the end of the reception pontoon which saves a walk to the capitainerie.

There are excellent marina facilities and some local shops. It is a long walk to town but there is a regular water-bus from the southwest corner of the marina.

Le Vieux Port

Le Vieux Port is in the centre of the liveliest part of the town and is the place to be if you want to enjoy the atmosphere. Pass through the towers and bear to port. The visitors' pontoons, H4 and H5, are straight ahead beyond the ferry pontoons. They only have depth of 1·0m but the mud is soft so deep-draught yachts remain upright. The pontoons have water and electricity and there are showers and toilets in the capitainerie by the lock gate into the Bassin des Yachts and at the Bassin des Chalutiers.

Looking NW across Vieux Port and Tour de l'Horloge on left
Nick Chavasse

Entrance to Bassin des Yachts showing lifting bridge down
and entry gate closed *Nick Chavasse*

Entrance to Bassin des Chalutiers is to starboard just before
the entrance to the Vieux Port. Lifting bridge is down and
entry gate is closed *Nick Chavasse*

Le Bassin des Yachts (Le Bassin à Flot)

This may be preferable for boats over 12m, or for those staying a few days. The lock gate is to starboard just inside Le Vieux Port. The sill dries 1·2m and 3m depth is maintained in the basin. Access is from HW-0200 to HW+0130 by day. Call the Bureau du Vieux Port to ask for space and for the lock gate and footbridge to be opened.

Bassin des Chalutiers

The Bassin des Chalutiers is used for special events but, space permitting, it is also available for visitors. It is particularly suitable for larger boats and multihulls. It has 5m depth. Contact the harbourmaster to arrange for a berth and for the entry gate and lifting bridge to be opened.

ASHORE IN LA ROCHELLE

La Rochelle has every imaginable yachting facility. There are boat builders, chandlers, engineers and sail makers. Most major marine manufacturers have agencies.

In town there is so much to do that a guidebook or a visit to the tourist office (Quai Georges Simenon, south of Le Bassin des Yachts) is the best approach. Try to visit the museums early as they can become crowded later in the day.

The covered market is open every day and the street market fills the surrounding streets twice a week.

Looking NE over Bassin des Yachts *Nick Chavasse*

83 Île d'Aix

46°01′N 1°11′W

Shelter
Fair weather only

Depth restrictions
Visitors' buoys 2·0m

Night entry Approaches well lit

HW time
PdG HW -0015

Mean height of tide (m) Île d'Aix

HWS	HWN	LWN	LWS
6·1	4·9	2·4	0·9

Tidal stream in approach
SE – PdG HW–0530 to +0030 (2·1kn)
Slack – PdG HW +0030 to +0130
NW – PdG HW+0130 to –0530
 (1·7kn)

Berthing
Anchorages and visitors' buoys

Facilities
A few shops, restaurants and cafés

Charts
SHOM *7405, 7415*
Imray *C41*

Small island with history

Île d'Aix is a small island surrounded by beaches.

There are pretty white houses with multi-coloured hollyhocks, no cars, good walking or biking and two museums. It was here that Napoleon last stood on French soil before being transported to St-Helena.

The island is about 8M south of La Rochelle and is a good stopover on the way to Rochefort or an interesting day trip from La Rochelle. There are some visitors' buoys and a choice of anchorages. The island is protected from Biscay swell by Île d'Oléron.

PILOTAGE

Île d'Aix western approach and entrance

By day The western approach is straightforward from any direction. Note that Fort Boyard 1·6M west-southwest of Île d'Aix light marks the shallows at the southern end of the Longue. Avoid the reef, marked by two west cardinal beacons, that extends 0·5M to the northwest. When close in, avoid the oyster beds, marked by a yellow buoy, Aix SE special purpose buoy, that extends 0·75M to the southeast.

By night From the northwest, keep in the white sector of the Île d'Aix light until Chauveau light turns from red to white, bearing 342°. Steer 162° down this boundary, passing through the red sector of Île d'Aix light. When it turns white again, use the Charente leading lights bearing 115°. When Île d'Aix light bears north steer 020° and anchor in 3m, or pick up a mooring. (*See plan page 281.*)

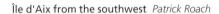

Île d'Aix from the southwest *Patrick Roach*

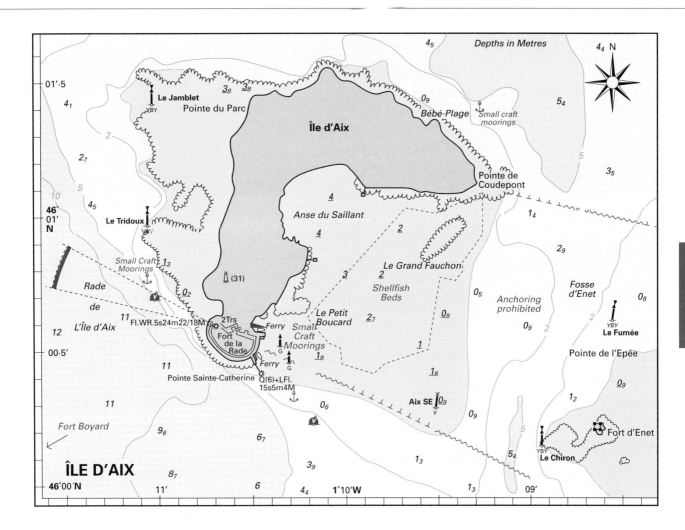

The passage E of Île d'Aix

By day Fosse d'Enet is a narrow channel between Île d'Aix and the mainland.

From the north, leave the east point of the Île d'Aix at least 0·5M to starboard to avoid a rocky spur. Steer 195° toward the west cardinal beacon just west of the conspicuous Fort d'Enet. A yellow buoy marks the dangers southeast of Île d'Aix.

BERTHS AND ANCHORAGES

⚓ Southeast of Pointe Ste-Cathérine

46°00'·26N 1°10'·18W

Well sheltered from north and northwest with some shelter from other directions, there is an anchorage with three white visitors' buoys off the southeast tip of Île d'Aix in 2·4m. Other moorings with a dayglo green band dry further in. Approach from the

Fort Boyard and Pointe Ste-Cathérine on left *Nick Chavasse*

Visitors moorings SE of Pointe Ste-Catherine *Nick Chavasse*

southeast and go in as far as depth allows. The mud is very soft so the holding is poor. The area is so well lit that it would be easy to leave at night and move to La Rochelle. Yachts that can take the ground can anchor inside the moorings, close northeast of the Fort de la Rade, by approaching close east of the ferry pier and leaving the two starboard hand beacons to starboard. However it would be wise to view the position of the oyster beds and other obstructions at LW beforehand.

⚓ Northwest of Pointe Ste-Cathérine

46°00′·70N 1°11′.04W

Sheltered from the east and partially sheltered from the southeast, there is an anchorage with visitors' buoys northwest of Fort de la Rade.

⚓ Bébé-Plage

46°01′·38N 1°09′·35W

Sheltered from the southwest, Bébé-Plage off the northeast coast makes a pleasant fine weather anchorage. Night departure to La Rochelle would be very easy. There are two visitors' buoys.

ASHORE IN ÎLE D'AIX

The village has modest shops and some cafés and restaurants. Bicycles and horse drawn carriages are also available for a tour of the island. A walk round the island will take about two and a half hours. There are two museums and two forts.

The visitors' moorings and beach northwest of Pointe Ste-Cathérine with Fort Boyard and Île d'Oléron beyond *Jeremy Parkinson*

Île d'Aix lighthouse is made up of two towers which produce the sector light in service since 1906 *Nick Chavasse*

85 La Charente

45°59′N 1°07′W

Hazard
Dangerous bar at Fouras
Bore above Rochefort at big springs

Depth restrictions
Bar at entrance has 0·8m
River has 0·8m

Night entry Lit to Port-des-Barques

HW time Île d'Aix La Rochelle-La Pallice −00·05

HW time Rochefort La Rochelle-La Pallice +00·15

Mean height of tide (m)
Île d'Aix

HWS	HWN	LWN	LWS
6·1	4·9	2·4	0·9

Rochefort

6·5	5·3	2·2	0·8

Tidal stream in river
Flood – PdG HW−0530 to +0030 (2.0kn)
Slack – PdG HW +0030 to +0130
Ebb – PdG HW+0130 to −0530 (2.0kn)
Stream can be 4.0kn in narrows

Berthing
Anchorages and visitors' buoys
Marina at Rochefort

Facilities
All facilities at Rochefort

Charts
SHOM *7415*
Imray *C41*

Communications
www.ville-rochefort.fr

River with fishing huts and sunflowers

Despite leading to Rochefort, the margins of the Charente are completely rural with fishing huts and fields of sunflowers lining the banks. It is a very attractive river with masses of wildlife.

It is navigable for masted yachts for about 16M to Tonnay-Charente, about 3M beyond Rochefort. Motorboats can continue to Saintes, which is reported to be a delightful trip. Even quite large ships regularly make the passage to Rochefort and it is quite a surprise to be overtaken by a coaster in this idyllic rural setting.

PILOTAGE

La Charente to Tonnay-Charente

Warning There is a dangerous bar at the mouth of the river, near Fouras. Seas break heavily on the ebb in wind against tide conditions so it is best to cross the bar as close to HW as possible on the flood if the wind is from west or northwest.

By day Start from a position south of Île d'Aix and close north of Les Palles north cardinal buoy. The first transit is on the land south of the town of Fouras. It is a very tall red-topped white lighthouse in line with a stubby red-topped white lighthouse on

115°. The second transit is two lighthouses in Port-des-Barques in line on 135°. The rear lighthouse has a black, pointed roof and the front light is white with ears and a small black window.

Once the river has been entered it is generally sufficient to keep in midstream. There are beacons on the shore that provide a succession of transits. Each one carries a conspicuous letter, running from (T) at Port-des-Barques to (A), just below Rochefort. These are fun to follow but they are only really necessary for the coasters.

By night The leading lines are lit as far as Port-des-Barques. Night passage beyond there is not permitted for small craft.

Stay alert for coasters using the river
Nick Chavasse

Fontaines Royales 0·75M beyond Port des Barques on starboard bank with prominent tower on foreshore
Nick Chavasse

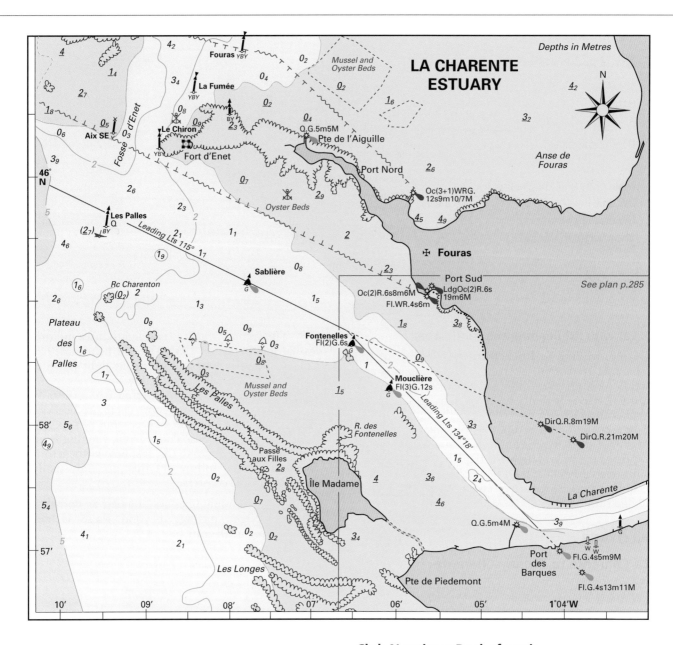

BERTHS AND ANCHORAGES

Port-des-Barques

Sheltered from the northwest by a jetty running north from the south shore there is a visitors' pontoon with a fuel berth and also two visitors' mooring buoys in 2–3m. There are also two large white mooring buoys marked with a 'V' at Fontaines Royales, about 0·75M upstream of Port-des Barques on the south side of the river with a landing slip close-by.

The Club Nautique Rochefortais at Le Port Neuf, 1·5M beyond Pte de la Sablière on East bank *Nick Chavasse*

Club Nautique Rochefortais

The Club Nautique Rochefortais is on the east bank about 1·5M beyond Pte de la Sablière. It has landing facilities and a number of moorings along the opposite bank.

Soubise

Soubise, about half way to Rochefort, has a visitors' pontoon and some visitors' moorings. Alternatively, anchor on the south side of the river as near to the bank as possible. Soubise is an attractive village with a boulangerie but no other shops. The supermarket is 20 minute walk. Frequent buses to Rochefort.

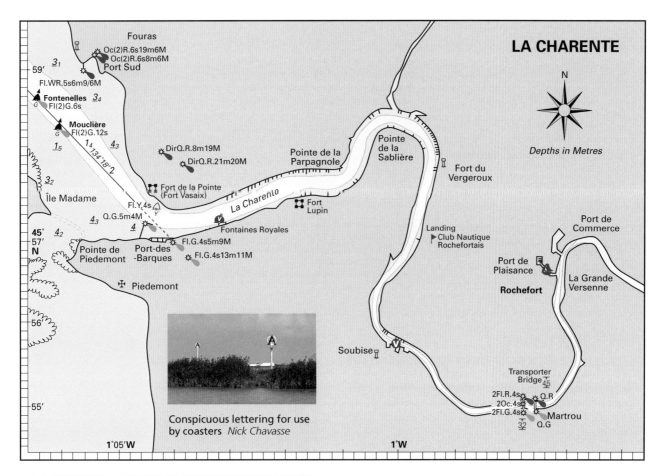

LA CHARENTE

Depths in Metres

Conspicuous lettering for use by coasters Nick Chavasse

Soubise pontoon and moorings *Nick Chavasse*

Rochefort See page 285

Tonnay-Charente

Tonnay-Charente is 3M beyond Rochefort at the limit of masted navigation. It has a modern pontoon that may be available for visitors but the depth is unknown. There are shops, cafés and restaurants and a splendid, historic suspension bridge.

Looking downstream at La Charente transporter bridge with Viaduc de Martrou behind *Nick Chavasse*

At Martrou, the D733 road bridge with 32m clearance and aerial transporter cross the river. The transporter bridge is the last of its kind in France. It is an airborne platform suspended about 4m above the water and moved by a trolley affair about 45m above it. Give way when in use!

La Charente transporter bridge in operation
Janet Spinlove

86 Rochefort

45°57'N 0°57'W

Shelter
Good in Rochefort marina

Depth restrictions
River has 0·8m
Marina has 1·5m or more

Rochefort lock and bridge opening
Rochefort HW–0100 to +0100

Night entry Forbidden

HW time Rochefort
La Rochelle - La Pallice +0015

Mean height of tide (m) Rochefort

HWS	HWN	LWN	LWS
6·5	5·3	2·2	0·8

Tidal stream in river
Flood – PdG HW–0530 to +0030 (2.0kn)
Slack – PdG HW+0030 to +0130

Ebb – PdG HW+0130 to –0530 (2.0kn)
Stream can be 4.0kn in narrows

Berthing
Marina at Rochefort

Facilities
Marina facilities, good shops, restaurants and museums

Charts
SHOM *7415*
Imray *C41*

Communications
VHF 9
HM ① 05 46 83 99 96 or 06 86 01 64 29
www.ville-rochefort.fr/plaisance-et-nautisme
  and download *Horaires des marées et ouverture de l'écluse*
www.francethisway.com/places/rochefort.php

Historic naval shipyard

Rochefort is a delight. It was created by Colbert in the 17th century as a naval arsenal to rival Toulon. The dignified architecture from that period is still largely preserved. The original ropewalk is particularly fine and has been made into a rope museum.

Rochefort has all the facilities of a regional centre. This and the good facilities for yachtsmen, helpful marina staff and reasonable prices make it a good place to keep a yacht.

The old transporter bridge is a couple of miles south of the marina. It was restored in 2016 and takes cyclists and pedestrians across the river.

Built as a secret dockyard, Rochefort was raised from the marshes. The weight of buildings has taken its toll and several are listing!

The old dock is home to the replica of the 1779 frigate *L'Hermione*, which was built using traditional methods. She is a very popular tourist attraction and sails from Rochefort on long and short trips. She is not always at home. In the neighbouring dock there is another replica of the ship showing the materials used in the reconstruction.

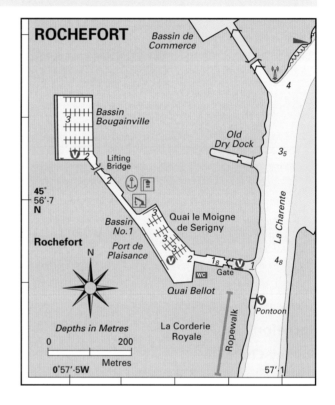

L'Hermione's home port *Nick Chavasse*

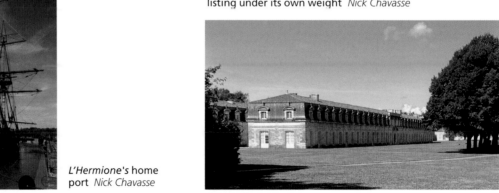

La Corderie Royale rope walk is one of the buildings that is listing under its own weight *Nick Chavasse*

Looking E at visitors'pontoon and closed lock gate on right
Nick Chavasse

PILOTAGE *See page 283*

BERTHS

Rochefort Port de Plaisance

The lock to the marina usually opens at about HW La Rochelle and remains open for about 30 to 60 minutes. The exact times are given in a booklet *Le Guide de la Plaisance Rochefortaise* that is given away in port offices throughout the region. Alternatively call the port on ☎ 06 86 01 64 29 to find the lock times or to book a space. Excellent website at www.ville-rochefort.fr. See info box for details.

The entrance to the marina requires a sharp turn to port just after the splendid 17th-century ropewalk. There is a waiting pontoon in the river outside and another at the entrance to the lock, which dries at spring tides but has 2m at neaps and the bottom is soft mud.

The outside pontoon, which has access to the shore as well as water and electricity, may be used for up to 24 hours but is shared with a ferry. The end of the pontoon closest to the lock is used for waiting and rafting may be necessary.

When the lock opens, visitors are directed to a berth. Those staying longer than one night normally go into the inner basin, Bassin Bougainville. The lifting bridge which allows access to Bassin Bougainville is opened when boats are ready to go through.

The berths are not well labelled and there is often a queue of boats entering when the lock opens, so manoeuvring can be interesting. It is best to leave as much space as possible behind the boat in front and be prepared to secure temporarily to the wall or another boat. The lock does become silted and boats have sometimes had to stay longer than planned due to insufficient water, effectively being neaped.

ASHORE IN ROCHEFORT

The marina has all facilities except a fuel berth. There are chandlers, engineers and repairs. The marina has a small 15-T crane for masting and a 16-T mobile crane for lift out. There is storage afloat and ashore.

Rochefort is a wealthy town with an excellent range of shops, cafés and restaurants. There is a supermarket upstream on the road by the river and an excellent street market in town on Tuesday and Thursday. Car hire is by the marina and the railway station is within walking distance.

Lifting bridge permitting access to Bassin Bougainville
Nick Chavasse

87 St-Denis-d'Oléron, Île d'Oléron

46°02'N 1°22'W

Shelter Good in marina

Depth restrictions
Sill dries 1·5m
Waiting buoy 0·7m to 1.0m
Marina 1·5m to 2·5m but silts

Night entry Lit

HW time
PdG HW -0015

Mean height of tide (m) Île d'Aix

HWS	HWN	LWN	LWS
6·1	4·9	2·4	0·9

Tidal stream in approach
E – PdG HW–0530 to –0030 (1·9kn)
Slack PdG HW–0030 to +0030
W – PdG HW+0030 to –0530 (2·3kn)

Berthing Marina

Fuel Marina entrance

Facilities
Limited repairs but good shops, cafés and restaurants

Charts
SHOM *7405*
Imray *C41*

Communications
VHF 9
HM ☏ 05 46 47 97 97
www.port-oleron.com
www.oleron-island.com
www.saintdenisoleron.fr

Île d'Oléron

Île d'Oléron is slightly larger than Île de Ré and, similarly, linked to the mainland by a viaduct which leads to Marennes. The island, which is mainly given over to tourism has numerous forests and marshes, as well as some fabulous beaches and miles of bicycle tracks. There are three main ports suited to cruising yachtsmen: St Denis-d'Oléron, Port du Douhet and Boyardville, which are covered in this chapter. *See plan on page 262.*

Friendly modern marina

St-Denis-d'Oléron, on the northeast tip of Île d'Oléron, makes a perfect base for exploring the north of the island. It is also a good jumping off point to cross Biscay and a suitable start point for navigating under the Viaduc d'Oléron, before progressing to La Seudre and Marennes.

Given the right conditions, it is possible to pass under the Viaduc d'Oléron and cruise out through the Pertuis de Maumusson at the southern tip of Île d'Oléron and on to La Gironde. Planning on large scale charts is crucial to pull this off!

There are sheltered family beaches nearby and the wilder beaches of the windward west side are not far away. Île d'Oléron is particularly well set up for cyclists, with many attractive cycle tracks away from roads. Bikes can be hired near the marina.

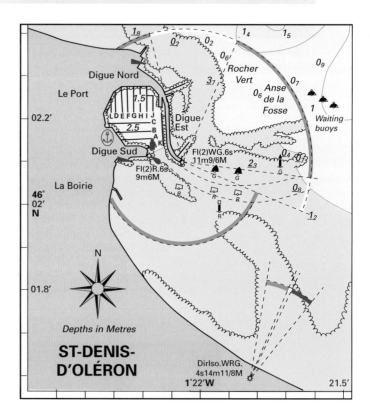

Looking SE from St-Denis marina at entrance channel. Note people walking with RIB in channel at LW *Nick Chavasse*

The modern, purpose-built marina offers good shelter and facilities. The attractive village is about 0·25M away. The marina has been dug out of the sand and has a sill at the entrance. At low water the bay outside the marina dries.

PILOTAGE

St-Denis approach and entrance

By day Avoid the shoals north of the island and start the approach from a position quite well east of the town. Approach with the church spire in line with the green starboard hand beacon pole on 250°. Beware drying patch 0·9m to south of the leading line 0·3M from starboard hand lateral beacon. In the final approach, leave the green beacon 100m to starboard and alter course to starboard to leave the red port hand beacon well to port. In the season the channel is marked with small red and green buoys.

By night Start from a position about 2M north-northeast of the harbour. Approach in the narrow white sector of the directional light on 205°. This lighthouse is 0·6M south of St Denis d'Oléron (see plan). On entering the white sector of the east breakwater light, alter to starboard to enter the marina. Leave the east breakwater 40m to starboard to avoid an outcrop of sand and stones encroaching on the channel.

The sill is 1·5m above CD and there is a tide gauge on the west side of the entrance. At mid-tide there is 1·9m over the sill. The marina silts so note the depth at the sill on entering to be able to calculate the depth of water in the marina when the sill dries.

BERTHS

St-Denis Marina

The visitors' pontoon (A) is to port just beyond the fuel dock. There are finger berths on its north side and yachts over 10m berth alongside on the south side. There are three waiting buoys 1M east-northeast of the entrance.

Looking NE across marina towards capitainerie *Nick Chavasse*

Fuel pontoon on port hand side at entrance and sill depth guage on right *Nick Chavasse*

ASHORE IN ST-DENIS D'OLÉRON

The marina has a fuel berth at the entrance but there are no repair facilities on site. Bicycles may be borrowed from the capitainerie for an hour for free. There are restaurants and a bike hire shop close to the marina. Further along is the village with shops, including a good supermarket and a daily market.

Looking SE at Pointe de Chassiron lighthouse *Nick Chavasse*

88 Le Douhet, Île d'Oléron

46°00'N 1°19'W

Shelter
Good in marina

Hazard
Overfalls in entrance in NE wind against ebb

Depth restrictions
Entrance dries 1·6m
Sill dries 1·8m
Visitors' pontoon 2·0m

Night entry Not lit

HW time PdG HW -0015

Mean height of tide (m) Île d'Aix

HWS	HWN	LWN	LWS
6·1	4·9	2·4	0·9

Tidal stream in approach
SE – PdG HW–0530 to +0030 (2·0kn)
Slack PdG HW+0030 to +0130
NW – PdG HW+0130 to –0530 (2·0kn)

Berthing Marina

Facilities Limited facilities

Charts
SHOM 7405
Imray C41

Communications
VHF 9
HM ☎ 05 46 76 71 13
www.oleron-island.com

Quiet marina with good beaches

Le Douhet is about 3M southeast of St-Denis-d'Oléron. It is quiet, well sheltered and attractively set amongst pine trees. There are some excellent beaches nearby.

PILOTAGE

Le Douhet approach and entrance

Warning The entrance is a narrow, dredged channel across 0·5M of sand and rock that dries 1·6m or more. It must be positively identified before attempting an entrance. Note that the channel can be quite rough in north and east winds.

By day Coming from the north, keep at least 2M offshore. Start the approach from Douhet west cardinal buoy. Steer 250° towards the marina and locate the red and green buoys that mark the channel. Follow the buoyed channel past two port hand beacons into the marina.

Once inside the entrance turn sharply to port into the first basin over a sill which is marked by a tide gauge left to starboard. The visitors' pontoon is Pontoon D in 2.0m in the northwest of the basin. The southeast of the basin carries 1·5m.

The basin is accessible for a boat with a draught of 1·5m on a tide with a co-efficient of 80, HW –0300 to HW +0300.

Approach channel to Port du Douhet *Nick Chavasse*

Entrance to Port du Douhet *Nick Chavasse*

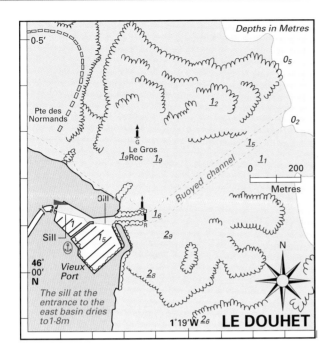

The sill at the entrance to the east basin dries to 1·8m

Looking E out of the entrance channel *Nick Chavasse*

ASHORE IN LE DOUHET

Facilities include water and electricity on the pontoons, showers and toilets ashore, a boatbuilder and chandler but no fuel berth. There are a few small shops, including a baker and bike hire. Otherwise, the nearest shops are at La Brée les Bains (3km) or St-Georges d'Oléron (4km).

Douhet is well placed for visiting the swell-protected family beaches and pine forests between Douhet and Boyardville.

Sill beyond the tide gauge showing at LW on right. Entry sill is this side of guage *Nick Chavasse*

Entrance to first basin leaving tide gauge to starboard at right, with visitors' berths on right-hand side of right-hand pontoon
Nick Chavasse

89 Boyardville, Île d'Oléron

45°58'N 1°14'W

Shelter Good in marina

Depth restrictions
Entrance dries 2·0m
Automatic gate
Visitors' pontoon 1·5m

Night entry Partially lit

HW time
PdG HW -0015

Mean height of tide (m) Île d'Aix

HWS	HWN	LWN	LWS
6·1	4·9	2·4	0·9

Tidal stream in approach
As Île d'Aix
2kn in river

Berthing Marina

Facilities All facilities

Fuel SE bank outside marina

Charts
SHOM *7405*
Imray *C41*

Communications
VHF 9
HM ☎ 05 46 47 23 71

Small marina in a pleasant fishing town

Boyardville has a small marina in a locked basin accessed by a tidal river. The basin is perfectly sheltered, in the centre of town, surrounded by shops and cafés. The ambience is pleasant but it does become busy in season.

On the weekend after 14 July a spectacular firework display takes place at Fort Boyard, 2M off the port. This can be watched from the beach, north of the town or from a boat at anchor off the beach.

Boyardville marina and the river entrance looking northeast. On the west side of the marina are a row of cafés and shops. The car park to the south is used for the market. The marshes are close by for walking or cycling and on Île d'Oléron a beach is never far away *Patrick Roach*

PILOTAGE

Boyardville approach and entrance

By day Approaching from the north beware of a large mussel farm north of Pte des Saumonards. It is marked by north cardinal and east cardinal lightbuoys.

Start from a position close to La Perrotine starboard hand buoy, which is about 2M south of the conspicuous Fort Boyard. Steer about 260° towards the breakwater with port hand beacon on head of breakwater. The channel shifts so watch the depth and be prepared to follow the deepest water. Once past the breakwater head, the best water is usually on the south side of the channel.

Waiting pontoon

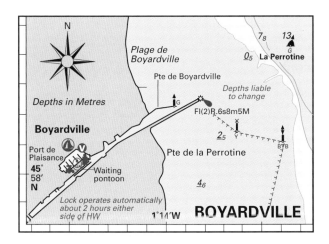

Looking into the marina through the lock gate with visitors' pontoon on right *Nick Chavasse*

Continue into the river entrance and be prepared for a very sharp turn to starboard into the marina. When the turn comes it is important not to cut the corner: almost go past the entrance before turning.

The gates into the wet basin are automatically operated by the water level. They open approximately HW±0130 at neaps and HW±0300 at springs (24 hours). The sill dries 1·8m. There is a waiting pontoon 50m beyond marina entrance on starboard side (*see photo*).

By night The mole head is lit but night entry is not recommended.

BERTHS AND ANCHORAGES

Port du Boyardville

Visitors berth on the pontoon to starboard of the entrance or on a pontoon berth as directed by the harbourmaster.

Drying out, alongside one of the quays in the river, may be possible but the bottom is uneven in places so check with the harbourmaster first.

Visitors' moorings

About 0·75M north-northwest of La Perrotine starboard hand buoy there are four white waiting buoys (marked PL29-32) and a large number of small craft moorings. Boyardville charges for their

Looking SW at *Wild Bird* on waiting pontoon *Nick Chavasse*

use and, in return, provides a taxi service to the beach. Alternatively, anchor nearby but note that the bottom shoals rapidly.

ASHORE IN BOYARDVILLE, ÎLE D'OLÉRON

The marina has all facilities.

Boyardville is a small town with a full range of shops close to the marina. It is a good base for exploring the coast by bicycle. The Atlantic beaches are spectacular and run for miles along most of the west coast of Île d'Oleron. The southeast coast is devoted to oyster and mussel farming, which is operated out of picturesque shacks in muddy creeks.

Looking towards waiting pontoon on right hand side from abeam the entrance to the marina *Nick Chavasse*

90 La Seudre to Marennes

45°49'N 1°10'W

Shelter
Excellent in Marennes marina

Hazard
Pertuis Maumusson is not advised in
any conditions (see blue box below)

Depth restrictions
Marennes canal dries 2·2m

Height restriction
Road bridge 18m above ML and NOT HAT

Night entry Not lit

HW time La Cayenne (Seudre River)
Pointe de Grave HW +0010

Mean height of tide (m) La Cayenne

HWS	HWN	LWN	LWS
5·6	4·6	2·4	0·8

Tidal stream in N approach
S – PdG HW–0530 to +0115 (2·1kn)
N – PdG HW+0115 to –0545 (1·7kn)
Complex at mouth of Seudre
4kn in Seudre

Berthing
Marina

Facilities
Basic facilities, good supermarket

Charts
SHOM *7405, 7414*

Communications
Marennes marina ☏ 05 46 76 47 97 /
06 08 70 08 26
www.tourisme-marennes.fr

Oyster capital of France

Marennes is the centre of a huge area of marshes and
tidal mud flats that stretch from Rochefort to Royan
and include much of the east side of Île d'Oléron.
The water is mostly shallow, the tides are strong and
the area is dedicated to the culture of the renowned
Marennes-Oléron oyster. Visiting boats are neither
appropriate nor particularly welcome. Nevertheless,
it is a fascinating area with outstanding seafood and
can be visited in suitable conditions. There are
several anchorages and a small marina at Marennes.

Coureau d'Oléron from the north

By day Le Coureau d'Oléron leads south to the
entrance to La Seudre River and the Pertuis de
Maumusson. The first challenge is to select the best
route under the Pont de L'Île d'Oléron. There are
two options; one with 18m and the other to the
southeast with 15m. The channel is intricate and the
pilotage is mostly buoy hopping so an up to date
version of the large-scale chart SHOM 7414 is
recommended. Note that the direction of buoyage is
from the south and that buoys may have been
respositioned due to shifting sand banks.

Start from a position close to waypoint
45°57'·00N 01°11'·02 and steer 157° with
Marennes church spire in line with the Juliar east
cardinal tower beacon. Leave Juliar beacon to
starboard and continue on the same course using the
Charret beacon (black rectangle with a white circle
on a tall pole) in line with Marennes church, still on
157°. About 0·5M from the Charret beacon,
45°52'·93 01°8'·67 turn to starboard and steer
about 220° to leave Agnas east cardinal buoy to
starboard and follow the buoys round the south side
of Bank d'Agnas to the bridge.

The two preferred routes under the bridge
(heights 18m or 15m) are marked with a red square
and a green triangle on a white square. The
southeast route is easier but is 3m lower. Pass under

the bridge, taking care to avoid the wreck at
45°49'·75N 01°10'·71W south of the bridge, and
follow the buoys towards La Palette port hand buoy
which should be left to starboard when going south.

Bridge heights for this area (SHOM 7414) are given as above
Mean Sea Level. Our mast height is 19m which meant that we
had to wait until below half-tide to get under the viaduct. We
were bound from the north, for La Seudre and the Marennes
canal entry point.

We managed to squeeze under the bridge by lowering the
burgee and watching in horror as the VHF antennae bent to the
horizontal. Having waited for the tide to drop sufficiently to get
under the bridge, we now had insufficient water to take the
direct route to La Seudre. We, therefore, had to take the long
route southwest to the Pertuis de Maumusson, and had to wait
for the tide before progressing up La Seudre and under the
bridge, 18m, at La Cayenne to the entrance of the Marennes
canal. The challenge here is to get there before the tide rises too
much to prevent access under the bridge. We made it in time
and found a mooring in the dark opposite La Tremblade on the
south side of the river.

I have been reminded that this trip is not for everyone!

VHF antenna horizontal under the Pont de L'Île d'Oléron
bridge *Nick Chavasse*

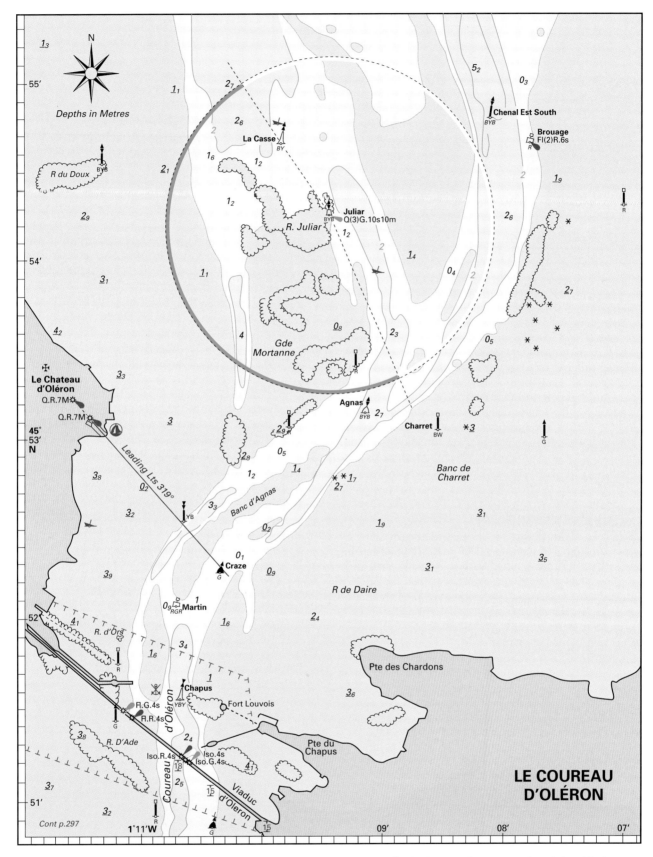

N

55'

Depths in Metres

R du Doux   BYB

2_9

54'

3_1

4_2

Le Chateau
d'Oléron
Q.R.7M

Q.R.7M

45°
53'
N

3_8

3_2

3_9

52'

4_1

R. d'Org

3_8 R. D'Ade

3_7

51'

3_2

Cont p.297

$1°11'W$

1_3

1_1 2_7 5_2 0_3

2 2_6 Chenal Est South   BYB

La Casse   BY   Brouage   Fl(2)R.6s   R

1_6 1_2

2_1 1_2 2 1_9 R

1_2 Juliar   Q(3)G.10s10m   BYB

R. Juliar 1_2 2 2_6

1_4 2_7

1_1 0_4 2

4 0_8 Gde   Mortanne 2_3 0_5

Agnas   BYB 2_7

Charret   BW $*3$ G

2_9 R

2_8 0_5 1_4 Banc de   Charret

1_2 $*1_7$ 3_1

2_7

3

Leading Lts 319°

0_2 YB

3_3 Banc d'Agnas 1_9

3_2 0_2 3_5

0_1 3_1

Craze   G 0_9 R de Daire

0_9 Martin   RGR 1 2_4

1_6 Pte des Chardons

3_4 3_6

1_6 T

1

Chapus   YBY   Fort Louvois

R.G.4s   G
R.R.4s   Pte du
Chapus

Iso.R.4s   Iso.4s
18 Iso.G.4s 4_1

2_4 LE COUREAU
D'OLÉRON

2_5

15 Viaduc d'Oléron

R   G 15 09'   08'   07'

Looking SW at Pont de L'Île d'Oléron with Fort Louvois on left   *Nick Chavasse*

Looking SE up La Seudre *Nick Chavasse*

Le Château d'Oléron

45°52'·44N 1°10'·70W

This is an oyster port on the east coast of Oléron just before the bridge. Yachts are not particularly welcome but a new oyster harbour is being built just to the south so that there may be more room in the future. There are two pontoons in the avant port where a yacht drawing 1m would stay just afloat on a neap tide but otherwise a boat would have to take the ground. Approach from Mortanne Sud south cardinal beacon and make good 319° towards the leading lights. The rear light is a red-topped white light tower. The front light is a squat white tower with a red board above it but beware of oyster beds marked by rather insubstantial withies close to the channel. There are no specific facilities for yachts but the citadel is worth seeing.

La Seudre river entrance

When La Palette port hand buoy is abeam turn to port through 90° and steer 145° towards Soumaille west cardinal buoy which is left close to port and into the start of the River Seudre. Between La Palette port hand and Soumaille west cardinal buoy a bank which dries 0·8m will have been crossed requiring an adequate rise of tide. Follow the buoys up the river and under the road bridge (height 18m above ML) to La Cayenne at the entrance to the Marennes canal. Beware that the sandbanks and buoyage are subject to change.

PILOTAGE

Marennes

The entrance to the Marennes canal lies just downstream of the ferry pier, on the port side as you head up river. There is a shallow patch in the entrance marked by a port hand beacon with the best water on the starboard side. The perches marking the channel are high on the mud, and the best water lies roughly halfway between them. At the end of the canal is the wet basin, the gates of which open automatically at about HW±0100 at neaps and HW±0200 at springs but they only operate when the tidal co-efficient exceeds 50. A power cable (height 24m) crosses the canal above the entry gate. Both above ML.

Entrance to Marennes canal *Nick Chavasse*

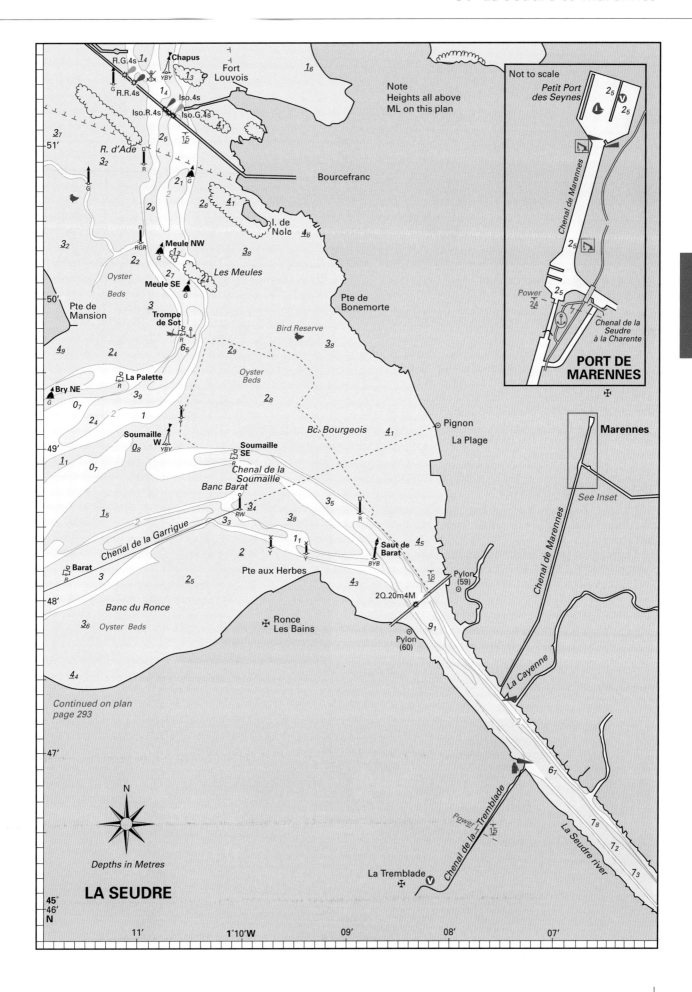

Note
Heights all above
ML on this plan

Not to scale

*Petit Port
des Seynes*

2_5

2_5

Chenal de Marennes

2_5

2_5

Power

2_4

2_5

*Chenal de la
Seudre
à la Charente*

**PORT DE
MARENNES**

⛨

R.G.4s 1_4

Chapus

YBY

1_3

Fort
Louvois

1_6

G R.R.4s

1_4

Iso.4s

Iso.R.4s

Iso.G.4s

4_1

Bourcefranc

3_7

51′

R. d'Ade

2_5

$\frac{T}{15}$

3_2

R

2_1 G

2_9

2

2_6

4_1

G

I. de
Nolo

4_6

Marennes

3_2

RGR

Meule NW

1_2

G

Les Meules

3_8

Pte de
Bonemorte

50′

2_2

2_7

Meule SE

G

*Oyster
Beds*

Pte de
Mansion

3

**Trompe
de Sot**

R

6_5

Bird Reserve

3_8

4_9

2_4

2_9

*Oyster
Beds*

2_8

3_8

La Palette

R

3_9

Bry NE

G

0_7

2

1

Bc. Bourgeois

4_1

Pignon
La Plage

See Inset

2_4

**Soumaille
W**

YBY

0_8

**Soumaille
SE**

R

49′

1_1

0_7

*Chenal de la
Soumaille*

Banc Barat

3_5

R

1_5

2

RW 3_4

3_3

3_8

Chenal de la Garrigue

2

1_1

Y

Y

**Saut de
Barat**

BYB

4_5

Barat

B

3

Pte aux Herbes

4_3

$\frac{T}{18}$

Pylon
(59)

48′

2_5

2Q.20m4M

Banc du Ronce

3_6

Oyster Beds

Ronce
Les Bains

Pylon
(60)

9_1

La Cavenne

4_4

Chenal de Marennes

Continued on plan
page 293

47′

6_7

N

Power Tremblade

$\frac{T}{15}$

La Tremblade

V
⛨

La Seudre river

1_8

1_2

1_3

Depths in Metres

LA SEUDRE

45°
46′
N

11′   1°10′W   09′   08′   07′

Marennes church spire *Nick Chavasse*

BERTHS

The marina is in an old dock. Visitors do occasionally arrive and yachts under 12m can be accommodated but it would be wise to telephone first or make contact on VHF 09 before transiting the canal. There is a marina building with showers, toilets and laundry. Repairs of all sorts can be undertaken through the harbourmaster. No fuel in the canal or the marina.

ASHORE IN MARENNES

Marennes has limited marina facilities but is charming and well-maintained and the town is attractive.

There is a good selection of shops, cafés and seafood restaurants as befits the oyster capital of Europe. A large hypermarket is at the rear of the post office a few minutes' walk through the municipal gardens. There are markets on Tuesdays, Thursdays and Saturdays. The fine church tower can be climbed to see the panoramic view over the marshes.

Looking N at Port de Marennes lock gate *Nick Chavasse*

Looking N inside entrance to Chenal de Marennes
Nick Chavasse

Looking N from N end of lock towards Marennes and conspic spire *Nick Chavasse*

ANCHORAGES

⚓ La Cayenne

The best anchorages are near the disused ferry slips at La Cayenne (north bank) and at the entrance to La Tremblade canal about 0·5M upstream on the south bank. Anchor near the side of the river and land at the ferry slip. Above the entrance to La Tremblade canal is a wreck, marked by a green buoy.

La Tremblade

There is a drying canal to Tremblade with a quay at the end of the canal beyond a power cable (height 15m) but there is very little room for visitors. It is very attractive with much oyster farming activity, but best visited by dinghy.

La Tremblade is a small market town with a boatyard, marine repair facilities and a range of shops and restaurants.

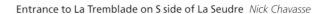

Entrance to La Tremblade on S side of La Seudre *Nick Chavasse*

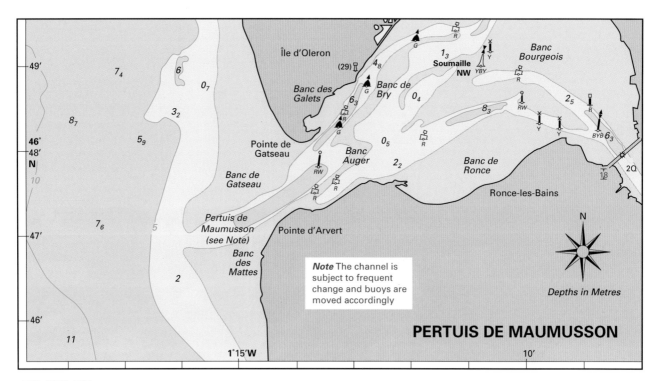

PERTUIS DE MAUMUSSON

Note The channel is subject to frequent change and buoys are moved accordingly

Depths in Metres

PILOTAGE

Pertuis de Maumusson

Warning The Pertuis de Maumusson is the passage south of Île d'Oléron. It has a very dangerous bar that moves and may be shallower than shown on the chart. The strong tide over this bar combined with any onshore swell causes breaking seas even in good weather.

Although the Pertuis de Maumusson is often given a bad press, in fair weather at neaps and above half-tide it was a perfectly acceptable route, in the author's opinion. Note that the channel markers are frequently moved to reflect the ever-changing conditions.

Looking SW down channel of Pertuis de Maumusson *Nick Chavasse*

Gatseau buoy in Pertuis de Maumusson *Nick Chavasse*

Looking SW at Pertuis de Maumusson *Nick Chavasse*

South side of entrance to Pertuis de Maumusson *Nick Chavasse*

Cap Ferret east cardinal buoy towards Dune du Pilat *Jane Russell*

IX. La Gironde and Bassin d'Arcachon to Hendaye

The Gironde is much used by North European yachtsmen with yachts of moderate draught as a short-cut to the Mediterranean via the Canal du Midi, but it is an interesting cruising area in its own right. The currents are fast and the water is silt-laden but for connoisseurs of fine wine it could be a mecca.

Arcachon itself is a useful stop-over between North Biscay and the Basque ports of France always assuming that there is not too much swell to make entry impossible. Once inside the basin a shoal-draught yacht or a boat that can sit on the mud at low tide has a big advantage over fin-keelers. All yachts are welcome in Arcachon Marina. Oyster culture is a major industry and many of the small harbours are given over to it entirely.

The three small harbours of the French Basque are holiday resorts with a main emphasis on their splendid beaches. But they are all interesting and quite different from one another so that they are all worth a visit.

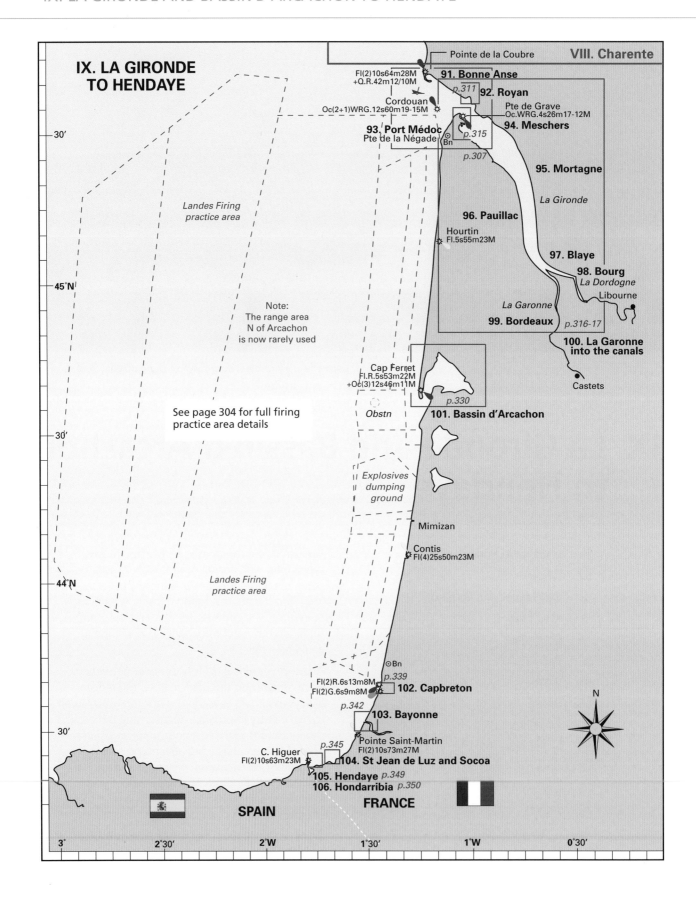

IX. LA GIRONDE TO HENDAYE

Pointe de la Coubre

VIII. Charente

Fl(2)10s64m28M
+Q.R.42m12/10M

91. Bonne Anse

p.311

92. Royan

Cordouan
Oc(2+1)WRG.12s60m19-15M

Pte de Grave
Oc.WRG.4s26m17-12M

93. Port Médoc
Pte de la Négade

94. Meschers

p.315

⊙
Bn

p.307

95. Mortagne

La Gironde

96. Pauillac

Hourtin
Fl.5s55m23M

97. Blaye

98. Bourg
La Dordogne

Libourne

*Landes Firing
practice area*

99. Bordeaux

La Garonne

p.316-17

**100. La Garonne
into the canals**

Note:
The range area
N of Arcachon
is now rarely used

Castets

Cap Ferret
Fl.R.5s53m22M
+Oc(3)12s46m11M

p.330

See page 304 for full firing
practice area details

Obstn

101. Bassin d'Arcachon

*Explosives
dumping
ground*

Mimizan

*Landes Firing
practice area*

Contis
Fl(4)25s50m23M

⊙Bn

p.339

Fl(2)R.6s13m8M
Fl(2)G.6s9m8M

102. Capbreton

p.342

103. Bayonne

Pointe Saint-Martin
Fl(2)10s73m27M

C. Higuer
Fl(2)10s63m23M

p.345

104. St Jean de Luz and Socoa

105. Hendaye *p.349*
106. Hondarribia *p.350*

N

SPAIN

FRANCE

Gironde to Hendaye tidal streams

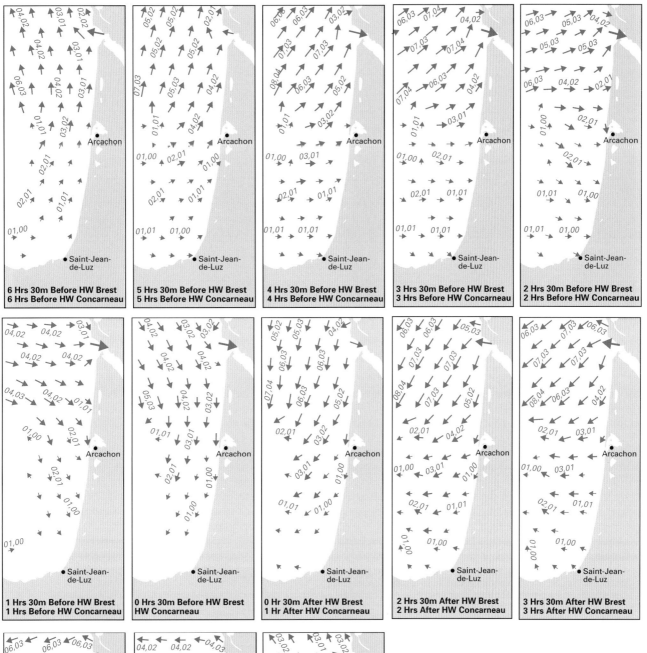

6 Hrs 30m Before HW Brest
6 Hrs Before HW Concarneau

5 Hrs 30m Before HW Brest
5 Hrs Before HW Concarneau

4 Hrs 30m Before HW Brest
4 Hrs Before HW Concarneau

3 Hrs 30m Before HW Brest
3 Hrs Before HW Concarneau

2 Hrs 30m Before HW Brest
2 Hrs Before HW Concarneau

1 Hrs 30m Before HW Brest
1 Hrs Before HW Concarneau

0 Hrs 30m Before HW Brest
HW Concarneau

0 Hr 30m After HW Brest
1 Hr After HW Concarneau

2 Hrs 30m After HW Brest
2 Hrs After HW Concarneau

3 Hrs 30m After HW Brest
3 Hrs After HW Concarneau

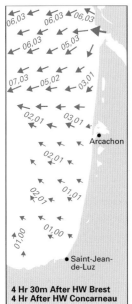

4 Hr 30m After HW Brest
4 Hr After HW Concarneau

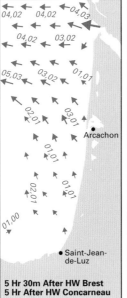

5 Hr 30m After HW Brest
5 Hr After HW Concarneau

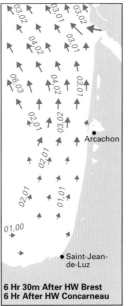

6 Hr 30m After HW Brest
6 Hr After HW Concarneau

TIDAL STREAMS EXPLANATION

The figures shown against the arrows are the mean rates at neaps and springs in tenths of a knot.

Thus *07,15* - mean neaps rate *0·7* knots, mean springs rate *1·5* knots

Looking SE over Bassin d'Arcachon *Nick Chavasse*

Introduction

South of Île d'Oléron for the next 140 miles lies the largely featureless and flat pine-covered coast of Les Landes, only marked by the major estuary of the Gironde in the north, the large land-locked basin of Arcachon halfway down, and the four small ports in the southeast corner of the Bay, before the border with Spain is reached.

Unless proceeding up the Gironde to Bordeaux to enter the French canals, the temptation is to bypass this stretch of coast and sail direct to the north Spanish coast. This is a pity as the Arcachon basin is a fascinating area for the family holiday in a shoal draught or bilge keeled boat; there are excellent facilities for yachts both here, at Capbreton, Anglet, St-Jean-de-Luz and Hendaye; tidal streams are no longer significant except in the river mouths or harbour entrances, the tidal range is much reduced and there are no dangers offshore. These ports all provide interesting and pleasant diversions on the outward or inward passage to the eastern end of the Spanish north coast.

Landes Firing Range

Firing danger areas exist from Pointe de la Négade in the north (6M south of La Gironde entrance) to Capbreton in the south. Co-ordinates of range area are:

45°27N 01°13'W (inshore N)
45°12N 02°00'W (NW corner)
44°00N 02°25'W (SW corner)
43°41N 01°30'W (inshore S)

They extend up to 35 miles offshore. There is a 3M-wide safety corridor between the range and the shore which may be used subject to clearance by the coastguard. The range is managed by Centre d'Essais des Landes (CEL) and the Range Control can be seen from the sea and is about 7M south of the LF buoy for Arcachon Basin. See plan on page 302.

Live Firing Information

The range is patrolled by range craft when firings take place.

Information on range activity:

☎ +33 (0)5 58 82 22 58
for 24 hr recorded message

☎ +33 (0)5 58 78 18 00
Monday–Thursday 0800–1700 and Friday 0800–1100 LT

VHF 16 from Socoa, Messanges, Cap-Ferret and Pointe de Grave Coastguard Stations. Or call them on VHF 6, then VHF 06 or VHF 10.

These stations can give advance information of activity:

* CROSS Etel broadcasts at 0703, 0715, 0733 and 0803 LT or phone before leaving port. Some English is spoken.
  ☎ +33 (0)5 58 82 22 42
  ☎ +33 (0)5 58 82 22 43
  ☎ +33 (0)2 97 55 35 35

* CEL broadcasts on VHF 06 and Ch 10 at 0815 and 1615 LT (Monday–Thursday) and at the same times on Friday only if the ranges are in use.

  Information is also available from CEL on request on the same VHF channels between 0800 and 1700 (Monday–Thursday and at the same times on Friday if the ranges are in use).

* Local NMs can be viewed at
  Arcachon Marina Office
  ☎ +33 (0)5 56 22 36 75 or
  Affaires Maritimes in Arcachon
  ☎ +33 (0)5 57 52 57 00

The Préfet Maritime publishes notices of firing at www.premar-atlantique.gouv.fr/avis-urgents-aux-navigateurs.html

Currents and tidal streams

There is a north-going current 5–6M off the coast of 0·5–1kn but this will increase after prolonged westerly gales. This starts as an east-going current along the Spanish coast turning northward to follow the coastline. A south-going countercurrent within a mile of the shore will often be found.

Tidal streams in the Gironde estuary are very strong and do not always follow the expected direction in the estuary. Out at sea tidal streams are very weak. In the other areas, tidal streams are only of significance in the rivers and entrances and these can be strong especially on the ebb. Details are given in the port information where appropriate.

Swell

A feature of this part of the coast is swell which can appear without any warning, caused by a disturbance far away in the Atlantic. The French weather forecasts for shipping include forecasts of swell (*la houle*). As the coast is relatively steep-to and there are no off-lying shallows or dangers, swell only presents a problem entering or leaving harbours. It would be unwise to enter or leave the Gironde, Arcachon, Capbreton and Anglet if there is any swell especially on the ebb. St-Jean-de-Luz, Hendaye and Rada de Higuer can be entered in these conditions provided the off-lying shallow patches are avoided.

Fishing

Fishing activity in this area is confined to some netting in the Gironde, extensive oyster and shellfish beds in Bassin d'Arcachon and a few small boats working out of Capbreton, Bayonne and Biarritz. There are small fleets of middle water boats at St-Jean-de-Luz and Gurutzeaundi.

Traditional oyster boat *Jane Russell*

Typical fishing huts found in the Gironde *Nick Chavasse*

LA GIRONDE

Approaches to the Gironde Estuary

45°34'N 01°26'W (BXA LF buoy)

Shelter
Very good in Royan and Port Médoc

Depth restrictions
12m minimum on leading lines
0·1m in Royan approach
1·0m in Port Médoc approach

Night entry
As by day. The Grande Passe de l'Ouest is extremely well lit but the buoys of the Passe Sud are not lit

Tidal information
As at Pointe de Grave (Pte de G)

Hazards
The tidal streams are very strong and do not always follow the line of the estuary in the mouth; constant checks are required to avoid being set off the intended track. Overfalls are severe and dangerous (5m). Do not attempt to enter the estuary in strong winds from the SW through W to N if there is any swell or on the ebb tide. If in doubt, stand off. Particular care is needed between Nos. 2A, 3, 4 and 5 entrance buoys where the channel is narrow and shoals quickly on either side. Only use the south channel in fine weather, good visibility and favourable tidal conditions. Keep to the main channel unless indicated otherwise as there are a number of wrecks outside it.
The sandbanks change their positions and depths during the winter storms and an up-to-date chart (SHOM 7425) should be used.

Wind effect on tidal level
Winds between S and NNW raise the water level up to 1m and advance the time of HW by up to 15 minutes. Winds from the N through E to S decrease the level by up to 0·3m and retard the time of HW by up to 15 minutes.

Tidal streams
The following is a simplification based on the times at Pointe de Grave:

	Flood begins	Spring rate knots	Ebb begins	Spring rate knots
BXA buoy	−0430	2·6	+0100	3.3
Off Royan	−0445	3.8	+0045	3.8
Off Mortagne	−0415	2·8	+0145	3.8
Pauillac	−0315	2·8	+0215	3.8
Bordeaux	−0115	2·8	+0315	3.8
Libourne	+0045	3.8	+0410	4·7

After Bordeaux there is no noticeable flood and the downward stream is significantly lessened.

Kilometre marks
They are on both banks and show the distance from Bordeaux (Pont de Pierre) and appear on all the charts. On the Dordogne they run from Libourne (0km) to Bourg (40km) and then revert to the Garonne distances.

Weather
On Ch 79
From Chassiron at 0703, 1533, 1903 LT (French)
From Soulac at 0715, 1545, 1915 LT (French)
Navtex from Corsen (A) (English) and (E) (French)
☎ 08 92 68 08 33 or VHF 63, 80 (recorded in French)

Charts
SHOM *7070, 7426, 7425, 7427*
Imray *C41, C42*

Radio
Port Control Bordeaux to BXA Ch 16 and 12 (24 hrs)
Radar guidance on Ch 12 on request
Gironde tide height Ch 17 (every 5 minutes)

Lifeboat
An all-weather lifeboat is maintained at Royan.

This extensive estuary leads to the city of Bordeaux and to the large rivers Garonne and Dordogne. Above Bordeaux the Canal Latéral à la Garonne and the Canal du Midi for access to the Mediterranean can be entered and may be used by craft smaller than 30m long, 5·25m wide, 1·5m draught and 3m high.

PILOTAGE

Warning It is essential to keep at least 5M off the coast in the later approaches to the BXA buoy to avoid the dangerous shoals north and south of the entrance to the Gironde. Do not cut the corner. When passage planning, take into account swell, height of tide and wind over tide situation.

Tidal Stategy
Between No.3 starboard hand and No.9 north cardinal buoys, wind against tide conditions generate very steep seas. In strong west winds against the ebb, the seas are dangerous and may break right across the channel.
Inward bound the best time to arrive at the entrance is at the commencement of the flood.

Outward bound, Royan or Port Medoc should be left well before HW to be clear of the narrow part of the channel between buoys No.3 starboard hand and No.9 north cardinal before the ebb sets in.
In light weather, reliable auxiliary power is necessary to keep out of the breakers on the banks.

Approach from south

By day Make for the BXA buoy on a track of 000° and outside the 20m line. This will clear all dangers. Do not be tempted to cut a corner through La Passe Sud unless the three conditions for its safe use are realised (*See Passe Sud, Entrance on page 308*).

By night As for by day. The lights of Pointe de Grave (Oc.WRG.4s26m17-13M) of which only the white will be visible in passing and Cordouan (Oc(2+1)WRG.12s60m19-15M) will assist.

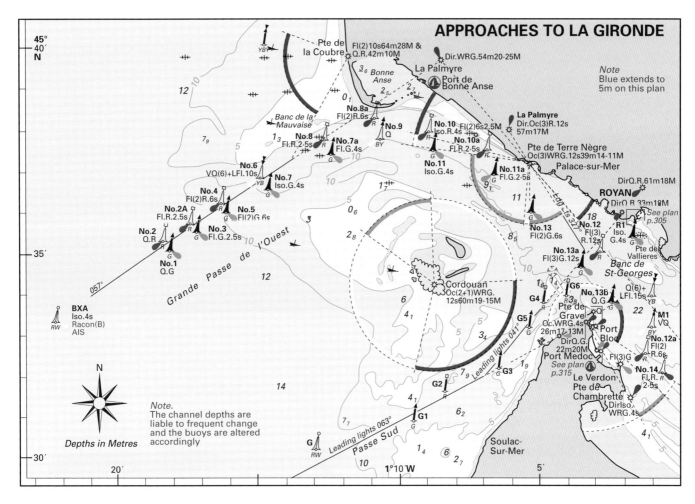

APPROACHES TO LA GIRONDE

Note
Blue extends to
5m on this plan

Pte de la Coubre Fl(2)10s64m28M & Q.R.42m10M

Dir.WRG.54m20-25M

La Palmyre
Port de Bonne Anse

Bonne Anse

La Palmyre Dir.Oc(3)R.12s 57m17M

Pte de Terre Nègre Oc(3)WRG.12s39m14-11M
Palace-sur-Mer

DirQ.R.61m18M

ROYAN

DirQ.R.33m18M

See plan p.305

R1 Iso. G.4s

Pte de Vallieres

No.8a Fl(2)R.6s

No.9 Q

No.10 Iso.R.4s Fl(2)6s2.5M

No.10a Fl.R.2.5s

No.8 Fl.R.2.5s

No.7a Fl.G.4s

No.6 VQ(6)+LFl.10s

No.7 Iso.G.4s

No.11 Iso.G.4s

No.11a Fl.G.2.5s

Banc de St-Georges

No.4 Fl(2)R.6s

No.2A Fl.R.2.5s

No.5 Fl(2)G.6s

No.2 Q.R

No.3 Fl.G.2.5s

No.1 Q.G

No.13 Fl(2)G.6s

No.12 Fl(3) R.12s

No.13a Fl(3)G.12s

Banc de St-Georges

Q(6)+LFl.15s

M1 VQ

No.12a Fl(2) R.6s

Cordouan Oc(2+1)WRG. 12s60m19-15M

Leading lights 041°

G6 No.13b Q.G

G4

G5

Pte de Grave Oc.WRG.4s 26m17-13M

Port Bloc

No.13b Q.G

BXA Iso.4s Racon(B) AIS

DirQ.G. 22m20M

Port Medoc See plan p.315

Fl(3)G

No.14 Fl.R. 2.5s

Le Verdon Pte de Chambrette DirIso. WRG.4s

057°

Grande Passe de l'Ouest

G3

G2

G1

Passe Sud

Leading lights 063°

G RW

Soulac-Sur-Mer

N

Note.
The channel depths are liable to frequent change and the buoys are altered accordingly

Depths in Metres

1°10'W

Grande Passe de l'Ouest

By day From the red and white BXA buoy make good a track of 057° until the entrance buoys can be picked out. Proceed on this line keeping in the channel between the buoys, leaving Royan to port and Port Bloc and Port Medoc to starboard. For Royan leave the channel at port hand buoy No.12 on a bearing of 055° and follow pilotage for Royan on page 310. For Port Médoc leave the channel at starboard hand buoy No. 13B on a bearing of 190° and follow pilotage for Port Médoc on page 314.

By night At the BXA buoy (Iso.4s7M) bring La Palmyre leading lights into line on 056° and enter the channel between No.1 and No.2 buoys (Q.G and Q.R). follow the lit channel, leaving Royan to port

Pointe de la Coubre lighthouse and the coastguard tower looking northeast *Patrick Roach*

Corduan lighthouse at the mouth of the Gironde
Jeremy Parkinson

Looking north from Pauillac across La Gironde *Nick Chavasse*

and Port Bloc and Port Médoc to starboard. For Royan leave the channel at port hand buoy No.12 (Q.R) on a bearing of 055° and follow pilotage for Royan on page 316. For Port Médoc leave the channel at starboard hand buoy No.13B (Q.G) on a bearing of 190° and follow pilotage for Port Médoc on page 314.

Passe Sud (or Passe de Grave)

From safe water buoy G at 45°30'·37N 01°15'·53W it is 9M to Pointe de Grave and 11M to Royan.

> **Warning** The minimum depth in the Passe Sud is 5m but this may vary. Entry should only be made in the absence of swell, the last quarter of the flood and in good visibility. The safest channel into La Gironde estuary is Grande Passe de l'Ouest.

By day Navigate to safe water buoy G, 45°30'·37N 01°15'·53W with a ball topmark and align the St-Nicolas (white tower) and Pointe de Grave (white tower with black corners and top) lighthouses on 063°. Proceed up this line leaving G1 starboard buoy and G2 port hand buoy on either side of the Passe Sud.

About 0·5M before G3 starboard buoy turn on to 041° and align Le Chay (white tower, red top) and St-Pierre (red water tower just to the left of Royan church) on this bearing. On reaching G4 port hand move to starboard of the leading line to avoid Platin de Grave (dries) and leave G6 port hand buoy to port. Cross the estuary, passing No.13a starboard buoy towards No.12 port buoy. Join Grande Passe de l'Ouest.

By night All the buoys to Pointe de Grave are unlit, so not recommended.

Looking west from Blaye across La Gironde *Nick Chavasse*

91 La Palmyre, Bonne Anse

45°42'N 12°00'W, 111km mark

Shelter
Good except in SW winds near HW

Depth restrictions
Dries 3·0m in approach
1m in marina

Night entry Not lit

Tidal Information
HW as for Pointe de Grave

Mean height of tide (m) Pointe de Grave

HWS	HWN	LWN	LWS
5·3	4 4	2·1	1·0

Tidal stream in approach
E – PdG HW–0440 to +0020 (2·5kn)
W – PdG HW+0050 to –0510 (4·2kn)

Berthing
On pontoons

Facilities
All but no fuel

Charts
SHOM *7425, 7426*
Imray *C41, C42*

Communications
VHF 09
☎ 05 46 22 44 31
www.la-palmyre-les-mathes.com

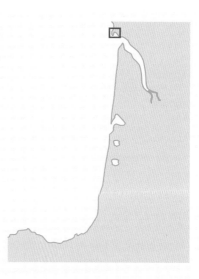

A small shallow marina in a wooded area near the mouth of La Gironde estuary

PILOTAGE

Approach and entrance

See plan page 307

> **Warning** The channel is very shallow with continually shifting sands. Take extra care when following the marked channel and only on the flood-tide.

From the vicinity of No.10 buoy make good a northerly track in the last quarter of the flood to pick out the winding entrance channel through the sandbanks, which is re-buoyed every season.

In the bay there are a number of oyster beds marked with the ubiquitous stakes which should be avoided; the bottom is flattish sand and mud.

The entrance is very narrow, marked by two spindly posts with sharp turn-in. There are crowded pontoons in the harbour in 1–1·5m with the deepest water at the ones on the southwest side.

Narrow entrance to Bonne Anse near HW Nick Chavasse

Looking E at visitors' berths on hammerheads *Nick Chavasse*

ANCHORAGE

Anchorage with 1·2m and coefficient >80 may be found 0·5M to the west of the entrance. Should be possible at neaps but beware depths at springs due to shifting sands.

ASHORE IN BONNE ANSE

The marina is a 10 minute walk from the holiday village of La Palmyre, where you will find some shops. Excellent beaches and unspoilt pinewoods are close by.

92 Royan

45°37′N 1°02′W

Shelter
Good in Royan Marina

Hazard
Gironde entrance dangerous in strong W wind
or swell against ebb
Wreck with 3m over it 200m E of R1 buoy

Depth restrictions
Dredged channel 1·2m at LW springs
Marina 2·5m

Night entry Well lit

HW time Royan
As for Pointe de Grave

Mean height of tide (m) Pointe de Grave
HWS	HWN	LWN	LWS
5·2	4·3	2·1	1·0

Tidal stream in Gironde entrance
Flood – PdG HW–0445 to +0015 (1·3kn)
Ebb – PdG HW+0045 to –0515 (2·2kn)

Berthing
Alongside N side of reception pontoon
or as directed in marina

Facilities
All facilities. 26-T travel-lift,
1·5-T crane

Charts
SHOM *7426, 7425*
Imray *C41, C42*

Communications
Gironde tide height VHF 17
Royan Marina VHF 9, 16
Ⓣ 05 46 38 72 22
www.royan-tourisme.co.uk
www.port-royan.com

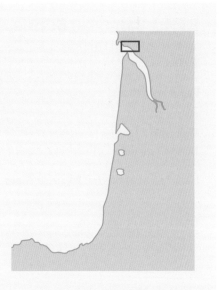

Holiday resort at the mouth of the Gironde

Royan was one of the most fashionable 19th-century holiday resorts, with magnificent hotels, casinos and villas. It was bombed flat by the British in April 1945 and has risen from the ruins around the Church of Notre Dame de Royan, which is built of concrete and has a strikingly modern design. It is now undergoing a period of refurbishment.

Royan is a welcoming place with lots going on. In August, there is a fantastic firework display and the beaches are attractive with clear water.

If going up the Gironde, be prepared for dark muddy water. Royan is a good place from which to cross Biscay.

PILOTAGE

Tidal strategy *See pages 306–307 Approaches to the Gironde* for information about entering and leaving the estuary. Outward bound, Royan should be left well before HW so as to be clear of the narrow part of the channel between buoys No.9 and No.3 before the ebb sets in. The danger is when the ebb flows strongly against the SW wind over the shoals.

Beware that the entrance channel to Royan harbour can be quite shallow at LW springs and watch out for the frequent Port Bloc ferries arriving at and departing from their terminal west of the entrance channel.

Royan marina looking west. The fishing harbour is to port inside the entrance. The harbourmaster's office and facilities are on the central spur opposite the entrance. *Office de Tourisme de Royan*

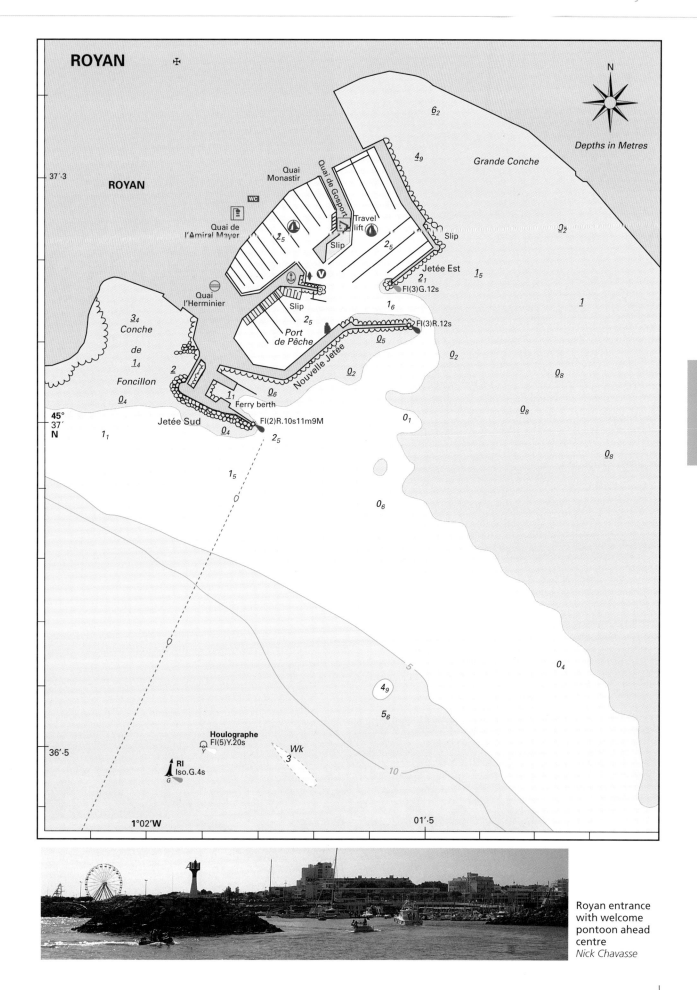

ROYAN

ROYAN

37'.3

Quai Monastir

Quai de Gosport

WC

Quai de l'Amiral Mayer

Travel lift

Slip

Slip

Jetée Est

Quai l'Herminier

Slip

Port de Pêche

2₅

1₆

Fl(3)G.12s

2₁

Fl(3)R.12s

0₅

Conche de Foncillon

3₄

1₄

2

1₁

0₆

Ferry berth

Jetée Sud

0₄

Fl(2)R.10s11m9M

Nouvelle Jetée

0₂

45° 37' N

1₁

2₅

1₅

0₄

Grande Conche

6₂

4₉

9₂

1₅

1

0₂

0₈

0₈

0₈

0₁

0₆

0₄

N

Depths in Metres

36'.5

4₉

5₆

Houlographe
Fl(5)Y.20s

Wk
3

10

5

RI
Iso.G.4s

1°02'W

01'.5

Royan entrance with welcome pontoon ahead centre
Nick Chavasse

Looking SE from capitainerie towards fuel dock
Nick Chavasse

By day From the northwest leave the main channel at No.13 buoy and continue on about 115° to R1 starboard buoy. Just before arriving at R1 starboard turn to port on to 035° and head for the harbour entrance. Leave the head of the breakwater close to port.

From the southeast beware of the shallow Banc de Saint-Georges (0·4m) and either navigate outside it by leaving No.12 port hand buoy to starboard and then altering on to 067° to R1 starboard buoy or pass inside the bank by leaving Pointe de Suzac close to starboard and leaving R1 buoy to starboard on a course of 320° before heading for the harbour entrance on 035°.

By night Make the R1 starboard buoy as by day but from the southeast it would be best to make the passage outside the Banc de Sainte-Georges. From R1 head for the east end of the south breakwater Fl(3)R.12s.

Royan visitors' pontoon *Nick Chavasse*

Looking NE over marina towards Royan *Nick Chavasse*

BERTHS

Royan Marina

The reception berth is on the north side of the central spur to the left of the inner harbour entrance directly below the harbourmaster's office. Secure here and report to the helpful staff in the office unless met by the harbour launch in the entrance. The fuel dock is just inside the entrance on the port hand side. De-mast facilities include a 1·5T crane but is limited to masts less than 15m and less than 300kg. Maximum boat weight lift is 26T using a travel-lift.

ASHORE IN ROYAN

Royan has all the facilities of a major marina and is a good place for de-masting prior to entering the Canal du Midi.

There are some shops, restaurants and cafés at the marina and plenty of shops in town. Royan has an interesting modern covered market.

There are few tourist attractions in the town since Royan is chiefly famous for its beaches, known locally as *conches*. Conche Foncillon is the small, family-friendly beach near the marina. The largest, longest and most famous beach is the Grande Conche.

Looking E over the welcome pontoon towards the entrance beyond
Nick Chavasse

Cockleshell Heroes

For those interested in the history of the Second World War, a pleasant 2km walk can be had eastwards along the beach to Pointe de Vallières and the memorial to the Cockleshell Heroes, which stands on the cliff edge near the disused lighthouse.

In December 1942 a daring operation by the British Royal Marines, code-named Operation Frankton, was launched to disrupt shipping in the German-occupied port of Bordeaux. On a moonless night, five armed canoes, known as cockles, left their launch submarine HMS *Tuna* near the Cordouan light for the 60-mile journey upriver to Bordeaux. Only two canoes reached the docks but limpet mines were successfully laid and exploded on five merchant ships and a patrol vessel, all of which settled on the bottom.

The two canoes escaped downriver and the four marines landed on the east bank where they split up to return to the UK with the help of the Resistance. Two were caught and shot by the Germans; the only two survivors of the original 10 were Major Hasler and Marine Sparks, who were back in England by April.

After the war Major Hasler initiated single-handed racing across the Atlantic in his junk-rigged folkboat *Jester* in which he invented servo pendulum type self-steering by windvane.

Memorial to the Cockleshell Heroes

Pointe de Vallieres on which is the memorial to the Cockleshell Heroes.
The old lighthouse at St Georges-de-Didonne *Nick Chavasse*

93 Port Médoc and Port Bloc

45°34'·00N 01°04'·00W

Shelter
Excellent in marina

Hazards
Strong cross stream at entrance

Depth restriction
2·2m at entrance Port Médoc
+2m over all marina

Night entry Lit

HW time
As for Pointe de Grave

Mean height of tide (m) Pointe de Grave

HWS	HWN	LWN	LWS
5·2	4·3	2·1	1·0

Tidal streams
Flood – PdG HW –0445 to +0100
Ebb – PdG HW +0115 to –0445

Berthing
Finger pontoons

Facilities
All in marina and shops in village

Charts
SHOM *7426*
Imray *C41, C42*

Communications
VHF 09
HM ☎ 05 56 09 69 75
www.port-adhoc.com/les-ports/port-medoc

Large modern marina with most facilities

At the mouth of the Gironde, opposite Royan, Port Médoc is a good place to stop if going down La Gironde or crossing Biscay. With some of the world's most famous vineyards on your doorstep, it would seem remiss not to visit Médoc, Saint Julien and Margaux to name but a few.

PILOTAGE

Approach and entrance to Port Médoc

Directions for the approach using Passe de l'Ouest or Passe Sud may be found on pages 306–308 *La Gironde approaches and estuary*. From starboard hand buoy No.13b (Q.G) or between it and the steep-to Pointe de Grave (Iso.G.4s) leave Port Bloc (Fl.G.4s and Fl.R.4s) to starboard and identify Port Médoc entrance 0·75M to the south.

Head for the entrance on a track of about 270° and round the east breakwater head to starboard allowing for a strong cross set until inside.

BERTHING

The reception is on the northernmost quay in front of the marina office. The fuel berth is on the first quay as you enter on the starboard hand side. The main channel in the marina is dredged to 3m and the remainder of the marina to 2m. On fingers on pontoons, 25m maximum. There is a pontoon for multihulls on the south wall.

ASHORE IN PORT MÉDOC

The marina occupies an unpromising position between the ferry port of Port Bloc and the oil terminal of Verdon. However, the marina has all facilities and a welcoming feel to it with friendly staff. De-mast facilities are available through Tyalan Accastillage who also run the local UShip franchise.

Port Bloc

45°34'·14N 1°03'·71W

Visiting yachts are not wanted or welcomed here and it is unlikely that there will be a vacant berth. Visitor berthing requires prior approval from AUPB (Port Bloc Users' Association; ☎ 05 56 09 84 02). In an emergency call on VHF 09 before going in and keep clear of the ferries entering and leaving.

Port Médoc is a friendly place with bars, shops and three restaurants. A taxi is needed for serious provisioning from Verdon. There is a small memorial to the cockleshell heroes on the marina office wall.

Port Médoc entrance *Nick Chavasse*

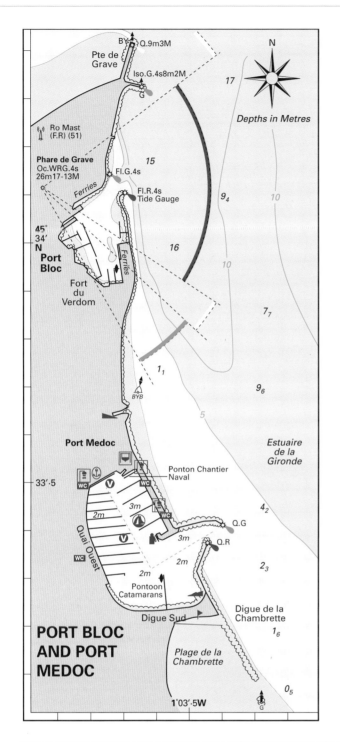

PORT BLOC AND PORT MEDOC

Map labels:

BY Q.9m3M
Pte de Grave
Iso.G.4s8m2M
G
Ro Mast (F.R) (51)
Phare de Grave
Oc.WRG.4s
26m17-13M
Ferries
45° 34' N
Port Bloc
Fort du Verdom
Fl.G.4s
Fl.R.4s Tide Gauge
Ferries
N
Depths in Metres
17
15
9₄
16
10
10
7₇
9₆
Estuaire de la Gironde
5
1₁
BYB
Port Medoc
33'·5
WC
V
WC
V
WC
3m
Ponton Chantier Naval
2m
3m
Q.G
3m
Q.R
2m
4₂
2₃
Quai Ouest
2m
Pontoon Catamarans
Digue Sud
Digue de la Chambrette
1₆
Plage de la Chambrette
1°03'·5W
0₅
G

Looking NE over Port Médoc. Port Bloc can be seen top left
Patrick Roach

Looking W over Port Bloc and Pointe de Grave beyond
Patrick Roach

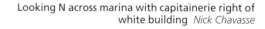

Looking N across marina with capitainerie right of white building *Nick Chavasse*

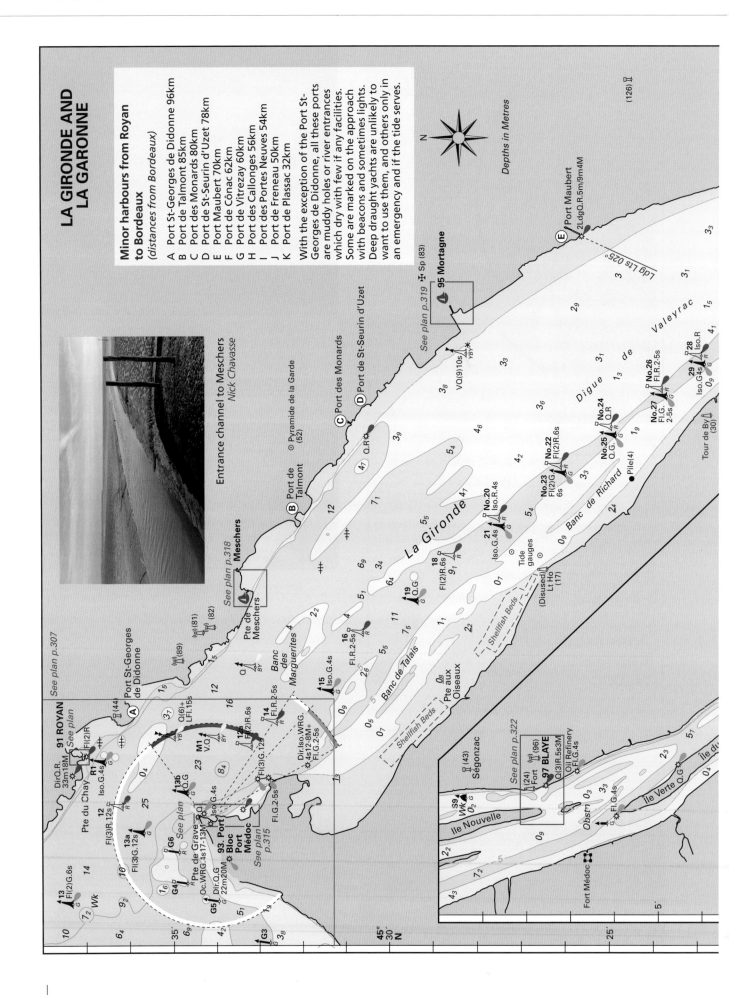

Entrance channel to Meschers
Nick Chavasse

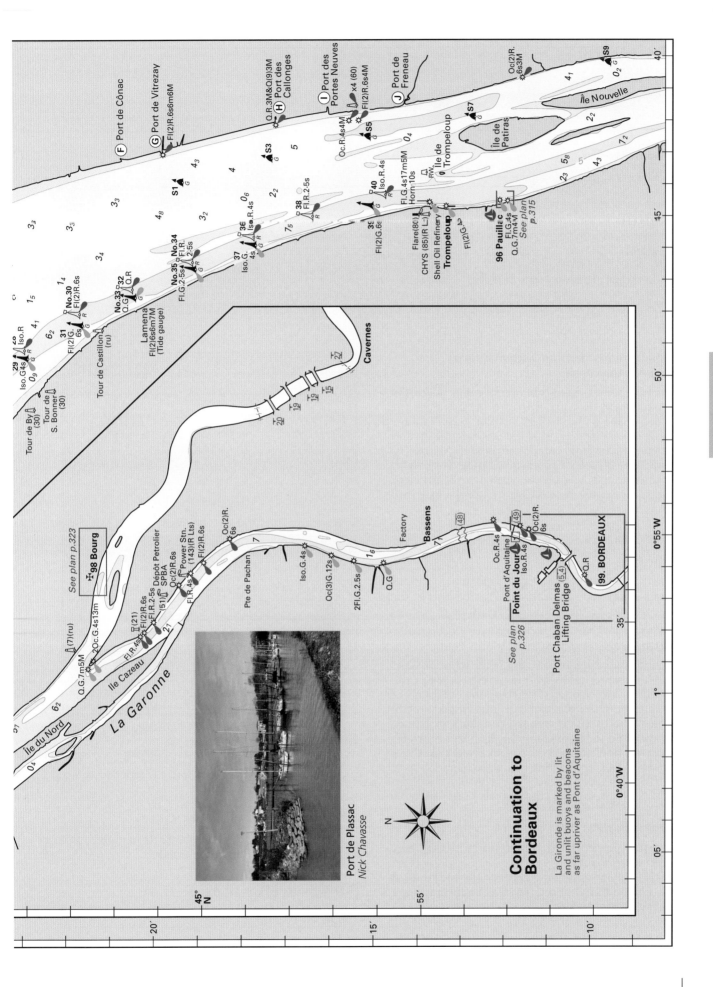

F Port de Cónac

G Port de Vitrezay   Fl(2)R.6s6m6M

H Port des Callonges   Q.R.3M&Q(9)3M

I Port des Portes Neuves   x4 (60)   Fl(2)R.6s4M   Oc.R.4s4M

J Port de Freneau

S9   Oc(2)R.6s3M

0₂ G

Île Nouvelle

4₁

▲S7 G   2₂

Île de Patiras

2₃   5₈   5   4₃   1₂

S5 ▲ G   Fl(2)R.6s4M

S3 ▲ G

S1 ▲ G   5

40 ▲ G   Iso.R.4s

38 Fl(2)R.6s   Fl.R.2-5s

Fl.G.4s17m5M Horn 10s   RW   Île de Trompeloup   0₄

CHYS (85)(R L)   0   Trompeloup

Flare(80)   Shell Oil Refinery   Fl(2)G.6s

Fl(2)R.6s   **35**   Fl(2)G.6s

96 Pauillac   Fl.G.4s   Q.G.7m4M   See plan p.315

Oc.R.4s4M

37 Iso.G.   Iso.R.4s   **36** Fl.R.   Fl.R.2-5s

7₅

No.34 Fl.R.2-5s   **No.35** Fl.G.2-5s   2₂   3₂   0₆   4₈

No.33 Q.G.   **32** Q.R.   **No.30** Fl(2)R.6s   3₄   3₂   4₈   3₃   4   4₃   3₃   3₃

Lamena Fl(2)6s6m7M (Tide gauge)

31 Fl(2)G.   6s   Tour de Castillon (ru)

1₄   1₅   6₂   4₁

29 Iso.G4s   Iso.R   0₉   0₃   C   3

Tour de By (30)   Tour de S. Bonner (30)

Cavernes   27   25   15   17   19   20

98 Bourg   See plan p.323

Q.G.7m5M   (7)(ru)   2Oc.G.4s13m   Fl.R.4s   Fl(2)R.6s   (21)   Fl.R.2-5s   (51)   Oc(2)R.6s   Fl.R.4s   Dépôt Petrolier Power Stn. (143)(R Lts)   SPBA   Fl(2)R.6s   Oc(2)R.6s

Île du Nord   0₄   Île Cazeau   2₁

La Garonne   6₂

Pte de Pachan   7   Iso.G.4s   1₆   Oc(3)G.12s   2Fl.G.2.5s   Q.G   Factory   Bassens   7₁   48   Oc.R.4s

Point du Jour   Pont d'Aquitaine   49   Oc(2)R.6s   Iso.R.4s   Port Chaban Delmas Lifting Bridge   (5.4)   Q.R

99. BORDEAUX

See plan p.326   35′

Port de Plassac *Nick Chavasse*

N

Continuation to Bordeaux

La Gironde is marked by lit and unlit buoys and beacons as far upriver as Pont d'Aquitaine

45°N   20′   15′   55′   10′   05′

0°55′W   0°40′W   1′   50′   45′   40′

94 Meschers

45°33'·00N 00°57'·00W

Shelter
Good in the inner basin

Hazards
Strong cross set on approach

Depth restriction
Dries 2·1m in approach channel
Dries 1·5–2m in outer basin
Sill dries 1·5m
2m in inner basin

Night entry
Ldg Line lit

HW time
HW and LW as for Pointe de Grave

Mean height of tide (m) Pointe de Grave

HWS	HWN	LWN	LWS
5·2	4·3	2·1	1·0

Tidal streams
Flood – PdG HW -0440 to +0030
Ebb – PdG HW +0100 to -0520

Berthing
On pontoon ends in inner basin

Facilities
Water/electricity on pontoons
Showers/toilets/laundry ashore

Charts
SHOM *7426*
Imray *C41, C42*

Communications
☎ 05 46 02 56 89 (Office hours)
www.ot-meschers.fr

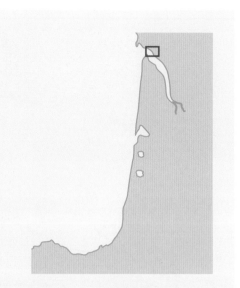

A small muddy harbour with marina in a locked inner basin

Meschers is the first stop, when going down the Gironde river, 6M east of Royan. At this stage the colour of the water will be coming a dull sludge shade of brown. It is quite disconcerting and becomes increasingly dark the nearer you get to Bordeaux. Meschers is an interesting place with good shops but needs to be visited with sufficient height of tide, to gain access through the gate into the marina.

PILOTAGE

Approach

Identify the entrance from conspicuous Talmont church 2M to the southeast close to the shore at the extremity of the same bay. The best time to enter is between HW–0200 and HW.

Entrance *(see photo page 316)*

Align the two green panels with white stripe on 354° (QG lights)and hold this line exactly between the port and starboard posts marking the outer end of the channel. There is a further south cardinal beacon to the east of these two posts which is left to starboard on the approach. The channel is buoyed. There will be a strong cross stream at any time other than HW slack until within the inner channel.

BERTHS AND ANCHORAGE

Outer basin

Reception pontoon with four drying berths on port side of entry channel.

If able to dry out, find a berth on the ends of A, B or C pontoons in the outer basin or on the northeast side just outside the lock.

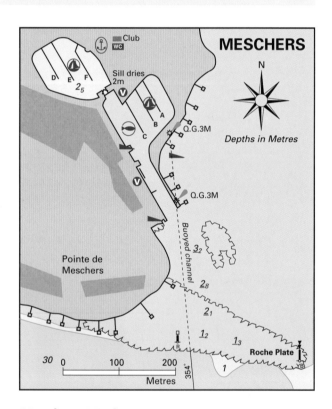

Meschers Marina

The automatic lock opens HW ±0230 hours day and night and the sill dries 1·5m. There is reported to be 2m in the basin. Berth alongside end of pontoons E or F. There is a fixed green light displayed on the side of the lock keeper's hut when the lock is open.

⚓ Outside to the east of the beacons in mud sounding in as far as possible out of the stream.

ASHORE IN MESCHERS

Small restaurant and several shops. The nearest beach suitable for swimming is Plage des Nonnes half an hour walk to the northwest past man-made caves which have regular guided tours. Supermarket west of the church and markets on Tuesday, Wednesday, Friday and Saturday.

95 Mortagne

45°28'·00N 00°48'·00W

Shelter
Good

Hazards
Strong cross set on approach

Depth restriction
Channel dries 1·5–2·0m in approach
2m in outer basin
Up to 4m inside locked basin

Night entry
Not lit

Tidal information: Pointe de Grave
HW +0018
LW +0030

Mean height of tide (m) Pointe de Grave

HWS	HWN	LWN	LWS
5·3	4·3	1·7	0·5

Tidal streams: Pointe de Grave
Flood – HW –0415 to +0115
Ebb – HW +0145 to -0445

Berthing
On pontoons in both basins

Facilities
All, but no laundry and no travel-lift
Fuel from garage

Charts
SHOM 7427
Imray C41, C42

Communications
VHF 09 from HW-0100 to HW+0100
① 05 46 90 63 15 / 06 43 48 91 93
www.ot-mortagne.com

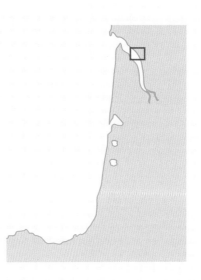

An attractive town and small harbour with a locked basin

A pleasant entry up a narrow channel into a secure basin. A good place to stop.

PILOTAGE

Approach

There is a minimum of 3·7m in the river off the entrance whence the village of Mortagne can be seen on the hill above. Alternatively make good a track of 050° from main channel buoy No.22 until the entrance marks can be identified.

Entrance

The entrance marks are a west cardinal buoy, a port-hand main channel buoy and port and starboard markers. Follow the channel on a track of about 060°. The dredged channel is almost straight for 0·65M to the harbour entrance and marked by the occasional stake.

BERTHS AND ANCHORAGE

There is a reception pontoon (dries) on the northwest side on entering. Berth on pontoons inside the lock in up to 4m. The lock is open HW±0100 regardless of tidal co-efficient and open HW±0200 with coefficient >40.

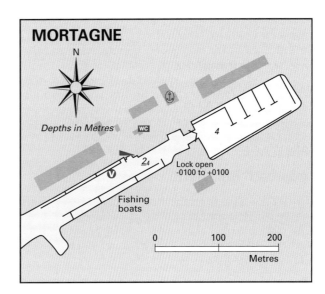

⚓ Anchor to the southeast of the entrance as far in as depth allows, in mud. Quite exposed except from the east.

ASHORE IN MORTAGNE

Restaurants and bars on quay, shops in the attractive old town running up the hill. There is also a small boatyard.

Mortagne with lock gate open leading into marina
Nick Chavasse

96 Pauillac

45°12'·00N 00°45'·00W

Shelter
Good in the marina

Hazards
The tidal stream sweeps through the marina
so it is safer to enter or leave near slack water

Depth restriction
1m in entrance, 4m at visitors' pontoons

Night entry
Lit but not recommended

Tidal information
PdG HW +0100
PdG LW +0150

Mean height of tide (m) Pointe de Grave

HWS	HWN	LWN	LWS
5·5	4·4	1·1	0·5

Tidal streams
Flood – PdG HW –0315 to +0200
Ebb – PdG HW +0215 to –0330

Berthing
Alongside the visitors' pontoon

Facilities
All facilities. 8 tonne haul-out on
trailer and 1tonne mast crane

Charts
SHOM *7427*

Communications
VHF 09 (office hours)
☎ 05 56 59 12 16
mob 06 21 86 48 93
www.pauillac-medoc.com

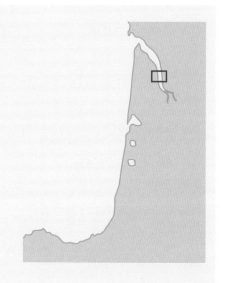

A useful halfway stop in good wine country

A useful yacht harbour halfway between Bordeaux and the sea in the centre of a famous wine growing region. The management is welcoming and friendly. English yachts have wintered afloat here. The marina suffers from silting up but is occasionally dredged. You might find your boat settling into soft brown mud.

PILOTAGE

Approach from north (heading upstream)

By day Pauillac is on the western bank, 1·5M south of the conspicuous oil refinery at Trompeloup. Leave the main channel at Nos.43 and 44 buoys (Fl(2)G. and Fl(2)R.) and head for the outer harbour wall (Fl.G.4s and Q.G).

Approach from south (heading downstream)

By day Leave the main channel at Nos.45 and 46 buoys (Iso.G and Iso.R) and head for the entrance.

Entrance

Entry and departure should only be attempted near slack water. The shuttering on the sides of the marina does not extend to the bottom and the stream flows through it. There is a white buoy with pick-up to the south of the marina to moor to while waiting.

Pauillac with marina entrance on left *Nick Chavasse*

BERTHS AND ANCHORAGES

The visitors' pontoon is just inside the entrance on the port side.

⚓ Anchoring is prohibited for up to 500m south of the harbour due to cables. Anchor to the north, off the slip, to wait for the tide.

Mast stepping and unstepping

The crane is no longer used. There is a cherry picker or similar which can manage masts up to 16m. There is haul-out on trailer facility for boats max 12m/15T.

ASHORE IN PAUILLAC

La Maison du Tourisme et Les Vins de Médoc near the marina can arrange vineyard tours. There is a market on Saturday.

Rail and bus services to Bordeaux (50km) and Merignac (Bordeaux) airport with internal and international flights.

Chicane entrance to Pauillac marina keeping close to starboard hand side to avoid mud on port hand side
Nick Chavasse

There is 2m of water at the entrance ±2 hours LW at coefficient of 100. Keep close to the east breakwater head when entering or leaving as the mud shoals rapidly. There is reasonable light inside the marina but a night entry is not recommended unless it has been done before in daylight.

Looking S over Pauillac marina with entrance beyond
Nick Chavasse

97 Blaye

45°07'·00N 00°40'·00W

Shelter
Reasonable in SW winds

Hazard
Very strong currents at berths

Depth restriction
None at pontoon
Small dinghy harbour dries

Night entry
Q(3)R.5s at N end of dinghy harbour
Lights on pontoon

Tidal information
PdG HW +0140
PdG LW +0305

Mean height of tide (m) Pointe de Grave

HWS	HWN	LWN	LWS
5·2	4·1	0·8	0·3

Tidal streams
Flood – PdG HW –0315 to +0245
Ebb – PdG HW +0315 to -0345

Berthing
On massive steel pontoon

Facilities
An active YC, otherwise few except shops

Charts
SHOM *7427*

Communications
VHF 12 with Bordeaux Port
☎ 05 57 42 12 09 tourist office
www.tourismeblaye.com

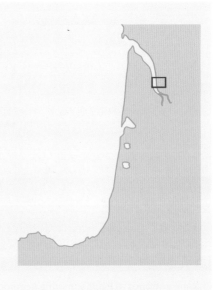

Historic town providing a fine-weather stop with good shopping

An important town with a visitors' pontoon and a small drying harbour only suitable for dinghies. The conspicuous and historic citadel is of much interest.

PILOTAGE

Approach

With a 2m+ draught, SHOM chart 7427 is essential for an approach to Blaye via the channel to the east of Îles Patiras, L'île Bouchard and Nouvelle. Otherwise leave the main channel between Nos.52 and 52a port hand buoys, make good a track of 125° and leave the south end of Île Nouvelle 500m to port to head for the visitors' pontoon in front of the citadel.

BERTHING

There is little shelter from the west off Blaye and the ebb can run at up to 3·5 knots; it will be distinctly uncomfortable in these conditions but the yacht berths are on the inside of a very substantial pontoon which would provide some protection. However berthing when the ebb is running hard can be tricky with the very substantial walkway close downstream. It is best to berth on the downstream end of the pontoon if possible. The outside of the pontoon is used by ferries.

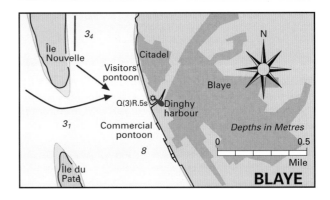

ASHORE IN BLAYE

Water and electricity are available on the pontoon which requires a code for access. A 2-pin plug is needed for an electrical connection. For the code and details on how to switch on the electrics call ☎ 05 57 42 12 09. There is a large motorhome park close to the pontoon which might have amenable showers and toilets available.

The tourist office, which is responsible for the visitors' pontoon, is inside the citadel complex. There is a good range of restaurants and small shops. Market days are Wednesday and Saturday.

Blaye pontoon looking NW towards Île Nouvelle *Nick Chavasse*

98 Bourg

45°02'·00N 00°33'·00W

Shelter Poor in W winds

Hazards
Strong W winds and ebb tide very
uncomfortable
Large drying wreck outside W end of pontoon

Depth restriction
3m at pontoon

Night entry Unlit

Tidal information
PdG HW +0145
PdG LW +0300

Mean height of tide (m) Pointe de Grave

HWS	HWN	LWN	LWS
5·1	4·0	0·6	0·1

Tidal Streams
Flood – PdG HW -0200 to +0245
Ebb – PdG HW +0315 to -0230

Berthing
Visitors' berth on outside of W end of
pontoon
No rafting

Facilities
No electricity or water on pontoon.
Fuel from garage

Charts
SHOM 7427

Communications
Bordeaux Port Control on VHF 12 in
emergency
☎ 05 57 68 40 04 (town hall)
☎ 05 57 68 44 41 (YC)
www.tourisme.bourg-en-gironde.fr

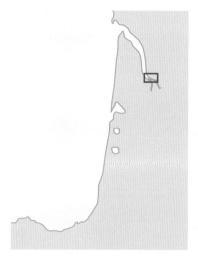

Attractive and historic town with a pontoon berth and some facilities ashore

Bourg is an attractive old fortified town on the Dordogne just upstream of the junction with the River Garonne.

PILOTAGE

Approaches

Heading upstream from Blaye, leave the Gironde by west cardinal buoy No.62 and head to port to enter the Dordogne, leaving Bec d'Ambès with its refineries and the Île d'Ambès, with its drying shoal at the west end, to starboard. Avoid the long, conspicuous drying wreck just to the south of the visitors' berths, which are at the west end of the long pontoon.

Confluence of rivers La Dordogne and La Garonne at Bec D'Ambes looking W from mouth of La Dordogne *Nick Chavasse*

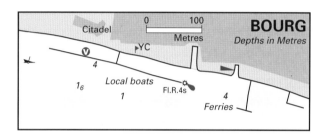

Wreck at Bourg off W end of visitors pontoon *Nick Chavasse*

Bourg visitors' pontoon in poor state of repair
Nick Chavasse

BERTHING

Doubling up on the pontoons is not allowed but yachts also berth on the inside where there appears to be plenty of water. If both sides are full there are no alternatives and anchoring off is not a happy option except at neaps and in fine weather. The pontoons are somewhat dilapidated which suggests that they are at times exposed to violent motion. Water and electricity on quay. Code needed for access can be obtained at the swimming pool or at the campsite. Showers and toilets are available at both places.

Above Four bridges 4·5M upstream from Bourg
Nick Chavasse

ASHORE IN BOURG

Good restaurants and shops; there are two yacht clubs. The citadel is worth a visit.

PILOTAGE ABOVE BOURG

Warning Yachts may be prohibited from going up to Limbourne when a tidal bore is expected. This is to avoid the swimmers and surfers riding the bore.

Approach

16km above Bourg is the small village of Cavernes on the south bank of the Dordogne. There is a pontoon here but it is prohibited for visitors. It is a further 24km to Libourne but access is not possible for masted craft due to a low bridge (height 7m) 0·5M below Libourne. Above this the Dordogne is tidal for 22km and navigable by unmasted vessels for 65km.

The kilometre distances marked intermittently on the river banks of the Dordogne start at Libourne.

The passage upstream from Bourg is easy with or without SHOM chart 7427. The river is buoyed occasionally but not lit. The depth in the channel is generally over 2m. Keep to the outside of the bends and follow the lateral buoyage. The river is crossed by three electricity cables just above Bourg (height 27m) and four bridges (least height 19m above ML) below Cavernes.

Cavernes is on the south bank on a left-hand bend just after the last of the four bridges and the power cables.

99 Bordeaux

44°53'·00N 00°32'·00W

Shelter
Good in Bassins á Flot but streams are strong in river

Hazards
The ebb runs at 5kn and the flood at 3kn
Much debris comes down on the ebb

Depth restriction
+6m in channel
3m at Lormont pontoons
3m at waiting pontoon for basins

Height restriction
Chaban Delmas (clearance 5·4m above ML) is the limit of navigation for masted vessels unless the lifting bridge is in the raised position. See further details on page 326.

Night entry
Night movement not advised

Tidal information
HW PdG +0215
LW PdG +0345

Mean height of tide (m) Pointe de Grave

HWS	HWN	LWN	LWS
5·3	4·2	0·4	0·0

Tidal streams
Flood – PdG HW –0115 to +0315
Ebb – PdG HW +0315 to –0130

Berthing
No.2 Basin through lock with waiting pontoon outside
Bègles Marina 4km upstream of Pont de Pierre (air draught 3·9m)

Facilities
Crane and water and electricity in No.2 Basin
Marine engineer in Basin No.2

Charts
SHOM 7427

Communications
Port Control VHF 12 (24H), Lock Ch 9

1. **River pontoons**
   www.bordeaux.fr and follow menus Découvrir et Sortir > Visite et Tourisme > Venir à Bordeaux/En Bateau > Lieux d'escale à Bordeaux
   ☎ 05 56 93 93 56

2. **Port de Plaisance des Bassins á Flot** (Bassin No 2)
   www.bordeaux-port.fr and follow menus Grand Public > Plaisance
   ☎ 06 27 34 48 05 Capitainerie
   ☎ 05 56 90 59 34 Lock keeper for basins

3. **Lormont YC** ☎ 05 56 31 50 10
   www.bordeaux-port.fr/en/marina

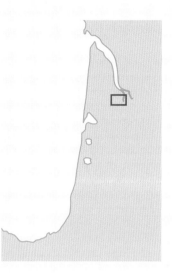

Large industrial city in the centre of a famous wine growing region

Bordeaux is a large and pleasant city in the centre of a renowned wine growing region. It is also a busy port and industrial centre and the passing yachtsman usually only sees the latter aspects.

However, an explore ashore will lead to some of the numerous old and interesting buildings, churches, ruins and museums, some dating from Roman times and the English occupation (1152–1453). Tours can be arranged through the Office du Tourisme, 12 cours du 30 Juillet, who will supply maps and directions.

Bordeaux dock area adjacent to the bassins à flot is being refurbished over a period of several years. It has been transformed since 2016 when it was in a very poor state of repair. It is now in a position to welcome visiting yachts which will enjoy excellent facilities and a great opportunity to experience a visit to Bordeaux.

Looking NW at Bassin entrance lock gate left of La Cité du Vin *Nick Chavasse*

PILOTAGE

Approach to Bordeaux

It is 47km between Pauillac and Bordeaux, less from Blaye or Bourg, and there should be no difficulty in navigating this wide, well-marked and lit estuary with the use of SHOM charts and benefiting from the flood and ebb streams. Poor visibility in the area is infrequent.

The ebb increases in strength upriver and with much rain up-country can exceed 5kn, with the addition of a lot of debris including whole trees. Anchoring above Bec d'Ambès, the confluence of the Garonne and the Dordogne, is not recommended and there are no safe or convenient stopping places for a yacht en route.

There is much commercial traffic in the river. Large ships unable to keep to the starboard side of the channel display a black ball forward and a red light by night and should be given right of way.

Masted navigation ceases at Pont Chaban Delmas (5·4m air draught).

There are two options for mooring and it is important to understand that the river pontoons are under different management to the Bassin à Flot No.2. See the Communications information in the info box on page 325 for website details.

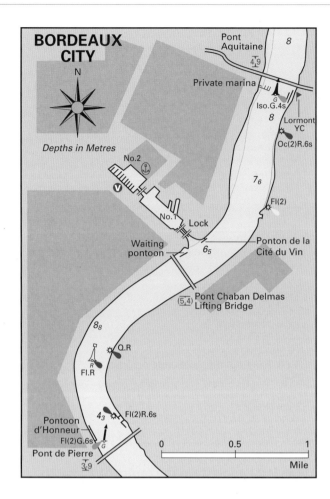

Waiting pontoon for entering the basins, just downstream of N end of Pont Chaban Delmas *Nick Chavasse*

Swing bridge in lock just before inner lock gate *Nick Chavasse*

Stay in the river option

For overnight stays it is possible to stay at the Ponton de la Cité du Vin. Alternatively you can go through the Pont Chaban Delmas lifting bridge when it coincides with a bridge lift for a tall ship or cruise liner. You may be able to reserve a berth on the Ponton d'Honneur but this must be booked in advance. The Pont de Pierre has an air draft of 3·8m and therefore yachts will need to de-mast before venturing further up stream. The Lormont YC used to be an option but is only likely to be an option by prior arrangement.

Lock in to Bassin à Flot No.2

The longer-term option is to lock in to Bassin No.2. The lock opens every day and the timings may be found on the website (details in the info box above). There are now showers and toilets and the marina area is secure. There is a Waiting Pontoon just up stream of the lock entrance, on starboard side, towards Pont de Chaban Delmas. There are de-masting facilities in Bassin No.2 by arrangement through the capitainerie.

BERTHS AND ANCHORAGES

The normal berthing options are either at Ponton de la Cité du Vin or in No.2 Basin. There is a waiting pontoon upstream of the lock gate to No.1 Basin. It is not recommended that yachts berth on the walls on the west bank in the city which are high, rough and subject to strong streams. It is also possible to berth at Ponton d'Honneur, provided you are able to access the lifting bridge, Pont Chaban Delmas (*see p.328*).

Ponton de la Cité du Vin

Ponton de la Cité du Vin is situated in the river just downstream of the Bassins á Flot (No.1 and No.2 Bassin). The pontoon is suitable for short overnight stays but the Bassins á Flot are more convenient for longer stays.

Lormont Yacht Club

The Lormont Yacht club used to be a viable option for visitors but is now unlikely to have space. It may be possible to stay overnight but would have to be by prior arrangement.

Nos 1 and 2 basins

Lock 20m wide, 4m deep. The lock opens at HW daily. Entry must be requested one hour before HW (30 minutes before HW on leaving) on Ch 12 and/or Ch 09 or ☎ 05 56 90 59 34. There is a waiting pontoon in 3m outside, just upstream.

Pass through No.1 basin but stay in the middle as it is surprisingly shallow and, after passing through the swing bridge between the two, select a berth as convenient in Bassin No.2. There is a waiting pontoon in the northwest corner of Bassin No.2.

Looking NE at Cité du Vin pontoon *Nick Chavasse*

Lifting bridge between Basin No.1 and No.2 *Nick Chavasse*

ASHORE IN BORDEAUX

There are modest restaurants within walking distance of the berths at Ponton de la Cité du Vin and there are several restaurants adjacent to the marina in Bassin No.2.

There are toilets and showers and the whole area has been revitalised due to major refurbishment. The submarine pens opposite the yacht berths serve as a grim reminder of the Second World War, but Bordeaux is a lovely city to explore. The excellent modern tram system stops near the basin lock and, closer still, there is a bus which connects with the tram system near McDonalds. There is an international airport at Merignac, Bordeaux. Bus and rail connections run in all directions.

British Consul
At 353, Boulevard du Président Wilson, 30373 Bordeaux Cedex. ☎ 05 57 22 21 10.
postmaster.bordeaux@fco.gov.uk

Bordeaux medieval gate *Nick Chavasse*

100 La Garonne into the canals to the Mediterranean

Masted navigation ceases just beyond the basins at Pont Chaban Delmas, unless you coincide with a cruise ship when the bridge is lifted. In its 'down position' the headroom is 5·4m above ML. Masts can be lowered at Royan, Port Médoc, Pauillac or Bordeaux. Yachts must demast in Bassin No 2 if they have not already done so.

About 1M upstream of Pont Chaban Delmas, the many narrow arches of Pont de Pierre bridge, headroom is 3·9m, obstruct the flow on the flood and the ebb, causing an appreciable fall of water through the bridge and many violent eddies on the downstream side. These difficulties are only surmountable with a very powerful engine and normally the bridge must be passed with the current. Use one of the arches marked by a white disc, but avoid those with No Entry signs. Passing through the Pont de Pierre at slack water is preferable.

The flood stream becomes negligible above the bridge and only causes a stand or diminution of the river flow.

There are three bridges above Pont de Pierre, all with greater headroom and larger arches. There is a small marina on the west bank at Bègles upstream of the third bridge and some 4km above Pont de Pierre.

Looking upstream at Ponton d'Honneur towards Pont de Pierre
Nick Chavasse

Pont Chaban Delmas looking up stream from S bank
Nick Chavasse

Bègles

44°47'·0N 00°31'·0W

A small marina with 80 berths in 2·5m and arrangements for transients who are expected to berth on the N end of the wave breaker. This is in the full flow of the current and any debris coming down, so it is worth trying to get a berth inside when the current slackens.

Water and electricity on the pontoons; showers and toilets, fuel berth, boatyard, 9-tonne crane and chandler; shopping centre nearby. Bègles is reasonably close to Bordeaux Merignac airport and is a possibility for changing crew.

VHF 09, ☎ 05 56 85 76 04 or 06 18 60 26 78 (weekday working hours).

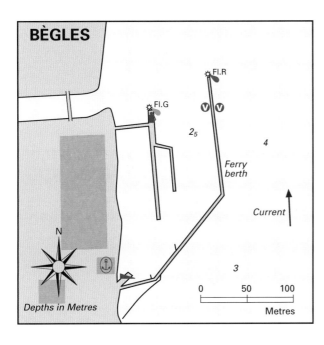

INTO THE CANALS

The Canal Latéral à la Garonne and Canal du Midi form a popular route to the Mediterranean, despite some 120 locks. The transit can be done in about a week, but 2-3 weeks is more relaxed.

The first, largest and deepest lock of the Canal Latéral à la Garonne is at Castets, about 50km upstream of Bordeaux. Approximately 1M short of the lock are some unmarked rocks which boats drawing 1·5m will hit before HW−0200. It would be wise to wait downstream at Langon until HW−0100 or later before proceeding. The locks will not open until just before HW anyway.

Heading upstream, the right-hand lock is the one in use. There are vertical bars to secure warps to but they are widely spaced. Once through the lock, a narrow lake leads to a second lock with a 3·3m rise and warping bars. Both locks have keepers and open during working hours at HW. There is a shady, wooden quay on the south bank just through the second lock.

Inland waterways

The rules and regulations for the French inland waterways apply to those entering the Canal Latéral à la Garonne above Castets. The minimum requirements for any vessel of less than 15m is that the helmsman should possess an RYA Helmsman's Overseas Certificate of Competence and that a current tax disc (*vignette*) is held. Details of the latter may be obtained from Voies Navigables de France, 175 rue Ludovic Boutleux, B.P. 820 62408, Béthune CEDEX. The French Government Tourist Office, 178 Piccadilly, London W1V 0AL ☎ 0906 824 4123 can help further and will supply details of any closures (*chômages*). Any boat drawing more than about 1·4m may have a problem in the summer months due to lack of water on this inland route. Enquiries should be made before lowering masts and committing to the transit.
The following references may be of further help:

Inland Waterways of France, Vols I, II & III David Edwards-May, Imray

Map of the inland waterways of France, David Edwards-May, Imray

Euroregs for Inland Waterways, Marian Martin, Adlard Coles Nautical

Through the French Canals, David Jefferson, Adlard Coles Nautical

Looking NE from capitainerie over Bègles marina
Nick Chavasse

101 Bassin d'Arcachon

44°35'N 01°18'W

Shelter
Good inside Cap Ferret, none in approaches

Hazards
Dangerous entrance

Depth restriction
Shallow bar at entrance to N channel depth
  variable over time
1·5–4m in Arcachon marina

Night entry
Not recommended. Not lit

Tidal information
HW Cap Ferret PdG HW-0005
LW Cap Ferret PdG LW+0010
HW Arcachon Marina PdG HW+0010
LW Arcachon Marina PdG LW+0015

Mean height of tide (m) Cap Ferret

HWS	HWN	LWN	LWS
4·2	3.3	1·4	0·6

Tidal streams at entrance
Flood PdG HW –0520 to –0115
Ebb PdG HW –0045 to –0550

Berthing
Arcachon marina

Facilities
Extensive

Charts
SHOM *7428*
Local (see below)

Communications
Arcachon Marina VHF 09
  ☎ 08 90 71 17 33 / 05 56 22 36 86
Cap Ferret VHF 13/16 for conditions at
  entrance
  ☎ 05 56 60 60 03 for buoyage and
  navigational updates
www.port-arcachon.com
www.arcachon-tourisme.com
www.bassin-arcachon-info.com

Lifeboat
A lifeboat is stationed at La Vigne inside
the entrance on the inside of Cap Ferret

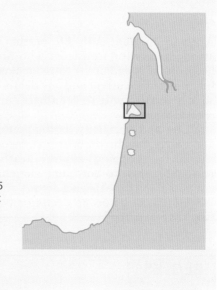

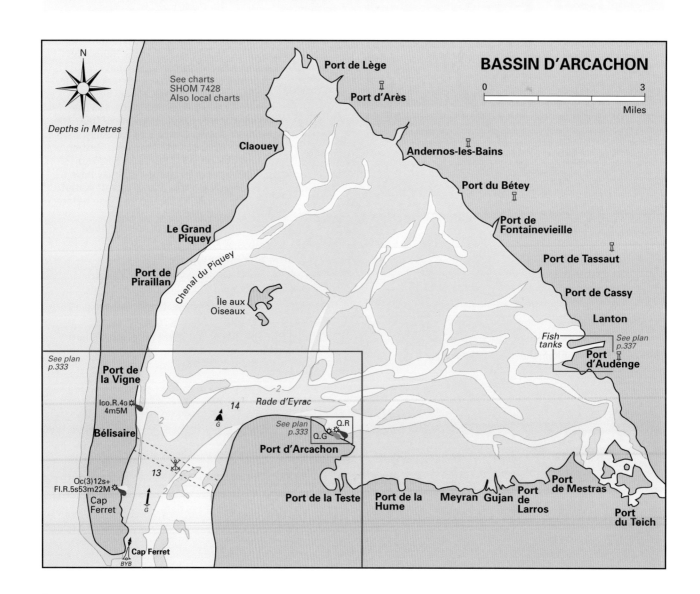

Typical oyster bed at Belisaire, looking SE towards Dune de Pilat *Nick Chavasse*

Extensive shallow basin with a large marina and many small harbours

The Bassin d'Arcachon, enclosed behind the wooded Cap Ferret peninsula, is an ecologically important tidal salt water lagoon with several protected conservation zones. The surrounding area is popular with week-enders and for holidays and much of it has a laid-back, beach resort feel. There is a network of cycle and walking routes, including old pilgrimage routes, which connect the communities around the basin. The forests surrounding the basin are home to wild boar.

At high tide and in settled weather the whole basin appears an enticing sailors' playground of protected water. However, this appearance is somewhat deceptive: Opposite Cap Ferret the imposing Dune du Pilat, the highest sand dune in Europe, towers over the entrance to the basin. The same sand which has formed this monstrous dune also forms shifting banks in the entrance and within the lagoon. As the basin fills and empties with each tide, the tidal flow of up to 3·5kn helps to scour out navigable channels, but most of the area dries out completely, including nearly all the so-called ports and marinas around the periphery. A few which do not dry entirely are small private marinas or oyster boat harbours known as *Ports d'ostreicole*. The tidal

replenishment of water helps to sustain numerous oyster and mussel beds which have been farmed across large areas of the basin since Roman times and this industry still dominates the whole region.

Anchoring in the basin is possible on the edges of the channels outside of restricted zones, shell fish beds and moorings, but is only allowed for 48 hours in the peak season (from 1 July to 31 August) and for 72 hours during the rest of the year. Visiting yachts which can take the ground, particularly those less than 7m in length, will find numerous *Ports de Plaisance* in which to sit in mud or dry out on firmer sand. There are also a large number of moorings, known as *corps-morts* (literally 'dead bodies') but, again, these are mostly drying. Moorings are usually overseen by the neighbouring communities and permission to use them is granted by the relevant *Mairie*. Deeper draught visiting yachts really only have the option of the marina or moorings at Port d'Arcachon, but here they will have access to a good range of facilities at the hub of the Bassin. Arcachon is a large, modern, beach resort town with a wide range of shops and restaurants, good transport links and ferries to Cap Ferret.

Looking SW from Dune du Pilat over the entrance to Bassin d'Arcachon *Jane Russell*

Dangerous entrance

When planning a visit to Bassin d'Arcachon, it would be sensible to telephone the Semaphore station at Cap Ferret for navigational updates 24 hours in advance.

The entrance channels are continuously shifting. The former South Channel has silted and is now closed and the buoyage removed. The North Channel, running between Banc du Toulinguet and Banc D'Arguin, is now the only access channel and there is a shallow sand bar at its seaward end, the depth of which also changes over time. In conditions of wind over tide, particularly on the ebb which can run at 3·5 kn, or if a swell of more than 1m is running, the bar can quickly become very dangerous. Good visibility is also important as the buoys are far apart and there are no leading marks. If in any doubt as to the prevailing conditions at the entrance, contact Sémaphore du Cap Ferret signal station on VHF 16 (or ☎ 05 56 60 60 03). Local regulations require the wearing of buoyancy aids in the approach from 01° 18'W to the No 8 port hand buoy and between the Phare du Cap Ferret lighthouse and the Wharf de la Salie, 44°30'·74N 01°15'·79W.

The North Channel is buoyed and is re-marked each year after the winter storms but changes do continue throughout the year and the shifting sands sometimes reveal old oyster bed structures. Enter at HW −0230 Arcachon (HW −0130 at the bar) to allow you to reach Arcachon on the end of the flood.

There is an air-to-air, air-to-sea and land-to-sea firing range on both sides of the entrance (see page 304 in the Introduction to Section IX). It is unlikely that entry to Arcachon will be prevented by its activities but there may be some restriction from north or to the south.

Local charts

There are two local charts on a larger scale than SHOM 7428, produced by Feret et Fils from drawings by Jean-Marie Bouchet and available in local bookshops. A local government publication *Bassin D'Arcachon Guide de la Plaisance et des Loisirs Nautique* contains a great deal of information relevant to yachts, including charts of restricted zones and channel buoyage within the basin. The guide is available from marinas and ports in the region or on line at www.gironde.gouv.fr.

PILOTAGE

Approach from north

A featureless coast extends from the mouth of La Gironde along which the beacon at Pointe de la Négade, Hourtin lighthouse, and Cap Ferret lighthouse are conspicuous. Do not cut the corner if entering Arcachon; head for the ATT ARC safe water buoy (LFl.10s4M), which lies approximately 4M southwest of Cap Ferret, before turning into the entrance channel. The huge sand dune of Pilat (103m) is located 2M southeast of Cap Ferret and is a conspicuous feature.

The firing range area north of Arcachon is very seldom used but confirmation must be obtained. (*See page 304.*)

Approach from south

From Capbreton a similar featureless coast stretches for 60M along which the Contis lighthouse, Biscarosse beacon and the firing range buildings stand out (*see page 304 for details of the firing range*). There may be a 3M wide safe passage between the shore and the range area but confirmation must be obtained. The 20m line provides a good danger limit from the shore which should be watched carefully when approaching the extended Arcachon shoals. A lit isolated danger mark lies approximately 1·5M west-southwest of the wharf at La Salie. The South Channel is closed, but just off its old entrance lies a sediment monitoring platform which is marked by an unlit isolated danger buoy, CNRS. Head to the ATT ARC safe water buoy (LFl.10s4M) before turning into the entrance channel.

Entrance by North Channel (Passe Nord or Chenal d'Accès)

If in any doubt about depths and conditions over the bar, contact the Sémaphore du Cap Ferret signal station on VHF 16 (or ☎ 05 56 60 60 03). Enter the buoyed channel from the vicinity of the ATT ARC approach buoy (red buoy with white stripes and ball top, LFl.10s) during the last half of the flood, HW − 0230 Arcachon (HW −0130 at the bar). The bar reportedly has a MEAN depth of 3·7m-4·5m, but the depth shifts continuously and could be significantly less than this. The bar is impassable from HW+1 to LW because of the steep seas generated by the outgoing tide. Follow the channel marked by a series of unlit red and green pillar buoys. The channel leads northeast before turning north towards the southeast tip of Cap Ferret. In any sea or swell there will be breakers on the sand banks on either side of the channel. Entry should not be attempted with a swell of more than 1m or on the ebb.

Once under the lee of Cap Ferret follow the buoyed channel northwards and then round to the east past the piers and town of Arcachon to the marina entrance.

The channel into the marina is 50m wide and leads in on 180° between port and starboard buoys. The entrance itself is lit (Q.R and Q.G). A large stone sculpture of an anchor is conspicuous on the port-hand side of the entrance. The welcome pontoon is on the port hand side by the fuel berth underneath the main marina office. The helpful marina office staff are English-speaking and can be contacted on VHF 9.

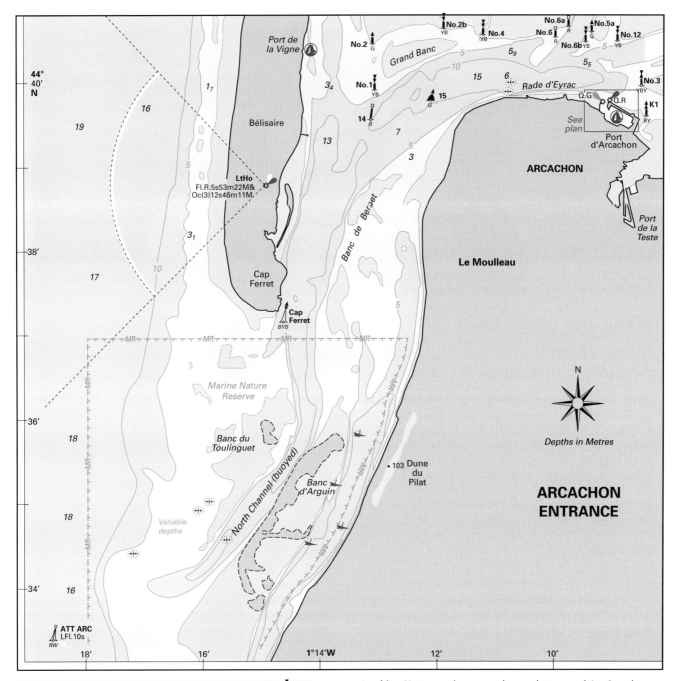

PORT DE LA VIGNE / BÉLISAIRE / CAP FERRET / ARCACHON ENTRANCE

44° 40' N

Port de la Vigne

No.2b YB
No.2 G
Grand Banc
No.4 YB
No.6a R
No.6 R
No.6b YB
No.5a G
No.12 YB

Bélisaire

No.1 YB
No.3 YBY

15 G
14 R
No.3 YBY
Rade d'Eyrac
Q.G
Q.R
K1 BY

38'

Banc de Berset

LtHo
Fl.R.5s53m22M&
Oc(3)12s46m11M

See plan
Port d'Arcachon

ARCACHON

Cap Ferret

Cap Ferret BYB

Port de la Teste

Le Moulleau

36'

Marine Nature Reserve

N

Banc du Toulinguet

Depths in Metres

103 Dune du Pilat

ARCACHON ENTRANCE

18

Banc d'Arguin

North Channel (buoyed)

Variable depths

34'

16

ATT ARC LFl.10s RW

18'   16'   1°14'W   12'   10'

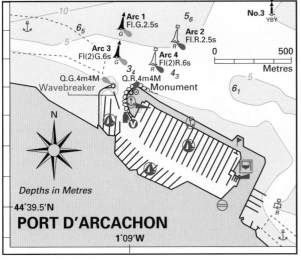

10
Arc 1 Fl.G.2.5s
5₆
No.3 YBY

6₅
Arc 2 Fl.R.2.5s
5

Arc 3 Fl(2)G.6s
Arc 4 Fl(2)R.6s

0   500
Metres

Q.G.4m4M
Wavebreaker
Q.R.4m4M
Monument

6₁

N

Depths in Metres

44°39.5'N

PORT D'ARCACHON

1°09'W

Looking N at conspicuous anchor sculpture and Arc 2 and Arc 4 port hand channel markers *Nick Chavasse*

Looking N out of the marina entrance - note wavebreaker (on left) inside entrance. Fuel berth and welcome pontoon are opposite, underneath the capitainerie *Jane Russell*

BERTHS AND ANCHORAGES

Arcachon Marina

The welcome pontoon and fuel dock are on the port hand side after entry under the capitainerie. The visitors' pontoon is opposite the fuel berth in the southwest corner of the marina and convenient for the town. Depths within the marina range between 1·5m and 4·0m. The marina can accommodate vessels up to 50m by 12m. It might be prudent to call the marina 24hrs in advance to reserve a berth. The old port is just to the east of the main marina basin and may offer alternative berthing for smaller vessels able to take the ground.

Moorings

There are a small number of swinging moorings just west of the marina entrance channel which are

Welcome pontoon and fuel berth from the capitanerie with Arcachon beyond *Jane Russell*

operated by the marina and suitable for yachts up to 25m. However, even in settled weather these suffer from the wash of passing vessels.

⚓ Outside Arcachon Marina

In 2m or more outside the marina, clear of moorings and the entrance. But note the anchorage restrictions: anchoring anywhere in the basin is possible on the edges of the channels outside of restricted zones, shell fish beds and moorings, but is only allowed for 48 hours in the peak season (from 1 July to 31 August) and for 72 hours during the rest of the year.

ASHORE

Everything expected in a large modern marina. The two travel-lifts (180-T and 45-T), slips and workshops are at the eastern end of the marina. Card operated fuel berth (24 hour). There is an active yacht and dinghy sailing club at the eastern end of the main breakwater.

The Dune du Pilat to the south of the town has a magnificent view from the top (103m) to reward the effort of the climb. The sliding run back down takes a fraction of the time. Banc d'Arguin in the approach to the basin is a nature reserve. Ferries run between Arcachon and Bélisaire on Cap Ferret from where you can access walks, surf beaches and a multitude of eateries. See ferry details at www.bassin-arcachon-info.com

Good rail and bus services. The nearest major airport is at Merignac, Bordeaux (70km).

EXPLORING THE BASSIN D'ARCACHON

There are many small, drying harbours around the edge of the Bassin d'Arcachon but very few have facilities for visitors. A few of the harbours retain water behind sills but most dry to soft mud and are not suitable for deep draught boats without legs. Nevertheless, with an appropriate vessel there are a number of places to explore. Most of the harbours

Moorings off Ares, a typical scene in the Bassin d'Arcachon *Jane Russell*

are *Ports d'Ostreicole* and home to fleets of working oyster boats but a few are designated *Ports de Plaisance*. All the harbours have water and electricity points and WCs and some also have showers. The working harbours usually have repair facilities.

SHOM chart *7428*, or the two large-scale charts available locally, are essential to explore further than the main channels although, even then, it is likely that you will need to feel your way to some extent. The bottom is soft and sandy mud but the water is clear and the bottom can often be seen. The channels are marked by beacons at all junctions and bear a letter and number as shown on SHOM *7428*. The banks of the channels are marked by stakes on the 0m line. It is advisable to explore on a rising tide and allow plenty of time to visit several harbours in search of a berth. Moorings can extend up to 300m from the shore, reducing the anchoring possibilities in some areas, even for the shoalest draught.

Île aux Oiseaux in the centre of the Bassin is the only island of any significance and is in a protected zone. It is possible to visit the island but only under strict regulations. Information boards placed around the island indicate the boundary of the protected zone as well as giving guidance about visits.

Warning Keep clear of the oyster beds and working boats, particularly between HW+0300 and HW−0300. The beds are easily identified by the grid patterns of posts sticking up out of the sand and mud. Be aware that tidal streams in the larger channels can reach 6kn at springs.

Looking NE from above Port de Piraillan across the extensive moorings *Jane Russell*

POSSIBLE ANCHORAGES AND PORTS

In a clockwise direction from the main entrance channel (*see plan page 330*):

Bélisaire

A long pier used by car ferries from Arcachon with a large area of moorings to the south of it and an oyster farm. Anchoring is not allowed within 100m of the shore in a zone which runs from the tip of Cap Ferret to north of Bélisaire.

Port de la Vigne

A private harbour for small boats (up to 8·5m) which does not usually cater for visiting yachts but has a fuelling berth on the port side of the entrance channel. HM ☏ 05 56 60 54 36.

Warning A bank with least depth of 0·8m lies 200m offshore for some distance north and south of the entrance. An approach from Bélisaire Pier keeping 100m offshore will avoid it.

Port de Piraillan

A small, completely drying, working oyster port. There may be space to anchor off to the east outside the large area of moorings.

Le Grand Piquey

A mooring area with a pier for landing and a slip. Anchoring depths up to 5m offshore but the streams in the channel run at up to 2·75 knots. Boatyard with haul-out, storage and repair facilities, mechanic and chandlery. Shops in the village. Good fish restaurant.

Port de Lège, seen here close to high tide, is typical of the many drying oyster ports *Jane Russell*

Fuel berth at Fontainevieille at half tide *Jane Russell*

Visitors' pontoon (in the foreground) in front of the capitainerie at Cassy/Lanton, looking out along the entrance channel *Jane Russell*

Claouey

A popular launching site with a large area of drying moorings. There is a large slip, club nautique, WCs, showers, boatyard, chandlery and shops in the village. Surrounded by pine trees.

Port d'Arès / Port de Lège

The two communities share a small drying harbour for working oyster boats. There are some drying moorings outside the harbour. Several of the oyster shacks sell shell fish and a couple serve as small restaurants. The shops of Arès are a 10 min walk from the harbour. There is a WC at the inner end of the port. Southeast of the harbour an extensive area of moorings parallels the shore. All of these moorings dry to soft mud or rather firmer sand.

Andernos-les-Bains

A large harbour exclusively for fishing and oyster boats with drying yacht moorings outside the harbour.

Port du Bétey

A small drying harbour for local yachts and workboats. Yachts secure alongside quays or bows to the wall. Facilities include water points, fuel nearby, two WCs and showers, a slip and shops at Andernos-les-Bains.

Port de Fontainevieille

A drying yacht basin with pontoon berths. Fuel is available at the entrance quay on the port side. There is a launch slip next to the fuelling quay. The sailing club overlooking the entrance has a restaurant.

Port de Tassaut

A very small harbour used by oyster boats and with restaurant shacks amongst the surrounding buildings. There is a small dinghy sailing club at the entrance. A submerged wall to starboard on entry is marked by stakes.

Port de Cassy / Lanton

An attractive but completely drying harbour for yachts and a few oyster boats, with space for 2 visitors on a short pontoon in front of the harbourmaster's office. A water tower to the north of the harbour helps identification. There are WCs, showers, water, a slip and crane plus a sailing club and shops in the village.

Port d'Audenge

A medium-sized drying harbour with facilities for yachts. Workboats use the centre basin, yachts are in the Nouveau Bassin on southeast side or in the Ancien Port (Old Harbour on northwest side). Maximum length 10m. Water and electricity, WCs

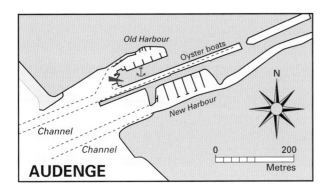

Audenge Nouveau Bassin (New Harbour) looking SW
Jane Russell

and showers, and a swimming lido which would be popular with younger crew. There are restaurants on the quay. Shops and fuel are available in Audenge, about 1 km from the port.

Port du Teich

A small drying harbour for yachts in the River L'Eyre on the south bank, adjacent to a bird reserve and visitor centre. The entrance channel is buoyed and marked by perches further in. Boats moor to pontoons and sit in the mud. Maximum 12m. Normal supplies from the village of Le Teich.

Ports de Mestras, Larros and Gujan

These are all working harbours with ship and boat building and repair facilities, including for yachts. Larros is the most yacht friendly; with a boatyard, WCs, several restaurants and a small museum.

Port de Meyran

A small harbour with drying berths each side used by oyster and fishing boats.

Port de la Hume

A medium-sized harbour for yachts, oyster and fishing boats located right next to a train station, which could make it useful for crew changes.

Port de la Teste

One of the larger drying harbours tucked behind Port d'Arcachon with a long and winding entrance channel from K1 beacon. Most of the berths are private and all dry to soft mud.

Entry channel to Port de la Hume *Jane Russell*

Port de Larros towards high tide *Jane Russell*

102 Capbreton

43°39'·00N 01°26'·00W

Shelter
Good once inside

Hazards
Le Fosse (or Le Gouf) de Capbreton, a deep
submarine valley rising from 1300m, runs at
right angles to the coast and ends 2M offshore.
Confused and breaking seas will be found here
in heavy weather especially round the edges.
Avoid it in these conditions.
Currents in the entrance run very strongly.

Depth restriction
Min 1·3m in the entrance
Min 1·5m in the marina

Night entry
Lit but no Ldg Lts

Tidal information: Pointe de Grave
HW PdG HW–0035
LW PdG LW–0035

Mean height of tide (m) Pointe de Grave

HWS	HWN	LWN	LWS
4·2	3.3	1·7	0·7

Tidal Streams
Up to 8kn in entrance,
1kn or less inside

Berthing
On pontoons. Max length 23m

Facilities
All, but a long walk to the shops

Charts
SHOM *7440*
Imray *C42*

Communications
VHF 09 (working hours)
☎ 05 58 72 21 23
www.francethisway.com
www.port-capbreton.fr

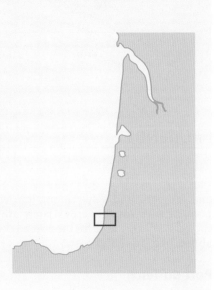

Holiday resort with a large marina but challenging entrance

Le Gouf de Capbreton is a remarkable deep sea canyon which influences the sea state in the approaches to Capbreton. The entrance can be challenging, even dangerous, and certainly should be approached with caution, but the large number of boats in this extensive marina are testament to the fact that in fair weather it is usually less daunting than it sounds.

PILOTAGE

Approach from north

A straight and featureless coastline with only Contis lighthouse breaking the monotony until the houses of Capbreton appear and the lighthouse at the end of the north breakwater can be identified. (*See page 304 regarding the firing ranges.*)

Approach from south

A similar featureless coastline from Bayonne northwards until the breakwaters can be identified.

By night The lights at Contis and Bayonne will assist and the 20m contour line provides a danger limit from the shore which is hazard-free in both directions. Otherwise it is GPS navigation in deep water.

Entrance to Capbreton *Jane Russell*

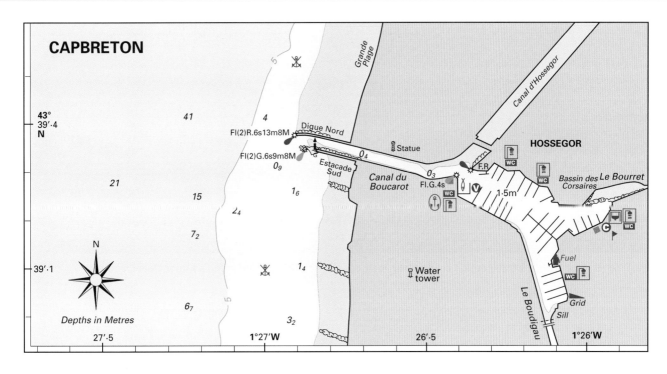

Entrance

In fair weather and with no swell running the entrance can be attempted at any time when draught permits (least depth 1·3m). In moderate seas or swell only attempt to enter between HW−0200 and HW+0100. Do not enter if the waves break right across the entrance, although they will usually be breaking on either side. If in doubt as to conditions at the entrance call the harbourmaster on ☎ 05 58 72 21 23.

Currents in the entrance channel run very strongly: two rivers, Le Bouret and Le Boudigau, feed into the marina basin. A man-made tidal lagoon to the north of the marina is fed by the Canal d'Hossegor, which branches off the entrance channel, and fills and empties with each tide.

Depending on the tidal coefficient and the prevailing weather conditions, the combined effect of tidal flow and river flow can result in peak streams of up to 8 knots in the entrance channel.

The south breakwater has an underwater extension at its end for 30m which is awash at half-tide, so the recommended inward track is to favour the port side of the channel until inside the moles and then to cross to the starboard side of the channel up to the marina entrance. Beware rocks and a concrete shelf which project a few metres from the port hand side of the channel on the corner opposite the marina entrance, adjacent to a walkway railing.

At any time other than slack water be aware that the flow in or out of Canal d'Hossegor creates a cross set at the entrance to the marina.

Marina entrance to starboard and underwater shelf to port

Looking SE across marina with reception pontoon hammerhead just beyond the fishermens' pontoon *Nick Chavasse*

Looking E to marina entrance *Nick Chavasse*

BERTHS, ANCHORAGES AND MOORINGS

The marina office is in the large building on the starboard side of the marina entrance. Call them ahead of arrival on VHF 09. The reception berth is pontoon B, the first pontoon on the starboard side after the pontoons allocated to the small fishing fleet. The marina is dredged to 1·5m but most of the outer part carries 2m. However, depths on the end of the reception hammerhead can be a problem as sand tends to build up here. 58 visitors' berths are on finger pontoons. Maximum length 23m.

No moorings. Anchorage is prohibited outside on either side of the entrance.

Looking N over **Capbreton** *Capitainerie, Cap Breton*

ASHORE IN CAPBRETON

Capbreton is a busy holiday resort town with good facilities and numerous restaurants and shops. There is a hypermarket within walking distance of the marina. A dinghy trip up the Canal d'Hossegor into Lake Hossegor may amuse, though the rapids in the canal should not be underestimated.

Bus services run in all directions ('yégo' bus www.mobi-macs.org). Rail stations at Labenne, Dax and Bayonne, and an airfield (mostly internal flights but some packages) at Biarritz (25km).

A 30-T travel-lift, 1·5-T crane, small boatyard, chandlers and sailmaker can all be found.

Several theories exist about the origin of the Gouf de Capbreton (deep-sea canyon). One of the most likely is that it is a seismic fault linked to the forming of the Pyrenees, but equally, it could be a former valley of erosion from the ice age.

When bad weather comes in from the west, the sea remains calm in the canyon but rough in the shallower depths (under 50m) which border it to the north and south. Furthermore, the bottom has firm mud, allowing ships to drop anchor in 60m of water in high winds.

The remarkable form of the canyon, one of the deepest in the world, with its steep-sided valleys just off the coast, makes Capbreton an exceptional geological phenomenon.

FRENCH BASQUE PORTS

103 Anglet

43°31′N 01°31′W

Shelter
Good in Anglet

Hazards
Give way to merchant ships in entrance or channel.
Only attempt entrance from HW–0400 to HW+0100
in any sea or swell.

Depth restriction
12m in entrance as regularly dredged
3m in marina
8·5m in harbour channel as regularly dredged

Night entry
Well lit plus Ldg Lts

Tidal information
HW PdG HW–0032

Mean height of tide (m) Pointe de Grave

HWS	HWN	LWN	LWS
4·2	3·3	1·7	0·7

Tidal streams
Flood PdG HW –0550 to +0030
Ebb PdG HW +0100 to +0540

Berthing
On pontoons in Anglet

Facilities
All in Anglet. Shops 2km

Charts
Admiralty 1292
SHOM 7440
Imray C42

Communications
Anglet marina VHF 09 (working
   hours)
① 05 59 63 05 45
www.bayonne.port.fr
www.anglet-tourisme.com/fr

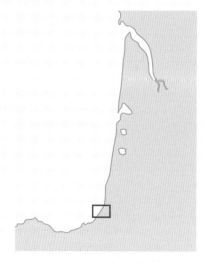

Historical town and commercial port with large marina accessible in most weathers

Anglet marina in Brise-Lames, about 1M upstream from the L'Adour river entrance, is somewhat isolated but lies in a well-protected basin and has adequate facilities, including a welcoming yacht club. There is an industrial feel to the area with a backdrop of factories and warehouses around Boucau on the opposite shore. Commercial shipping works up and down the river.

A taxi or bus will be needed to reach the city of Bayonne, 5M from Anglet, but it is worth the trip to see the 13th-century cathedral, Roman remains, two museums and the citadel. The old port and town were created by the Romans around 100 BC and many Roman remains including the foundations of Le Vieux Château can still be seen. Gascony (which includes Bayonne) became an English province in 1150AD and the English held it for 300 prosperous years. However, with their departure and the loss of trade with Britain, the river silted up and the town

Looking W out of entrance to L'Adour

fell on hard times. The river was eventually dredged in the 18th century and the town prospered again with a free port and a large fishing fleet.

PILOTAGE

Approach from north

Head for the landfall BA safe water buoy and steer 140° for 1M to the end of the breakwater which is conspicuous as are the warehouses and silos at Boucau.

Approach from south

The low coastline is broken by the rocky outcrop of Pointe St-Martin and its lighthouse in front of Biarritz town. Head for the breakwater end and buildings at Boucau will be identified.

By night The lights of Pointe St-Martin, Capbreton and the landfall buoy, BA safe water (LFl.10s) will assist until the well-lit entrance is identified.

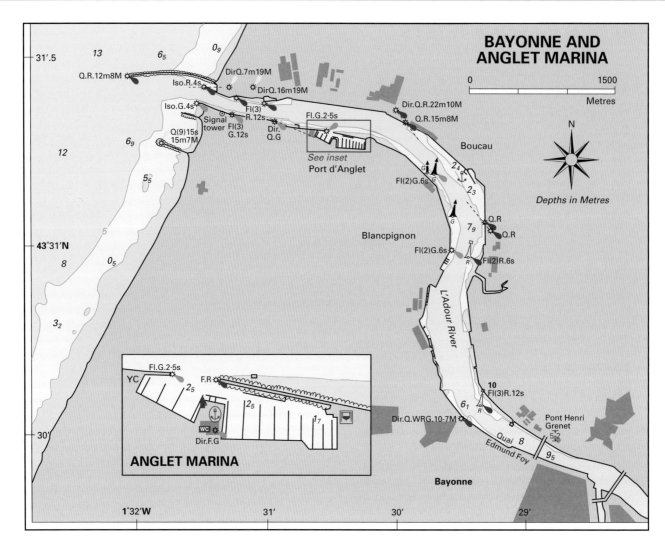

Entrance

By day and night The first set of leading marks on 090° (both white lattice structures. Front – thin red vertical stripe on white ground, Rear – white vertical stripe on red ground and Q.W intense on line) and proceed on this line to leave the outer breakwater end 100m to port (Q.R). Before reaching the inner breakwater heads pick up the next leading line on 111° (Front – lattice structure, vertical green band on white ground Dir Q.G; Rear – Dir Q.G) and pass through the inner entrance on this line.

The inner entrance ends are lit by Iso.R and Iso.G both 4s. When the conspicuous signal tower is abeam to starboard alter to about 095° to proceed up the centre of the channel. The entrance to the marina is marked on its west side by a white pylon, green top Fl.G.2·5s. The stream sets strongly across this entrance except for HW and LW slack.

Coaster heading up the channel to Bayonne commercial docks *Nick Chavasse*

Conspicuous signal tower on starboard side of channel just inside inner breakwaters *Nick Chavasse*

Anglet Marina from the river

BERTHS

Anglet Marina

Up to 45 visitors' berths up to 16m LOA, are available on finger pontoons. The marina basin is dredged to 3m. The welcome pontoon is just opposite the port side of the marina entrance underneath the harbourmaster's office. Visitors should call on VHF 09 or telephone ahead for a berth.

It used to be possible to moor further up river but now anchoring is prohibited in the river and there are no visitors' berths beyond Anglet Marina.

Capitainerie inside entrance to marina *Nick Chavasse*

ASHORE

There is a 25-T travel-lift and a 1·1-T crane. A few shops and restaurants are within walking distance of the marina but it is 4km to a larger supermarket on the road to Bayonne.

ANCHORAGES

⚓ Biarritz

Only 3·5M south of the river entrance lies the fashionable watering-place of Biarritz 43°29'·12N 01°33'·97W, where it is sometimes possible to anchor off in fair and settled weather. Dinghies can be taken into the tiny harbour.

SOUTH FROM BIARRITZ

Warning The Plateau de St-Jean-de-Luz lies between 1·5–4 miles offshore with a minimum depth of 10m. The sea breaks over some of the rocky shallows in heavy weather or swell and should be avoided.

Looking E over the marina from the capitainerie towards the commercial docks beyond *Nick Chavasse*

104 St-Jean-de-Luz

43°24'·00N 01°41'·00W

Shelter
Good in Larraldénia
Anchorage exposed in northerlies

Hazards
A number of off-lying banks break in heavy weather

Depth restriction
Larraldénia 1·9m on approach

Height restriction
La Nivelle bridge has 1·9m clearance

Night entry
Well-lit ldg lines

Tidal information
HW PdG HW−0042

Mean height of tide (m) Pointe de Grave

HWS	HWN	LWN	LWS
4·3	3·4	1·6	0·6

Tidal streams
The flood (0·5kn) enters by the E entrance and the ebb (1kn) exits by the W entrance
Flood PdG HW −0600 to −0030
Ebb PdG HW 0000 to +0530

Berthing
Pontoons at Larraldénia (up to 8 visitors, max LOA 16m)
La Nivelle only for 8m LOA and lowering mast
Anchorage areas and some moorings in bay

Facilities
All facilities

Charts
Admiralty *1292, 1170*
SHOM *6786, 7440, 7431*
Imray *C42*

Communications
Larraldénia VHF 09 (working hours)
Larraldénia ① 05 59 47 26 81
Socoa ① 05 59 47 26 81
Basque YC (Socoa) ① 05 59 47 18 31
www.saint-jean-de-luz.com

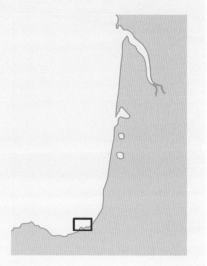

Large bay with seaside resorts and a small marina

St Jean de Luz offers a useful passage anchorage in settled conditions but becomes uncomfortable or untenable when swell finds its way in. The marina is at Larraldénia opposite St Jean de Luz. The facilities for visitors are minimal.

PILOTAGE

The directions below are given for approach in heavy weather to avoid the shoal patches which have a least depth of 9m over them. In fine weather or little swell more direct lines may be taken.

Approach from west

By day or night A good offing should be maintained after Cabo Higuer to clear Les Briquets 1M off the conspicuous Pointe St-Anne. Proceed outside the Belhara Perdun shoal to pick up the Socoa/Bordagain leading line 138° (*Front* – DirQWR, *Rear* – DirQW) and then Sainte-Barbe leading line 101° (*Front* and *Rear* – DirOc(4)R.12s) transferring to the inner leading line 151° (*Front* and *Rear* – DirQ.G) to pass through the west entrance.

Approach from north

By day or night Pick up the Socoa/Bordagain leading line on 138° and proceed as directed from west (above) to pass through the west entrance.

Approach from east or northeast

By day Follow the coast about 1M off and outside the 20m line inside the shoal patches until the Tour de Bordagain (tall stone tower on top of hill with trees round it) bears 193°. Keep on this bearing to pass through the east entrance. Do not cut the corner because of Les Esquilletac shoal.

By night It would be prudent to proceed outside the shoals until the inner leading line (both Q.G) on 151° is identified and proceed down this through the west entrance.

Looking NW at entrance which is left hand passage and Socoa anchorage on left *Nick Chavasse*

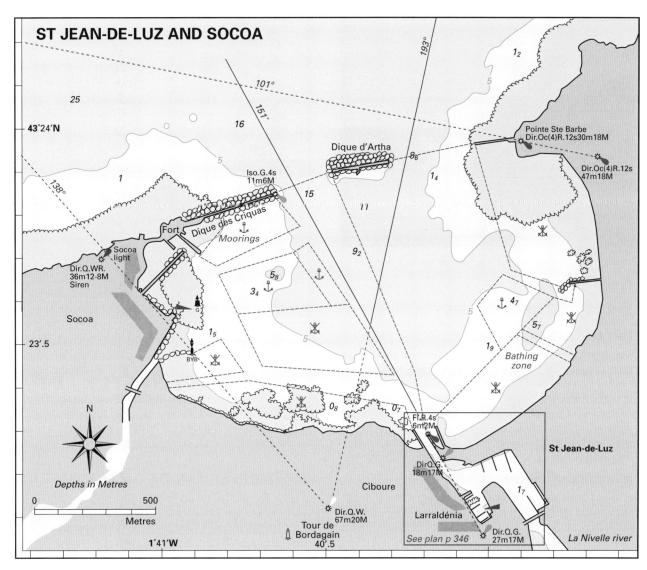

ST JEAN-DE-LUZ AND SOCOA

Dique d'Artha

Pointe Ste Barbe
Dir.Oc(4)R.12s30m18M

Dir.Oc(4)R.12s
47m18M

Iso.G.4s
11m6M

Fort   Dique des Criquas

Moorings

Socoa
light

Dir.Q.WR.
36m12-8M
Siren

Socoa

Bathing
zone

St Jean-de-Luz

Fl.R.4s
6m2M

Ciboure

DirQ.G.
18m17M

Larraldénia

Dir.Q.W.
67m20M

Tour de
Bordagain
40'.5

See plan p 346

Dir.Q.G.
27m17M

La Nivelle river

Depths in Metres

0   500

Metres

Entrance

The entrance to the Nivelle river is between two rocky training walls just southwest of the leading line. At night be careful not to go between the eastern Finger Mole and the east training wall as the front leading light is well back. The entrance is dredged inside the wall-ends to 3m but it shoals to 0·7m outside. Delay entrance to HW if there is any swell as it can break right across.

Entrance to La Nivelle river and Larraldénia marina beyond

Looking NW from capitainerie across marina *Nick Chavasse*

LARRALDÉNIA MARINA

BERTHS AND ANCHORAGES

Larraldénia marina

An attractive but tiny basin in the middle of the picturesque old town, occupied by small motor and sailing vessels with little room for visitors. In theory it could cater for as many as eight visiting yachts up to 16m in 2·5m on finger pontoons. In practice the marina is likely to be full and there is little space for manoeuvring. Fuel can be brought by road tanker around HW to an alongside berth ☎ 05 59 26 06 98.

Moorings off Socoa

It may be possible to pick up a mooring here; contact the yacht club for more information. The drying harbour at Socoa is on unforgiving and rocky ground and is not recommended.

⚓ Socoa

The normal yacht anchorage is outside the moorings off Socoa under the Digue des Criquas. A tripping line is advised. Holding is variable and two anchors would be wise in heavy weather, although the anchorage is unlikely to be tenable in these conditions. Dinghies can be left just inside the Socoa harbour entrance.

An alternative anchorage is off the beach in the southeast corner of the bay clear of the bathing zone in 3m or more. There is a landing pier in the corner of the bay.

ASHORE IN ST-JEAN-DE-LUZ / SOCOA

There are plenty of attractive places to visit ashore with numerous restaurants and shops. Socoa has the very friendly Yacht Club Basque with restaurant and showers and there is also a diving club for those needing emergency underwater work.

Travel

Good rail and bus services in all directions. An airfield at Biarritz (15km) offers European and international flights.

Looking NW towards Socoa moorings and anchorage

105 Hendaye

43°23'·00N 01°47'·00W

Shelter
Excellent in marina

Hazards
River Bidasoa entrance

Depth restriction
4·4m on bar in entrance channel
0·7m W of Hendaye Marina
3m in marina

Night entry
Well lit but no Leading Lights

Tidal information
HW PdG HW–0040

Mean height of tide (m) Pointe de Grave

HWS	HWN	LWN	LWS
4·2	3.4	1·6	0·6

Tidal streams
Not significant except in rio entrance where ebb can reach 5kn

Berthing
At pontoons in both marinas
In Baie de Chingoudy if space allows

Facilities
All, in both marinas

Charts
Admiralty *1292, 1170*
SHOM *6786, 7440, 7431*
Imray *C12*

Communications
Hendaye VHF 09 (24hr)
Harbourmaster ① 05 59 48 06 10
www.port-hendaye.fr/port-
   plaisance-hendaye.html
www.euskoguide.com

Beach resort at the foot of the Pyrenees

The bay, estuary, harbours and Río Bidasoa lie on the border between France and Spain. A large part of the bay is a neutral area and the boundary between the two countries is complex. The Pyrenees form a mountainous backdrop to the town, which is primarily a beach resort. There is plenty going on ashore, including a number of excellent restaurants.

PILOTAGE

Warning Do not enter if the seas are breaking across the entrance to the river. Go to Puerto Gurutzeaundi instead.

Approach from west

By day or night Navigate to the north of Cabo Higuer (Fl(2)10s63m23M) and enter the Baie de Fontarabie leaving the headland 0·5M to starboard and the fishing port of Gurutzeaundi close to starboard. A track of 205° will then lead between the training wall heads of the Río Bidasoa (Fl(3)G.9s5M, LFl(3)R.9s5M). This track will leave Banc Iruarri (7·9m), on which the seas can break, 200m to port. Gurutzeaundi has Q(3)5s on its east corner and the entrance is marked by FlR.7s and FlG.7s lights.

Approach from east

By day or night Cabo Higuer LtHo (Fl(2)10s62m23M) should be approached on a track of 240° or less to avoid Les Briquets rocks to the northeast of the bay.

Looking S over Hendaye Marina with Baie de Chingoudy beyond

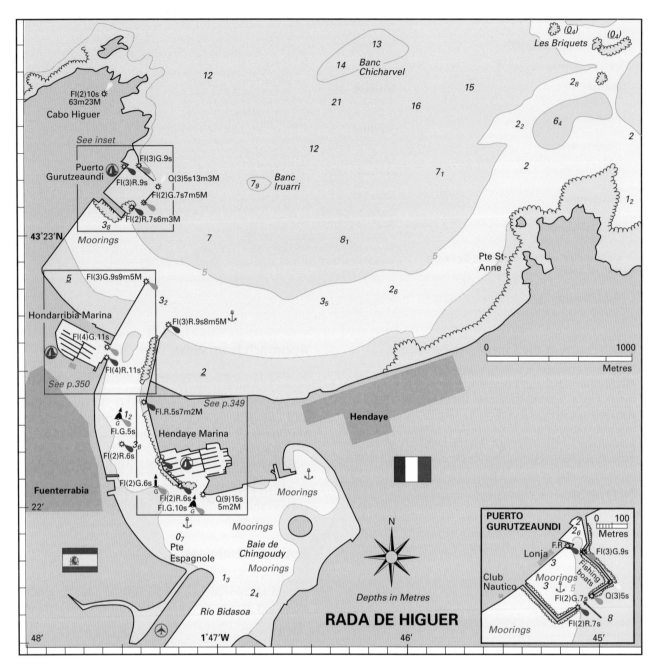

RADA DE HIGUER

Depths in Metres

Cabo Higuer
Fl(2)10s ✿
63m23M

Puerto
Gurutzeaundi
Fl(3)R.9s   Fl(3)G.9s
Q(3)5s13m3M
Fl(2)G.7s7m5M
Fl(2)R.7s6m3M
3₈

43°23'N
Moorings

5   Fl(3)G.9s9m5M
3₂
Hondarribia Marina   Fl(3)R.9s8m5M
Fl(4)G.11s
Fl(4)R.11s
See p.350
2
See p.349
Fl.R.5s7m2M
1₂
G
Fl.G.5s
3₆
Fl(2)R.6s
Hendaye Marina
Fl(2)G.6s
Fl(2)R.6s   Q(9)15s 5m2M
Fl.G.10s
G
Fuenterrabia
22'
Moorings
0₇
Pte
Espagnole
Baie de
Chingoudy
Moorings
1₃
Moorings
2₄
Río Bidasoa

N

12   13   Banc
14   Chicharvel
21   16   15   2₈
2₂   6₄   2
12   7₁
Banc   2   1₂
7₉   Iruarri
7   8₁   Pte St-
Anne
5
2₆
3₅
⚓
Hendaye
🇫🇷

48'   1°47'W   46'   45'

0 ─────── 1000
Metres

**PUERTO
GURUTZEAUNDI**
2   0 ─── 100
2₆   Metres
F.R   Fl(3)G.9s
Lonja
3   Fishing boats
Club   *Moorings*
Nautico   3   5
Fl(2)G.7s   Q(3)5s
8
Moorings   Fl(2)R.7s

In heavy weather this should be reduced to 215° to avoid Banc Chicharvel (13m). When 0·5M from the headland proceed as above. Do not turn short if there is any sea or swell which may break on Banc Iruarri (7·9m).

Looking S down entrance channel from Hondarribia entrance *Nick Chavasse*

Approach from north

By day or night A southerly course towards Cabo Higuer clears all dangers. The lighthouses of Cabo Higuer (Fl(2)10s23M and Le Socoa (Q.WR.12M) assist. The houses of Hendaye above a long sandy beach stand out clearly.

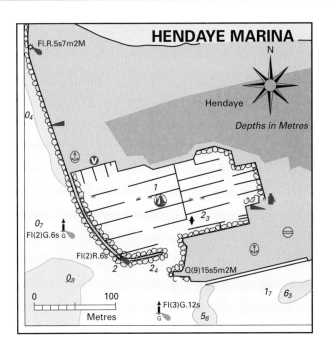

Looking N from marina entrance towards capitainerie
Nick Chavasse

Capitainerie Hendaye *Nick Chavasse*

Entrances to Río Bidasoa

The least depth outside the ends of the Río Bidasoa training walls is 2·7m and it deepens inside to about 4m. Follow the channel, with least depth of 0·7m, to Hendaye Marina.

Hendaye Marina

Continue up the río leaving a starboard hand buoy (Fl.G.5s) and a starboard hand beacon (Fl(2)G.6s) to starboard, follow the marina wall round to port at about 50m off passing a Fl(2)R.6s on its elbow and turn sharply to port into the entrance.

BERTHS AND ANCHORAGES

Hendaye Marina (France)

The reception pontoon has finger berths in the northwest corner of the marina. Continue turning to port inside the entrance and go up the channel between the pontoon ends and turn to port to berth on this pontoon. Maximum length 20m, depths mostly 3m.

There are many private moorings in Baie de Chingoudy to the southeast of Hendaye Marina. Ask at marina office before picking one up.

⚓ Outer bay

Anchorage in 2–5m, mostly sand, is available anywhere in the main bay clear of any moorings but will be subject to swell.

⚓ Baie de Chingoudy

A sheltered anchorage may be possible in the northeast corner of Baie de Chingoudy clear of the moorings which are now extensive. Alternatively, there may be room to anchor beyond the channel to the south of the marina entrance. To reach the anchoring area, leave a starboard hand beacon (Fl(2)G.6s) and a starboard hand buoy (LFl.G.10s) to starboard. Keep a careful eye open for aircraft if passing the line of the runway and anchor well clear of it.

ASHORE IN HENDAYE

Hendaye has all the facilities of a first-class marina including a 30-T travel-lift, a secure laying up area and a welcoming yacht club. Hendaye is a popular family seaside resort with much activity in the season.

Travel

Locally there is a half-hourly bus service which runs between Hendaye and Fuenterrabía. Otherwise there are the usual bus services in all directions in France and Spain. The large railway station at Irun is 4km from Hondarribia and connects with the French and Spanish networks; the latter includes a slow line along the north coast to La Coruña.

The local airport at Fuenterrabía (also known as San Sebastián airport) services local flights and international flights via Madrid; Biarritz, 25km away, has the occasional charter and international flight, otherwise connects with Paris.

106 Hondarribia, Spain

43°23'·00N 01°47'·00W

Shelter
Excellent in marina

Hazards
Do not enter if the seas are breaking across the entrance to the river

Depth restriction
3m in Hondarribia

Night entry
Well lit but no Leading Lights

Tidal information
HW PdG HW–0040

Mean height of tide (m) Pointe de Grave

HWS	HWN	LWN	LWS
4·3	3.4	1·6	0·6

Tidal streams
Not significant except in entrance where ebb can reach 5kn

Berthing
At pontoons in marina

Facilities
All facilities in marina

Charts
Admiralty *1292, 1170*
SHOM *6786, 7440, 7431*
Imray *C42*

Communications
Hondarribia VHF 09 (24hr)
☎ 00 34 943 641 711
hondarribia@ekpsa.eus
www.ekpsa.eus
https://tourism.euskadi.eus

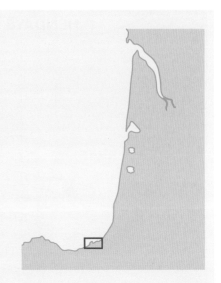

First-class Spanish marina on the border

The bay, estuary, harbours and Río Bidasoa lie on the border between France and Spain. A large part of the bay is a neutral area and the boundary between the two countries is complex. There are two first-class marinas (see previous page for Hendaye) and plenty going on ashore, including a number of excellent restaurants. Hondarribia has an old town behind a fortified mediaeval wall. The church of Santa Maria has a long history and is built on Roman foundations. The Charles V castle is now a Parador hotel but the bar is open to non-residents.

PILOTAGE

See Pilotage for Hendaye on page 347

Hondarribia Marina

Turn to starboard into the marina 400m up from the west training wall end. The entrance is marked by Fl(4)R.11s and Fl(4)G.11s on prominent pylons.

Reception berth is the first pontoon on the port side marked G and with a yellow light at its end. Maximum length 16m, depths 3m and 2m at finger pontoons. Office is in centre of south side.

For anchorage information, see details for outer bay and Baie de Chingoudy on page 349.

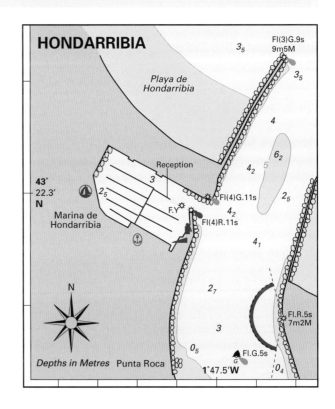

Hondarribia marina looking E with Harbour office on right
Nick Chavasse

Hondarribia Marina

ASHORE IN HONDARRIBIA

The marina has all the facilities including a 35-T travel-lift and 3-T crane plus fuel (24 hours). Shops, supermarkets and restaurants are a five-minute walk away in the attractive old town of Fuenterrabía where Charles V's castle, Guadaloupe church, Mont Jaizkibel and Castillo San Telmo are worth a visit, and a wander round the old fortifications provides a pleasant interlude.

PUERTO GURUTZEAUNDI (SPAIN)

This fishing harbour may be used as a refuge in the worst weather and sea conditions if the entrance to Río Bidasoa is impassable. The entrance is straightforward from an approach course of from 280° to 350° after taking particular care to avoid Banc Iruarri. Either anchor in the outer harbour, pick up a mooring or go alongside in the inner harbour which has a least depth of 2m. *See plan on page 348.*

Looking N out of entrance to Rio Bidasoa towards Puerto Gurutzeaundi

Appendix

Obtaining charts

Imray charts

Imray chart coverage for Atlantic France is detailed on their website at
www.imray.com

Imray is also able to help with enquiries and supply French charts.

Imray Navigator

Imray charts, as well as those from other official Hydrographic Offices, are available on Imray's new navigation app for iPad and iPhone. Download the free app Imray Navigator from the App Store for navigation software and demonstration charts. Subscribe to chart sets by area for updates throughout the year.

The chart sets covered by this book are:

ID40 Imray Atlantic France, Iberia and Atlantic Islands

FR1 Bay of Biscay (derived from SHOM charts)

French charts

French (SHOM – Service Hydrographique et Océanographique de la Marine) charts, which offer more comprehensive coverage, are listed at
www.shom.fr

Note that SHOM chart numbers change and the SHOM website should be checked for the latest details.

Charts

Planning charts – north to south

	SHOM	Scale
Île d' Yeu to Pointe de La Coubre	(7069)	1:200,000
Pointe de la Coubre to Pointe d'Arcachon	(7070)	1:200,000

Passage charts – north to south

	SHOM	Scale
Goulet de Brest to Portsall	(7149)	1:50,000
to Chaussée de Sein	(7172)	1:50,000
Chaussée de Sein to Pointe de Penmarc'h	(7147)	1:50,000
Pointe de Penmarc'h to Pointe de Trevignon	(7146)	1:50,000
Île de Penfret to Plateaux des Birvideaux	(7031)	1:50,000
Île de Groix to Belle-Île	(7032)	1:50,000
Quiberon to Croisic	(7033)	1:50,000
Approaches to La Loire	(7395)	1:50,000
Pointe de St-Gildas to Goulet de Fromentine	(7394)	1:50,000
Les Sables d'Olonne to Île de Ré	(7403)	1:50,000
Pointe du Grouin du Cou to Pointe de Chassiron	(7404)	1:50,000
La Rochelle to Pointe de la Coubre	(7405)	1:50,000
Approaches to La Gironde	(7426)	1:50,000

Large scale charts – north to south

	SHOM	Scale
Approaches to Brest	(7401)	1:22,500
Rade de Brest	(7400)	1:22,500
Baie de Douarnenez	(7121)	1:30,000
Raz de Sein	(7423)	1:20,000
Cours de l'Odet – De Bénodet à Quimper	(6679)	1:20,000
Îles de Glénan, partie Sud	(6648)	1:20,000
Ports et mouillages en Bretagne Sud	(7138)	Various
Île de Groix	(7139)	1:20,000
Passes et Rade de Lorient	(7140)	1:10,000
Belle-Île	(7142)	1:25,000
Abords des Îles de Houat et de Hoëdic	(7143)	1:20,000
La Baie de Pont-Mahé to Piriac-sur-Mer	(7136)	1:15,000
La Turballe to Pornichet	(7145)	1:25,000
Île d'Yeu	(7410)	1:20,000
La Charente Île d'Aix to Tonnay-Charente	(7415)	1:20,000

Imray charts for North Biscay

C18 Western Approaches to the English Channel and Bay of
Biscay - Passage Chart
1:1,000,000 WGS 84

C35 Baie de Morlaix to L'Aber-Ildut
1: 75 000 WGS 84
Plans L'Aber-Ildut, Argenton, Portsall, Approaches to
L'Aber Wrac'h & L'Aber Benoît, Port du Pontusval,
Moguériec, Roscoff, Port de Morlaix

C36 Île d'Ouessant to Raz de Sein
1: 80 000 WGS 84
Plans Baie de Lampaul (Ouessant), Port du Conquet,
Port de Brest & Marina du Moulin Blanc, Marina du
Moulin Blanc, Port de Camaret-sur-Mer, Port de
Morgat, Port de Douarnenez, L'Elorn - Continuation
to Landerneau

C37 Raz de Sein to Bénodet
1: 80 000 WGS 84
Plans Île de Sein, Audierne, St Guénole, Le Guilvinec,
Lesconil, Loctudy, Bénodet, L'Odet Fleuve

C38 Anse de Bénodet to Presqu'île de Quiberon
1: 80 000 WGS 84
Plans Port la Forêt, Concarneau, Port Manec'h,
Ports Brigneau & Merrien, Doëlan, Îles de Glénan
North, Lorient, Lorient Yacht Harbour, Port Tudy (Île
de Groix), Étel

C39 Lorient to Le Croisic
1: 80 000 WGS 84
Plans Sauzon, Le Palais, Port Haliguen, La Trinité-
Sur-Mer, Port Du Crouesty, Piriac-sur-Mer, La
Turballe, Le Croisic, Baie de Pouliguen, Continuation
of La Vilaine

C40 Le Croisic to Les Sables d'Olonne
1: 110 000 WGS 84
Plans Le Croisic, Saint-Nazaire, Pornic,
L'Herbaudière, Goulet de Fromentine, Port-Joinville
(Île d'Yeu), Port de Saint-Gilles-Croix-de-Vie, Les
Sables d'Olonne

C41 Les Sables d'Olonne to La Gironde
1: 110 000 WGS 84
Plans Bourgenay, Approach to Jard-sur-Mer,
Approach to Ars-en-Ré, Approach to St Martin-de-
Ré, Approach to La Flotte-en-Ré, Rade de la Pallice,
La Rochelle and Port des Minimes, St-Denis-
d'Oléron, Douhet, Boyardville, Rochefort, Royan,
Port Médoc, La Gironde & La Garonne,
Continuation to Bordeaux

C42 La Rochelle to Santander
1: 350 000 WGS 84
Plans Approach to Arcachon, Capbreton, Rada de
Higuer, Getaria, Zumaia, Abra de Bilbao, Laredo,
Santoña, Santander, La Gironde & La Garonne,
Continuation to Bordeaux

Tidal charts

Admiralty Tidal Stream Atlases
NP 265 France West Coast

Shom
560-UJA Goulven to Penmarc'h
559-UJA St-Nazaire-Royan
565-UJA Goye de Gascoigne

Imray Tides Planner

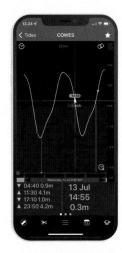

The essential companion for sailors, divers, canoeists, fishermen, surfers, swimmers and anyone involved with sport and leisure at the seaside.

Instant access to tide data for 8,000 world locations, no connection needed.

Rich in features and advanced tools to give you customized access to the information you need.

Current day's data is free. In app purchases offer more options

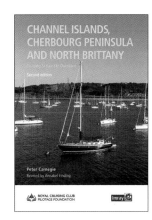 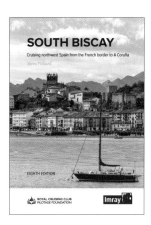

Index